THE NEW SUFFERINGS OF YOUNG W.

and Other Stories from the German
Democratic Republic

The German Library: Volume 87

Volkmar Sander, General Editor

THE NEW SUFFERINGS

OF YOUNG W.

and Other Stories from the German Democratic Republic

Edited by Therese Hörnigk and
Alexander Stephan

CONTINUUM · NEW YORK

1997
The Continuum Publishing Company
370 Lexington Avenue
New York, NY 10017

The German Library
is published in cooperation with Deutsches Haus,
New York University.
This volume has been supported by Inter Nationes;
and by a grant from Daimler-Benz-Fonds; and
The University of Florida, Division of Sponsored Research.

Printed in the United States of America

Library of Congress Cataloging-in-Publication Data

The new sufferings of young W. and other stories from the German
  Democratic Republic / edited by Therese Hörnigk and Alexander
  Stephan.
      p.   cm. — (The German library ; v. 87)
    ISBN 0-8264-0953-9 (alk. paper). — ISBN 0-8264-0952-0
  (pbk. : alk. paper)
    1. Short stories, German—Germany (East)—Translations into
  English. 2. German fiction—20th century—Translations into
  English. 3. Germany (East—Social conditions—Fiction.
  I. Hörnigk, Therese, 1942–   . II. Stephan, Alexander, 1946–   .
  III. Series.
  PT3740.N42   1997
  833'.9140809431—dc21   96-53312
                                                                         CIP

Acknowledgments will be found on page 349,
which constitutes an extension of the copyright page.

Contents

Introduction

The German Democratic Republic officially ceased to exist on October 3, 1990. Little more than forty years after its founding, the first socialist state in Germany—dismissed by the other Germany (the Federal Republic) as the "Soviet Zone," as the "so-called GDR," or as "the GDR" in quotation marks—had peacefully dissolved after its citizens staged bloodless demonstrations in the waning days of the Soviet empire. Official statements then and now used the term *Beitritt*, "entry" or "accession," to describe the act by which the new federal states were joined to the old Federal Republic of Germany. The word *Wiedervereinigung*, "reunification," rapidly became established long after it seemed to have lost its concrete meaning. Artists and intellectuals from both parts of Germany, who would have preferred a gradual blending of the two nations, used the word *Anschluß* or "junction"—a loaded term ever since 1938, when it was meant to describe Nazi Germany's more or less forcible annexation of Austria—or even spoke of the GDR as having been "occupied." When the Berlin Wall came down on November 9, 1989, many nations of Europe were haunted, openly or secretly, by fear that Germany might be resurrected as a great power at the center of Europe. Other voices, mainly in the United States, spoke of the final victory of democracy and of the free-market economy over socialism.

The way to the collapse of the GDR had been paved in the 1980s by the policies of Mikhail Gorbachev. *Glasnost* ("openness") and *perestroika* ("reform") were the guiding principles of that era, first in the Soviet Union and then throughout Eastern Europe, where the Polish Solidarity movement had already created unrest. The call went out to abolish the last remnants of Stalinism. Comprehensive reforms in every sphere of life, the arts among them, would—it was thought—revive a petrified socialism, which had been economically devastated by the arms race with the West, and start it moving again on its long march to a better future.

But the GDR, a one-party state governed by the Socialist Unity Party, bogged down in rigid structures and paralyzed by a hopelessly out-of-date leadership, seemed no longer capable of introducing reforms and thus of saving itself from internal collapse. And to the shock of the hidebound party officials, the Soviet Union, which had come to the rescue of its most loyal ally during the crisis years of 1948–49, 1953, and 1961, this time did not send tanks but instead offered suggestions on how to restructure GDR society. For decades, the GDR had been the showpiece among the moldering Warsaw Pact nations and was credited with notable successes: a program, far more comprehensive than that in the Federal Republic, to purge the country of National Socialism; an education system with an emphasis on practical application; wide gains in social welfare that particularly eased the burdens on working women; and a degree of economic productivity that had turned the GDR into a leading industrial nation even though it had only seventeen million people, had relatively little industry prior to 1945, and after 1945 was economically drained by the Soviet occupation forces. But however impressive the achievements of this stronghold of socialist unity, they could no longer conceal the dismal condition of the country, and were now clearly and irreversibly outweighed by its deficits. In the area of consumer goods, which was of key importance to the everyday well-being of its citizens, there was no prospect of an economic miracle similar to what had brought to Germans in the Federal Republic a steady rise in their standard of living and, with some exceptions, in their quality of life as well, ever since the 1950s. The miracle, if it came at all, would be too little and too late. The shock of June 17, 1953, when Russian tanks moved against striking GDR workers, had left a deep imprint on the population. The erection of the Berlin Wall in August 1961, and the restrictions on travel, which were stringent even for an Eastern-bloc nation, made GDR citizens feel locked up inside their country, which in any case was quite small and lacking in obvious tourist attractions. And finally, the party and government leaders found it increasingly difficult to explain to the younger generation why the gap was continuing to widen between the propaganda about a perfectly functioning communist society and the gray humdrum of actual socialism that they saw around them.

Long before the collapse of the GDR, increasing numbers of its citizens, disenchanted about their future prospects, withdrew from public life into the private sphere of family, friends, or a weekend hideaway in the country with the Russian nickname *Datscha*. Many writers, including Sarah Kirsch, Günter Kunert, Reiner Kunze, and Erich Loest, moved to the West, disillusioned by the government's expatriation of singer–poet Wolf Biermann in 1976. Of those who remained, a growing number chose as a theme the isolation of people in the panel-built suburban housing developments, protested the environmental destructiveness of the industrial districts and the buildup of weapons, favored literary experimentation over efforts to effect social change, and drifted further and further away from the ideals of the positive hero and the better world that many officials still expected writers to emulate, in line with the supposed tenets of Socialist Realism. Then in the 1980s, under the aegis of the Protestant Church, peace and human rights movements formed in the GDR, and their members addressed proposals for reform to a public that was increasingly eager to listen. Protest assemblies grew rapidly into peaceful mass demonstrations. When the border between Hungary and Austria was opened in May 1989, hordes of young people began to flee from the GDR, leading to the fall of the Berlin Wall a few months later.

Although the German Democratic Republic has been dissolved by formal treaty, the literature that painstakingly portrayed the rise and fall of the first Workers' and Peasants' State on German soil, which became progressively more critical as time went on, cannot be said to be over and done. Pollsters report that many Germans, especially in the new Eastern states, believe it may take twenty years or more before all traces of the GDR have vanished. Civil rights advocates and artists who contributed to the fall of the Honecker government at the end of the 1980s, continue to maintain that a gradual merger of the two nations would have better prepared East Germans for their "entry" into the Federal Republic of Germany. Working people, including many intellectuals who lost their jobs following unification, see themselves as permanently excluded in the harshly competitive new society. A never-ending series of revelations about alleged collaboration between citizens and the GDR's notorious Ministry of State Security—the secret police, *Stasi* for short—have caused continual unrest, particularly among writers. Increasingly, former East Germans, especially those in their middle years, are resisting the demand that they should erase from their lives all the years before 1989. And of course, GDR writers who have not yet achieved emotional distance from historical events of such magnitude as the creation and demise of their country, may take some time to process these events into literature.

The goals set by the GDR and by its writers following the defeat of the Third Reich in 1945 were more ambitious in many respects than in the Western zones of occupation. Artists and intellectuals who had lived in the Nazi period were rigorously isolated in the Soviet-occupied part of Germany, and the crimes of the Nazis were brought up for intensive review—although as Christa Wolf and other writers made clear thirty years later, the old thought patterns still lingered under the surface and remained to be described. Writers who had gone into exile under the Nazis—among them Friedrich Wolf, Stephan Hermlin, Anna Seghers, and Stefan Heym—returned to East Germany after the war, or were called back to help rebuild their society. Organizations founded by exiles and opponents of Hitler—the League of Culture *(Kulturbund)*, the writers' association P.E.N., and the academies of arts and sciences—were marshaled to promote antifascism and democratic reform. Right after the ceasefire, theaters were restored, publishing houses opened, and journals such as *Aufbau* and, later, *Sinn und Form,* were founded, all with the active encouragement of the Soviet occupation forces.

But the Soviet forces, whom most Germans did not treat as liberators, owing to Nazi propaganda and to the Soviet military excesses in the final days of the war, soon suppressed diversity of opinion in the Eastern part of Germany, in response to the burgeoning of the Cold War. The experiments of modern literature from expressionism to Kafka and James Joyce were dismissed as formalistic and cosmopolitan. So-called artistic freedom was replaced by the prescriptive aesthetic of Socialist Realism, which with some variations would dominate GDR literature for many years to come. The new literature was to be socialist in content, that is, to be class conscious and consistent with the goals of Marxism–Leninism as decreed by Stalin and Andrei Zhdanov, a Soviet party official who had defined the parameters of Socialist Realism since the 1930s, and their mouthpieces in East Germany. The form was to be realistic, that is, to show a unified structure and to adhere closely to actual everyday life, so as to make artistic products accessible to relatively uneducated workers and peasants on the one hand, while at the same time excluding the experimental literature produced by bourgeois authors who were concerned not so much with ongoing projects to create a better future as with revealing the flaws in society, the dark sides of man, and the indissoluble and destructive conflicts of modern life. Following the model of the worker-correspondent movement of the 1920s, the officials hoped that the authors of socialist–realist literature could be recruited from the working class, which produced Hermann Kant, Helga Schütz, and Erwin Strittmatter, and could, if necessary, be trained in special courses like those offered by the Johannes R. Becher Institute for Literature, founded in Leipzig in 1954, which educated Werner Bräunig and Sarah Kirsch. Socialist Realism took an optimistic view of the future in line with the Marxist interpretation of history, and depicted positive heroes and so-called non-antagonistic conflicts, that is, conflicts which could be overcome in a way that served as an example to others. Themes and figures from the bourgeois cultural heritage were to be used as models, much as Goethe functions as a model in Ulrich Plenzdorf's *The New Sufferings of Young W.*, as long as it was made clear what progress had meanwhile been achieved by the socialist society.

The aesthetic of Socialist Realism as it applied to GDR literature had been formulated by the Hungarian philosopher and literary theorist Georg Lukács, and gained dominance before the GDR was officially founded in 1949. At approximately the same time, Walter Ulbricht, who was to govern the GDR for a quarter of a century, made it eminently clear to writers that the new country would allot paper for them only if their works depicted contemporary themes such as the collectivization of agriculture and industrialization in line with the provisions of the first Two-Year Plan. Whereas many authors of the older generation, who had returned home from exile, were reluctant to adopt the slogans of Ulbricht and Lukács, the literary generation that followed addressed their new assignments without hesitation, produced worker–heroes of the type of Hans Garbe, an actual political activist and brick-furnace designer (cf. Käthe Rülicke's "Hans Garbe Tells His Story"), portrayed smoking chimneys galore, and were critical of the class enemy who—so they believed—was trying, aided and abetted by the Federal Republic, to sabotage the construction of the new world. And they all, young and old, former exiles, resistance fighters, and newly minted socialists alike, were convinced that whoever wanted to put an end to fascism, whoever viewed the restorationist regime in Adenauer's Germany with distrust, and whoever—like writer Stefan Heym, who left the United States in 1952 to move to the GDR—felt reservations about the capitalism of the Western nations, should place their hopes in socialism and in the new Germany proclaimed by the Socialist Unity Party.

But the literature of the GDR was by no means as monolithic as it may appear from a present-day vantage point. The global pronouncements made in the West about "official state literature" or "government poets-for-hire" are particularly untrue when applied to writers who began their careers before the formal creation of the GDR, and to those who were writing toward the end of its history. And members of the West German press who, after the *Wende* ("turning point") in 1989, dismissed the whole of GDR literature for its "moralism" and "aesthetic of ideology," are likewise unjust. Of the three generations of writers represented in this anthology, the eldest—whose members include the likes of Bertolt Brecht and Anna Seghers—brought with them, when they returned to Germany, a background steeped in the experimental techniques of the 1920s avant-garde, and the demand for social relevance to be found in the revolutionary, proletarian literature of that period. Writers of the next generation, after their experience of living under National Socialism, began by identifying more or less unconditionally with their young country; but in the 1960s, once the everyday realities of life in the GDR had become established, they started to call for innovative forms, to pursue the right to portray individual failure and the individual's unsatisfied claim to happiness, or to withdraw into myth or everyday concerns. Ulrich Plenzdorf achieved unusual success with his novella *The New Sufferings of Young W.*, written in 1972 in the comparatively liberal climate created by the changing of the guard, when Erich Honecker replaced Walter Ulbricht as first party secretary and head of state— a story that created an explosive mixture by combining the controversy over the bourgeois cultural tradition and the frustration of young people caught in intergenerational conflict, with the themes of job failure and untimely death, and for the first time turned people's eyes all the way toward the United States, with references to blue jeans and to J. D. Salinger's novel *The Catcher in the Rye*.

Before the West had begun to develop a literature by, for, and about women, many women writers in the GDR (Irmtraud Morgner, Maxie Wander, Irina Liebmann, Angela Stachowa, Christine Wolter) had addressed the special experiences and perceptions of women and experimented with a "feminine aesthetic." In the writings of Helga Schütz and others, fantasy, science fiction, and fairy tales became the vehicles of antiutopian models. And finally, a young generation of writers produced texts that bypassed socialism as it existed in reality or in the minds of functionaries issuing their comments from outside or underneath via characters who were victims or voyeurs, or, using techniques reminiscent of West German literature, expressed their generation's loss of utopia in images such as the *Titanic* (Joachim Walther, Wolfgang Hilbig).

The stories in this volume, the great majority of which have never before appeared in English translation, have been chosen to reflect the most important features in the literary development of the GDR. The tales of Franz Fühmann, Johannes Bobrowski, Anna Seghers, and Heinz Knobloch mirror the antifascist, democratic roots of this new alternative Germany, while Käthe Rülicke, Erwin Strittmatter, Erik Neutsch, and Friedrich Wolf present the edifying, upbeat themes of the so-called literature of Building Socialism. In Wolfgang Kohlhaase, Werner Bräunig, Fritz Rudolf Fries, Jurij Brězan, Helga Königsdorf, Günter de Bruyn, and Günter Kunert we find critical or straightforward descriptions of everyday life under socialism. Some texts are explicitly political, others withdraw into the private sphere. Maxie Wander experiments with documentary material, while Stephan Hermlin, Heiner Müller, and Hermann Kant use the forms of autobiography. And the last part of the anthology testifies, in the writings of Wolfgang Hilbig, Erich Loest, F. Hendrik Melle, Daniela Dahn, and others that the themes of the so-called unification of Germany and the historical legacy of the GDR—themes that are treated here with hesitation and caution but also with irony and anger—will remain integral to German literature for a long time to come. This collection includes both well-known authors and new arrivals, established figures and minor ones, the offspring of a middle-class milieu, and, not surprisingly, a large number of working-class children. Some of the writers became dissatisfied with the GDR and moved to the West, while others, once the archives had been opened, were revealed to have had contacts with the Stasi.

The selection of texts attests to the wide variety of narrative literature generated in the German Democratic Republic during its brief lifetime, and shows this literature to have been frequently critical in tone, as uneven in quality as other national literatures, and distinct from the literature of the former Federal Republic of Germany, although at many points it works with themes and forms that are familiar in any modern society. And finally, the assembled stories illustrate, directly and indirectly, that GDR literature is far from being a closed issue, a mere collector's item or, as some in a united Germany now try to state, an episode to be fundamentally rewritten or altogether eliminated from the history books. Rather, we are still far from having written the last word of this chapter in the chronicle of German literature as the older texts of the kind found in this anthology will need to be compared to the memories currently recorded by contemporaries, as well as the commentaries of future generations looking back at the rise and fall of the German Democratic Republic.

In conclusion, an editorial note. Stories by Bertolt Brecht, Jurek Becker, and Volker Braun were omitted due to copyright restrictions. Ulrich Plenzdorf's novella was selected by the publishers. Christa Wolf is absent since The German Library is devoting half of a separate volume (number 94) to her work.

ALEXANDER STEPHAN
Translated by Jan van Heurck

Ulrich Plenzdorf

The New Sufferings of Young W.

Notice in the "Berliner Zeitung," December 26:

On the night of December 24, Edgar W., a youth, was found critically injured in a garden house in Paradise II Colony in the district of Lichtenberg. According to police reports, Edgar W., who had been illegally inhabiting the condemned structure for some time, had been carelessly tinkering with electric current.

Obituary in the "Berliner Zeitung," December 30:

On December 24 an accident ended the life of our
young colleague
Edgar Wibeau
He was a promising young man!
People's Works WIK Berlin
Local Trade-union Administration Free German Youth
Director

Obituaries in the "Volkswacht," Frankfurt/O., December 31:

A tragic accident completely unexpectedly took the life of
Edgar Wibeau
our unforgettable member.
People's Works (Communally Managed) Hydraulics of
Mittenberg
Trade School   Director   Free German Youth
Yet inconceivable to me, on December 24 my dear son

Edgar Wibeau
died as a result of a tragic accident.
Else Wibeau

"When did you last see him?"

"In September. The end of September. The night before he left."

"Didn't you ever think of a police search?"

"If anybody has the right to blame me, it's not you! Not the man who for years didn't show any more concern for his son than an occasional postcard!"

"Pardon me! That's what you wanted, wasn't it, what with my lifestyle?!"

"That's your old irony again! Not going to the police was perhaps the only right thing that I did. Even that ended up wrong. But I was simply fed up with him. He'd put me in an impossible situation at the trade school and in the factory. The son of the director, until then the best apprentice, A-average, turns out to be a rowdy! Rebels against the school! Runs away from home! I mean . . . ! And then the news came from him pretty quickly and regularly. Not to me. God forbid. To his buddy, Willi. On tapes. Strange messages. So affected. Finally this Willi let me hear them; even he thought the whole thing was getting weird. Where Edgar was, in Berlin you know, he didn't want to tell me that at first. Anyway, nobody was able to get a thing out of those tapes. No matter, at least they told us one thing. That Edgar was well. That he was even working, and not wasting his time. Later a girl was mentioned, but then that broke up. She got married! As long as I had him *here* he never had anything to do with girls. But that still wasn't any reason for calling the police."

Stop, just stop! That's a lot of crap. You bet I had something to do with girls. The first time when I was fourteen. Now I can say it. You'd heard all kinds of stuff, but nothing definite. I wanted to know for sure, that's the way I am. Her name was Sylvia. She was about three years older than me. It took me exactly sixty minutes to bring her 'round. I think that's pretty fast work for my age, especially when you consider that I didn't have all my charm yet, or my distinct chin. I'm not saying that to brag, people, but just so that nobody gets a false impression of me. A year later mother enlightened me. She really exhausted herself doing it. Idiot that I am, I could have died laughing, but I played the naive, good little boy, like always. That was disgusting.

"What do you mean, he turned out to be a rowdy?!"
"He broke his teacher's toe."—"His toe?"
"He threw a heavy iron plate on his foot, a foundation plate. I was dumbfounded. I mean . . . !"
"Just like that?"
"I wasn't there, but my colleague, Flemming, told me—he's the teacher, an old and experienced teacher, dependable—that that's how it happened: Every morning he passes out the materials in the shop, these foundation plates to be filed. And the boys file them down, and while he's checking measurements he notices that Edgar's neighbor, Willi, has finished a plate, but he hasn't filed it himself. It was from the machine. In the factory the foundation plates are machine-made, of course. The boy has managed to get a hold of one, and now he presents it as his own. Naturally it's exact to the hundredth. He says to him: That's out of the machine.
Willi: Out of what machine?
Flemming: Out of the machine in plant two.
Willi: Oh, there's a machine there?! I can't be expected to know that, Sir. The last time we were in plant two was at the beginning of our apprenticeship, and then we still thought those things were egg-laying machines. And that was Edgar's cue, they'd of course arranged everything ahead of time: OK, let's assume there is a machine there. Can be. You have to ask yourself, why do we have to file down those foundation plates then? And that in our third year."

I did say that. That's true. But all off the cuff. Not a single thing was arranged. I know what Willi and the others were planning, but I wanted to keep out of it, like always.

"Flemming: What did I tell all of you when you first started here? I told you: You get a hunk of iron! When you can make a watch from it, you've finished your apprenticeship. Not before and not after. That's his standard motto.
And Edgar: But we didn't really want to become watchmakers."

I wanted to tell Flemming that for a long time. That was not only his stupid motto, that was his whole attitude out of the Middle Ages: the era of handmade articles. Until then I'd always kept my mouth shut.

"And then right afterward Edgar threw the foundation plate on his foot, and with such force that his toe broke. I felt like I'd been hit by a bolt of lightning. I couldn't believe it at first."

It's all true. Except for two minor details. First of all, I didn't *throw* the plate. I didn't have to. The plates themselves were heavy enough to break a stupid old toe or anything else for that matter, just with their weight. All I had to do was drop it. Which I did. And secondly, I didn't drop it *right afterward,* but first Flemming made another little crack, specifically, he bellowed: You're the last person I would have expected that from, Wiebau!

By then I'd had it. I dropped the plate. Just the way that sounds: Edgar Wiebau! It's Edgar *Wibeau!* Only an idiot would say nivau instead of niveau. I mean, after all, every person has the right to be correctly called by his correct name. If you don't attach any great importance to it—that's your business. But I do attach importance to it. That'd been going on for years. Mother didn't let it bother her to be called Wiebau. She was of the opinion that that had simply come into common use, and it wouldn't have killed her, and besides, everything she'd become in the factory she'd become under the name Wiebau. And it was only natural that we'd be called Wiebau! What's the matter with the name "Wiebeau"? If it'd been "Hitler" maybe, or "Himmler"! That would've been truly decent. But "Wibeau"? Wibeau is an old Huguenot name. So? In spite of all that, I suppose that really wasn't reason to drop that stupid old plate on stupid old Flemming's stupid toe. That was a real mess. Right away I knew that not a living soul would talk about our apprenticeship, only about the plate and the toe. Sometimes I would suddenly get hot and dizzy, and then I would do things, and afterward I didn't know what I'd done. That was my Huguenot blood, or maybe my blood pressure was too high. Too high Huguenot blood pressure.

"Do you mean Edgar was afraid of the consequences, and that's why he ran away?"
   "Of course. What else?"

I just want to say this: I wasn't exactly looking forward to the epilogue. "What does Edgar Wiebau (!), member of the Free German Youth, have to say about his behavior in front of Master

Flemming?" People! I'd rather've ordered hamburger than to've
had to season my steak with crap like: I realize . . . in the future I
will . . . I hereby commit myself to . . . and so on! I had something
against self-criticism, I mean: when it's public. Somehow it's de-
grading. I don't know if you understand me. I think that a person
should be allowed to have his pride. It's the same with good examples. Somebody's always coming up to you and wants to know
who you want to be like, or you have to write three essays about
it every week. Can be that I have a model, but I don't make a point
of telling everyone about it. Once I wrote: my best good example
is Edgar Wibeau. I want to be just like what he's going to be like.
Nothing more. That is: I *wanted* to write that. But I left well
enough alone, people. The most that could've happened would've
been that they wouldn't have graded it. Not one damn teacher
dared to give me an F or something.

"Can you remember anything else?"
"You mean a fight, I suppose? We never argued. Oh, once in a
fit of rage he threw himself down the stairs, because I wouldn't
take him with me somewhere. He was five then, if that's what
you're referred to. Just the same I suppose it's all my fault."

That is a crock of shit! It's nobody's fault, only my own. Let's be
clear about that! Edgar Wibeau broke his apprenticeship and ran
away from home *because he'd been planning to for a long time.*
He made his way in Berlin as a painter, had his fun, had Charlotte,
and almost made a great invention, *because he wanted to.*
   That I passed into the Great Beyond doing it, that was really
dumb. But if it consoles anyone: I didn't notice much. Three hundred eighty volts are no joke, people. It went very fast. As a rule,
regrets in the Great Beyond are not the usual thing. All of us here
know what we're in for. That we cease to exist when you cease to
think about us. My chances are probably lousy. I was too young.

"My name is Wibeau."
"Glad to meet you—Linder, Willi."

Greetings, Willi! My whole life you were my best friend, do me a
favor now. Don't start grubbing around in your soul after guilt or
something. Pull yourself together.

"There are supposed to be tapes from Edgar which he mentioned.
Are they available? I mean, can I hear them? At your convenience?"
"Yeah. That's OK."

The tapes.
    to sum it up/wilhelm/i have made an acquaintance/which touches
my heart closely—an angel—and yet i am not in a position/to tell
you/in what respect she is perfect/why she is perfect/enough/she
has taken possession of my whole being—end
    no/i do not delude myself—i read in her black eyes true sympathy
for me and for my fate—she is sacred to me—all physical desire
is mute in her presence—end
    enough/wilhelm/the betrothed is here—fortunate that i was not
present to witness his reception—that would have rent my
heart—end
    he wishes me well/and i surmise/that that is Lotte's doing/for in
that respect women have a fine instinct and a sound one/if they
can keep two admirers on good terms with each other/that is bound
to be to their advantage/however rarely it succeeds—end
    that was a night—wilhelm/now i can survive anything—i shall
not see her again—here i sit and gasp for air/try to calm myself/
and await the morning/and the horses are ordered for sunrise
    o my friends/you ask why the stream of genius so seldom bursts
forth/so seldom sends its sublime floods rushing in to make your
souls quake with astonishment—dear friends/why there along both
banks of the river dwell the placid conservatives/whose summer
houses/tulip beds and cabbage fields would be ruined/and who consequently manage to avert betimes with dams and drainage ditches
any future threat—all this/wilhelm/forces me into silence—i return
into myself and find a world—end
    and for all this you are to blame/who talked me into undergoing
this yoke and prated so much about activity—activity—i have petitioned the court for my dismissal—feed this to my mother in a
sweet syrup—end

"Understand it?"
    "No. Nothing."

Of course you can't. Nobody can, I'd guess. I got it from an old
book, a paperback. A Reclam paperback. I'm not even sure what

it was called. The stupid old cover got flushed down the stupid old john in Willi's garden house. The whole thing was written in this impossible style.

"Sometimes I think—a code."

"It makes too much sense for a code. But then on the other hand it doesn't sound thought-out either."

"You could never tell about Ed. He came up with some really weird stuff. Whole songs, for example. Words *and* music! There wasn't a musical instrument that he couldn't learn to play in two days. Or at least in a week. He was able to make calculators out of cardboard that still work today. But most of the time we painted."

"Edgar painted?" What kind of pictures were they?"

"Always GIN A2."*

"I mean: what kinds of motifs? Or can I see some of them?"

"Impossible. He had them all with him. And you can hardly talk about motifs. We always painted abstract. One was called physics. Another: chemistry. Or: the brain of a mathematician. It was just that his mother was against it. Ed should've had a "decent job" first. That used to really tick Ed off, if you're interested. But he got maddest when he found out that she, his mother, had gotten a card from his progenitor . . . I mean: his father . . . I mean: you, and had hidden it from him. That happened every once in a while. Then he was really ticked.

That's true. I thought that really stunk. After all, there was such a thing as the privacy of letters, and the cards were plainly addressed to me. To Mr. Edgar Wibeau, the stupid old Huguenot. Any idiot could have seen that I wasn't supposed to know anything about my progenitor, the slob who drank and chased after women. The bad man from Mittenberg. Him with his paintings that nobody could understand, which was always the paintings' fault of course.

"And you believe that that's why he ran away?"

"I don't know . . . Anyway, what most people think, that Ed ran away 'cause of this thing with Flemming, that's pure bullshit. Why

---

*GIN (German Industrial Norms) is an abbreviation used by the GDR government. It means: "meeting government standards" or "satisfactory." A2 means: "second class."

he did that, I don't really know that either. Ed had it easy. He was tops in all his classes, without hitting the books. And he never got himself involved in anything. There was always a lot of trouble there. People called him "mama's boy." Not to his face, of course. Ed didn't let it get to him. Or maybe he didn't hear it. For example, that business with the miniskirts. The broads, I mean: the girls in our class, they just couldn't stop themselves from showing up in the shop in miniskirts, on the job. In order to give the teachers a thrill. It had already been forbidden umpteen times. That really ticked us off, so we, us guys, showed up at work one morning with miniskirts. That was really quite a spectacle. Ed didn't take part. That was probably too silly for him.

Sorry. I just didn't have anything against short skirts. You drag yourself completely zonked out of bed in the morning, see a woman through the window, and already you begin to feel better. Beyond that, as far as I'm concerned anyone can wear what they please. Just the same, I thought the whole thing was a good joke. Could have been my own idea. The only reason I stay'd out of it was that I didn't want to cause any trouble for mother. That was really my big mistake: I never wanted to cause any trouble for mother. In fact, I'd gotten into the habit of never causing any trouble for anybody. Do that, and you never have any fun. After a while it really begins to bug you. I don't know if you know what I mean. That brings us to the subject of why I split. I was just sick of running around as living proof that you can raise child very well without a father. That was what I was supposed to be. One day I had the crazy idea, what would've happened if I'd suddenly croaked, smallpox or something. I mean, what would i have gotten out of life. I just couldn't stop thinking about it.

"If you ask me—Ed went away because he wanted to be a painter. That was the reason. It's just too bad that they turned him down at the art school in Berlin."
    "Why?"
    "Ed said: untalented. No imagination. He was really ticked."

Was I ever! But the *fact* was that my collected works weren't worth a damn. Why do you think we always painted abstract? Because, idiot that I am, I could never in my whole life have painted something real so that you would have recognized it, a stupid old dog or something. I guess that the whole thing with painting was genuine insanity on my part. Even so, that wasn't a bad show, where I came charging into this art school and right into this professor's room and slammed my collected works down on the table right in front of him.

First he asked: How long have you been doing that?

I: Don't know! A long time.

I wasn't looking at him.

He: Do you have a job?

I: Not that I know of. Why should I?

He should have at least thrown me out at that point. But the man was tough. He stuck with it.

He: Is there any order to this? Which one's last, which one's first?

He was referring to my exhibit on the table.

I: The earlier works are on the left.

The early works! Man! Did I pull that off well. That was a low blow.

He: How old are you?

This guy was really tough!

I mumbled: Nineteen!

I don't know if he believed me.

He: Imagination you've got. There's no question there, none at all, and you can draw too. If you had a job, I'd say: draftsman.

I began to pack up my stuff.

He: I could be mistaken. Leave your things here for a few days. It's a known fact that four or even six eyes see more than two.

I packed up. Stubborn. There never was a more unrecognized genius than me.

"You stayed in Berlin in spite of that."

"Ed—not me. I couldn't. But I encouraged him. Theoretically that was right too. After all, there's no better place than Berlin to go underground and then make a name for yourself. I mean, I didn't tell him to stay here or anything. You couldn't get anywhere with Ed like that. We had a garden house in Berlin. We moved from Berlin when my father got transferred here. We didn't get rid of the garden house, they were supposed to put up new houses. In any case I had the key. The place was still in pretty good shape. We looked it over, and I talked the idea down the whole time. The roof was caving in. Someone had swiped the stupid old slipcover off the sofa. Our old furniture was still there, like that always happens. And the house was about to be torn down, because of the new housing project. Ed was getting more and more determined. He unpacked his things. His things! Actually he didn't have any more than the pictures, only the clothes on his back. His burlap jacket that he'd sewn together himself, with copper wire, and his old jeans.

Naturally jeans! Or can you imagine a life without jeans? Jeans are the greatest pants in the world. For jeans I'd give up all of the synthetic rags in Jumo* that always look squeaky clean. For jeans I would give up everything, except maybe for the *finest thing*. And except for music. I don't mean just an old Händelsohn Bacholdy, I mean genuine music, people. I didn't have anything against Bacholdy or the others, but they didn't exactly sweep me off my feet. Of course I mean real jeans. There's a whole pile of junk that just pretends to be jeans. If that's all I could get I'd rather not have any at all. Real jeans, for example, don't have a zipper in front. There is only one kind of real jeans. A real jeans wearer knows what I mean. That doesn't mean that everyone who wears real jeans is a real jeans wearer. Most of them don't even know what they're wearing. It always killed me when I saw some twenty-five-year-old fogy with jeans on that he's forced up over his bloated thighs and then belted up tight at the waist. Jeans are supposed to be hip pants, I mean they're pants that will slip down off your hips if you don't buy them small enough, and they stay up by friction. You naturally can't have fat hips and certainly not a fat ass, because otherwise they won't snap together. People over twenty-five are too dense to grasp that. That is, if they're card-carrying communists and beat their wives. I mean, jeans are an attitude and not just pants. Sometimes I think that people shouldn't be allowed to get older than seventeen—or eighteen. After that they get a job or go to college or join the army and then there's no reasoning with them anymore. At least I haven't known any. Maybe nobody understands me. Then you start wearing jeans that you don't any more have a right to. It's also great when you're retired and then wear jeans, with a belly and suspenders. That's also great. But I

---

*A large department store in East Berlin.

haven't known any, except Zaremba. Zaremba was great. He could've worn some, if he'd wanted to, and it wouldn't have bothered anybody.

"Edgar even wanted me to stay. 'We'll make it' he said. But that wasn't planned, and besides, I couldn't. Ed could, I couldn't. I wanted to, but I couldn't.

Then Ed said: When you get home tell 'em I'm living, and that's all. That was the last thing he said. Then I left."

You're OK, Willi. You can stay that way. You're a stubborn bastard. I'm pleased with you. If I had written a will I'd have made you my sole inheritor. Maybe I've always underestimated you. That was really sly, the way you talked me into the garden house. But I wasn't being honest with you either when I said you should stay. I mean, I was being honest. We'd have gotten along good together. But I wasn't being really honest. When somebody has never in his whole life had a chance to be really alone and suddenly *gets* the chance, then it can be really hard to be honest. I hope you didn't notice. If you did, forget it. Anyway, as soon as you left I got into a really crazy mood. First I just wanted to crash, automatically. My time had come. Then I began to see that from now on I could do anything I felt like. That nobody could tell me what to do anymore. That I didn't have to wash my hands before dinner anymore if I didn't want to. I really should have eaten, but I wasn't *that* hungry. So I scattered all my rags and other crap around the room as unsystematically as possible. The socks on the table. That was the crowning glory. Then I grabbed the microphone, flicked on the recorder, and began one of my private broadcasts: Ladies and gentlemen! Boys and girls! Just and unjust! Relax! Shoo your little brothers and sisters off to the movies! Lock your parents in the pantry! Here is your Eddie again, the irrepressible. . . .

I began with my blue jeans song, which I had written three years ago and which got better every year.

> "Oh, Blue Jeans"
> *White Jeans?—No*
> *Black Jeans?—No*
> *Blue Jeans, oh*
> *Oh, Blue Jeans, yeah*

Oh, Blue Jeans
Old Jeans?—No
New Jeans?—No
Blue Jeans, oh
Oh, Blue jeans, yeah

Maybe you can imagine it. All of that in this very rich sound, in *his* style. Some people think that *he's* dead. That's bullshit. Satchmo can't be killed, because Jazz can't be killed. I don't think that I'd ever before done a better job with this song. Afterward I felt like Robinson Crusoe and Satchmo at the same time. Robinson Satchmo. I, idiot that I am, I pinned all my collected works up on the wall. Just the same, at last everybody could tell immediately: Here lives the unrecognized genius, Edgar Wibeau. Maybe I was an idiot, people, but I was really high. I didn't know what to do first. Actually I wanted to go right downtown and check out Berlin, all the nightlife and everything and the Huguenot museum. I probably already said that I'm a Huguenot on my father's side. I was positive that I'd be able to find traces of the Wibeau family in Berlin. I think, idiot that I am, that I was hoping that maybe they'd be noblemen. Edgar de Wibeau and everything. But I told myself that no museum would be open so late. Besides that, I didn't know where it was.

I analyzed myself quickly and decided that I really wanted to read, at least until morning. Then I wanted to crash until noon and then see what was going on in Berlin. That's what I wanted to do everyday: sleep until noon and then live until midnight. I never really came alive until noon anyway. My problem was only that I didn't have any stuff—I hope that nobody thinks I mean hash or opium. I didn't have anything against hash. Of course I'd never tried any. But I think that I, idiot that I am, would've been idiotic enough to have taken some if I'd been able to get hold of some somewhere. Out of pure curiosity. Old Willi and I had once collected banana skins for a half a year and dried them. That's supposed to be as good as hash. I didn't notice a damn thing, except my spit got thick and glued my whole throat together. We lay on the carpet, turned the recorder on, and smoked these skins. When nothing happened I started to roll my eyes around in my head and to laugh ecstatically and to spin around like a maniac as if I was somehow high. When old Willi saw that he started to do the same thing, but I'm convinced that it wasn't doing any more to him than it was to me. By the way, I never tried that banana stuff or any of that other crap again, ever! What I meant was, I didn't have any stuff to read. Or did you think I'd dragged my books along with me? Not even my favorites. I thought, I don't want to drag all that crap from my childhood around with me. Besides, I practically memorized those two books. My opinion about books is that nobody can read all of them, not even all the good ones. Consequently, I concentrated on just two. Anyway, my opinion is that almost *all* books are in each book. I don't know if you understand me. I mean, in order to write a book you've got to have already read a couple a thousand others. At least I can't imagine it any other way. Say, three thousand. And each one of those was written by somebody who'd read three thousand himself. Nobody knows how many books there are. But by simple calculation there are at least . . . umpteen billion times two. I thought that that was enough. My two favorite books were: Robinson Crusoe. I know one of you's going to smirk. Never in my life would I have admitted that. The other was by this Salinger guy. I got my hands on it by pure accident. No one had even heard of it. I mean, no one had recommended it to me or anything. That's just as well. Then I wouldn't have touched it. My experience with recommended books was extremely lousy. I, idiot that I am, I was so stupid that I would think a recommended book was dumb, even when it was good. Even so, I still get pale when I think that I might never've gotten a hold of this book. This Salinger is a great guy. How he creeps around in New York in the rain and can't come home 'cause he's run away from school when they wanted to kick him out anyway, that really got to me. If I'd known his address I'd have written him, he should come over here. He must have been exactly my age. Mittenberg was of course a hole compared to New York, but he would've recovered magnificently over here. Above all, we'd have gotten rid of his dumb sexual problems for him. That's probably the only thing that I could never understand about Salinger. Probably that's easy to say if you've never had sexual problems. I can only say, If you've got problems like that, you should get yourself a girl friend. I don't mean just any old girl friend. Never that. But if you notice, for example, that you both laugh about the same things. That's always a good sign, people. I could've told Salinger right away about at least two in Mittenberg who would have laughed about the same things as him. And if not, then we'd have gotten them to.

If I'd wanted to I could have plopped myself down and could have read the whole book from cover to cover or Crusoe for that matter. I mean, I could have read them in my head. That was always my technique at home when I didn't want to cause a certain Mrs. Wibeau any trouble. But after all, I didn't have to resort to that anymore. I started to scour Willi's garden house for books. It almost blew my mind. His parents must have suddenly gotten affluent. They'd stored the complete furnishings for a four-room apartment here with everything that goes with it. But not one damn book, not even a piece of newspaper. No paper at all, in fact. Not even in that hole of a kitchen. Complete furnishings, but not one book. Willi's folks must've really clung to their books. Suddenly I felt sick. The yard was as dark as a dungeon. I ran so fast I practically cracked my stupid old skull open on the pump and then on the trees before I found the outhouse. Actually, I only wanted to take a leak, but like always the rumor spread itself through both intestines. That had always been a real pain in my life. I've never been able to keep the two affairs apart. If I had to take a leak, then I always had to take a shit, there was no stopping it. And no paper, people. I fumbled around in the john like a madman. And that's how I got my hands on this famous book, this paperback. It was too dark to recognize anything. First I sacrificed the cover, then the title page, and then the last few pages, where, according to my experience, the epilogue is located, which nobody ever reads anyway. When I got out into the light again I found out that my work had in fact been perfect. Before hand I paused for a moment of silence. After all, I had just gotten rid of the last remains of Mittenberg. After two pages I threw the turkey into the corner. People, absolutely nobody would have read that trash. With all good intentions. Five minutes later I had the turkey in my hands again. Either I was going to read until morning or not at all. That's the way I am. Three hours later I had it behind me.

Was I ticked! The guy in the book, Werther, he was called, commits suicide in the end. Just turns in his cards. Blows his stupid old brains out because he can't get the woman he wants and really feels sorry for himself doing it. If he wasn't completely retarded he had to see that she, this Charlotte, was only waiting for him to *do* something. I mean, when I'm alone in a room with a woman, and I know that nobody's coming in for the next half hour or so, people, then I try *everything*. Can be that I'll get slapped a few in the process. So what? Still better than to let an opportunity slip by. Besides, getting slapped is involved in only two out of ten cases at the most. That's a fact. And this Werther was alone with her hundreds of times. In this part, for example. And what's he do? He looks on peacefully while she gets married. And then he kills himself. He was beyond help.

I only really felt sorry for the woman. There she was stuck with her husband, that sissy. Werther should at least have thought of her. OK, let's suppose that he really couldn't have moved in on her. That was no reason to blow his brains out. After all, he did have a horse! I'd have been off in the woods in no time. There was enough of them then. Thousand to one he'd have found at least a million friends. For example, Thomas Münzer* or someone. That just wasn't real. Pure bullshit. Besides that style. That reeked of heart and soul and joy and tears. I can't imagine that anybody ever really talked like that, not even three centuries ago. The whole concoction consisted of nothing but letters from this impossible Werther to his buddy at home. That was probably supposed to be fantastically original or sound not thought-out. Whoever wrote it should read Salinger sometime. *That's* real, folks.

I can only tell you, you've got to read it, if you can just get your hands on it. Swipe it if you have to, wherever you can find it, and don't give it back. Check it out and don't return it. Just say you've lost it. That'll cost you five marks, so what? Don't let the title fool you. I admit it doesn't really do anything for you. Maybe it's badly translated or something, but who cares? Or see the movie. That is, I don't exactly know if there is a movie of it. That's the way it was with Robinson. I could picture everything to myself, every scene. I don't know if you know what I mean. You can envision everything like it would be in the movie, and then you would find out there isn't any movie. But if there really isn't any Salinger film I can only advise every producer to shoot one. He's got it made. I don't know if I would have gone myself. I think it would have scared me to have my own film destroyed. I was never a big movie fan. If it wasn't Chaplin or something like that, these overdone

---

*Religious revolutionary at the time of Martin Luther. Known for his "Christian communism."

bowler hat films where they make the pigs in those idiotic jungle hats look like asses, you couldn't force me into the theater. Or *To Sir with Love* with Sidney Poitier, maybe somebody's seen that one. I could've seen that one every day. I'm not talking about those required films for history class of course. You *have* to go to those. They were in the curriculum. By the way, I liked going to those. You get in an hour what it would take you forever and three days to read in the history book. I've always thought that was practical. I'd like just once to have talked to somebody who makes those films. I'd have said to him: Keep up the good work. I think that people like that should be encouraged. They save you a lot of time. I once knew a guy from the movies. He wasn't a producer, but he did write the scripts, even though I don't think they were the ones for the history films.

He just grinned when I told him what I thought about it. I couldn't make it clear to him that I was serious. I met him one day at the trade school when they dragged us off to one of those films, that he'd supplied the script for. Afterwards: discussion with the creators. But not everyone who wanted to—only the best, the model students—as a reward. The whole show took place during class time. And Edgar Wibeau was naturally right up there at the front, this intelligent, educated, disciplined boy. Our finest specimen. And all the other finest specimens from the other grades, two from each grade.

The film took place in the present. I don't want to make a big deal out of it. Naturally I'd never have gone voluntarily, unless of course the Medium Soft had done the music for it. I assume they wanted to get into the film business. It was about this dude who'd just gotten out of the clink and wanted to start a new life. Until then he'd always been a little suspect, I mean politically, and the cooler hadn't done a lot to change that. His crime was assault and battery. He'd once attacked a veteran because he'd gotten him mad in a conversation about too loud and piercing music. Right out of jail he went to the hospital, because of jaundice, I guess. Anyway, nobody was allowed to visit him. He didn't know anybody anyway. But in the hospital there was this propagandist or whatever that was supposed to be in the same room with him. At least he talked like it. As soon as I saw that I knew right away what was coming. The man would talk to him until he realized his mistakes, and then they would make him conform beautifully. And that's the way it really happened. He joined a splendid work crew with a splendid foreman, met a splendid coed, whose parents were against it at first, but they accepted it splendidly when they saw what a splendid boy he'd become, and finally he was allowed to join the army. I don't know who's seen this splendid film, people. The only thing that still interested me, besides the music, was the hero's brother. He dragged him with him everywhere he went, because he was supposed to conform too. They were always looking for this propagandist. That's supposed to be touching or something. The brother let himself be dragged along, he even got a kick out of all the traveling, and he even got to like this splendid coed, and she him, and one time I thought, just one word and he'll bring her around, if he wants to. Anyway, from that moment on I started to like her. He cooperated with everything, but he didn't conform for a long time. He wanted to be a clown in the circus, and he wouldn't let himself be talked out of it. They said he just wanted to fool around instead of getting a steady job. A steady job, people, I'd heard that line before! Naturally he wanted to join the circus because there he could see the world, among other things, or at least part of it. What's wrong with that? I understood him completely. I couldn't see why that should be bad. I think that most people want to see the world. Whoever claims he doesn't is lying. I was always turned off when somebody claimed you can find everything in the world in Mittenberg. And this brother was turned off, too.

This guy that wrote it started to interest me. I watched him the whole time we sat in the classroom and talked about how great we thought the film was and everything that we could learn from it. First all the teachers and the educators who were there told us what we could learn from it and then we told them what we'd learned from it. The man didn't say anything the whole time. He looked as if this whole show with model students really bored him. Then there was a tour for the film producers through all of our classrooms and everything. At the first opportunity we threw ourselves at the man, me and Old Willi. We hung on to him and stayed behind with him. I had the feeling he was thankful for that, at least at first. Then I told him what I really thought. I told him that a movie in which people are supposed to do nonstop learning could only be boring. That everyone can tell right away what they're supposed to learn, and that nobody who's spent the whole day learning wants to learn at night when he goes to the movie thinking he can have fun. He said that he'd always thought that himself, but that it had to be that way. I advised him just to give it up and to start making those history films where everybody knows from the start that they're not supposed to have fun. Then he saw to it that he caught up with his group which was getting a lecture from Flemming on our outstanding educational facilities. We let him go. Anyhow, I had the feeling that he was raging on the inside about something that had happened that day or maybe just things in general. I'm only sorry that I didn't have his address. Maybe he was in Berlin, then I could have visited him, and he couldn't have taken off.

"Do the Schmidts live here?"
   "Who'd you want to see?"
   "Mrs. Schmidt."
   "That's me. You're in luck."
   "Good. My name is Wibeau. Edgar's father."
   "How'd you find me?"
   "It wasn't easy."
   "I mean, how'd you know about me?"
   "From the tapes. Edgar'd sent tapes to Mittenberg, like letters."
   "I didn't know anything about that. And there's something about me on them?"
   "Only a little. That your name is Charlotte, and that you're married. And that you have black eyes."
   Easy, Charlie. I didn't say anything. Not one word.
   "What do you mean, Charlotte? My name isn't Charlotte."
   "I didn't know. Why are you crying? Please don't cry."

Stop howling, Charlie. Knock it off! That's no reason to howl. I got the name from that dumb book.

"I'm sorry, but Edgar was an idiot. Edgar was a stubborn, obstinate idiot. There was no way to help me. Excuse me."

That's right. I was an idiot. Man, was I ever. But stop howling. I don't think anybody can imagine what an idiot I was.

"Actually I came to see if you maybe had a picture he'd made."

"Edgar couldn't paint at all. That was also one of his idiocies. Everyone knew it, but he just wouldn't listen. And if you said it to him right to his face he'd babble some nonsense that nobody could understand. Probably not even himself."

That's when you were at your best, Charlie, when you'd really gotten yourself worked up. But that everybody could see right away that I couldn't paint is not exactly correct. I mean, you might have seen it, but I was really good at acting as if I could. That's really one of the greatest tricks, people. It doesn't matter whether or not you can do something, the main thing is to act as if you can. Then it works. At least with painting and art and that stuff. A pair of pliers is good if it grips. But a picture or something like that? Nobody really knows whether it's good or not.

"It started already on the first day. our kindergarten had a playground in the housing project, with a sandbox, swings, and a teeter-totter. In the summer we spent the whole day there when we could. Now everything's been torn up. The children always charged straight from the sandbox onto the jungle gym and into the bushes. They were on the neighboring lot, but it practically belonged to us. The fence had disappeared a long time before, and we hadn't seen anybody there for ages. The whole subdivision was going to be torn down. Suddenly I saw someone coming out of the garden house, a guy, unkempt and really degenerate looking. Right away I called the children to me."

That was me. People, was I ever zonked. I was really outstandingly zonked. I didn't see anything. I dragged myself to the privy and from there to the pump. But I just couldn't touch the pump water. I could have drunk an ocean, but the pump water would have killed me. I don't know if you can understand it. I'd just plain woken up too early. Charlie's brats had woken me with their screaming.

"That was Edgar?"
"That was Edgar. I immediately forbade the children to go there again. But you know how children are—five minutes later they were all gone. I called them, and then I saw: there they were, with

Edgar. Edgar sat behind his garden house with his painting gear, and they were all behind him, dead silent."

That's true. I was never a child lover. I didn't have anything against children, but I was never a child lover. They can really bug you in the long run, at least me, or men in general. Or did you ever hear of a *male* kindergarten teacher? It's just that it always really pissed me off when somebody was supposed to be a degenerate or immoral or something because he had long hair, unpressed pants, didn't get up at five, and didn't wash himself down with pump water first thing in the morning and didn't know what income bracket he'd be in when he got to be fifty. So I fished out all my painting gear and planted myself behind the garden house and started to take my bearings with a pencil like all painters are supposed to do. And five minutes later Charlie's brats were all behind me in full strength.

"What was he painting?"
"Actually, nothing. Lines. The children wanted to know too."
Edgar said: We'll see. Maybe a tree?
Instantly: What do you mean, maybe? Don't you know what you're going to paint?
And Edgar: That all depends on what the morning holds for me. How can you know ahead of time? First of all a painter has to loosen himself up. Otherwise the tree that he wants to paint will be too stiff.
They enjoyed themselves. Edgar knew how to get along with children, but he certainly couldn't paint. I could tell that right away. I'm kind of interested in painting."

Stop it, Charlie! They enjoyed themselves all right, but the joke about the tree was yours. I was still thinking: That's the way it always is. You're having fun and then the kindergarten teacher comes along and gives you a serious explanation. And then I turned around and looked at you. I thought I'd been hit by a truck. I had underestimated you. That was plain irony. I think that the whole thing, this tug of war of ours, began right there. Both of us wanted to pull the other one over the line. Charlie wanted to prove to me that I couldn't paint worth a damn, and that I was just an overgrown child, that I couldn't live like that and that I needed help.

And I wanted to prove the opposite to her. That I was an unrecognized genius, that I could live my own life, that I didn't need any help, and above all, that I was anything but a child. Besides, from the beginning I wanted to have her. To lay her, no matter what happened, but to have her too. I don't know if you know what I mean, people.

"You mean, he couldn't draw realistically? He couldn't even sketch?"

"He couldn't draw at all. It was also clear to me why he pretended he could: He wanted people to think he was an unrecognized genius. I've just never understood why. That was a real tick with him. I got the idea of bringing him to our kindergarten and letting him paint on one of the walls. He couldn't have hurt anything. Our school was going to be torn down. the principal didn't have anything against it. I thought Edgar would try to get out of it. But he came. It's just that he was so shrewd. Excuse me, but he was really shrewd. He just gave each of the children a paintbrush and let them all paint anything they wanted. I knew right away what would happen. In half an hour there was the most beautiful fresco on the wall. And Edgar hadn't made a single brush stroke or at least as good as none."

The thing came off fantastically, I knew it would. I knew that nothing could happen. Children can really bore you but they can paint so it'll just knock you over. If I wanted to look at pictures I'd rather go to a kindergarten than a stupid old museum. Besides, they just love to smear up the whole wall.

The teacher's aides were astounded. They thought it was just fantastic, what their kids had painted. I thought it was pretty good myself. It really knocked me right over, the way kids can paint. And Charlie couldn't do anything about it. The others delegated her to bring me some lunch. They'd probably noticed that Charlie could mean something to me. They'd have had to have been stupid not to. I just sat there watching her starry-eyed the whole time. I don't mean I really stared at her like a wild-eyed kid the whole time. Not that, people! I didn't have especially impressive optical organs in my stupid old Huguenot skull. They're regular pig slits in comparison with Charlie's headlights. But brown. Brown is dynamite, serious.

Back at my *kolkhoz** I got the best idea of my life. At least it's gotten me a lot of laughs. It was really dynamite. I got my hands on this book again, this paperback. Automatically I started to read it again. I had the time, and above all I had the *idea*. I shot into my room, flipped on my recorder, and dictated to Willi:

I'd gotten that directly out of the book, even the Wilhelm. To sum it up, Wilhelm I have made an acquaintance which touches my heart closely . . . An angel . . . And yet I am not in a position to tell you in what respect she is perfect, why she is perfect; enough! she has taken possession of my whole being. End.

That's how I first got onto the *idea*. I got the tape off to the post office right away. I owed Willi a letter anyway. It was only too bad that I couldn't see Willi fall over. He must've keeled over. He must've gotten cramps. He probably rolled his eyes around in his head and fell out of his chair.

"Could I see this mural?"

"Unfortunately not. The building has been torn down. We're in a new building now.

I do have one of Edgar's pictures. But there's nothing to see in it. It's a silhouette. I told you: he wouldn't believe me. That was a day later. I came to him. We wanted to pay him a fee. Then I got the idea of asking him to draw a picture of me, this time without help. We were alone, of course. What'd he do? This silhouette. Anybody can do that. But I saw his other pictures in his garden house. I can't describe them. They were just jumbled confusion. That was probably supposed to be abstract. But it was only jumbled! Really as a matter of fact, everything was always jumbled at his place. I don't mean dirty, but jumbled and sloppy as can be."

You're a hundred percent correct, Charlie. Jumbled and sloppy and everything, just like you say. At first I thought I'd been run over by a bus, people, with Charlie standing there in my room. Luckily it was the afternoon and I was pretty much awake. But that with the money was clear to me from the start. Because of a fee! That was Charlie's own money and beyond that an excuse. She just couldn't get her mind off me.

---

*Russian word for *collective farm*. Here it means as much as "my place."

At first I acted modest. I said: What for? I didn't even raise a finger.

And Charlie: Just the same!—Without your supervision it would never have worked.

Then I said it right to her face: That's your own money, and you know it. A fee? No way!

Then she got an idea: OK. But I'll get it back again. Just has to be approved from upstairs. I thought you could use it.

I still had some money, but I definitely could've used it. People, you can always use money. But I didn't take it anyway. I knew what it would mean. It would mean she thought I was a bum or something. I didn't do her that favor. When that was settled she actually should've left. But that isn't the way Charlie was. That just wasn't her. Her skull was at least as thick as mine. I mean head. With women you should probably say head.

Besides, the whole time I was telling her that she really could mean something to me. I mean, naturally I didn't say it in so many words. Actually I didn't say anything at all. But she still noticed, I think. And then she started with her idea about my painting a picture of her. Supposedly just for fun. And I was supposed to believe that! Charlie was talented maybe, but she was a lousy actress. That didn't suit her. For about three seconds I looked pretty worried, until I got the idea with the candle. I put Charlie on a stupid old stool, darkened the room, pinned a hunk of paper on the wall and started twisting her head around in the light. Naturally I could have moved the stupid old candle around instead, but I wasn't that dumb. I took a hold of her whole chin and turned her head. Charlie swallowed hard, but she went along with it. I used every trick I could think of: the painter and his model. Supposedly there's nothing erotic in that, but I think that's bullshit. That's probably something the painters dreamed up so their models won't all run away. In my case, something clicked, and in Charlie's too, at least. But she didn't have a chance! She just wouldn't take her eyes off me. These headlights of hers. I was just about to try *everything*. But I analyzed myself and decided that I didn't want *everything*. I mean I did, but just not right away. I don't know if you understand me, people. For the first time in my life I wanted to wait with that. Besides, I probably would have gotten slapped. For sure. Then I still would have gotten slapped. I just kept my cool and made this silhouette of her. When I was done she started right in: give it to me! For my fiancé. He's in the army.

If one of you thinks that that really got on my nerves or something, that about the fiancé, he's wrong, people. Being engaged is a long way from being married. Anyway, at least Charlie had figured out what the name of the game was. *That* was exactly it! She started to take me seriously. I'd heard that one before. Fiancés always pop up when it starts to get too serious. Naturally I didn't give her the silhouette. I mumbled something like: It's still too rough . . . Needs some life. As if you could put life into it. Especially not without her eyes. And Charlie's eyes were regular headlights, or did I already say that? I just had to keep it. I wanted to varnish it and keep it for myself. That really got her angry. She dug in her heels and told me to my face: You can't paint at all, at least not correctly. That's all just an excuse for something. You're also not in from Berlin, anyone can see that. You don't have a real job, and anyway you don't earn any money painting, how you do otherwise, I don't know. She'd really gotten herself wound up.

But I wasn't lazy either: I thought for a minute and blurted out the following:

Uniformity marks the human race. Most of them spend the greater part of their time in working for a living, and the scanty freedom that is left to them burdens them so that they seek every means of getting rid of it.

Charlie didn't say a thing. She probably hadn't understood a word of it. Which isn't surprising, what with that style. Naturally I had gotten it from that book. I don't know if I told you that I can memorize things from books fantastically. That was a real pain in my life. It had its advantages, of course, in school for example. I mean every teacher is satisfied when he hears a passage from a book he knows. I couldn't blame them. They don't need to check if it's all right, like they do with their own words. And they were all satisfied.

"Am I mistaken, or did you have a fight with him?"

"We didn't fight. I told him to his face that I thought he was lazy. I almost thought maybe he was involved in something crooked. He must have gotten money somehow. I'm sorry. I know that's nonsense, but you really couldn't figure him out."

"And him? Edgar?"

"Edgar did what he always did in such cases, only that day was the first time for me: He talked rubbish. I can't think of anything else to call it. You couldn't even remember it. The stuff was really that insane. Maybe it had some meaning, but it was really queer. And it wasn't his own. Probably from the Bible, that what I think sometimes. He just wanted to flabbergast you with it, that's all."

Maybe I shouldn't have even tried that joke on Charlie. Even so, her reaction was priceless.

Then she asked me: How old are you actually? My age! She just wanted to show me that she could have been my mother. She couldn't have been more than two years older than me. I said: three thousand seven hundred and sixty-seven years old, or is it seventy-six? I always confuse those two. Then she left. I admit that this question always bugged me. Even from a woman who could have meant something to me. It always forced you to lie. I mean, you can't help your age. And if you're more mature than the average seventeen-year-old it's pretty dumb to tell the truth, if you want to be taken seriously. If you want to see a movie and you've got to be eighteen, you don't stand there and scream: I'm only seventeen, do you? By the way, I used to go to the movies quite a bit. At least that was better than sitting at home with Mother Wibeau in front of the boob tube.

The first thing I did when Charlie'd left: I stuck in a new tape and reported to Willi:

No, I do not delude myself! I read in her black eyes true sympathy for me, and for my fate. She is sacred to me. All physical desire is mute in her presence. End.

People! Was that ever a crock. Especially that stuff about desire. But on the other hand, it wasn't really so dumb. I just couldn't come to grips with that language. Sacred! I could hardly wait to see what Willi would do with that one.

After that I really wanted to hear some music. I shoved in the cassette with all the records by the Medium Soft on it and started to move. Slowly at first. I knew that I had time. The tape lasted at least fifty minutes. I had just about everything those guys did. They played so it just knocks you over. I couldn't dance very well, at least not in public. I mean, still at least three times as good as anybody else. But I really only got warmed up between my own four walls. Outside the eternal breaks in the music always messed me up. You're just beginning to get started and bang—they cut. That always made me sick. This music has to be played nonstop, preferably with two bands. Otherwise no one can get into proper form. The Negroes know that. I mean the Blacks. You should say Blacks. It's just, where else could you find bands like the Medium Soft. You should just be glad that they existed. Especially the organist. In my opinion they only could have gotten him from a seminary, a heretic or something. I'd almost busted my ass trying to round up all these guys' albums. They were dynamite. Fifteen minutes and I was really high for the second time in the last few days. Usually I only accomplished that once a year at the most. I was beginning to see that coming to Berlin was the perfect thing for me. If for no other reason, then because of Charlie. Man, was I high! I don't know if you know what I mean. If I could have I'd have invited all of you. I had at least three hundred and sixty minutes of music in the cassettes. I believe that I'm a really talented dancer. Edgar Wibeau, the great rhythmist, equally great in Beat and Soul. I could also tap dance. I'd nailed taps on an old pair of gym shoes. It was fantastic, serious. And if my cassettes hadn't held out we'd have gone to the "Eisenbahner" or even better to the "Grosse Melodie" where the Medium Soft played or the SOK or Petrowski or Old Lenz, depending on who was there. We always went on Mondays. Or does one of you think maybe I didn't know where to go in Berlin for real music? After *one* week I knew that. I don't think there was much in Berlin I missed. I was like in one constant stream of music. Maybe you can understand me. I'd been like starving. I'd estimate that there wasn't one decent group that had any idea of what music is in a two hundred kilometer radius of Mittenberg. Old Lez and Uschi Brüning! Whenever that woman started I just about died. I don't think she's any worse than Ella Fitzgerald or anybody else for that matter. I'd have given her everything, the way she'd stand up there with her huge glasses and practice with the group. And the way she'd communicate with the leader with just a look, that must have been transmigration of souls or something. And the way she'd thank him with just a look when he let her start in. I could've cried every time. He'd hold her back until she just couldn't stand it anymore, and then he'd let her start in, and then she'd always thank him with this smile, and I'd just about go out of my head. Could be that it was completely different with Lenz. Just the same, the "Grosse Melodie," it was a kind of paradise for me, like heaven. I don't think that I lived on much besides milk and music then.

At first my only problem at the "Grosse Melodie" was that I didn't have long hair. I really looked out of place. As a genuine model student in Mittenberg I naturally wasn't even allowed to have a shag, much less *long* hair. I don't know if you can imagine what a pain that was. I cringed when I saw the others with their manes, naturally only on the inside. Otherwise I claimed that long hair didn't mean anything to me 'cause as long as everybody had it it didn't take any courage. Besides, having long hair was a non-stop hassle. Just the way people looked at it. I don't know if you know what I mean, people. That face that they make when they tell you that you can't have long hair in the shop or someplace else, for safety reasons. Or else head protection, hairnets, like the women, so you look branded, like you're being punished. I don't think any of you can imagine how much satisfaction that gave someone like Flemming. Most of them wore head protection and when no one was looking they naturally took it off. With the result that Flemming immediately went through the ceiling. He didn't have anything against long hair, but in the shop . . . *unfortunately* . . . and so on. When I saw the way he'd grin then, I'd just about explode. I don't know what you'd call that when people constantly get harassed because of their hair. I'd like to know who you're hurting with it. I always thought Flemming was a real bastard then. Especially when he said: Look at Edgar. He always looks proper. Proper!

Somebody'd once told me the story about a model student like that, A-average or better, son of splendid parents, only he didn't have any friends. And there was this gang in his neighborhood that tipped over park benches and smashed windows and stuff like that. Nobody could catch them. The leader was an absolutely sly dog. But one more or less beautiful day it happened anyway. They got him. The guy had hair down to his shoulders—typical. Only it was a wig, and the truth was he was that same splendid model student. One day he'd had enough, and he'd gotten himself a wig.

In Berlin at first I thought of getting a wig somewhere, for the "Grosse Melodie." But in the first place wigs don't grow on trees, and secondly, my hair grew at a fantastic rate. Whether you believe it or not—my hair grew approximately two centimeters a day. That had always been a pain in my life. I could hardly get away from the barber. But this way I at least had a respectable mop in two weeks.

"Then you saw him more often after that?"

"That couldn't be avoided. We were after all practically neighbors. And after the thing with the mural he couldn't get the kids off his back anymore. What else could I have done? He had a way with children, which is something most men don't, I mean, most boys. Besides, I'm convinced that most children know exactly who really likes them and who doesn't."

That's the truth. Charlie's brats couldn't be helped. That's the way kids are. You can't give them an inch. I knew that. They probably think you enjoy it. Just the same, I cooperated, patient as a cow. First of all because Charlie was of the opinion that I got along with children magnificently. Sort of crazy about kids. I didn't want to disillusion her. Me? Crazy about kids? Secondly because the brats were my only chance to stay close to her. Do what I would I couldn't get Charlie back on my kolkhoz, let alone in my garden house. She knew why, and I did too. Day after day I hung around that playground. I pushed the merry-go-round or whatever that thing with the four beams is called, or I played Indian. That way I slowly learned how you can shake them off when you want to. At least for ten minutes. I divided them up into two groups and let them play war.

About that time I got the first answer from Willi. Good Old Willi. That was too much for him. He couldn't get over it. On his tape was the following text: Greetings, Eddie! I don't get it. Give me the new code. Which book, which page, which line? End. What's with variant three?

Give me the new code! That killed me. It was too much for him. It wasn't really fair of me, I admit it. Usually we talked to each other like that—in code. But that was too much. A new code. I could've kicked myself in the ass. When we were in the mood, for example, we'd shoot off dumb proverbs at each other a mile a minute: There are two ends to a loaf of bread.—Right. But when you don't dry the dishes in the morning, they're still wet.—You don't have to be stupid to be dumb.—Work makes your feet dry. In that vein. But *that* was too much for Old Willi. Man, you should have heard his voice. He didn't understand the world anymore. By variant three he meant whether or not I was working. He probably thought I was starving. Just like Charlie. She was always bugging me about it.

I didn't have anything against work. My opinion about it was; when I work, then I work, and when I mess around, I mess around. Or didn't I deserve any vacation? But nobody should think I planned to sit on my kolkhoz forever or something. At first you might think that'll work. But any halfway intelligent person knows how long. Until you go crazy, people. Always to see only your own mug, that just about guarantees you'll go crazy after a while. That just doesn't work anymore. All the fun's gone and everything. For that you've gotta have friends, and a job. At least I do. I just hadn't gotten that far yet. For the time being, it was still OK. Besides, I didn't have any time for work. I had to stick around Charlie. Charlie meant something to me, but I probably already said that. In a case like that you've got to stick around. I can see myself squatting next to her on that playground and the brats were running around us. Charlie was crocheting. An idyll, people. All that was missing was that I didn't have my head in her lap. I didn't have any inhibitions, and I'd already managed it once. The feeling on the back of my head was not bad. Serious. But ever since that day she'd brought her crocheting stuff along and fooled around with it in her lap. She came in the afternoon with her brats, sat down and got out her crocheting stuff. I was always already there. Charlie had a way of sitting down that'd just about make you flip. She probably only had full skirts, and before she sat down she'd grab hold of the hem, lift the whole thing up, and then sit down on her panties. She did that very precisely. That's why I was always right there when she came. I didn't want to miss it. I also always made sure that the bench was dry. I don't know if she noticed, but she knew for sure that I was watching her when she sat down. Nobody can tell me different. That's the way they are. They know for sure that you're watching them, and they do it anyway. It was also a show in itself everytime when she'd look down with her headlights. I think that Charlie had a slight squint. That's why you always got the impression she was looking right at you. I don't know if you've ever seen these portraits of people that hang on the wall and always look at you no matter where you stand. The trick that the painters have is simply that they paint the eyes so the optical axes are exactly parallel, which is never true in real life. It's a known fact that there are no real parallels. By that I don't mean that it wasn't pleasant for me. Not that. It's just that you never knew for sure if she was taking you seriously or making fun of you. That can really bug you.

I probably already said that I'd practically become part of the kindergarten furnishings. A sort of ex-officio caretaker or something. All that was missing was for me to paint the fence. This toy repairing and merry-go-round pushing was just part of the job. And balloon blowing. One day, I think it was a party, I'd already blown up about two to the sixth power balloons and by the two to the seventh power balloon I started to black out, and I fell over. I just fell right over. I could stay under water for four minutes, starve for three days, or go a whole half a day without music, I mean: genuine music. But that made me fall over. When I surfaced again I was lying in Charlie's lap. I noticed that right away. She'd undone my shirt and was massaging my chest. I pressed my skull into her belly and held still. Unfortunately I am insanely ticklish. I had to sit up. the brats were standing around us. Charlie was pale. Almost immediately she burst out: If I was hungry I'd eat!

I protested: It came from all the blowing.

Charlie: If *I* didn't have anything to eat I'd buy myself something.

I grinned. I knew exactly why she was ranting so. Because she was fantastically happy that I was still alive. Any half-way intelligent person could've seen that. She nearly gobbled me up with her headlights, people. I almost went crazy. Only I could've sent the brats to the moon.

Charlie: If *I* didn't have any money, I'd get a job.

I said: He who doesn't eat, shall also not work. I always thought that such distortions were rather clever. Then I got up, shot onto my kolkhoz, which wasn't more than two steps away, and dug up the first head of lettuce that I could get my hands on. I probably haven't told you yet that one day I'd scattered all the seed packages I could find in Willi's garden house in the yard, just as a joke. The first thing to appear was the lettuce. Lettuce and radishes. I started to cram the lettuce down my throat. The sand crunched, but I just wanted to get out the following:

How fortunate it is for me that my heart can feel the plain, naive delight of the man who puts on the table a cabbage that he has grown himself.

Naturally I'd gotten that from that Werther. I guess I had more charm that day than ever.

Charlie just said: You're crazy.

She'd never said that before. She always went right through the ceiling when I came up with this Werther stuff. I wanted to grab my chance and lodge my skull in her lap again, and I guarantee it would've worked, if that stupid Werther paperback hadn't slipped out of my shirt at that moment. I'd gotten in to the habit of carrying it in my shirt. I really didn't know why myself.

Charlie got her hands on it immediately. She flipped through it without reading anything. I looked pretty worried. I would've really felt stupid if she'd figured everything out. She asked what it was. I mumbled: toilet paper. A second later I'd grabbed it back again. I put it away. I'd estimate that my hands were shaking the whole time. After that day I left it in the garden house, people. I wanted to keep on playing the charmer and everything, only right then the principal came charging out onto the playground. At first I thought that maybe she had something against my esteemed presence. But she didn't even see me. She only looked at Charlie, sort of strangely.

She said: You can quit for the day. I'll finish up for you.

Charlie didn't understand it at all.

The principal: Dieter is here.

Charlie turned white as a sheet, then bright red. Then she looked at me like I was some kind of criminal, and she took off.

I didn't know what was going on.

The principal explained it to me. Dieter was her fiancé. He'd come home from the army that day, honorable discharge and all. I asked myself how come Charlie didn't know that. They usually write and tell you. Then I thought of the you're-a-criminal look. *I* was the guilty one, *I,* Edgar Wibeau, the lazy kid, the pseudo painter, the crazy man! It was supposed to be my fault that she hadn't met Dieter at the train station with flowers and everything. I felt like I'd been kicked by a horse. I think I already said that I've got a lot of charm. That I was pretty successful with women, with females, I mean. I mean: spiritually, or whatever you want to call it. Sylvia was almost three years older than me, but hardly a woman. I don't know if you can understand me. Sylvia was way below my niveau. I didn't have anything against her for it, but she was way below my niveau. Charlie was the first real woman I'd ever had anything to do with. I hadn't thought that I'd fall for her so fast. I was almost out of my mind, people. I think that happened 'cause I hung around her so much. I shot back into my garden house, that is, I wanted to. But before that I saw Dieter. He was coming toward Charlie. He was wearing a jacket and tie, and he had a suitcase, one of those stupid attaché cases, an air rifle in a case, and a bouquet of flowers. I guessed him to be about twenty-five: I mean, this Dieter. In that case he must have served longer. He's probably gotten to be a general or something. I waited to see if they'd kiss. But I couldn't see anything.

Back in the garden house I immediately grabbled the mike. Old Willi had to hear about this. About one second and I'd found the appropriate text:

Enough, Wilhelm: the betrothed is here! . . . Fortunate that I was not present to witness his reception! That would have rent my heart. End.

"If his painting wasn't worth anything, I ask myself, how did he actually support himself?"

"At the most he could've gotten a job somewhere as temporary help. But we would have noticed that, my husband and I. That is, we weren't married yet then. We'd known each other for a long time, since we were children. He'd been in the army for a long time. I introduced him to Edgar. Dieter, I mean my husband, had been in charge of garrison duty. I don't know if that means anything to you. Anyway, with that job he came into contact with a lot of boys Edgar's age. I thought that he might have some influence on Edgar. They did get along well together, too. We visited Edgar once, and he was at our place occasionally. But Edgar couldn't be helped. He just couldn't be helped. Dieter really had the patience of Job with him, maybe too much so, I don't know. But Edgar just couldn't be helped."

That's true. They both moved in on me one day. As long as she had Dieter with her Charlie dared to go into my garden house again. She hadn't been on the playground for a few days. Her brats had, but not her. Then she popped up with Dieter at my place. She treated me like a kid. I'd been through that before. She wanted to make it clear to Dieter that she thought of me as a harmless jerk. Immediately I put up my dukes. I mean, not really. On the inside.

I probably haven't told you that since I was fourteen I'd been in a boxing club. That and Old Willi were probably the best about Mittenberg. Of course I didn't know what kind of a partner he was. At first glance I guessed him to be pretty flabby. But I'd learned that you can never judge your partner by first glance. But that he wasn't the right man for Charlie, that was my opinion from the start. He could have been her father, I mean, not according to his age. But otherwise. He carried himself with at least as much dignity as Bismarck or somebody like that. He was looking over my collected works. Charlie'd probably dragged him along mostly for that reason. She still wasn't really sure whether I wasn't really an unrecognized genius. Most of the time she stuck close to Dieter. I still had my dukes up. Dieter was taking a long time. I thought he wasn't going to say anything. But that was the way Dieter was. I don't think he ever said a damn thing in his life that he hadn't thought over three times, or maybe more. Then he began: I would say that it wouldn't hurt him if he were to orient himself more toward real life in the future, toward the life of the construction workers, for example. He has all the subjects he needs practically right outside his door. And then there are naturally here as in all professions certain rules which he simply must observe: perspective, proportion, foreground, background, etc.

That was it. I looked at Charlie. I looked at the man. I could have screamed shit at the top of my lungs. The man meant that all seriously, completely seriously. At first I thought: irony. But he meant that seriously, people.

I could have knocked him around the ring a while longer, but I decided to put my strongest weapon into action. I thought for a moment and then shot out the following gem:

One can say much in favor of rules, about the same things as can be said in favor of civil society. A person who trains himself by the rules will never produce anything absurd or bad, just as one who lets himself be modelled after laws and decorum can never become an intolerable neighbor, never an outright villain; on the other hand any "rule," say what you like, will destroy the true feeling for nature and the true expression of her!

This Werther had really thrown together some worthwhile things. I could see right away that I could safely lower my fists. The man was finished. Charlie had prepared him for at least everything, but *that* was too much for him. He acted as if he were dealing

with a maniac who you didn't dare provoke, but he couldn't fool
me. Any half-way intelligent trainer would have taken him out of
the fight. Technical knockout. Charlie wanted to go then. But Dieter still had something to say: On the other hand it's very original,
what he paints, and very decorative.

I don't know what he meant by that. He probably though *he'd*
knocked me out, and now he wanted to sugarcoat the pill. You
poor ass! I felt sorry for the man. I let him go. And then, of all
stupid things, this silhouette that I'd made of Charlie caught his
eye. Charlie said immediately: That's supposed to be for you. He
just hasn't given it to me yet. Supposedly because he hasn't finished
it yet. But he hasn't *done* anything to it since then.

And Dieter: Now I have you in the flesh.

God! That was probably supposed to be charming. He was a
real charmer, dear old Dieter.

Then they split. Charlie'd draped herself around him the whole
time. I mean, not really. With her headlights. Just so I saw it. But
that ran off me like water off a duck's back. Not that you should
think I had something against Dieter because he was in the army.
I didn't have anything against the army. I admit I was a pacifist,
especially when I thought of the unavoidable eighteen months.
Then I was an outstanding pacifist. But I wasn't able to look at
any Viet Nam pictures or anything like that. Then I saw red. If
somebody's asked me then, I'd have signed up for the rest of my
life. Serious.

I've got one more thing to say about Dieter: He was probably a
very nice guy. After all, not everyone could be an idiot like me.
And he was probably exactly the right man for Charlie. But there
was no point in thinking about it. I can only tell you, people, not
to think about it in a situation like that. When you're face to face
with your opponent you can't stop to think about whether he's a
nice guy or not. That gets you nowhere.

I grabbed the mike and gave Willi the latest:

He wishes me well, and I surmise that that is Lotte's doing . . . ,
for in that respect women have a fine instinct, and a sound one: if
they can keep two admirers on good terms with each other, that
is bound to be to their advantage, however rarely it succeeds. End.

I was slowly getting used to this Werther, but I still had to hang
in there. I knew that you've got to hang in there, people. You might
win the first round, but you can't let up your guard. I stayed hot

on their tails and didn't let up. "I'll get you yet," in this vein. Charlie clung to Dieter's arm. She gave her other one almost instantly to me. That almost drove me out of my mind. I had to think of Old Werther. That man knew what was what. Dieter didn't even open his mouth.

We landed in Dieter's apartment. In an old building. One room and a kitchen. That was the tidiest room that I'd ever seen. Mother Wibeau would've loved it. It was about as homey as the waiting room at the train station in Mittenberg. Except that one was at least never straightened up. *That* I could've put up with. I don't know if you know what I mean, these rooms that always look as if they're only lived in two days out of the whole year and then by the head of public health. And the best part was: Charlie suddenly thought the same thing. She said; That's all going to change. Once we're married, right?

I started with a sort of grand tour. First I took a look at the pictures he had. The one was a lousy print of Old Gogh's sunflowers. I didn't have anything against Van Gogh and his sunflowers. But when you start finding a picture hanging in every stupid john it begins to make you sick. At the least it'd make me want to puke. Usually I couldn't stand it for the rest of my life. The other was in one of those convertible frames. I don't want to say anything more about that. Whoever's seen it knows which one I mean. Enough to make you sick, serious. This splendid couple there on the beach. After all: convertible frame. When I want to see all the pictures in the world I'll go to the museum. Or if a picture really gets to me I hang it up in three different places so I can see it no matter where I am. Whenever I saw one of those convertible frames all I ever thought is that the people have committed themselves to look at twelve pictures a year.

Suddenly Charlie said: The pictures go back to our school days.

But I hadn't opened my mouth *once* the whole time. I hadn't even groaned or rolled my eyes or anything. I turned and looked at Dieter. I gotta tell you, the man was standing in his corner, had his fists down, and stood still. Can be that he hadn't yet realized that the second round had already begun. Charlie was constantly making excuses for him, and he didn't budge. People, at least I knew what to do. My next move was to take a look at his books. He had a million of them. All behind glass. All arranged according to their size. I just about flipped. Whenever I saw something like that I just about flipped. I've probably already stated my opinion about books. I don't know what all he had. Guaranteed, all of 'em good books. Marx, Engels, Lenin, all in neat rows. I didn't have anything against Lenin and the others. I also didn't have anything against Communism and all that, the abolition of the exploitation of the world. I wasn't against that. But against everything else. That you arranged books according to their size, for example. It's the same with most of us. They don't have anything against Communism. No half-way intelligent person can have anything against Communism these days. But they're against the other things. Being for something doesn't take courage. But everyone wants to be courageous. Consequently they're against things. That's the way it is. Charlie said: Dieter's going to study German. He's got a lot of catching up to do. Most of them his age who weren't in the army so long have already been assistant professors for a long time now.

I looked at Dieter. If I'd been in his shoes I'd have attacked by now. But he hadn't even put up his dukes yet. A fantastic situation. Slowly I was beginning to see that there was going to be an explosion if I kept this up and if Charlie didn't stop making excuses for him.

The only thing in the whole room was Dieter's air rifle, the kind you can break down. He'd hung it over his bed. I took it down, carelessly, without asking, and started fooling around with it. I aimed it at this couple on the beach, then at Dieter, and then at Charlie. When I got to Charlie Dieter finally leapt into action. He pushed the barrel away.

I asked: Loaded?

And Dieter: Just the same. Too much has happened already.

Grandfather sayings like that one always pissed me off. Still I didn't say anything. I just held the barrel up to my temple and pulled the trigger. That finally brought him out of hibernation: That's not a plaything. Even you've gotta have *that much* sense!

And he grabbed the flintlock away from me.

Then I went for my most powerful weapon, Old Werther:

My friend . . . human beings are human, and the bit of common sense a man may have counts for little or nothing when passions rage and the bounds of humanness press in on us. Say rather— We'll come back to this.

The bounds of humanness, Old Werther wasn't satisfied with any less. But I'd gotten to Dieter. He made the mistake of thinking about what I'd said. Charlie stopped listening altogether. But Dieter made the mistake of thinking about it. I really could've gone. Then Charlie started in: I"ll make us something to munch on, OK?

And Dieter: OK with me! But I've got things to do. He was already in gear. He planted himself behind his desk. With his back to us.

Charlie: He's got to take his entrance exams in three days.

Charlie must've had a bad day. She just wouldn't give up. I was still standing around.That was when Dieter hit the ceiling. He said coldly: You can tell him more about me *along the way.*

Charlie turned pale. We'd just been thrown out, both of us. I'd gotten her into a splendid situation, and I, idiot that I am, was happy about it. Charlie was pale, and I, idiot that I am, stood there and was happy. Then I left. Charlie followed me. When we got out onto the street I managed to get my arm around her shoulder.

Charlie jabbed me in the ribs right away and hissed: Are you crazy?

Then she ran away. She ran away, but I got into a completely crazy mood. Slowly I began to see that it was a losing fight with Charlie. Still and all I was somehow really high. At least I was suddenly standing in front of my garden house with a tape from Old Willi in my paws. Consequently I must have been at the post office. I don't know if you know what I mean, people.

Dear Edgar. I don't know where you are. But if you want to come back now, the key is under the doormat. I won't ask any questions. And from now on you can come home whenever you want. And if you want to finish your apprenticeship in another factory, that's OK too. The main thing is that you are working and not just fooling around.

I thought I'd been kicked by a horse. That was Mother Wibeau.

Then came Willi. Greetings, Eddie! I just *couldn't* get rid of your mother. Sorry. She's really down. She even wanted to give me money for you. Maybe that idea about working isn't so bad. Think about Van Gogh or one of them. All the stuff they had to do just in order to paint. End.

I listened to it, and right away I knew what Old Werther'd have said:

That was a night! Wilhelm! now I can survive anything. I shall not see her again! Here I sit and gasp for air, try to calm myself, and await the morning, and the horses are ordered for sunrise . . .

The stupid tape wasn't any longer, and I didn't have any more in reserve. I could have erased some music, but I didn't want to. To go out and get a new tape would've been a pain too. I analyzed myself quickly and figured out that the whole Kolkhoz and everything just didn't turn me on any more. I didn't think of going back to Mittenberg, not that. But it just didn't turn me on any more.

"But sometime or other Edgar must've started working, construction. At WIK."

"Yes, of course. I just lost track of him. I had enough to do. The wedding. Then Dieter started going to the university. German. It wasn't easy for him at first. I was only working half-days, in order to make it easier for him at the start. Then our kindergarten moved into the new building, the old one was torn down, because they were putting up the new ones. The playground next to Edgar's lot went too. We would've only had to go to the police. Somebody's living in the garden house illegally. I don't know if that would've helped him. In any case, then it wouldn't have happened."

"May I ask you something? Did you like Edgar?"

"What do you mean 'like'? Edgar wasn't even eighteen, I was over twenty. I had Dieter. That's all there was to it. What do you think?"

That's right, Charlie. Don't tell everything. There wouldn't be any point to it, telling everything. I've never done it in my whole life. I didn't even tell you everything, Charlie. You can't tell everything. If you tell everything, maybe you're not even human.

"You don't have to answer me."

"Of course I liked him. He could be very funny. Even touching. He was always moving . . . I . . . ."

Stop bawling, Charlie. Do me a favor and stop bawling. I was a loser. I was just some idiot, I was a screwball, just a lot of hot air. Nothing to bawl about. Serious.

"Hi. I'm supposed to speak to a Mr. Berliner."

"Yeah. That's me."

"My name is Wibeau."

"Are you related to Edgar? Edgar Wibeau, the kid who was with us?"

"Yeah. I'm his father."

Addi! You old grubber! How'ya doing? Right from the start you were my best enemy. I pissed you off whenever I could, and you gave me a hard time everyway you knew how. But now that it's all over, I can tell you: You're a real stubborn bastard. Our immortal souls were related. Just that your brain waves were straighter than mine.

"That was a tragic thing with Edgar. At first we didn't know what to make of it. Everything's clearer to us now. Edgar was a worthwhile person."

Addi, you disappoint me, and I thought you were a stubborn bastard. I thought you wouldn't go along with all that, saying that bull about somebody who's bitten the dust. Me, a worthwhile person? Schiller and Goethe and those guys, they were maybe worthwhile people. Or Zaremba. It always killed me anyway, when they say that crap about somebody who's dead, what a worthwhile person he was and that. I'd like to know who started it.

"Right from the start we'd misjudged Edgar, that's the truth. We underestimated him, above all me as foreman. From the start all I saw in him was the faker, the good-for-nothing, who wanted to live off the sweat off our backs."

Of course I wanted to earn money. If you want to buy tapes you've got to have money. And where do you get it? Construction! The old saying: If you can't do anything and don't want to, work construction or for the railroad. The railroad was too dangerous for me. I can guarantee they would've asked for my ID and social security number and all that crap. So it was construction. They take everyone. I knew that. I was only ticked 'cause when I came to Addi and Zaremba and the crew they were renovating old Berlin apartments, one right after the other, and Addi said first thing: You say "Good Morning" when you come in here.

I knew *that* type. Ask one of them about Salinger or something. I'll guarantee they won't know. He'd think it was a technical manual that he'd missed.

Could be that everything would've been different if Addi had taken the day off that day or something. But *the way* he acted I felt personally challenged. It could also be that my nerves weren't very good, because of the thing with Charlie. That had gotten to me more than I'd thought.

The next thing Addi did was to hand me one of those paint rollers and ask me if I'd ever had one in my hand before. Every Pioneer* knows those things. Consequently I just refused to answer. After that he handed me a paint brush and sent me over to Zaremba. Undercoat the windows. Everybody's standing around gaping, of course, wondering what I'm going to do. But I felt better as soon as I saw Zaremba. It was sort of love at first sight. Right away I knew that the old guy was a real animal. Zaremba was over seventy. He could've retired a long time ago, but instead he stayed here and worked his ass off. And he wasn't just a stand-in. He could clamp a stepladder between his legs and dance around the room on it without wetting his pants. Besides the fact that he was only made out of skin, bone, and muscles. Where was the piss supposed to come from, anyway? One of his tricks was to have someone drop an open jackknife on his biceps. It popped back like rubber. Or he'd play the Hunchback of Notre Dame. For that he'd take one of his eyes out—he had a glass eye—bend himself in at the hips and stagger around. He'd gotten a hold of that glass eye in Spain. I mean: It'd been made for him by somebody in Philadelphia. Besides that he was missing part of one of his little fingers and two ribs. To make up for it though he still had all of his teeth and both arms and a chest full of tattoos. But not those fat women and hearts and stuff and anchors. It was filled with flags and stars and hammers and sickels, there was even a part of the Kremlin wall there. He himself was probably from Bohemia or something. But the neatest thing was that he still fooled around with women. I don't know if you're gonna believe me, but it's all true. Zaremba took care of the trailer. He kept it clean and always had the key. It was a pretty nice vehicle. With two bunks and

---

*Organization for children between the ages of six and thirteen in the German Democratic Republic.

everything to go with it. Once when it was dark I snuck up to it. Until then I didn't know anything, it was just that I had something I had to do under the trailer for a very special reason. I could hear clearly that he was just about to make some woman. Judging by her laughter she must have been very nice. You shouldn't think, however, that I'd have gotten all excited about Zaremba just because of that. No way. Especially not because the first thing he asked me was whether I was paid up on my union dues. He was the treasurer. That really pissed me off. If it hadn't been Zaremba I'd have split right away. Instead I just held out my book. He took it away from me and started snooping through it. Probably he only wanted to know where I stood. Naturally I hadn't paid in Berlin. Right away he got out his goofy little tin box and I was supposed to pay up. That's a real trick, when you can't even afford tapes. He probably just wanted to know that.

Then I started right in putting the undercoat on one of those windows. The paint ran all over the glass. I'd painted the windows umpteen times at home, but I just couldn't seem to manage it. If they hadn't been gaping so, wondering how I'd react, I'd have whipped off the cleanest window imaginable. Not as clean as Zaremba. Zaremba painted like a machine. But still as clean as any one of them, including Addi. Addi was obviously getting nervous. The only reason he didn't go right through the ceiling was because Zaremba was right next to me. That Zaremba couldn't be bothered was already clear to me. In any case, Addi finally couldn't take it any more and burst out: I was going to smear up the *whole* window.

What I did then is probably obvious. I started to smear up the whole window. I thought Addi was going to fall off his ladder. But then *I* almost fell of my ladder, if I'd been standing on one. Zaremba, who was right next to me, started singing. I thought I'd been kicked by a horse and run over by a bus and both at the same time. Zaremba bellowed away, and right away the others started doing it with him, and it wasn't even a hit or anything, but one of those songs where you only know the first verse. But the crew bellowed out the whole song. I think it was: Arise, you socialists, close the ranks, the drums are calling, the flags now blow. . . .*

---

*From the "Sozialistenmarsch," written by Max Kegel (music by Carl Gramm, 1891).

That was one hell of a crew, people. Arise you socialists! I almost dropped my paintbrush. That was Zaremba's way when Addi was about to go through the ceiling. I found that out the next time it happened. It was in some stupid old kitchen. The wall was pretty cracked and I was supposed to plaster it up. Addi said: Ever worked with plaster before? Then take a look at this wall.

In that vein.

So I started mixing plaster in some old bucket. I don't know if you know about that, people. In any case, all my life I've always put in too much plaster, then too much water, and so on. At this rate the bucket got slowly full, and I'd have to have been a magician to have kept the stuff from getting hard. I was looking pretty worried. Then help came. Addi blew his cool. He hissed: I'd fill the *whole* bucket.

Nothing better occurred to him. I took him at his word and dumped all the plaster into the bucket. At the exact same time Zaremba started singing. He couldn't even see us from the john or wherever he was hiding. But he must have smelled what was happening. It was another one of his jokes, this time with partisans, and the whole crew joined the fight. He really had them in the palm of his hand. Addi pulled himself together almost instantly and sent me into one of the rooms to sweep the floor for undercoating. If I'd been in his shoes I'd probably have dumped the whole bucket, plaster and all, on my head. But Addi pulled himself together. Then it dawned on me, what this singing was all about. I split. I was just wondering what Zaremba would do if I got to him. If he'd sing. Before that I heard Zaremba storm into the kitchen and snarl at Addi: Take it easy, fellow. Real easy. No?

And Addi: Just tell me, what does he want with us? He just wants to get rich off of our work. No question about it. That no-good.

And Zaremba went: No . . . no good?!

I probably already said that Zaremba was from Bohemia. That's probably the reason for this "no" business. He managed to get it out at least three times in every sentence. The man could say more with his "no" than other people say in whole novels. If he said "no?" and leaned his head over to the side, that meant: You better think that one over again, fella. If he went: "no?!" and raised his eyebrows at the same time, that meant: Don't say that again, buddy. If he squinted his pig slits everybody knew the Hunchback of Notre Dame was coming. I don't know if that's true. Somebody told me, after '45 Zaremba was supposed to have been the highest judge in Berlin for three weeks or so. He's supposed to have given some really weird and strict sentences.

No? Mr. Defendant, so you were always a good friend of Communism, d'cheer! In that vein. "D'cheer," that was also one of his words. It took me forever to figure out that "d'cheer" meant "did ya hear." Zaremba was a real animal.

I don't know if he got sick of singing or if he finally realized that Addi and I didn't get along. In any case *he* started giving me my orders himself. The first one was that I was supposed to whitewash the panel, I mean the stuff above the panel, in some old bathroom, and the ceiling. He left me alone and I mixed up the prettiest blue goo and started to roll it all over the ceiling and walls, like pop art. After a while it looked like the blueprints for expressway interchanges. And everything in this real neat blue. I wasn't even through, and there was Zaremba, standing there, and the whole crew behind him. They were probably anxious as hell to see what he was going to do with me, especially Addi. But he just went: "No?!"

That was probably the longest "no" I'd ever heard out of him. Besides that he leaned his head over to one side, raised his eyebrows, and squinted his pig slits, all at the same time. I could have burst with pride. I'm still proud of this new "no" variation.

"Sure he acted a little strange. No question about it. But that should've tipped us off, especially me. Instead I chased him away, even Zaremba wasn't able to stop me. Zaremba was maybe the only one of us who'd suspected what Edgar had in him. But I was hardheaded. It has to do with our VPS, vaporless paint sprayer. We'd already built a lot of things, but that was going to be our greatest. A machine that could spray any kind of paint without producing that awful vapor that every other kind of sprayer still makes. That would've been one-of-a-kind, even in the world market. Unfortunately we'd come to a standstill about that time. Not even the experts we called in were able to help. And then Edgar comes along and gives us his two cents worth. I really exploded. I don't want to apologize. I just wasn't all there."

Do me a favor, Addi, and save your breath. I can tell you exactly what I had in me: nothing. And as far as the VPS is concerned:

absolutely nothing. Your idea with the air-pressure and the hollow nozzle was lousy, but so was my idea with the hydraulic pressure. So what are you jabbering about? I'll admit that I really thought the hydraulic idea was great, actually from the start, almost as soon as I saw the thing. It was lying around under our trailer. I'd already tripped over it at least three times and had already looked it over. But I'd rather've died than ask someone what kind of machine it was. Especially not Addi. Until one day Zaremba opened his mouth. I think that dog was able to see through me like glass.

Haven't seen it yet, no? Can't, either. It's unique. This paint sprayer sprays every kind of paint under the sun, in the water or in the air, does as much in one day as three painters, no, works *without* this vapor, and for that reason is better than all other comparable machines on the market, even American, d'cheer. That is, when we get it working, no?

Then he wiped a little of the dust off the thing and stood around sighing. And then he said: It's not our first invention, but our best one, no.

It looked as if he wanted to prod the crew on a little, who'd naturally long since been standing there. That thing'd probably been lying around there for a long time. It didn't work at all, it just vaporized and vaporized, and beyond that nothing.

I said: The machine will never replace it.

And I held up my paintbrush. And started undercoating again.

That set off Addi: Listen here, my friend. That's all well and good. I don't know what's eating you, but something is. No question about it. And I don't care. But we're a crew here, and not a bad one, and you belong to it, and in the long run you've got no choice but to fit in and pull your own weight. And don't think you're our first case of that. We've straightened out a lot of others. Ask Jonas. In any case, we're still waiting for the guy who can pull us down to average.

There it was again. He turned around in his tracks and took off, with the others at his heels. I'd only understood about half of what he'd said. The line about the machine was, after all, harmless. I had a lot of other stuff I could've said. From Old Werther, for example. I analyzed the situation quickly and concluded that I'd hit Addi's weakest point with the sprayer.

On top of which Zaremba says: Gotta understand him, no. His baby, the sprayer. Christ, don't mess with it. Either going to be a flop or *the* success, no? His first!

And I:

He is the most punctilious fool that can exist; one step at a time and as fussy as an old woman; a person who is never content with himself, and whom consequently no one else can satisfy.

That was Old Werther again at last. Zaremba opened his pig slits wide and snarled: No! Don't say that!

He was the first one who this Old High German* didn't knock off his horse. That would've made me feel bad. I'll admit I'd picked out a fairly normal passage for him. I don't know if you know what I mean, people. A few days later it came to a showdown. Addi and the crew had set up the sprayer in the yard of one of these stupid old houses and were hooking it up. Two experts from some specialty shop had come with a whole box full of nozzles, all different. They were all going to be tried out. Big show! Just about everyone and his grandmother had shown up. All the potters and masons and everybody else who hung around in those houses. None of the nozzles worked. Either a stream as thick as your arm came out or it vaporized like a lawn sprinkler. The experts weren't very optimistic from the start, but they still forked over every one of their nozzles. Addi wouldn't give up. He was a stubborn bastard. Until he grabbed for the smallest caliber, and the pressure was too much for it. The old hose exploded, and everybody standing within a radius of ten yards was "as yellow as a Chinaman" or something. Especially Addi. That drew an incredible laugh from the whole crowd.

The experts said: Forget it. We didn't have any better luck, and we've got everything! Can't be done! Technically unsolvable, at least for the time being. It's not the fault of the nozzles.

And then I came and drew my Werther pistol:

Uniformity marks the human race. Most of them spend the greater part of their time in working for a living, and the scanty freedom that is left to them burdens them so that they seek every means of getting rid of it.

The experts probably thought I was the crew clown. They grinned anyway. But the crew itself came walking slowly up to me, with Addi at the front. They were still wiping the yellow sauce out

---

*It is customary to divide the history of the German language into three periods. The first of these, Old High German, dates from the beginning of literary tradition about the eighth century to around 1100.

of their faces. I put up my dukes, just in case, but nothing happened. Addi hissed coldly: Get out of here! Just get out of here, or I won't guarantee anything.

I couldn't see his face really clearly. I still had paint in my eyes. But it sounded as if he was just about to bawl. Addi was over twenty. I don't know when was the last time I bawled. In any case, it was quite a while ago. That was probably why I did, in fact, get out of there. Could be I'd gone a little too far or something. I hope none of you think I'm a chicken, people. As a boxer you're not really allowed to defend yourself anyway. If you hurt somebody you can go to jail. Besides, Zaremba was there, and he was signaling to me: get out of here. Now is the right time. That was, at least for the time being, the end of my guest appearance as a painter at Addi and company.

By the way, the weather that day was rotten. I took off for my kolkhoz. First thing was to dictate a new tape to Old Willi:

And for all this you are to blame who talked me into undergoing this yoke, and prated so much about activity. Activity! . . . I have petitioned the court for my dismissal. . . . Feed this to my mother in a sweet syrup. End.

I thought that fit magnificently.

"I just fired him! Not that we wanted to isolate ourselves. Jonas, for example, is an ex-con. But most of the people that come to us can't do anything and don't want to either. It's not easy to get a crew together that you can begin to do something with."

"You don't have to apologize. Maybe Edgar was only an obstinate faker, rotten-tempered, incapable of fitting in, and lazy, for all I know."

"Take it easy! He was never actually rotten-tempered, at least not around here. And obstinate . . . ? You must have known him better than we did."

"Know him? I haven't seen him since he was five!"

"I didn't know that. I mean, wait a minute. Edgar visited you. He was at your place!"

Shut up, Addi!

"He was raving about it. You have a studio apartment, faces the north, pictures all over the place, perfect disorder."

I said shut up, Addi!

"Excuse me. But I didn't get that from Edgar—I got it from Zaremba."
"When was that supposed to have been?"
"That must've been after we'd fired him, end of October."
"Nobody was at my place."

Unfortunately it's true. I don't know why I went there, but it's true. He lived in one of those magnificently nondescript modern apartments that Berlin's slowly getting full of. I knew his address. But I didn't know it was one of those magnificently nondescript modern apartments. He had an apartment. And it did face the north. I don't know if any of you thinks I'd be stupid enough just to walk up and introduce myself. Hi, Dad, I'm Edgar, in that vein. No way. I was wearing my work clothes. I just said; furnace man, when he opened the door. He wasn't really impressed, but he did believe me. I didn't have any plan, but I was pretty sure it'd work. A pair of blue pants and you're the furnace man. A stupid old jacket and you're the new janitor. A leather bag and you're the man from the telegraph office, etc. People'll believe anything, and you can't even hold it against them. You've just got to know how to do it. Besides, I still had a hammer with me. I took it and banged around for a while on the radiator in the bathroom. He stood in the door and watched me. I needed a little time to get used to him. I don't know if you can understand that, people. To know you've got a father, and then seeing him, they're *not at all* the same thing. He looked about thirty or so. That really surprised me. I had no idea. I always figured he was at least fifty! I don't know why. He was standing in the door in his bathrobe and a pair of brand new jeans. Around that time you were suddenly able to get real jeans in Berlin. No idea why. But you could. It was like always just before something. The rumor spread, at least in certain circles. They were selling them in some warehouse, because they knew that no department store in Berlin was big enough for people who'd come for those jeans. And there were millions of 'em. I guess none of you'll think that I wouldn't have been there. And how! I hadn't gotten up so early in years, just to be there on time. I'd have kicked myself in the ass if I hadn't gotten any jeans. There were about three thousand of us standing there in this hallway waiting to get

in. You can't imagine how crowded it was. That was the day of
the first snow, but I can guarantee that none of us froze to death.
A couple of people had music with them. It was an atmosphere
like at Christmas, when you get up in the morning and start opening gifts—that is, if you still believe in Santa Claus. We were all
on a genuine high. I was just about ready to do my "Blue Jeans"
song, when they opened up the door and the show began. Standing
behind the doors were four full-grown salesmen. We just pushed
them out of the way and plunged into the jeans. Unfortunately the
whole thing was a waste. They weren't genuine, the ones they had.
They were authentic, but not genuine. Just the same, it was a real
happening that day. The funniest thing was probably these two old
mummies from the boonies who were standing there in the hallway.
They probably wanted to get some genuine jeans for their little
boys back in Podunk. But when the mood reached its high point
they got weak knees. They wanted out, the dears. They wouldn't
have had a chance, even if one of us had helped them. They had
to stay, like it or not. I just hope they at least halfway survived.

In any case, this father of mine must have been somewhere in
the crowd that day. I was easily able to imagine it while he was
standing there in the doorway watching over me. Why he was
standing there, that was clear to me right away. There was a pair
of women's stockings hanging from a clothesline in the bathroom.
I'd have guaranteed he had one in his room, and *that's* where I
wanted to look before I gave myself away. So I said: Everything's
OK here. Wanta take a look in the other room.

And he: Everything there is OK.

I: Fine. But this is the last time we're coming this year.

Then he gave in. We went into the other room. The woman was
lying in bed. Next to the bed was one of those camping cots, that
he'd probably camped in. I liked the woman right away. She had
something of Charlie. I'm not sure what. Probably it was her way
of always looking at you, of always aiming her headlights right at
you. Right away I started imagining the three of us living there
together. We'd have gotten a hold of a wider bed, or I'd have slept
on the old one, or for that matter, on the camping bed in the
hallway. I'd have gone and gotten rolls in the morning and made
coffee, and we'd have all three of us eaten breakfast together in
their bed. And at night I'd have dragged them both to the *Grosse*

Melodie or sometimes her alone, and we'd have flirted with each other, decently, of course, like buddies.

Then I turned on my charm: Pardon me, Madam. Only the furnace man. Be done in a sec. In that vein.

I went for the radiator. I tapped on the pipes with the hammer and listened for the echo, like those furnace guys always do. Naturally I was looking over the whole room at the same time. Wasn't much there. Portable shelves with books. A TV, last year's model. Not a single picture in the whole place. The woman offered me a smoke.

I said: No thanks. Smoking is one of the main obstacles to communication.

I was playing the role of the young, well-trained specialist. Then I asked this father of mine: You're not much of a picture fan, are you?

He didn't get it.

I went on: I mean the walls. Tabula rasa. We get around. Everybody's got pictures, always different kinds, but you? But then, you've got other nice things.

The woman smiled. She'd gotten it instantly. But then, it probably wasn't all that difficult. We looked at each other for a second. I think she was the only thing in the whole room that didn't bug me. Everything else bugged me, especially the bare walls. That's the only way I can explain the fact that I suddenly started to babble like a fool: But that makes good sense. I always say, if you're gonna have pictures, then at least ones you've painted yourself, and naturally you don't hang those on your own walls if you've got any sense at all. Do you mind my asking: Do you have any children? Take a tip from me: Kids can paint so it'll just knock you over. You can hang 'em on the wall any time without being embarrassed. . . .

I don't know what other stupid things I might have said. I don't think I stopped talking until I was standing on the stairs, the door was already shut, and it suddenly occurred to me that I hadn't said a word about who I was and all that. But I just couldn't bring myself to ring the doorbell again and say it all. I don't know if you can understand that, people.

When it was all over I crawled back into my garden house, like always. I wanted to hear some music, and I did, too, but somehow it just didn't do anything for me. By then I knew myself well enough to know that something was wrong with me. I analyzed myself quickly and concluded that I wanted to start building *my own* sprayer, right away. *My* VPS. Of course I didn't know how. I only knew it would have to be completely different from Addi's. And I did know that it wasn't going to be easy without the right tools and all that. But it was never like me to let stuff like that scare me off. It was also clear the whole thing had to take place in secret. And then, when it worked, my sprayer, I'd show up at work with it, real casual like. I don't know if you know what I mean, people. In any case, I, idiot that I am, started combing the whole damn deserted subdivision for usable objects that same day. I don't know if you can imagine what all you can find in a place like that. I can only tell you, everything, serious, except what I needed. Just the same I dragged it all home, everything that looked halfway useful. First collect your material, I thought. That was the first stone on my grave, people, the first nail in my coffin.

"I could say that we got him back here pretty quickly again. But that was more on Zaremba's initiative than anybody else's. In principle it was already too late. Edgar'd already started working on *his* VPS. Zaremba didn't know that. We hunted him up in his garden house. But there was no trace of the fact that he was working on it. And we never thought of looking in the kitchen."

That with the kitchen wouldn't have done you a damn bit of good. It was locked up. I wouldn't have let anybody in there. Maybe not even Charlie. I was building away like mad. Then I saw Zaremba's skull with his moldy hair pop up from behind the hedge. Instantly I closed up shop. I threw myself on the stupid old sofa and started coughing. Not that I was sick or anything, at least not really. I did have a cough. Probably I'd gotten it rummaging around the old subdivision. Maybe I should've already started heating the place. But I could've stopped coughing if I'd wanted to. Only that I'd sort of gotten used to it. It had such a splendid effect. Edgar Wibeau, the unrecognized genius, selflessly works on his newest invention, his lung half eaten away, and he doesn't give up. I was a complete idiot, I mean really. But that spurred me on. I don't know if you understand me. So I was hacking away when the crew stormed into my *kolkhoz*. I mean, they didn't really storm into it. They came in quietly. First Addi and and then Zaremba. Probably the old man was shoving him. These guys obviously thought they were supposed to have a bad conscience or something. 'Cause they'd chased me away. And then me with my cough on the sofa! I don't know if you can imagine what a splendid cough I'd developed. Besides that, my feet were sticking out from underneath this stupid old blanket, as if it was too short.

For Zaremba it was too much! Ahoy! You've never coughed better in your life, no? And then he stepped aside, so that Addi could get out his speech. At first Addi was looking for something to hold onto, then he started in: What I wanted to tell you, sometimes I'm maybe a little too quick to react, that's just my way, no doubt about it. Both of us oughta think about that in the future. And it's all over now with the sprayer. All over and done with, no doubt about it.

It wasn't easy for him. I was almost touched. I couldn't say anything, because of the cough. Jonas, the reformed ex-con, took care of the rest: We thought you could specialize in floor covering. Roller 1a would be OK too. And on Saturdays we always go bowling.

Naturally the rest of the crew had gathered around in the meantime, in full strength. They'd just trickled in on me, one by one. I had the feeling that Addi or Zaremba had set up guards on all four sides, just in case I'd tried to disappear. I could've laughed my ass off. They were all standing around gaping at my collected works. It was obvious they thought they were dynamite. They thought I was a rare bird, someone you didn't dare get too close to. Except for Zaremba. I'd guarantee Zaremba had his thoughts about me. He started sniffing around my castle. At last he started to open the door to the kitchen. But it was locked, like I said, and as for all his trick questions, like whether or not I was going to stay here all winter, I could hardly answer them. This cough was really unpredictable. It came at the dumbest times, people. I really had a good one. Zaremba wanted to rush me to a doctor, the dog. For a second I must've looked pretty worried. Then it occurred to me that I get this cough every fall and that it's completely harmless. An allergy. Hay fever or something. One of a kind. A riddle for science. And then it'd suddenly stop. But my cough improved amazingly after that day, that is: it vanished, except for occasional minor attacks. A doctor, that's all I would've needed. My opinion about doctors is: I can live without 'em. I went to a doctor once, because of a rash on my feet. Half an hour later I was on this table, and he was jabbing two shots into every one of my toes. And then he pulled out my toe-nails. That was already outrageous. And when he finished, he sent me off to the waiting room, on foot, people, believe it or not. I was bleeding through the bandages like a wildman. He didn't even think about putting me in a wheelchair or giving me anything. Since then I haven't changed my opinion about doctors.

In any case, from that day on I was on the list of endangered species, as far as Addi was concerned. All those pictures and on top of that an unsurpassed cough. I probably could've afforded to do even more after that. But I was able to control myself. I had no real yearning to host them again on my kolkhoz. They could've caught on to the sprayer. I, idiot that I am, thought the whole time that I'd make headlines with my sprayer. I denied myself almost everything. I didn't even draw my Werther pistol once, for example. I painted my floors with the roller like a good little boy, and Saturdays I sometimes even went bowling. I sat there with ants in my pants, while they bowled and thought to themselves: This Wibeau, we've done a splendid job of straightening him out. It was as bad as in Mittenberg. And at home my sprayer was waiting.

About this time I managed to scare up that Huguenot Museum, by accident. I'd actually long since given up looking for it. At first I'd asked dozens of people, a sort of public opinion poll. Can you tell me where I can find the Huguenot Museum? With zero success. Not one damn person in all of Berlin knew anything about it. Most of them thought I was stupid, or maybe a tourist. And suddenly I was standing right there before it. It was in a dilapidated church. The building had interested me, because it was the first war ruin I'd ever seen. Not one shot had been fired in Mittenberg! General Brussilow or somebody had forgotten to capture it. And on the only entrance to the whole building that was still intact was: Huguenot Museum. And under that: closed for renovation. Normally I wouldn't have paid any attention to a sign like that. I was after all a Huguenot, and they couldn't shut me out. According to my estimates the head of the place would probably slobber all over me. A genuine, living descendant of the Huguenots. And far as I knew, we were in danger of dying out. But for some reason I stopped dead in my tracks in front of this sign. I analyzed myself quickly and concluded that I wasn't even interested in knowing whether or not I was noble, or what the other Huguenots were up to; probably not even whether I was a Huguenot or a Mormon or something else. For some reason I wasn't even interested any more.

On the other hand it was about this time that I got another crazy idea, namely writing to Charlie.

Since that one day I practically hadn't even seen her. It was clear to me that she'd made up with her Dieter a long time ago and that after all that had happened I didn't have a chance any more. I still couldn't get her out of my mind. I don't know if you know what I mean, people. My first thought was right away Old Werther. He'd written letters to his Charlotte nonstop. It didn't take long for me to find an appropriate one:

If you saw me, best of women, in this surge of distractions! and saw how desiccated my senses become; . . . not one hour of bliss! nothing! nothing!

I scribbled that on the back of a menu in this bowling alley. But I never sent it. It became clear to me, that I just didn't have a chance with her any more with Werther. That wouldn't work with her any more. It was just that I couldn't think of anything else. Just to go there wouldn't work. And then one night there was an envelope in my mailbox. I saw it already from a distance. I'd always had to pick up my mail at the post office. And there wasn't any stamp on it. In it was a card from Charlie: Are you still alive? Drop in some time. We've been married for ages.

Charlie must have been there herself. I almost fell out of my tree, people. My knees were knocking. Serious. I got the shivers. I left everything where it was and tore out of there, but fast. Eight minutes later I was standing in front of Dieter's door. I just assumed they'd be living together at Dieter's. And they were, too. Charlie opened the door. At first she just stared at me. I had the feeling that I hadn't exactly arrived at the right time. I mean, it was the right time, but not *exactly* the right time. Maybe she thought I wouldn't come the same day she'd brought the letter to my kolkhoz. In any case, she asked me in. They only had this one room. Dieter was sitting there. He was sitting behind his desk, exactly like he'd been sitting there a few weeks ago. That is, he wasn't sitting behind it, but rather in front of it. He'd put the desk in front of the window, and was sitting in front of it, with his back to the room. I understood that completely. If you've only got one room, and you've got to work in it too, you've got to be able to block yourself off somehow. And Dieter did it with his back. His back was practically a wall.

Charlie said: Turn around!

Dieter turned around, and fortunately I got an idea: Only wanted to ask if you had a pipe wrench.

I just couldn't get rid of the feeling that Dieter wasn't supposed to know that Charlie'd invited me. I went at the most one step into the room. Oddly enough Charlie said: Do we have a pipe wrench?

I analyzed the situation instantly and came to the conclusion that Charlie was only playing along with the thing with the pipe wrench. Right away I got the shivers again. Dieter asked: What do you need a pipe wrench for? Pipe burst?

And I: You could call it that.

By the way, I really did need this pipe wrench. For the sprayer. I'd scared up something like it in an old shed. Just that it was so dilapidated that the most you could've done with it would've been to chop a hole in your knee. Then we gave each other five, and Dieter went: Well?

That was his uncle-type well. All that was missing was if he'd added: Young man. Have we mended our ways since our last meeting, or do we still have those foolish ideas in our heads? Usually that drove me right up a tree, and this time too. I was up there in a matter of seconds. But I pulled myself together and came down again and played the humble, reasonable, mature young man, that I after all had just become, people. I don't know if you can imagine that, me being humble. And all that just because I thought I had this sprayer in my back pocket, idiot that I am. I don't even know anymore what I was actually thinking. I was probably just so certain that my idea with the hydraulics was exactly right that I was already beginning to act humble like a great inventor after his success. Edgar Wibeau, the great, congenial young man, who has nevertheless remained humble and so on. Like with these top-flight athletes. Man, people, was I ever an idiot. Besides I could naturally see that Charlie was turning red. I mean, I didn't *see* it. I just couldn't look at her the whole time. Otherwise I probably would've done something really stupid. But I *noticed* it. She probably thought that one of her greatest dreams was being realized, that Dieter and I were becoming good friends. Until then she'd been standing behind me in the door. Then she got all excited, wanted to make tea and all that, and I was supposed to sit down. the room was hardly recognizable. It wasn't just that it'd been renovated and all, but it had been completely refurnished. I don't mean with furniture. Actually only the pictures and the lamps and curtains, and all sorts of knick-knacks that Charlie'd probably brought into the marriage with her, were new. Suddenly I wanted to live there myself.

I don't mean that everything was perfectly matched. The chairs with the carpet. The carpet with the curtains. The curtains with the wallpaper and the wallpaper with the chairs. That sort of thing always bugged me. That's not what I mean. But the pictures, for example, were from the brats in the kindergarten. That kids can paint so that it just about knocks you over, I've probably already said that. One of the pictures was probably supposed to be a snowman. He was only with red crayon. He looked like Charlie Chaplin, after he'd been robbed of everything. He could really get to you. Next to it was Dieter's air rifle. All the books suddenly looked as if someone was always reading them. You suddenly felt the urge to plop yourself down somewhere and read every one of them. I started running back and forth in the room, looking at everything and talking about it. I praised everything like a fool. I can only tell you, if you're hot for a woman or a girl, you've got to praise her. In my case that was just a part of the standard service. Naturally I wasn't clumsy about it. More like I was doing, for example, right now in this room with Charlie. Entirely aside from the fact that I *really did* like it, I naturally saw that Charlie was turning alternately red and white. I considered it possible that Dieter'd never said a thing about all that. Which was entirely consistent with the fact that he immediately started to block himself off again. He was working again. When Charlie saw that, she sat down immediately and I had to too. I almost flipped. She always had this way of setting herself down with her skirt. People, I can't even describe what that did to me. Later she motioned me out of the room. Outside she explained to me: You've got to understand him, OK? He's *completely* out of everything because of all that time in the army. He's the oldest in his class. I suspect he doesn't even know for sure if literature is the right thing for him. She was just about whispering. Then she asked me: And you? how's your garden house?

I automatically started in coughing. Decently, of course.

Right away Charlie: You're not going to try to spend the winter there?

I said: Hardly.

Now I was coughing like never before.

Then she asked me: Are you working?

And I: 'Course. Construction.

You could see right away that turned her on. Charlie was one of those people who you could ask if they believed in the "good in mankind" and they could answer "yes" without turning red. And she was probably thinking that the good in me had finally won out and maybe because she'd been so frank with me that time before.

Whenever I read in some book that somebody was suddenly standing somewhere and didn't know how he'd gotten there, 'cause he was so deep in thought, I usually just bailed right out. I always thought that was a complete crock. But that night I was standing in front of my garden house and really didn't know how I'd gotten there. I must have been sleeping the whole way home or something. I immediately turned the recorder on. First I wanted to dance half the night, but then I started working on my sprayer like a madman. That night I was more certain than ever that I was on the right path with my sprayer. I was only sorry that I hadn't really taken Charlie's pipe wrench with me. Naturally that wasn't even brought up again. Mine was just plain rotten. But this way at least I had a good reason for turning up at Charlie's the next day. Dieter wasn't home. Charlie was tinkering away on the shade of one of her ceiling lamps. It wasn't holding. She was standing on a stepladder, like the ones we used on the job. One of those like Zaremba could dance on. I climbed up next to her, and we worked away together on the dumb lampshade. Charlie held it and I screwed. Believe it or not, people, my hand was shaking. I just couldn't get a grip on this grub screw. After all I'd never actually had Charlie so close to me as then. I probably still could've managed it. But she was aiming her headlights directly at me. It got to the point where I held and Charlie screwed. At any rate that was the best thing for the screw. She finally got it. Our arms were about ready to fall off. I don't know if you know what that's like, when you hold your arms up in the air for hours at a time. If you've ever painted ceilings or put up curtains you know what I mean. We were groaning in unison and massaging our arms, all that on the ladder. Then I started telling her about Zaremba, and how he could dance with the ladder, and then we held onto each other and wobbled around the room on the ladder. We almost tipped over about three times, but we'd made up our minds to get all the way to the door without getting down, and we finally made it. I talked her into it. That was just it: You could talk Charlie into something like that. Ninety-nine out of a hundred women would've given up or else they'd have shrieked a few times and then jumped down. Not Charlie. When we got to the door, Dieter was standing there on the threshold. Right away we jumped down off the ladder. Charlie asked him: Do you want to eat?

And I: I'll go then. I only came for the pipe wrench.

I was sacred to death that he was going to grab a hold of Charlie right there in front of me and maybe kiss her or something. I don't know what would've happened then, people. But Dieter didn't even think of it. He went straight to his desk with his briefcase. Either he never kissed Charlie when he came home, or he restrained himself because of me. Right away I had to think of Old Werther, how he writes to his friend Wilhelm:

Yes, and he is so decent that he has not kissed Lotte a single time in my presence. God reward him!

To tell the truth I didn't understand what that had to do with decency, but I understood everything else. In my whole life I never thought that I'd understand this Werther so well. Beyond that, though, he couldn't have kissed Charlie anyway. She took off for the kitchen pretty fast. Still I really should have gone. But I stayed. I put the ladder away. Then I stood around in the room. I wanted to start a conversation with Dieter, only I couldn't think of anything. Suddenly I had the air rifle in my mitts. Dieter didn't utter a word. When Charlie came back with the snake, she blurted out: Got an idea, men, OK? We'll all go shooting together, by the railroad embankment. You always wanted to teach me how.

Dieter snarled: Light's not good enough this late.

He was against it. He wanted to work. He thought that was kids' stuff. Just like with the ladder. But Charlie aimed her headlights directly at him, and he gave in.

The bad part about it for him was that he just didn't take part at the railroad embankment. We shot at an old parking sign that I pretty quickly ripped to shreds. That is: Charlie shot. Dieter gave the fire orders, and I corrected Charlie's technique. That just happened that way, 'cause it never crossed Dieter's mind to pay attention to Charlie. He just let the children play, so to speak. He was probably thinking of all the time this was costing him. I could see his side, but I still felt like knocking myself out for Charlie. I showed her how to pull the butt into your shoulder and how to stand with your feet at right angles to each other and that you start high and come down into the target and exhale while you're doing it, and I told her all that stuff from my pre-military training that they teach you there. Full sight, fine sight, medium sight, trigger slack and all that. Charlie shot and shot and willingly let me take hold of her until she noticed what was happening with Dieter or maybe until she finally *wanted* to take notice. Then she stopped. Dieter, by the way, had been right, it actually was too dark. Only Dieter had to promise to take her someplace the next Sunday, anywhere, the main thing was to get out. I wasn't mentioned, at least not explicitly. Charlie was really clever about that. She said: . . . let's go someplace.

That must've included me. But maybe I, idiot that I am, just imagined it. Maybe she really wasn't thinking about me. Maybe everything that happened wouldn't have happened if I, idiot that I am, hadn't flattered myself into thinking Charlie'd invited me. But I don't regret anything. Not one damn bit.

Next Sunday I was sitting next to Charlie on their couch in their room. It was raining like crazy. Dieter was sitting at his desk working, and we were waiting for him to finish. Charlie was already in her raincoat and everything. She hadn't even acted surprised or anything when I rang. Everything seemed to go perfectly. Or maybe she was surprised and just didn't show it. This time Dieter was *writing*. With two fingers. On the typewriter. He was writing right out of his head. A paper, I thought, and that was probably right. I could tell right away. It just wasn't flowing. I know what that's like. He was typing about one letter per half hour. That just about says it all. Finally Charlie said: You can't *force* it!

Dieter didn't respond. I had to look at his legs the whole time. He'd wound them around the chairlegs and hooked himself in with his feet. I didn't know if that was a habit of his. But it was obvious to me from the start that he wasn't coming with us.

Charlie started in again: Come on! Just leave everything where it is, OK? That can do wonders!

She wasn't furious or anything. Not yet. She was maybe about as gentle as a nurse is supposed to be.

Dieter said: Not with a boat in this weather.

I don't know if I already told you, but Charlie wanted to rent a boat.

Charlie shoots back: OK. Not a boat, a steamboat. Dieter was actually right. A boat in this weather was crazy.

He started typing again.

Charlie: OK. Not a steamboat. Just a couple of times around the block.

That was her last offer, and it really was a chance for Dieter. But he wouldn't budge.

Charlie: After all, we're not made out of sugar.

I think it was then that she lost her patience. Dieter answered calmly: Go then.

And Charlie: But you promised.

Dieter: I just said: Go!

Then Charlie got loud: We're going!

Just then I left. Anybody would've been able to figure out what was going to happen next. I was really out of place. I mean: I left the room. I really should've gone altogether. I realize that. But I just couldn't bring myself to do that. I stood around in the kitchen for a while. I was suddenly reminded of Old Werther, where he says:

Satiety and indifference, that is what it is! Does not any miserable business matter attract him more than his precious, delicious wife?

Dieter wasn't, of course, a business man, and Charlie was anything but the precious and delicious wife. And it wasn't a matter of satiety with Dieter either. Sure, Dieter must've gotten a pretty big scholarship because of the army. But I'd guarantee that guys like me got at least three times as much just daubing a little paint. I didn't know what it was. Personally I didn't have anything against Dieter, but it was a fact that it'd been an eternity since he'd taken Charlie out. That was the only thing that was a fact. About the same time I'd finished analyzing that, Charlie came shooting out of their room. I'm saying that purposely, people: shooting. All she said to me was: Let's go!

I was right with her.

Then she said: Wait!

I waited. She grabbed this gray poncho from a hook and shoved it into my chest. Dieter'd probably brought it back from the army. It smelled like rubber, gasoline, cheese, and burnt garbage.

She asked me: Can you drive a motorboat?
I said: Hardly.
Normally I'd have said; 'Course. Only I'd done such a good job of taking on the role of the well-behaved young man that I just went ahead and told the truth.
Charlie asked: What'd you say?
She looked at me as if she hadn't heard me right.
Right away I said: 'Course.
Three seconds later we were on the water. That is, it must have taken an hour or so. It's just that for the second time now being with Charlie gave me the feeling as if I didn't know how I'd gotten where I was. Like in a movie. Zoom—and you're there. Only I didn't have any time then to analyze it. This stupid boat had a lot of horsepower. It shot over the Spree like crazy, and on the other side was a concrete wall from some factory. I had a lot of trouble making the curve. Instead of just letting up on the gas, idiot that I am. We'd have drowned for sure, and there'd have been nothing left of the boat. These boats take right off when you start them. No transmission or anything. I looked at Charlie. She didn't make a sound. I guess the boat guy we got the thing from just about flipped. I saw him just standing there on the dock. How Charlie was ever able to weasel that boat out of him, that's a story in itself. I don't know if you'll believe me, that I was really shy and all. Or that I had inhibitions. But I'd have passed when I saw that shed for the FGY* boat rental. Everything was dripping wet. Not a single boat in the water. You couldn't, after all, have called it the "season" anymore, so close to Christmas. And the shed was boarded up as if for World War III. But Charlie found a hole in the fence and rang the boat guy out of the shed and pleaded so long with him that he finally handed over the boat from his boathouse. I wouldn't have thought it'd be possible. The boat guy probably wouldn't either. I think Charlie could've gotten *anything* that day. She just couldn't have been held back. She could've talked anybody into anything.
Out on the water she crept in under the poncho with me. It was still raining like crazy. Couple of degrees lower and we'd have had the most beautiful snowstorm ever. Probably none of you still remember last December. It was really cold as hell in the boat, but

---

*Free German Youth (Freie Deutsche Jugend).

I didn't even notice. I don't know if you know what I mean. Charlie
laid her arm over my seat and her head on my shoulder. I just
about flipped. I was slowly getting a feel for the boat. I didn't
know if there were traffic laws for on the water. Seemed like I'd
heard something about that. But that day there wasn't a single boat
or steamer out on the whole damn Spree. I opened it up. The bow
shot up in the air. This boat wasn't bad. It was probably for this
boat guy's private use. I started making all sorts of curves. Mostly
to the left, because that pressed Charlie up against me. She didn't
have anything against it. Later she started steering herself. Once
we just missed a pier. Charlie didn't say a word. She still had just
about the same look on her face as when she'd come shooting out
of their room.

Until then I hadn't known that you can see a city from behind.
Berlin from the spree, that's Berlin from behind. All the old factories and warehouses.

At first I thought the rain was going to fill the boat. But it didn't.
Probably we drove right out from underneath it. We were already
soaked to the bone, in spite of the poncho. There was nothing you
could've done about the rain anyway. We were so wet that we
didn't even care anymore. We might as well have gone swimming
with our clothes on. I don't know if you know what I mean, people.
You're so wet you just don't even care.

Somewhere or other the warehouses stopped. Only villas and
stuff. Then we had to turn, either left or right. Naturally I picked
left. I was only hoping we'd get out of this lake again. I mean: a
different way. My whole life I've never liked taking the same way
back that I'd come. Not because I'm superstitious or anything. Not
that. I just didn't like to. Probably it bored me. I think that was
one of my ticks. Like with the sprayer, for example. As we thun-
dered past an island Charlie looked uneasy. She had to go. I got
the message. That always happens when it rains. I looked for a
gap in the reeds. Fortunately there were a lot of them. Actually
more gaps than reeds. It was still coming down in buckets. We
jumped onto the shore. Charlie disappeared somewhere. When she
got back we crouched together in this sopping wet grass on the
island. Could be it was only a peninsula. I never went back there.
Then Charlie asked me: Want a kiss?

People, I just about flipped. I started shaking. Charlie was still
pissed at Dieter, that was obvious. Still I kissed her. Her face

smelled like laundry that was bleached about twenty times. Her mouth was ice cold, probably from all that rain. I just couldn't let go of her. She opened her eyes wide, but I just couldn't let go of her. She was really soaked to the bone, her legs and everything.

In some book I once read how this Negro, I mean this Black, comes to Europe and gets his first white woman. He started singing, some song from his homeland. I bailed right out. That was maybe one of my biggest mistakes, always to bail out when I didn't know something. With Charlie I really could've started singing. I don't know if you know what I mean, people. There was no saving me.

Then we went back to Berlin, the same way we'd come. Charlie didn't say anything, but suddenly she was in a big hurry. I didn't know why. I thought that it was just too cold for her. I wanted to get her under the poncho again, but she wouldn't, and she wouldn't say why. She wouldn't even touch the poncho when I gave her the whole thing. The whole way back she didn't say anything. I started feeling like a criminal. I started making curves. Right away I could see she was against it. She was just in a hurry. Then we ran out of gas. We paddled up to the next bridge. I wanted to go to the next station and get gas while Charlie waited. But she got out. I couldn't stop her. She got out, ran up this dripping wet iron stairway, and was gone. I don't know why I didn't run after her. When I'd been at the movies and had seen those films where the woman is always wanting to leave and he wants to stop her, and she runs out the door, and he just stands in the doorway and yells after her, I'd always bailed out. Three steps and he could've had her. And I still just sat there and let Charlie go. Two days later I had bitten the dust, and I, idiot that I am, just sat there and let her go, and just thought about how I was going to get the boat back by myself. I don't know if any of you ever thought about dying and that. About the fact that one day you're just not there any more, no longer present, over and done with, gone, passed away, and irreversible so. For a long time I thought about that a lot, but then I gave up. I just wasn't able to imagine what that would be like, in the coffin, for example. I could only think of stupid things. Like that I'd be lying in the coffin, and it'd be completely dark, and then I'd get this awful itch on my back, and I'd have to scratch myself or I'd die. But it'd be so narrow that I couldn't move my arms. That's almost half dead, people, if you know what I mean. But I was only, at the most, in suspended animation. I just couldn't do it. Could be, if you can, you're already half dead, and I, idiot that I am, probably thought I'd live forever. I can only advise you, people, never to just sit there and think about a shitty boat or something while someone you really care about's running away.

In any case, this boat guy had as much as alarmed the port authority by the time I finally got back with the boat. He was so happy to have gotten his boat back he could've shit. I thought: He wont' forget this day either. At first I thought he was going to make a scene. I put up my dukes. I was in just the right mood. The guy at the service station, for example, I'd given him so much shit he almost fell over. He didn't want to give me a gas can. He was one of those types: Who's-going-to-pay-for-the-can-when-you-don't-come-back-with-it? I can't live with people like that.

At home I hung up my wet things on a nail. I didn't know what to do. I *just didn't* know what to do. I was down like never before. I played the MS. I danced till I was all worked up, maybe about two hours, but I still didn't know what to do. I tried sleeping. But I tossed and turned for 3 hours and a day on the dumb old sofa. When I woke up World War III had broken out. A tank attack or something. I jumped up from the dumb old sofa and ran to the door. There was an animal with caterpillar tracks and an iron shield headed right for me. A bulldozer. Hundred-fifty HP. I'd estimate I started bellowing like an idiot. He stopped about a half a yard in front of me, and throttled his engine down. This guy, the driver, came down from his seat. Without any warning or anything he hit me with his right, so that I flew about two yards aback into my garden house. I did a backwards somersault. That's the best way to get back on your feet again. I pulled in my head for a counterattack.

I'd have given him a left hook that would have knocked him out. I don't think I've told you yet that I'm left-handed. That was about the only thing that Mother Wibeau couldn't break me of. She tried just about everything she could think of, and I, idiot that I am, went right along with it. Until I started stuttering and wetting the bed. That's when the doctors said stop. I was allowed to write with my left hand again, and I stopped stuttering and slept dry. The result was that later I made out fabulously with my right, better than most people with their left. But the left was still always a little better. Only that this tank driver didn't think of putting up his fists. He suddenly turned snow white and sat down on the ground. Then he said: A second later and you'd a been mush and I'd a been in the can. And I've got three kids. Are you crazy, still living here?

He was clearing the ground with his scraper for the new buildings. I probably looked pretty worried. I mumbled: Just a couple of days and I'll be gone.

One thing became clear to me in the course of that night, that there was nothing left for me in Berlin. Without Charlie there was nothing left for me. That's what it amounted to. Of course *she'd* started the whole kissing business. But slowly I began to see that I'd still gone too far. As the man I should've kept things under control.

Then he said: Just three days. Till after Christmas. Then you're out. Got it?!

Then he swung himself back into his tank. I was determined to finished the sprayer as fast as possible, but three days, that was tight. And I didn't want to miss work. I didn't want to take any risks at the last minute by missing work. Zaremba would've popped up within twenty-four hours and sniffed out the truth. Or Addi. I was, after all, his greatest pedagogic success. I wanted to finish the sprayer, slam it down on the table in front of Addi and then take off for Mittenberg and as far as I was concerned even finish my apprenticeship. I'd come that far. I don't know if you understand me, people. Probably I was just getting soft 'cause of Christmas. I'd actually never put a whole lot of stock in this Christmas stuff. "Hark! what mean those holy voices" and Christmas trees and cookies. But I'd still gotten soft somehow. That's probably why I went *straight* to the post office to see if there was another tape there for me from Willi. Otherwise I'd always waited until after work.

I got a funny feeling when I found a special delivery letter from Willi in my box. I tore it open. I almost flipped. The most important sentence was . . . say what you want to. I couldn't hold out any longer. I told your mother where you are. Just so you wont' be surprised when she shows up. He'd mailed it two days before. I knew what I had to do. I took off, instantly. If she took the early train from Mittenberg, she'd have already had to be there, even allowing for stopovers. That meant I still had a chance, till the evening train. I bought an armful of milk cartons, because milk fills you up fastest, and locked myself in my garden house. I closed all the curtains. Beforehand I put a note on the door: Be right back! Just in case. That's also work for the next stupid bulldozer. I thought. Then I hurled myself at my sprayer. I started working like crazy, idiot that I am.

"On Monday, the day before Christmas, he didn't come to work. We weren't really upset. It was amazingly warm, and we were able to make a good use of the day, but we'd already long since filled all our quotas for the year. Besides, it was the first time Edgar'd been absent since we'd gone to get him."

That was just my luck, if you want to call it that. Just about the only thing that'd gone right. I still don't understand, for example, why I was so sure about my sprayer. But I was, in fact, more sure than ever. The idea with the hydraulics was about as logical as you can get. This vapor you got when you were spraying came from the air pressure. If it disappeared and you got the necessary pressure without air, then the thing worked. It was just too bad that I didn't have enough time to get myself the necessary nozzles. I had to wait until after quitting time, preferably till after dark, and then swipe Addi's. Addi's sprayer was lying abandoned under the trailer. My next problem was getting the necessary HP for the two pressure cylinders. Luckily I'd actually been able to scare up an electric motor with 2 HP. I even had to throttle it. I don't know if you can imagine what all two HP can cause when you let 'em loose. Maybe you think the whole thing was just a game or something. A hobby. That's BS. What Zaremba had said, that was true. That thing would've been a genuine sensation, technically and economically. About on the same level as front-wheel drive on cars was, if you know what that is. Actually a step up. It could have made you famous, at least in the profession. I wanted to slam it down in front of Addi and say: Just press on this button here.

I'd estimated that he'd just about flip. Then I could've straightened things out with Charlie and taken off for Mittenberg. I mean, I wouldn't *really* have ever slammed it down in front of Addi. It was slowly getting to be too big for that. It was slowly beginning to look like a wind-driven piss pump. I had everything I needed, only nothing fit together right. I just *had* to start botching it. Otherwise I never in my life would've finished. What I needed most was an electric drill. Besides that the motor naturally had three hundred eighty volts. I'd have guessed it was out of an old lathe. That meant I had to do something to jack up the two hundred twenty in the garden house. I only hope that the transformer I had was OK. I didn't have any kind of measuring device. That was probably another nail in my coffin. And the time to find one, I obviously didn't have that. And you just don't find meters lying around like old truck shock absorbers. By the way, you couldn't find them just lying around either, but you could at least get a hold of some if you needed 'em. Without the shock absorbers I'd have been all washed up. The casing actually should've been thicker, for the pressure. If necessary I was planning to bore out the nozzles. That would've made the stream thicker, but I wanted to start with oil-base anyway. By twelve I was so far that I needed the nozzle for adjusting. I took off in the direction of the construction site. I wasn't of the opinion that I was already done and that it would work on the first try. But this way I at least had the whole night for improvements. I was calm again. Mother Wibeau could've shown up at the earliest the next morning. She'd given me another chance. At the site everything was dark. I dove under the trailer and started undoing the hasp nut. Stupidly enough the only tool I'd brought along was the half-dilapidated pipe wrench. Besides that, the nut was frozen. I almost tore half my ass off getting it loose. Just then I heard Zaremba in the trailer with a woman. I've already told you. I'd probably roused them. In any case, when I crawled out from underneath the trailer he was standing in front of me. He snarled: No?

He was standing right in front of me and staring at me. Even though, he was standing in the light that was coming out of the trailer. He had this little ax of ours in his hand. Then I thought he was just blinded, by the light. But he had this grin in his pig slits. At *that* distance he must've been able to see me. Still and all, I didn't move a muscle. I can only advise you in a situation like that not to move a muscle. My opinion is that Zaremba was the last person to see me and that he knew exactly what was going on.

The whole way home I didn't see a soul. At this time of the night you might as well have been in Mittenberg. Generally speaking Berlin looked exactly like Mittenberg after dark. Everybody sitting in front of the boob tube. And the few hoods beating themselves to a pulp in some park or sitting in movie theaters, or they were athletes and were in training. Not a soul on the street.

By about two I had the nozzle in the socket. I poured about half the oil paint in the cartridge. Then I gave the switch a final check-over. I took another look at the whole thing. I've already told you how it looked. By normal standards it wasn't technically accept-able. But I was interested in the principle. I'd estimate that was my last thought before I pressed the button. I, idiot that I am, had actually taken apart the doorbell button from the garden house. I could've used any normal switch. But I'd taken apart the doorbell button, just so I could say to Addi: Just press on this button here.

I was a complete idiot, people. The last thing I noticed was that it got bright and that I couldn't pull my hand away from the but-ton. That was all I noticed. It must have been that the whole hy-draulic press didn't even budge. That must have caused the voltage to get enormously high, and when you've got your hand on it then, you can't get it off again. That was it. Take care, people!

"When Edgar didn't show up on Tuesday we went looking for him, about noon.

The police were on the property. When we said who we were they told us what had happened. Also that there was no point in going to the hospital. We were stunned. Then they let us in the garden house. The first thing we noticed was that the walls were covered with paint, especially in the kitchen. It was still damp. It was the same paint we'd been using on the kitchen paneling. Every-thing smelled like paint and singed insulation material. The kitchen table was upside down. All the glass was shattered. On the floor were a burned-out electric motor, hunks of bent-up pipe, a piece of garden hose. We told the police what we knew, but we didn't have an explanation either. Zaremba told them where Edgar had worked. And that was it.

We quit for the day. I sent them all home. Only Zaremba stayed. He started pulling our old sprayer out from underneath the trailer. He inspected it, and then he showed me that the nozzle was miss-ing. We went right back to Edgar's garden house. We found the nozzle in the kitchen in an old piece of glass pipe. I gathered to-gether what was still lying around, even the small stuff. The stuff that was screwed to the table too. At home I cleaned off all the paint. Over Christmas I tried to reconstruct the whole arrangement. A kind of jigsaw puzzle. I couldn't do it. Probably half the parts were still missing, above all a pressure tank or something like that. I wanted to go back to the garden house, but it had been leveled."

It was probably better that way. I wouldn't have lived through this failure anyway. In any case, I'd almost gotten to the point where I could understand Old Werther when he said he couldn't continue. I mean, I'd have never turned in my cards voluntarily. Never hung myself from the next tree or anything. No way. But I never would've *really* gone back to Mittenberg. I don't know if you understand me. That was maybe my biggest mistake. My whole life I'd been a bad loser. I just couldn't swallow anything. Idiot that I am, I always wanted to be the winner.

"Just the same. Edgar's apparatus won't leave me alone. I can't get rid of the feeling that Edgar was on the track of something really sensational, something that you just don't think of every day. In any case, it wasn't just a tick. No doubt about that."
"And the pictures. Do you think that one of them could still be found somewhere?"
"The pictures. Nobody'd thought of that. They were covered with paint. They were probably leveled with the building."
"Could you describe some of them?"
"I don't understand that kind of thing. I'm only a simple painter. Zaremba thought they weren't bad. No wonder. What with his father."
"I'm not a painter. I was never a painter. I'm a statistician. I haven't seen Edgar since he was five. I don't know anything about him, not even now. Charlie, a garden house that's no longer standing, pictures that no longer exist, and this machine."
"I can't really tell you any more than that. But we can't just let his work go down the drain. I don't know what his mistake was. According to what the doctors said, it was something electrical."

Translated by Kenneth P. Wilcox

EVERYDAY LIFE
UNDER SOCIALISM

Wolfgang Kohlhaase

Suffer the Little Children . . . .

Every two weeks, on Friday or Saturday, Biesener the carpenter would climb on his motorbike and chug fifty miles to the home of his mother and father. When he arrived, he would push his machine along the garden path into the laundry room, take off his crash helmet, remove his bag of laundry from the rear seat, go around the little house and walk into the kitchen, his face red with health and the wind of his bike ride.

"Well, so you're back," his mother would cry, and her face bloomed like his; only in her case, the flush came from the heat that rose from the sizzling, seething saucepans. "Dinner will be ready in a jiffy. Wash your hands," she would call. Then she would race on heavy, sturdy legs from the stove to the table, from the table to the cupboard, and between times to the window nook where the pump stood, to pump water into a tin bowl for her son. The living room door would open, and Josef Biesener, the father, would blink his eyes as if he had been reading in poor light and say: "Well, so you're back, Jochen."

Then they would sit down in the main room, at the table which had space for more than three. There would be potatoes, along with chops or fried eggs and bacon or fresh grilled flounder from the nearby lagoon. The son would fill his plate a second or even a third time, and eat intently and in silence. If his parents wanted to know anything, they had to ask.

"Haven't you all finished building there yet?" Josef Biesener would query.

"I guess we won't finish as quick as all that," his son would reply.

"So you're still going to stay on there?"

"I s'pose I'll stay on there."

"I s'pose there's hardly any real carpentry work any more?"

"Nary any," their son would say, and might add in a fit of loquacity: "Cuz now they make everything out of concrete. And tomorrow they may make it out of something else. Maybe plastic, you know?"

"Ye-es, ye-es, 'tis everything is changing," his father would say.

Biesener Senior knew from television how things really looked out there where Jochen Biesener no longer framed roof timbers from living, aromatic wood but instead nailed up rough sheathing, flexed iron rods, and smoothed down a rich concrete mash. Now and then the TV showed cooling towers, pipelines, chimneys, and brightly-lit multi-family dwellings which stood like boxes in the landscape. Different types of workers were consulted about different tasks, the children went to new schools, and important people arrived in cars. Biesener had not yet glimpsed his son on these filmed occasions, nor did he actually expect to. It was enough for him to imagine that his son was somewhere out there in that ever-shifting landscape of miracle, that he lived in a barracks-like room, earned good money and yet—there really was no other way to put it—did not become frivolous.

Biesener Senior naturally felt annoyed now and then that his son was so close-mouthed. Jochen was still coming home, and the father would have liked, through his son, to learn many things about the world which he himself could no longer experience. But he took comfort in thinking that some people talked and talked without making a grain of sense. There were worse things than being quiet, even if quiet people had a harder life in some ways. Only one thing about his son gave Biesener Senior real concern.

"So tell us, do you still have no intended?" he had asked many and many a time.

At first the son's face would redden, or rather get redder than it was already. He would avoid answering. His mother would look reproachfully at his father and cry in a shrill voice: "Now leave the boy in peace! He'll tell you when the time comes."

All the same, she would have liked to hear the answer, too. The years had slipped by almost without their noticing. Their son would soon be thirty, and the father was no longer working in the sawmill but, now that he had retired, went strolling through the meadows by the river, usually following the same route to the public swimming pool and back. But his thoughts roved here and there, back and forth, to the war, to the moon, to the poor people in Vietnam. And when he thought about what was left of his life, he felt that he would like to have a grandchild. But their son had never spoken about a girl, never hinted at the subject, never asked for advice. Back when Jochen had just turned twenty, his father, wishing to stop him from making any hasty decisions, had used every occasion to impress on him that "'Tis foolish to marry young." That had been a mistake, he now thought, and felt guilty.

When Jochen Biesener was at home, he would clean up the chicken coop, split firewood, nail a few loose fenceboards, dig a garden bed, shoot at sparrows or old lightbulbs with his airgun, clean his motorcycle until it shone. And in fine weather he would ride at a fast clip around a few corners to a motorcycle repair shop where a schoolfriend was working. On Saturday or Sunday, young men in leather vests used to meet there to show each other their bikes, argue about speed and horsepower, and shout remarks to the girls who walked past. Some of the girls would giggle, or turn around. Jochen Biesener would sit there with the others, red-faced, strong-boned and broad-shouldered on his beautiful motorbike, and would feel the girls' glances touch him and pass by with indifference. Then the girls would continue on their light-footed way, carrying off their secrets under their clothes. The young men would gaze after them, laughing at some racy remark. But time by time and year by year, Jochen Biesener gradually became more shy and withdrawn. A torpid energy stored itself up in his body in the long summer afternoons, which seemed joyless and empty to him. He would race his motorcycle, while the trees lining the avenue beat the echo of the exhaust into his ears. He grew chilled by the wind rushing past, but no lighter in heart. And as the summer had its heat, so the spring had its fragrance, the autumn its early twilit evenings, and the winter its dancehalls smelling of beer and perfume, where you could always find a pal to have a couple of drinks with until midnight. The music would grind to a halt, the drunks would sing or babble, the last of the rejected girl friends would get into their coats with mannered pride, and Jochen Biesener did not have the looks or find the words to get them to smile that smile which is the beginning of everything. "Hey girls!" he would sometimes say in a challenging voice. But most of them pretended not to have heard him. And not one ever noticed the great and genuine longing that lay behind his crude offer.

So Jochen Biesener felt helpless when his father asked him questions, and kept a hurt silence, until finally the father almost stopped mentioning the subject. At most he would permit himself to crack a joke. At New Year's, for example, he asked his wife while his son was present: "I wonder if I'll have to get my black suit ironed this year?"

But there came a weekend in spring when Jochen would actually have liked his father to ask him if he had a fiancée. The mealtimes and the hours went by, it was Sunday afternoon already, and he had to think about the journey back. Then father Josef donned his Sunday jacket, put on his flat blue cap and said: "I'm just going to walk down to the swimming pool."

"I'll come with you a ways," said Jochen.

"That's nice," said the father.

They walked out into the field and past the peat holes, exchanged a few words about the carp which were bred in them: big strapping fellows, and reached the dark path flanked by poplars that ran straight as a die alongside the river. Now and then, Josef Biesener tapped the brim of his cap, greeting other strollers. It felt good to be seen with his grown-up son.

When a stretch of empty path lay ahead, Jochen Biesener said hesitantly: "I wanted to talk with you about this some time. I mean, I have to tell you about it first. The thing is, I plan to get married."

He did not look at his father as he spoke. His father, too, looked straight ahead along the path, because he felt that his emotion showed in his eyes. So he took several steps in silence before he said: "A person has to get married some time, my boy."

"Ye-es," the son said.

They were silent a while. Then the father asked, "How long have you known her?"

"Since winter. Our firm had a get-together. With music and dancing."

So, she is a sort of co-worker, the father thought. Why not? That's how things are today. His son had looked for a long time, really for a very long time, but then he had made his move. At a party.

"I thought you couldn't dance?" he asked in surprise.

"We talked. You get to know each other better that way, anyhow."

"That's true," the father said, savoring the good sense in his son's words.

"We already knew each other by sight, cuz she works in the canteen at our firm. She hands out the food. You should just see what a whiz she is at it."

The father pictured a cheerful, modern young woman with nimble hands, but who looked a little like the girls in his own youth, too. Without accounting for it, he had all his life judged people by how they worked. It appeared that his son was the same.

"What's her name?" he asked.

"Irmchen."

"Uh-huh," the old man said, and nodded approval.

He would have liked to go on walking beside his son a while longer, to ask this and that question and think about the replies, to drink a beer or even two to celebrate, and to keep the news to himself for a time before he brought it home to his wife. But unfortunately that could not be, because his son had to leave on the fifty-mile journey back to his work and to his girl.

So they turned around at the fence by the swimming pool, which lay empty and serene.

"There is one thing I'll tell you right away. There's something else," said Jochen Biesener. His father gazed at him questioningly. The son looked impatient, as if he could not understand why his father did not guess it for himself. He got up courage by putting a rough tone into his voice. "Well what do you think it is? She's got a kid."

"Oh, she already has a little one," the father repeated. He felt that he could not hide his disappointment. But he also felt awkward, and sensed that he must avoid saying the wrong thing, and that he had to be careful.

"Ye-es," he said in a lingering voice, trying to sort out his emotions while he spoke. "Yes, well of course that's up to you, isn't it? Things today aren't how they used to be. Though of course there can be problems when a child is not your own. Please don't think I'm old-fashioned. That sort of thing can easily happen these days, and a person shouldn't assume the worst. And if there's gossip, what does it matter what people say? Provided she's the right one for you. As I said, it's up to you. . . ."

Josef Biesener could not say more, not at the moment and not later, when his son climbed onto his motorbike feeling dissatisfied and a bit discouraged, and rode away. The father was also put off by the thought that he would find nothing of himself and nothing of his son in the long-awaited child who might now come into their home. The mother thought in more practical terms.

"They can have more children," she called from the kitchen. "It wouldn't have hurt you to tell him that you are happy about it."

Josef Biesener sat down in an armchair under the photograph of their first son, who had died in the war, and a colorful picture of the island of Helgoland made of mother-of-pearl, and tried to imagine the future.

Two weeks later, their son came home again. He sat silently at the table as always, and did not say a word about the important family issues that were on all their minds. The father felt that he had to make amends, and asked: "When are you going to introduce your intended to us?"

The mother immediately added, in her high voice that was always a little too loud, "You can bring her with you. I'll bake a nice cake."

"There's time enough for that," the son said evasively. And they spoke no more about it until the next day, when Jochen Biesener was already preparing to leave, and was polishing the frame of his motorbike with window cleaner. Josef Biesener came over, looked at his son's rough, skilled hands and said in a friendly tone: "Understand what I mean, my boy. The main thing is that you like her."

The son looked probingly at his father, as if he had to be on his guard.

"And a child is really nothing unusual. From the modern point of view," Josef Biesener continued.

His son went on cleaning his bike. Then, twisting the cloth back and forth between his fingers, he said: "I wanted to tell you something anyway. She has another child."

Josef Biesener looked into the obstinate face of his son and understood that it must be true. The generous mood that had filled him at the thought of one child left him now, and he said without thinking: "She must have done a lot of running around."

"Why must she have done a lot of running around?" his son asked angrily. "One kid is by her former husband. She didn't have to run around for that one. What dumb things you say."

Usually he did not address his father this way, but the father paid no attention to the tone, he was far too stirred up for that.

"Oh, so she's divorced, too. Well, well."

He dashed into the house, where he was heard repeating this same sentence, until he expanded on it by voicing his suspicion that she must have been searching for a long time for a dope who would marry her anyhow. And that's what had happened. His son, not man enough to find out what was up, had fallen into the trap, and thought he should be proud of it to boot.

"The last word hasn't been said about this yet," the mother called into the living room where the father was conducting his scornful soliloquy. She called it again into the hall where Jochen Biesener was silently packing his bag.

"Shall I give you a couple of fresh eggs to take with you?" she asked him. For the first time in years, he did not want any fresh eggs.

Nevertheless, he came home again two weeks later. But he did not talk with his father. He leaned the ladder against the shed, climbed onto the roof, tore down the remains of the old tarpaper, cut some new, nailed it on, and built a fire in the laundry to blend roof coating.

"You can't see a thing any more," his mother called when it got dark.

"I plan to leave at noon tomorrow," he said.

The father, Josef Biesener, prowled around the shed hoping that his son would reach the point of needing to ask him something. But his son was familiar with the roof and required no help. The father borrowed the son's hammer and drove a fresh and completely unnecesary nail through the handle of the rake. Their silence angered him more than if they had been fighting, so after supper he left the house and went to drink two beers which he did not enjoy.

While his mother was tidying the kitchen, Jochen stood and watched her, unable to make up his mind. She shook her head and wisely avoided coming directly to the point. "The way you two always have to get into a fight straight away," she said. He felt grateful that she did not reproach or question him. He leaned in the doorway and tried to explain in words which came to him with difficulty.

"If the woman says yes to me, then it doesn't matter whether she has children already. What use is it if she has no children but she doesn't say yes?"

"It's just that it's two children, and is that the right thing?" his mother objected cautiously. "Aren't there lots of nice young girls where you are?"

"It's up to me what I do with my life," Jochen Biesener answered, insulted. "What difference do two or three children make to the pair of you, if they don't make any difference to me?"

His mother put the towel down on the table and dropped her arms. Her eyes and mouth grew round. "My boy," she said. "Tell me, my boy, does she have another child? . . ."

"Some people are more susceptible than others," her son said. And his face took on a tender expression, because at that moment he was thinking of the woman.

"Dear God, I won't tell him that!" his mother cried shrilly. "Dear God, you must tell him that yourself."

Jochen Biesener fetched his bedclothes from upstairs and lay down on the sofa in the living room. If he pressed his nose into the cushioned back seat, it still smelled the way it did twenty years ago. He turned to the wall, and although he did not fall asleep for a long time, he did not move any more.

When it grew light he got up, rinsed his eyes and went outdoors to tar the roof for the second time. By nine o'clock he was finished with everything, had breakfasted, and was pushing his motorcycle out of the yard. Biesener Senior, his shirt open over his bony, grey-haired chest and his cap on his head, stood in the morning sun and watched the chickens pecking at the grain with senseless greed because they could not remember that every morning there was enough for all.

"G'bye," the son said.

The father behaved as if he had only now noticed his son.

"Ye-es, g'bye then," he said.

For a couple of days the mother managed to keep to herself her suspicions about the children of their prospective daughter-in-law. But one evening when they were sitting at the table under the lamp—she was mending clothes, he was reading—she said: "What do you think about it now?"

He knew what she meant, and without looking up he said: "I don't want to hear anything about it."

She was silent for a while. Then she said in a dismissive tone, as if she were far from believing any such thing: "He made a remark as if there were not two children but three . . ."

The father set down his book and took off his spectacles, and when he looked at her, she saw two helpless old man's tears in his eyes.

"Really?" he asked softly.

Shocked by the tears, she said: "Maybe he just expressed himself awkwardly." The old man shook his head and sobbed through his nose as children do, with the pain of a deep, undeserved injury.

"How cowardly," he said in a bitter voice. "Telling us the story piece by piece."

"It seems incredible," returned the mother. "She can't be so very old."

"Not old, but a tart," Josef Biesener said, raising his voice. "She's twisting him around her finger. A construction-site floozie who puts her arms around the men's necks. Especially on Fridays, when they have money. You know what? Those kids were all begotten on a Friday . . ."

He found increasingly extravagant terms to describe the good-natured stupidity of his son and the subtle cunning of this canteen siren. What work did she do there, anyway? Was she a cook? Who knows if she even has a respectable job? At the end he swore she would not enter his house.

"And what if he doesn't come back any more?"

"We'll see if he decides to do that to us," the old man cried. "In that case, he should stay away!"

At night he thought less with anger than with sorrow about his son who no longer listened to him, and perhaps no longer trusted him either. Am I a backward person? he wondered. Am I behind the times? Do people today marry anybody who walks through the door? Isn't a father allowed to give his opinion, if his son is making himself unhappy with a woman like that? Then he tried to picture the woman accurately. From the dim light of a faraway dance hall where he had waltzed to the newest American music after World War I, dressed in pointed shoes and with a spare paper collar in his pocket, out stepped the Hudeleit sisters with their loud and brassy laugh. Many men had gone behind the hedge with them, including himself, except that the sister he was with ran out on him. But even the Hudeleit sisters had not become mothers three times over without a permanent man. Whatever became of them, anyway? he brooded. And he felt surprised that the better-behaved girls were no longer so clearly etched in his mind.

He tossed and turned in his bed. He thought about his neighbors, his relatives, his brother-in-law Gustav, who liked to crack jokes. He heard his wife breathing peacefully beside him, felt lonely, and thought that he was the only one who was really worried.

But of course the mother worried too, because what she had feared came to pass. Their son seemed disinclined to visit home. Anyhow he wrote a card saying that he had a lot of work at the weekend and for the time being he would not come. The father merely nodded grimly, but the mother wrote back a letter, and the week after, she sent a little packet of fresh eggs, and then she would write another letter, or a card, telling her son about the garden, their health, and the door which they had just had painted. She did not send any greeting to the unknown woman, but occasionally she would include her in phrases addressed to her son. "I'm sure you two are taking advantage of the beautiful weather," she would write, or: "Have you two eaten fresh strawberries yet?" Once or twice she even slipped in a white lie which she hoped would prove true in the end: "Above all, Papa is angry because you did not tell him right away how things stand. He can't bear how you let it come out little by little."

In this way she kept up communication, while the father withdrew into a baffled silence. He suffered because his son did not come home any more. Sometimes he tended to blame himself, because he suspected that he was behaving in a petty way. But then a huge anger would well up in him again, because he could not remember hearing of any man who had married three children along with a wife, when he did not have to. He roamed restlessly through the meadows that smelled of warm grass. "Who knows how many more summers I have," he thought. "And I can't even enjoy them."

When the time came to take his vacation, Jochen Biesener cautiously asked his mother if she could look after a child for a couple of weeks, an eight-year-old girl who was the woman's daughter. His mother told his father, and in order to head off any possible objection, she immediately added in a determined voice: "Then at least I will have a little bit of diversion."

Josef Biesener did not say yes and he did not say no. He acted as if he were staying out of it. Even now, his son did not come home. Jochen wrote that he did not wish to carry the child on the back of his motorbike, and so she would come on the train.

"You go to the train station. What does it have to do with me?" Josef Biesener said to his wife. But then he went anyhow, claiming that he wanted an opportunity to chat with the station master, whom he had known for a long time. The train pulled in and people climbed out and dispersed, leaving behind a little girl with a tightly packed case. Old Biesener stood waiting near the barrier as if he still had the choice not to introduce himself. The child walked over to him hesitantly. At least she dresses the kid decently, he thought with reluctance.

"Are you Mr. Biesener?" the child asked.

"I am."

"My name is Bianca Gebel."

"Well, come along then," the old man said.

Outside the train station, he took the bag from the child. Then they walked along side by side, silent and embarrassed.

But Jochen's mother started to bustle joyfully when the two came home. She pumped water into the washbowl as she used to do for her long-absent son, and asked questions about a number of things in a loud and somewhat unnatural voice, the way people speak who have not talked with children for a long time and who therefore do not realize how grown-up an eight-year-old girl feels.

Bianca washed her fingers politely, sat up straight at the table, did not mix up which hand to use for her knife and fork, and reported patiently how she did in school, what games she liked to play, and whether she helped out at home.

"Would you like to go along and see the swimming pool after our meal?" the mother asked, and winked at her husband. He looked at her reproachfully because of the way she had taken charge of his afternoon walk; but he made no objection. "And when you two come back, we'll have cherry tart," the mother cried.

For a while Bianca did not dare to speak to the silent, strange old man. But when they came to the peat holes, she wanted very much to know if there were fish in them, and asked him about it. Josef Biesener told her that large, strong and wily carp lived in the black, opaque water, but that no doubt there were a couple of pike, too, which ate the carp while they were still small. Then they came to some cows who were chewing their cuds sleepily and were guarded only by a thin wire. Bianca already knew that it was an electrified wire, but she did not know if it hurt the cows when they ran into it.

"I 'spect it just gives them a fright," Josef Biesener said, and felt glad that the girl trusted him: a child is a child, he thought. She needs someone to explain things to her. And an old man like me needs a child to listen to him. Pain surged through him as he thought: but not three children all at once, or in such a way. He made up his mind never to think that thought again. "Won't it be boring for you to be so alone here?" he asked the child.

"Certainly not."

"But there are several of you children at home, aren't there?"

He wanted to hear it so that he could make his peace with it.

"Six," said Bianca.

Then she burst out laughing. She could not understand what the old man found so amazing and unbelievable.

One Sunday in autumn, Josef Biesener saw his daughter-in-law through the curtain. His son closed the garden gate from the inside, then his son's wife took his son's arm again and walked toward the house with a heavy tread and broad hips. Her seventh child was on the way. The son wore a hat.

The old man posted himself by the stove, which already was giving off a low heat. He heard the door, and after a moment when they most likely were taking off their coats, they entered the kitchen. It made the father cross to hear the voice of his wife saying eagerly, "Here you are at last!"

Then they came into the living room at once, led by the son dressed in white shirt and tie, which made him look very red in the face as if he were getting no air. He said formally, "May I introduce you? This is Irmchen."

The old man moved away from the stove. His son's wife walked across the threshold: a voluptuous, resolute woman with a fat belly and a harmonious, pleasant face. "Well, you are welcome," said Josef Biesener, and shook her hand.

"I am really happy to meet you," said his daughter-in-law. Jochen's mother, standing in the doorway, was waving a pot of cyclamen and half a bottle of cognac. "The cognac is for you."

"You didn't have to do that," Josef Biesener said, embarrassed.

His daughter-in-law hung her handbag on the back of a chair, and despite the mother's protest, she carried in the bowl of potatoes. There was chicken soup, roast cockerel, and plum compote. The lack of conversation during the meal could be blamed on the cockerels, whose stringy flesh and tender bones made eating them a matter for concentration. Occasionally, Josef Biesener raised his eyes from the table to look at his daughter-in-law sitting beside his son. She had just had her hair done. Josef tried to get used to her round face, because she would soon make him a grandfather: a task in which God knows she had had ample practice. He had already received a letter from his brother-in-law, Gustav the joker, in which Gustav wrote that if Jochen Biesener the doughty carpenter ever brought his new family to Berlin, they would qualify for a special group tour of the zoo all on their own!

By the time they reached the compote, it was clear that they finally had to talk about something. Old Biesener could not think of one sentence that he could address to his daughter-in-law. Therefore he asked his son: "I 'spose you're still going on with the building job, eh?"

His son answered, "I 'spect it will go on."

"Weren't you all s'posed to be finished in five years?"

"I 'spect the plans have changed," his son said. Happy that the silence had been broken, he considered what else he could tell his father, but his wife briskly got in ahead of him. "The plan is for forty thousand people to come there."

Josef Biesener looked at her and said, "Well, well." And his admiration was less for the plan than for how it sounded, coming from the mouth of his daughter-in-law.

The women carried out the dishes, the son went into the yard, and the old man sat down in his armchair and watched his daughter-in-law come back into the room again. In case she developed weak knees soon, she had powerful arms to make up for it. She bent her heavy, fruitful belly over the table and wiped off the oil tablecloth.

Translated by Jan van Heurck

Käthe Rülicke

Hans Garbe Tells His Story

Shortly before Christmas, Ring Oven Number 3 broke down and had to be given a general overhaul. A crucible oven of this kind has thirty-six chambers, four corner chambers and thirty-two central chambers. Each chamber is six by six feet across and about eight feet deep. The chambers are connected to each other by gas canals. The constant heat in the ovens, around one thousand degrees Celsius, destroys the walls and lids over time and the ovens have to be replaced at intervals.

Oven Number 3 had reached that point. The war had destroyed several ovens, oven space was very short as a result, and we could not get along without this one. When it broke down, we were unable to fulfill our two-year plan.

In the past, the whole oven was always shut down during repairs. Production stopped for four months until the remodeling was finished. The engineers, the managers, the foremen came to examine the oven, but nothing more could be done.

Then the brickworks manager came to me and said: "Oven Number 3 absolutely must be rebuilt. If we shut it down for four months, that means a production loss of four hundred thousand marks, and the rebuilding will cost two hundred thousand. Then our plan is done for. What should we do? Think it over."

"Well," I said, "can't the construction be done without letting the fire go out in the oven?"

"Man, if you could only do that."

"Let me think about it," I said. "I'll let you know tomorrow morning."

The thing gave me no peace. The oven could not be allowed to shut down, our production was needed urgently. I thought about it all evening.

When I was lying in bed—it was very cold, December, there was no fire, coal was so scarce—I said to Erika: "Mother, put on a jacket and get paper and pencil, you have to help me. I am planning something big, we have to figure it out."

"The things you think up," Erika said. "But if we've no choice, let's try it." She fetched paper and pencil. Erika has always helped me. I always say that my wife is my collective; without her I could not have achieved all the work I've done.

For hours we calculated how the oven could be rebuilt while it was in operation. It was such an unfamiliar idea. I had never been involved in such a big project before, more than half a million marks were at stake.

Next morning I said to the brickworks manager: "I'll rebuild the oven without closing it down." Immediately he hurried to Director H. and let me know that I should hand in my proposal in writing. God, then I had to start figuring and making plans again. I'm a mason after all, and I didn't study many things in school. Erika had to help again.

Next day I presented my plan to Director H., who himself is a former laborer. "You've done good calculations," he said. "You plan to build the oven in the same time as the private contractor, four months, but without suspending operation, so that we won't have any production loss. And you have estimated a cost of only eighty-five thousand marks, the private contractor wants two hundred thousand. But there'll be a big fight about it. The intellectuals will say no. Your foreman won't stand for it. Who'll take the responsibility? I'll call a meeting tomorrow morning. We're going to have a tough time."

At the meeting I sweated as if I were already in the oven. Doctor W., the technical manager, said: "No, it can't be done, that kind of thing is impossible. Gases will build up. The bricks will get damp. I won't take any responsibility for it. Two hundred thousand marks' worth of materials are at risk." Foreman Z. said: "You'll bungle it. The oven will break down in a week." The private contractor also said: "It's impossible." I got very excited and said: "Nothing is impossible, I'm asking now for you to let me build the oven. After all, we have a say in this too." Director H. took my side and said that they had to give me the chance to try it. Of course if things went wrong they could not lock me up, but at most strip me of my activist's badge. But I said: "I'll earn another badge besides. If we doubt ourselves, we'll never amount to anything. I'll build the oven, but I need support." Now that I was going to be allowed to build the oven, of course I needed help. Thirty of my co-workers reported for duty, even the ones who had called me a traitor to the working class and who had walked out on the meeting before it was over. Some of them in time became the best workers.

I picked out six co-workers, now we were a proper collective: Willi Gottschling, Gerd Brauer, Fritz Hesse, Alfred Schubert, Helmut Stein, and Paul Heide. That was the first brigade at Siemens-Plania; now there are over two hundred brigades competing with each other.

We made careful preparations for the job. We kept track of the supplies of fire-brick and mortar, and checked how the old and new bricks were being transported in and out.

We had four assistants: two at the oven, two to cart the bricks. We could not afford any stoppages. The time schedule had to be adhered to exactly, because we always had to conduct the fire onward at a certain time so that the batch in the oven would not suffer any damage.

The plan specified four months for completion. On May 1, 1950, the oven was supposed to be ready. We had just begun the third day of the Christmas celebration. On December 27, our first brick came rushing out of the oven.

We were still building the wall of the first chamber, when the Soviet general manager came to visit the oven. He asked me through the interpreter—at that time he could not yet speak much German—how I had come to take on this difficult job. After all, we were still badly off then, we had little to eat and so on. "I'm doing this job precisely because we have so little to eat and things are still so bad. Your Stakhanov* had a tough time, too." Then he laughed, clapped me on the shoulder, said "khorosho" and told me to go on working.

---

*Alexey Stakhanov, a Soviet model coal miner whose innovative work methods started a movement in 1935 to increase individual productivity.

That encouraged me and I thought: "Wow, so our Soviet friends know what I'm doing here." Then he announced right out in the open that the others should learn from my example.

He often came back to the oven and always asked if I was having problems. He even spoke to me when he met me out in the yard as I was going home in the evening: "Hey Garbe, we can still chat for half an hour." We walked some distance while he asked me in detail how the work was progressing.

But our problems began in the first few days. We got so much grief. The foreman came and laid down rules how I was supposed to do the job. I said to him: "This is my oven. I signed the contract and I have to answer for it if something goes wrong." The thing is, we were earning seven or eight marks an hour, and the company accountants did not want to be responsible for that. But we were working so much above the standard level. Then I signed a contract with the Labor Standards Office, the administration and the union, specifying the working hours for building the oven.

Engineer K. then prohibited Foreman Z. from interfering in the building.

In the first fourteen days, the technical experts came and watched how we worked. Each time, my heart started pounding when I saw them; I was scared that things could go wrong. After all, I had taken on a big responsibility.

Doctor W. had said that we must not build any damp bricks into the walls. I had already included this in my calculations and continually had a number of bricks drying out. But when we arrived in the morning, the dry bricks had been swiped and used somewhere else. Fortunately I usually had a few dry bricks in reserve that the foreman did not know anything about. But it took a lot of energy, always having to be on guard this way. Then the fire-clay went missing and we could not go on with the work. Finally, our hod carriers were put to work elsewhere, and no one cleared away our debris any more.

Once I really reached the point of thinking that we could not do the job after all. Then I went to the Soviet managing director. He knew right away what to do. He barred the foreman from all the building sites and had him give us the bricks; now we had all the bricks we needed.

We had only been working for two weeks when the thought came to me that we had to finish the oven ahead of schedule. I had to think about how we could save time. I got the brigade together, told them my idea and asked if they wanted to take part. I said: "We'll earn twice as much if we finish in half the time, but we have to use the money for our health, otherwise we won't be able to get through it. We have to buy milk and butter and keep ourselves fit." They all agreed.

But now we had to improve our work methods if we wanted to save time. I had to do a lot of thinking because I could not quite cope with the technical matters. That was the bad part, back then. Today I've learned enough that I can read a diagram.

In the evening when my workmates had gone home, I went into a corner with some bricks and arranged them in different ways to figure out the most practical way to do the bricklaying. Before that I used to draw on the ground with a stick. I could not let anyone see me, my workmates were so funny back then, they would have laughed at me. Today the world is very different.

Then I invented a new brick for the gas canal. It was a great help to us and saved a lot of time. The brick yielded efficiency savings of forty-five thousand marks a year, so I was given an award of four thousand marks on top of my pay.

Now we were managing fine with the bricks, but the sabotage campaign against us continued. In the early morning I hung my jacket in the storeroom and worked just in my trousers. My jacket was swiped. Crossing the yard without a jacket to get breakfast after working in one-hundred-degree heat was impossible, so I stayed in the oven until evening, and my mates brought me food. Next day my other jacket was taken, too. Then I put on my wife's knitted jacket, from which I had cut away the sleeves, and next I had a box made with a lock on it. They did not get my fourth jacket.

People continued to call me names. They threatened to catch me in the evening and fix me so that I would no longer be physically able to rebuild the oven. A couple of times, a few bricks actually whistled past my head. I also received anonymous threatening letters.

Then came fresh obstacles. I said to my wife: "I have the feeling they'll throw bricks into the gas canal." When I looked next day, there really were new bricks in it. I had to chisel everything out again and and wall it up once more. But we had to be finished by a particular time, because the fire had to come through the canal at a fixed hour.

In the first week, we completed only two of the thirty-six chambers. Later we did four or five a week, and at the end, we even managed six. That was how much the new bricks and the new method helped us.

Suddenly a new hurdle arose. The company doctor made things hot for us, saying that our way of working was suicide, and that I was the sickest of all and had heart problems. I said: "I feel just fine, it's what you are saying that is making me heartsick." But he insisted that we all get a medical exam. Then I went to the provincial union of the Socialist Unity Party, and my comrades there sent me to the head physician in the Weissensee district of East Berlin. My heart was okay, I was just exhausted. The others had already gotten discouraged and said there was no point in our going on. But I said: "Don't be afraid, we'll all go together to the doctor in Weissensee and get a check-up. We won't let them bar us from working." Then they plucked up fresh courage.

Foreman Z. was still making problems for me. He had said to some colleagues, "Damn it, the oven hasn't cracked yet." I answered: "If you don't get away from our oven, you can take a bath in the lime trough." The work brigade threw away their trowels and stopped laying bricks. Then he hurried to Engineer K. to complain.

Later I learned that he told K. that if they did not get rid of Garbe right away, there would be a disaster. Our colleague K. had to choose between him and me, he said. Then K. transferred him to another division, and I became foreman in the construction division. Later I also asked the firm to let go two fellow workers who were hounding us, and K. helped me in this case too.

We had now made a lot of progress in building the oven. In March the competition flag was to be brought out, and we wanted to win it for our plant. But that meant we had to build the oven in two months instead of four.

We only had three more chambers to build when S., the party secretary, arrived and said: "Don't build any more chambers."

"Why not?" I asked. "We want to finish by February 26. If we don't build them now, we'll have to wait another four weeks."

S. said: "The completion date is May 1, and I'll give you the party's order to stick to the plan." I didn't know what to do. Manager H. was at the provincial party training. I had to admit that I had neglected my party work while I was building the oven, and S. reproached me on that account. I was group subleader and had failed a couple of times to pick up the literature. But I could not always get out of the chamber, emerging from one-hundred-degree heat to cross the yard, and sometimes my mail went on lying there.

I tried to make it clear to the party secretary that the development of new work methods is important and that building the oven was also party work.

We had three more chambers to build. Then Manager H. got time off and immediately came to see the oven. I said: "I don't know what's wrong, the intellectuals never show up any more. At first they were here every day. Something isn't right." He laughed and said: "Buddy, you can be proud of that. They didn't find anything wrong. They see that your plan is succeeding and now they feel ashamed."

Manager H. was among the comrades who always helped me, and so did Division Manager K. If individuals, the party secretary for example, worked against me, I didn't think of it as the party. And he didn't stay on at Siemens-Plania either. In time the plant's Socialist Unity Party group took on a completely different complexion. Gradually they really became comrades, one and all. It always gave me strength to know that the party was behind me. I knew that if I couldn't do the job any more, they would help me. And then the party really did support me. I always looked on the party the way my grandfather, who was still a believer, looked on the Bible. I am a communist and don't read any Bible, but I believe in my party, and the party is my holy place. I will always fight for my party.

We really did finish our oven on February 26, in two months instead of in four. We quickly fixed up a little rostrum in the brickworks, put in a couple of tables and a bench, and dedicated the oven.

The technical manager, Doctor W., who was against the plan at first, gave the first speech. He said that he had been working at Siemens-Plania for forty years but that nothing like this had happened in living memory. Not only had we made a masterpiece, he said, but our work methods had been high-quality, too. He was also the first to apologize. He embraced me and shook hands with all my mates in my brigade. Then all the others acted the same way. We were very proud that we had achieved this great project.

Translated by Jan van Heurck

Erwin Strittmatter

Electric Power

Two pigs in a pen require old Adam to plant potatoes on an acre of sandy land behind the house, and to cultivate and harvest them. The potatoes travel through the pigs, turn into droppings, and he takes the manure to the field to plant new potatoes in it.

He feeds the chickens, tends the geese, saws and splits firewood, hauls ten to twenty buckets of water daily from the pump a hundred yards behind the house, transforms it into slops and carries it out again. With a spade he aerates the top layer of soil in the kitchen garden, plants and weeds vegetables, uses pruning shears to train the productive boughs of the fruit trees, protects their blossoms from the spring frosts with smoke, keeps track of the wild roamings of his grandson, helps his neighbor, doesn't talk much, prefers to think and consequently works more than others can see, does old Adam.

Roast meat wrapped in bed feathers standing on pale pink legs—that's what geese are. Why don't they fly away at Martinmas? They certainly have enough wings for it! Man has tamed them, bred them, fattened them up, gotten them used to not flying. Accursed biped, Man!

He has made the chickens line with eggs their lives that stretch from chick to chicken soup, he has compelled them to lay their eggs in boxes and baskets, he steals their eggs out from under them, and he has even fixed things so that they do not feel surprised if they never find more than one egg lying in the nest. A savvy cuss, Man!

From the tangle of weeds he grows this kind of radish and that kind, rutabagas and kohlrabi, red cabbage and white—Man, Man does that! He's proud of him, is old Adam.

He is some sixty summers old, and thirty of these he has spent in the forest. The forest is no longer that dark rank growth of plants where the gods Uran and Urina crouched, where serpents offered to man the high-grade fruit grown by monks, as we have seen it in the paintings of Paradise by old Italian masters. The forest is our vassal, and we, its overlords, plant its trees, poison its May beetles, eradicate its sedges, support its rampant growth of pine trees, and thin it out.

A tall pine fell at a bad angle in the swirling wind when it was being felled, grazed a neighboring tree and broke off one of its thick branches. The branch fell and smashed a knee, it was the right knee of old Adam. So as not to spend the money on the barber, he let his beard grow full while he was in the hospital.

He loves the forest. But that is not how you say things in the outwork; you don't throw high-sounding phrases around like worm-eaten plums. So, old Adam likes to creep about in the forest. He goes to pick mushrooms. Mushrooms are not plants, not eggs, but not animals either. One kind, the green agaric, grows in the wagon tracks on the forest paths where even the lowliest of plants, the couch grass, dares not tread. Green agaric perithecia are built of quicksand, shaped with a ruler and compass. Under their hoods they manufacture a nameless green; they can be pickled and taste good, old Adam knows.

Timber haulers carrying long-stemmed tree trunks unload them along the road. "There will be light," says Adam's son-in-law; says it serenely like that old guy in the Bible: "Let there be light!" Is man a god? There has been too much talk about light. Two governments have promised light to the people of the outwork, and the new government is only two years old. Old Adam doesn't believe in the light.

He lives in his daughter's household. In a box that can hold ninety cubic yards of air drenched in tobacco smoke. That is his little room. If you subtract the air space taken up by the table, the wardrobe, the bureau and the bed, you are left with seventy-five cubic yards of grandfather's air.

Photographs on the walls, a roebuck's antlers, the palmate antlers of an elk, and a big number twenty-five made of silver cardboard. In the bureau drawer are books, the corners of whose pages are brown from being turned in the damp.

On the brown-tinted daylight photo above the bed is a serious woman with a child's nose, Mrs. Adam. She died of blood poisoning. On another photo: He, his wife and three children; the children look as if they have just been chased out of the field to get photographed. The boys died in the war, devil take it! The little girl with the big hair ribbon is the daughter he is living with. On a black-rimmed photo: he, young and alone on horseback. Horse-drawn artillery, Rathenow, 1905. "Up, up, comrades, to horse, to horse. To the memory of my period of service."

His daughter, formerly a maid in the service of the landowner's wife and a person who used to keep her books clean even when she was still in school, is a bookkeeper on the public land; his son-in-law is a tractor driver, also on the public land.

Time flies. Man measures it with his life. The dream of light becomes reality.

Five men come, and lean their ramshackle bicycles against the tall pines. Bicycles, steel frames and metal legs that make man into a sprinter, have become a rarity. There are no more tires for them, made of elasticized tree resin. The war forced the people round about into using their feet again. Shoes are in short supply because cattle are in short supply. Grown-up people have been playing with fire, and they have set on fire more than their neighbor's houses and sheds. Fire has its laws.

A bicycle tire, even one that has been mended fifteen times, saves shoe leather. Worn-out tires are turned into shoe soles, and when they drop off people's feet in shreds, they are dumped at the edge of the forest. A man who has work to do in the forest and not enough coat, makes a fire with them and warms himself. One thing blends into another until it disappears from sight.

The men wear worn-out work clothes. Who knows where the blue color has gone! At midday they eat cold baked potatoes with turnip marmalade. They dig holes by the edge of the woods, stick one to two cubic yards of air into the earth's crust, and where they throw the earth they have lifted out, the forest air must move out of the way. Where one thing is, the other cannot be. They stick the tree trunks with their tarred ends into the holes, fill the holes up with earth again, and the air moves out of the way. Trade and commerce.

A man reverts to the animal kingdom, buckling iron claws onto his wooden clogs and using them to climb up into what used to be the top of a tree. The geese walk over the grave of Adolf Schädlich, eat the begonias and fertilize the geraniums with their pins of green dung. Old Adam has forgotten to tend them.

The man with the claws on his feet attaches porcelain leaves to the top of the bare tree. A pole is set every fifty yards. They stretch one mile to the main village; old Adam is an eyewitness.

The men stay away for two days, then they come back by the aerial route, as high-wire acrobats, and the denuded avenue of light-poles is endowed with two thin tracks running to the outwork, a road for the One who is to come.

The word "insulators" lodges in old Adam's vocabulary, along with other neologisms. He pronounces the word at the supper table so no one can miss it. The family are amazed. You could call the insulators "poles' hands" which the bare pine trees use to hand each other the wire; but each new invention flushes new names and concepts into mankind's storehouse of words, and those who do not use them look ridiculous. Can you use old words to address electricity, and call it "the power to bring light"?

He begins to get terribly interested in the conduction of electricity. He was not interested when the main village was fitted with cable, because the rich farmers there were so boastful about their possessions. Is a man supposed to stand under a rich farmer's window and admire the brightness of his lights? Now the people from the main village would no longer be able to call the people of the outwork "miserable lamp-huggers." Old Adam has developed a soft spot for the new government.

Three houses, four cottages—that is the outwork, and two insulators are plastered into the gable of each residence. Two days later all the houses are linked with wires, are leashed together like a pack of hunting dogs.

The workmen crawl around the attics and parlors. The house is given metal entrails. Tin-plated pipes trickle from the walls, ripple in the corners of the rooms and end at the ceilings. Covered wires hang like untied shoelaces from the tin pipes and wait for the lamps.

He presses his calloused thumb on the switch and the bulb lights up. Something mighty has occurred: The outwork is connected to the larger world outside by two nerve-cords, and old Adam believes in light.

It's sinfully bright in the rooms in the evening. They light the oil lamps once again and stage a contest. The oil lamps burn as brightly as they can and and try so hard that they smolder, but they can't compete with the little light bulb. No one pays attention any more to the deep yellow cosiness of the kerosene lamp. Cosiness is just inadequate light plus the smell of kerosene gas. The light bulb is a room-sized sun, and wins the victory. The grandson counts the hairs on the back of his hand. The daughter discovers that it's time to put on a fresh coat of whitewash in the parlor. The son-in-law puts the new light to the test by reading a book about diesel tractors. Old Adam tests the electric meter against his pocket watch to see if a kilowatt hour has sixty minutes. They are a bit dazed with sheer light, the folk in the outwork.

A mysterious energy is flowing into the house, but its effect is invisible until you make it go into the light bulb via the switch. What does it do when it is sitting hidden inside the wires? The children of the outwork have a yen to track it down. They take themselves off to the cemetery hill, carrying a wet bean pole. Schädlich's grandson taps on the wire.

"What's it like?"

"Like music."

Old Adam's grandson tries it but he hears no sound. They tell him he is hard of hearing and has to tap both wires; and he does it. There are sparks, green and yellow sparks, and the grandson claims later that there were red sparks too. The pole lands in the grass, and Adam's grandson lies next to it with burned arms. The children run away; the old man rushes to the place and takes the boy, who is petrified with terror, to the district hospital in Pfuhl's one-horse carriage.

When human inventions turn against man because he manages them incorrectly, he curses them. Uran, the primal man, cursed the fire he captured when he burned his hands on it. Old Adam does not curse, he thinks of the time when he was an adolescent boy:

It was autumn, already cool, they were tending the rich farmer's cattle, they lit a shepherd's fire and warmed themselves. They ran a trial to see which of them could hold himself over the fire the longest. He was the smallest, he wanted to prove himself and huddled over the flame until his trousers caught fire. He ran, and the draft set his trousers blazing. Then he lay in the grass, and the others put out the fire on his rear end with sand from a mole's hole. It left scars that you cannot see because they are inside his trousers.

Even when his grandson gets well, the old man cannot find out from him what sort of power electricity is.

In the spring he helps Grete Blume saw up the winter wood. It is a time of year when the blossoms of the sour cherries are reflected even in the eyes of widows. Grete Blume in her fiery-checked apron chats about older men in the neighboring villages who remembered their powers and married again. She is not only a widow but also a work-brigade leader among the forest women and even an activist. Old Adam has grown used to these new words too, but he cannot succumb to the springtime charms of his woodchopping partner. He is happy to help her, but his daughter would not put up with any complications. She is moral and watches out to see that he remains faithful to her mother; and who would carry out the housemaid's chores in her house if grandfather changed his life?

One evening the grandson says: "Grete Blume uses electricity to cook potatoes." This news travels into old Adam the way news about the moon travels into an astronaut.

Grete Blume shows him her electric stove, with glowing filaments like thin mattress feathers. He sees the little wheel in the meter box turn as fast as if there were three or more lamps burning. "You'll really have to dig deep into your pockets to pay for that," he says.

Grete Blume pouts and says: That wouldn't be necessary if she had someone in the house to heat the stove for her before she gets in from work. Old Adam is busy researching how the electrical current works: So, it turns into a flameless fire if it is run through spiral filaments, and it even replaces the man in the house. Later he will no longer find this thought amusing.

Electricity brought another miracle to the outwork: news, plays, lectures and weather forecasts. You sucked them out of the air into your parlor with a machine hooked to extended wires. Each family did it for themselves, as much or little as they wanted.

Until the war, only one person in the outwork had a radio. He got the electricity to run it from the bicycle mender in the neighboring village, and carried it in a rectangular preserving jar.

Adolf Schädlich stood in the open square in front of the big woodland barn, cupped his hands into a loudspeaker and bellowed: "Community radio broadcast! The Führer is speaking!"

One day the two men argued while they were having breakfast in the forest. "Only herd animals need a leader; people have intelligence and can agree together where they want to go," said old Adam.

This kind of breakfast conversation was not appropriate for a timber foreman, which was Adolf Schädlich's job. Then the accident happened in the woods when the tree branch fell on old Adam's knee, and Schädlich proclaimed that providence had struck down old Adam.

Schädlich volunteered to fight in the war, and the first time he had leave, he strutted around the outwork sporting a silver chevron in the field-gray solitude of his coat. "Can't you say hello, man?" he bellowed at the limping Adam.

Schädlich visited the chief forester, whose bird dog bit him in the back of the thigh. The wound smarted, but Schädlich waved it aside heroically. The bird dog was a boss's dog.

The front was still far away and Schädlich took a long time getting there. Rabies shimmered through his blood vessels and erupted when a mail sack dropped in front of his feet at a railroad station. He bit the sack in fury and was arrested, and in a regional headquarters at the front he also bit a colonel and a head official. Now he was past rescue! He went back to the outwork in a black uniform made of wood that was hammered together very roughly to fit him, and was buried in the cemetery surrounded by fir trees. That was when electrical current was still carried to the outwork in preserve jars.

Old Adam listens to scientific lectures and is disappointed when he does not find out what electricity is. Then he looks in the newspaper under the *Science and Technology* column. His daughter becomes uneasy. Is her father looking for marriage advertisements? Dissatisfied, he throws away the newspaper and swears at the editors, who assume that people know what is unknown and who explain things that people already know.

When a new energy first makes its appearance, there are spans of time in which it affects the world around it only quantum by quantum. These are the boring passages in our stories. We'll skip them and continue where there are visible changes:

Old Adam is sitting in the cemetery, sitting there on a grave and is not on good terms with himself. There are still holes in the cemetery fence. It must be horrid to lie unprotected under the earth and be regaled with goose shit! He goes after the geese with a shovel, he could kill them. The geese position themselves outside, and peep into the cemetery until he sits down again.

He has sat down on the grave of Adolf Schädling. A quiver of horror runs through him, but he suppresses it.

He sits down on his wife's grave. There is rustling in the blue spruces. This late-summer wind would be invisible if there were nothing in its way! The same as electricity. He still does not know what this power is, but he has personally experienced its effects . . .

Five more electricians came, they had motors on their bicycles and were as fast as galloping horses. Otherwise everything went the same as before: Two insulators to each pole; two additional wires, and the houses had a second supply point. "Electricity at last!" said the son-in-law and bought a pump engine. A mesentery of iron entrails was installed in the house from below, and the water came under human authority and had to crawl up the walls in narrow pipes. A pressure tank, kitchen sink and water faucets. The first water that was tapped in the kitchen elicited a song of praise from old Adam, praise of the wiliness of man.

But great troubles germinate unseen; you do not recognize the rock on which you will one day break your leg.

The water buckets were brought into the house and set down beside the kerosene lamps, and their handles, polished by calloused skin, longed there in the dark for the hands of old Adam. Who can know what they feel?

Neighbor Pfuhl, the land-reform farmer, bought a motor for his threshing machine, and from then on he stopped sending for old Adam to drive his draught horses; but he still let him work the machine that cleansed the grain after the threshing. Then the farmers' co-op was founded; Pfuhl's threshing machine became outmoded, and so did the old man who turned the barrel of the grain-cleanser. A use was found for the threshing machine motor, but not for old Adam. The motor was hooked up to a circular saw, and the motorized saw could chop up the winter wood for all the inhabitants of the outwork in just a few hours. That put an end to sawing wood at Grete Blume's in springtime!

But the vegetable garden, the pigs and the poultry were still there. Silently he took up the struggle against leftover time. His grandson was training as an electrician in the city. "Do you know

now what electrical power is?" asked old Adam. His grandson did not know.

A new wonder of the world arrived in the cottage: a machine the size of a chicken crate, with a wall of glass on one side. Electric power lured living and speaking pictures from all over the world onto the glass wall. "Grandfather should still get something out of life," the young people said.

They only washed off the worst of the dirt when they came in from work, wolfed down their supper and sat like a wall in front of the toy box. He had to be satisfied with what he could glimpse from behind them: Mongols on horseback, a fat humorless Berliner playing a comedian, harvest battles and floods, dredging machines as big as churches that were run by a single person, top league sports and iron foundry workers being awarded decorations by the Council of State, competitive dancing, competitive riding—everyone in the country had his place, his satisfying work, except for him, old Adam.

The young people turned refined and got rid of the pigs. The daughter and son-in-law were sick of salted meat and hard-smoked sausage. The potato patch no longer needed to be tilled.

The young people went after the chickens. He could not get any winter eggs from them in his little henhouse. Winter eggs were enticed from the hens in warmed and electrically-lighted henhouses on the co-op farms.

In spring his daughter brought fresh savoy cabbages from the co-op. He had only just finished planting his savoy cabbage plants, lettuce and kohlrabi—all too late, too late. "What's the point of the back garden?" His daughter took no notice of the hands that hid themselves under the table, the hands of old Adam.

They left him only the geese, which he was least fond of. Were they keeping them for the bed feathers' sake or for his? He became even more taciturn, turned to the familiar forest again, gathered mushrooms, sold them at the assembly point. But was it his business in life to transform mushrooms into printed banknotes?

In spring he thought about the encouragements of Grete Blume. It was a warm evening. The lilac emitted its fragrant gas, and the urge to reproduce shrieked out of the screech owls as he knocked on Grete Blume's door. He heard a "Come in!" and a giggle, and that was understandable: a widowed resettler from the main village was sitting in his shirtsleeves in Grete Blume's kitchen, and they were eating together, electrically baked potatoes and brawn.

On the way home there was weariness in his feet as after a long march. The scent of lilac weighed down his shoulders, and in the mating call of the screech owl he heard mockery.

That was last spring. Now it's the summer finale with slanting light and ebbing green. Once more he drives the geese out of the courtyard of the dead. The geese signal to each other and act as if they are turning toward the lake.

He remains standing in front of a gravestone, that practical shield for corpses that has been in use since the days of Uran, and reads the inscription composed for the dead man:

> *The clock's tick-tock, the hour's strike*
> *Stitch time from stillness, day and night;*
> *The moon steps a beat,*
> *Death stamps its feet.*

He starts to dig under the big Douglas fir, lifts out the green smile of the earth, the slices of turf, and stacks them up. An old man's tear, heavy with the salt of experience, hangs from his beard like a drop of dew from a tree lichen. It falls, like everything that must obey earth's gravity, into the crumbly humus and seeps away.

At the start of summer he had gone into the village and applied for a job as a herdsman. The dairy foreman and manager of the long co-op milk factory clapped him on the shoulder and pointed at old Adam's walking stick and his game leg.

He resorted to gathering medicinal plants and drying them on pastry boards. One day he brought them to the sidewalk in front of the cottage because there was the right amount of sun there, and his son-in-law rode his moped across the tea-trays.

What followed was not a quarrel but a sigh, and then a little fire in the meadow. A great quantity of good health went up in smoke.

Adam's grandson was now an electrician in the forest, in an atomic energy plant. He was a good worker and was awarded a decoration on May Day, but at home he was—music, music and fever. A radio receiver the size of a cigarette box operated on his wrist. Music came out of his wrist. The electricity for the box came from little roll batteries no thicker than goose pins. Drums and stopped horns scared away the boy's own songs. That is what produced the fever that made the old man uneasy about his grandson.

The young electrician brought home a salesgirl from the little forest town. They put their arms around each other, dislocated their legs and hips, managed to walk anyhow and went down to the sea. They exchanged feelings with the musicboxes chattering on their wrists, smiled, made monosyllabic sounds, were happy in their way, which was not necessarily a bad way merely because old Adam did not understand it.

The salesgirl, this child, was going to have a child. She was taken into the Adams' cottage. She was supposed to learn how to keep house before the child was born.

This was no new wonder of the world that came to the cottage now: the future daughter-in-law, whose name was Beatrix like the names on the TV. Her face was pale, her hair was bleached; she carried her growing belly through the little world reluctantly, and held her nose because pipe tobacco did not agree with her. Old Adam interpreted the nausea of pregnancy in his own way: To the very young he already smelled like a corpse. He avoided little Bea, but she seemed to be pursuing him in her baggy little skirt. A full bud was about to push a yellow autumn leaf off the branch.

She would fall asleep on the sofa while she was dusting, she would sleep while peeling potatoes, and most of all little Bea liked to sleep in the bed in the hidden room that belonged to the grandfather. Once upon a time Urina too no doubt would visit the warm cave when the bear was away. Bea slept, and the little machine on her wrist worked away. That's how he found her when he returned from the forest at noon. She would wake up when she smelled his pipe, hold her nostrils shut, use her other hand to fiddle with the tower of her hair, yawn and say: "We'll be so cosy living here."

There he had it from the source: They were waiting for his death. They wouldn't have to wait long!

Now he is digging his own grave, turning a commonplace metaphor into literal reality. He digs, and little stones cry out when the blade of the shovel touches them . . . A man goes down to the lake, thank God he is no swimmer, he sinks without further ado. Maybe he gets a heart attack from the cold water before he has to swallow the sludge of green algae. He trudges in behind the reeds, sinks up to his neck and deeper. The columbine-blue sky is traded for pale green twilight; an eel wriggles up around him, uses the swirling water to glide into his gulping mouth . . .

But things haven't gotten to that point yet. He has read the books with the brown-cornered pages in the bureau drawer; he knows stories. He wants to announce his death to the young people, wants to go and smash the little pump engine in the cellar. He will not cut off one head of the Electricity Dragon in the process, but he wants to leave this little enigma for the young people.

He goes down to the road, walks up to the meadow and stands before a miracle: The co-op's meadow is surrounded by a low electric-wire fence that reaches right up to the forest. Iron posts, insulators and wires—a miniature circuit line.

A modern death. All you needed was to touch the drooping wire. He grabs the upper wire with his bare hand and gets an electric shock, but it does not substitute for death in the lake.

Curiosity, that sly prolonger of life, awakens in him. Electricity lies at his feet. He must find out what electricity is, he must!

Seven and a half acres of meadow encircled by electricity, with the herd of dairy cattle grazing in the middle. The electricity has been made the herdsman while Adam has been thrown onto the scrapheap of humanity.

A little cabinet on a red iron pole. It crackles and sputters inside as if a woodpecker were trying to peck its way out. The pole and the little cabinet are under a tree in the meadow.

As he climbs over the fence his stiff leg, this obstacle to life, catches on the upper wire. Several jolts of electricity go through him, he falls, and the connection is broken. He stands up again and is alive.

Two men jump down off their bicycles. He strokes his full beard, embarrassed, and looks for an excuse. The leader of the co-op is not looking for an excuse, he wants someone to look after the meadow. Is old Adam willing to take on the job?

He tumbles out of nothingness into earthly life and asks for a place to stay in the main village.

A tractor drives up in front of the Adam cottage. Two tractor drivers excavate a room, reduce it to ninety cubic yards of air space.

"What's that for?" The young people tackle the grandfather.

"You'll find out what," says old Adam.

Pale Bea is sleeping on the sofa with her belly sticking out. A saxophone and a percussion group are working away on her wrist. He climbs onto the twin seat of the tractor. The young people wave—for the sake of the neighbors.—There is no law that says: Thou shalt die in the room thou wert born in!

The calves' meadow, the young livestock meadow, and the dairy herd meadow—he has to patrol them all. When deer or wild pigs tear down the wires on their nocturnal forays, he has to mend them. The insulators have to be intact and the accumulators full. A fragile fellow, this electrical herdsman, who stumbles over blades of grass and needs someone to tend him constantly.

The world needs him, old Adam, again. But he still does not know what electricity is. He flags down his grandson, who is whizzing to work on his motorbike at half the speed of a rifle bullet. There is no longer a music box on the boy's wrist. The music of the new child in the cottage has suppressed it. Every young thing is exuberant. The old people are afraid that this exuberance could spoil their plans for their planet; but the planet is round and is on the move.

"Ask your engineers at last what electricity is!" says the old man.

The grandson no longer dares to smile at his grandfather. He has brought enough disgrace on the household. In the factory library he looks in the lexicon and learns the answer by heart: "Electricity is the totality of phenomena based on electrical charges and the fields they emit."

"The cow eats grass and gives milk, and that's where it comes from. Is that an answer?" asks old Adam. He is dissatisfied with the engineers. He must continue to spy on the electricity itself: which is nothing alien: transformed coal, the transformed energy of flowing water, transformed uranium ore from the earth's mountains. It is no more alien than the wind that sailors greet gratefully in the morning.

It gives him a vast lot to think about, which makes him happy. But that is not how you say things in the outwork; you don't throw high-sounding phrases around like worm-eaten plums. Old Adam is alive with power.

Translated by Jan van Heurck

Erik Neutsch

Hartholz

One day—no, more precisely at the end of April this year—the journalist Eddy Merker drove into the housing development at the edge of the city. He had been given a clear-cut assignment: write about someone who has recently distinguished himself by his strong sense of duty and special achievements in his work. May Day was coming, and a personal portrait of this kind was the only thing the newspaper still needed to produce a well-rounded, successful holiday edition.

Eddy Merker, a long-time editorial secretary who was not really used to writing his own articles any more but was a bit tired of endlessly correcting and overseeing other people's manuscripts, found the assignment appealing and set to work at once. It would mean another sensational success at last, not only for the paper but for him. "Get me the right man, you can leave all the rest to me," he had said.

Now he had gotten hold of a name, and yesterday the construction workers' collective had supplied him the address. He had brought along a press photographer too, who no sooner got out of the car than he draped himself with several pieces of equipment, including a heavy black leather bag that dragged his shoulder down, and started shooting pictures without delay: the little house on the left, the little house on the right, a backlit photo of the little house itself.

It sat in a row of other houses of the same type, on a hill from which, on this day polished till it shone with brilliant sunshine, you could look down across the land to the far-off waste heaps of the coppermines. In the front garden the forsythias were blooming yellow, the first tulips red, and the bluebonnets already as blue as ever. The house seemed to have already been through its spring cleaning. It had been dipped from head to foot in a fresh glowing white. But opposite it, on the other side of the yard, rose a crude structure with walls of hollow gray cinder blocks and a roof of corrugated asbestos tiles, evidently an unfinished garage.

In suburban housing projects like this, the doors are locked only at night or when the occupants are away. So Eddy Merker was able to walk right into the yard. But then he came face to face with a man in worn-out overalls covered with whitewash stains, and at once he got the feeling that he had met him before. But where, but when? It must have been a very long time ago. Alfons Wein came into his mind, not for the first time since he began to think about this article. That was twenty years ago. But it couldn't be. This man had a different name, and he was a different person too. Eddy did not even know if Alfons Wein was still alive.

Hilmar Hartholz—Hille as his workmates called him—had heard the sound of the engine as the car made its tortured way up the incline, which though gentle was riddled with potholes, and observed the two men through the kitchen window. Actually he was waiting for the dump truck. Then, seeing the photographer with his camera gear and realizing that these had to be the news-paper people, he thought: "So they've caught you anyway, all your running away and jumping the tracks has been for nothing . . ."

He didn't want to hide any longer, he wasn't a woodlouse. He said to his wife Bärbel, who was busy at the stove behind him and was clattering the pot lids: "Put the potatoes on the fire soon. By the time lunch is ready they'll be gone." His elder son was due home from school any minute now too, and as always he would be hungry as a bear.

Then he went out into the yard. A single glance was enough. But even he hadn't expected this. *Aha, old friend, so we know each other. You've gotten a bit bloated. Each year you buy your suits a size larger, don't you, and you get your trousers shortened. You've lost some of your hair too, and what's left has gotten mouldy . . .* He estimated that Merker must be about fifty by now.

But Merker no longer seemed to remember him, and introduced himself. Hille Hartholz did the same. He saw no reason to betray himself. *On the contrary,* he thought, *it's all the better if we two don't have to take any notice of those days: Good old Alfons and the first Socialist Work Brigade here and there and everywhere, building away.* The photographer roamed around them snapping photos.

But Hille could not be so impolite as to just leave them standing there. He invited them to sit down in the garden, in the summerhouse of split oak trunks that he had built himself. The forsythia were blooming here too. The dense jungle of clematis that his father had planted and raised on trellises was only now showing little shoots. He called to Bärbel through the veranda door to make coffee.

"The sun is making an effort today, isn't it? But it's deep in the red and needs to pay off some of its debt to us after this beastly winter." The best thing was to talk about the weather.

Merker tried to explain what he had in mind. The editors' intentions were such-and-such, and his own plan was this. An entire page, one hundred and fifty typed lines of text, the rest nice little pictures.

"Fine . . . So . . . Just stay in that pose," said the photographer, scenting business in the air. "No. Not like that. Don't look into the camera. Natural, you understand, as natural as possible."

"As soon as it's printed, you'll be famous," Eddy said, selling his article.

But Hille was barely listening. He had already known since yesterday what lay in store for him. Very early in the morning his union head had told him that a reporter wanted to interview him when his shift was over. Why, and for what? Then around noon he abruptly fled from the building site. The tile plant had left them in the lurch again anyhow and not delivered any of the materials. Up until last weekend they were still being told: We need to put out extra efforts to catch up on the backlog, but now it was all twiddling one's thumbs and slacking off . . . . He would rather run away, he would rather prepare the bed of gravel and wait for the dump truck with the asphalt. But instead it was a Moskvitch that came crawling up the hill to him; he could tell by the noise. No one else but he in the housing development owned such a Rolls Royce of the steppes. But his own Moskvitch was standing under the pear trees, covered with a tarpaulin. Although admittedly that was about to change, because he finally had time to level off the entrance to the garage. But he could do without an audience for that. The day had gone wrong pretty much from the first cockcrow. He was an unlucky guy, Hille was, even if other people believed he was a big success. In the breast pocket of his overalls he still had the envelope with the police summons. He had found the letter in the mailbox that morning and so far had kept it secret even from Bärbel, although she knew the reason for the summons because he had told her the story on the evening of the day it happened. No, he was not a hero, not in the least the sort of person who should be smiling at everyone from the newspaper on May Day.

Merker was thinking that he wasn't going to get close to the man this way. He didn't lack experience, but maybe he was a bit out of practice? He had to find some other method to tackle him. Once again, he remembered the business with Wein. What angles had he played back then? But could he still reconstruct that affair in all its details, after so many years?

It was a long, long time ago. My God, I earned my spurs on that job. Our pal Alfons had let himself be talked into it without putting up too much resistance. It was he, Eddy, who ran the show, or to put it more amiably: guided the pen.

Back then, the Wein Brigade made headlines for several months straight, was on the schedule for at least two quarter terms. That was the time in which socialist group-work techniques were born and innovative methods were given cosy names—the Seifert Method, the Kowaljow Technique, the Steffens Approach—after those who invented them. Work, learn and live the socialist way. The collectives even used to book theater seats as a group for a whole season.

But what happened then? What was left of that, what survived?

The last Eddy had heard of Alfons Wein was that he had gone downhill, that his brigade had broken up a short time later.

A reporter from the financial section, which Merker had once been in charge of, told him the news. He made it sound like a reproach. Yeah, so what? Merker did not know how to defend himself except to reply: "Revolutionaries come and go. Wein affected the economy and so he affected history too. Other people found out about him through our articles and imitated what he did. So he fulfilled his purpose. He supplied the right headlines at the right time. . . ."

Today, Eddy felt a little guilty all the same.

He had to get at Hartholz through his sense of honor. The way Hartholz was behaving now, puffing away at one cigarette after another, blowing smoke rings into the air and evidently more interested in their fate than in him, Eddy, and in what Eddy was saying—this just couldn't continue.

"I was told you are an outstanding worker. You mentioned the sun and the winter just now. It shouldn't surprise you if we want to know something more about you than that. Your brigade called for special shifts of workers to make up the backlogs. There is your commitment to residential building in general. The business of the wallpaper. Your personal efforts at the tile plant to reconstruct the outer-wall production line . . ."

How well-informed he is, Hille thought—*almost better than I am. Whoever clued him in to all that? But I also socked two teenage louts in the kisser, no older than sixteen they were, with faces like fire alarms. That's why the cops sent me a summons, sent it overnight by express messenger. I have to expect punishment for it, because it's forbidden to beat people up. I admit I saw red. But I couldn't simply sit there and watch like the other passengers. Newspaper hack, why don't you blow? Any minute now I'm expecting the dump truck, and besides I made a crooked deal, you know, since petroleum got scarcer and there's barely enough asphalt to fill in the holes in the road that the frost left.*

Bärbel brought the pot of coffee and three cups on a tray. She was wearing a head scarf that hid her curlers. Softly she asked Hille if she shouldn't turn down the heat under the potatoes.

He said: "If you two guys are hungry, of course you can eat with us. On Saturdays we always have soup."

The photographer nodded. He said it was a good theme, he would put some fresh film in the camera for that.

"No," said Merker. "We don't want to disturb you. We just have to hurry it up."

So, Alfons Wein, in the headlines back in 1959, a go-getter, the kind of guy you only meet in newspaper stories written by men like Merker! Everything fit the picture, the marriage, bringing up the children, meeting the daily quota and his high monthly contribution to the group; and what didn't fit was—at the very least—kept under wraps.

Despite all his bitterness, maybe Wein had really been what he seemed, a star, a doubting Thomas turned saint. Eddy had interviewed him a hundred times and he ought to know. At the time he had traveled around with Wein from one construction site to another. The multiple shift system was in great demand. Alfons resisted at first, then let himself be talked into it and was told that he ought to teach his method to others; then he really kicked up a fuss. A socialist aid program. So what do you think? It meant living abroad, living in lousy barracks again. His wife was even more fed up with his migratory existence than he was. "If you can convince her," Alfons said, "then fine, maybe I'll cooperate." Eddy caught him at home one day and sat down opposite him, exactly the way he was sitting across from this Hartholz guy today. The wife was violently opposed and tried to salvage what was past rescue. Soon she was writhing under Eddy's blunt words as if they were blows. "Well go ahead you two, shut the door behind you."

But in Klagnitz, the first stopping point for Alfons and his brigade, weeks went by before they found any allies at the construction site for the new carbide plant. Often they pottered around alone. No one supplied them with cement or lime, not even with the most essential materials. So we're supposed to work in shifts and even at night? Where has that ever been done in the building trade! Are we supposed to fall off the scaffolding and break our necks? Many workers treated Wein's crew like strikebreakers and threatened them with their pickaxes in the bars in the evening; and once the rungs of a ladder had been partly sawed through.

Alfons said: "I'm going to throw up this job. My wife is right. I want to go on being a good father for a long time yet."

Of course Hille had heard this remark before too. He also knew what Merker had said to Alfons in reply:

"You're staying here," Eddy had answered. "That's our mission for the Party. But so you can get your courage back, we'll broach the subject in the newspaper. You'll write an article against the reactionaries."

"Why me, man? At school I always got D's in essay writing."

So Eddy told him what to write.

At that moment a horn honked in front of the house, or rather it was more the death rattle of a honk. The dump truck stood outside the door.

Hille hesitated. How could he explain what the truck was doing there? He had been in his trade for twenty years. He had worked at every job from the ground up, he was an old hand. He had suffered through all the ups and downs from the building program for the chemical industry to the residential building program. He knew everybody, including a few dump-truck drivers. Recently he had waved a couple of bills at one of them. "Set something aside for me, pal. I need a load for the ramp to my garage." That kind could always be found. Whether it was sand or asphalt—what was the difference? But . . . But there was a difference. Oil was getting scarce, gravel pits weren't.

Just last weekend, during the extra shift that he had called for, he had someone dump a pile of sand in front of his construction vehicle. Bärbel was away from home that day too. Her brigade was traveling, they planned to see a museum somewhere and visit the beautiful green countryside to celebrate an award they had received. But what should she do about their youngest child? Hille promised her that he would look after him. "I have an idea. Count on me." He took the boy along to work with him, and to make sure that his son would have something to do, he had a load of sand brought up especially for him to build a castle. "Don't you dare move from this spot when Daddy's working." Once when the boy began to whine, the foreman played "Patticake, patticake, baker's man" with him.

Now the dump truck had arrived with the asphalt. The photographer was taking pictures. That wasn't so pleasant. No, it wasn't. *If you want to write about me, Merker, and want to write the truth, the whole unvarnished truth, then write that too. Do we have to hide? To keep silent what we're really like, and print only what we ought to be? Well so what? Tell your readers the sort of man Hille Hartholz is, the whole picture. That he isn't afraid to slip someone a couple of bills, because there's no other way, no honest course by which he can get hold of building materials.*

But Eddy did not appear to understand him. His was a more theoretical mind, he often missed the mark when it came to knowing how the world was run on the practical level. He could not even keep track of the exact prices of butter, bread and the most common types of sausage. So he did not take offense when Hille excused himself, saying that he had to go and check on things outside, to see if the asphalt he had swiped—"Yes, I swiped it, you understand!"—from the Neustadt central railroad station was worth the two bills he had paid for it. Eddy meanwhile spent his time philosophizing and thinking about Alfons again. That first article was published, and several others promptly followed it. The series was called *The Diary of Wein the Iconoclast.*

But good old Alfons had never written a diary, not even during the war, when he served with the ground personnel of the Luftwaffe and would have had time for it. He grumbled: "People who know me won't think I'm capable of that. They'll laugh themselves silly at me. And I don't like being the butt of jokes."

Eddy responded: "Take it easy. That's for me to worry about. You do have to let me use a bit of imagination. It can't hurt us, or the job either."

After that, a diary page was published every week, fifty to eighty lines of type. A crackerjack text, and what's more—don't look so surprised, ladies and gentlemen!—it's all signed with the unimpeachable name of Carpenters' Brigade Leader Wein. But not one sentence, not one word of it came from him. Alfons had nothing to do but approve and confirm on Monday morning what Merker had diligently collected and written down by Sunday. His work on it was limited to shaking his graying head at some passage now and then. But for him the worst thing was that he got money for it, a fee of thirty pennies for each line of print. He always drank up the money along with his men. "It's Judas's pay, boys, believe me." He didn't even feel happy when his brigade became the first in the construction business to be given the title "socialist" and was awarded a decoration.

Hille could tell people a thing or two about all that. He had just turned seventeen when it happened. In many ways it was the period of his apprenticeship. He came back and sat down again on the bench in the summerhouse. The asphalt had been unloaded and smoothed out. Bärbel brought in the potato soup with little sausages, grilled bacon, and roasted onions. Besides this there were some slices of coarse brown bread from the baker's, spread with mustard.

"Enjoying your meal?"

The photographer said: "In America they're already showing films where, when flowers bloom or food is served, the scents are pumped into the movie theater through mechanical jets."

Merker reminded Hille of the wallpaper story.

"What's so unusual about that?" asked Hille. "I suggested that when we were doing up the new apartments, the future tenants should be asked what wallpaper patterns they wanted on the walls.

In the past we slapped on any old thing, regardless of the taste of the occupants. Most tenants tore the wallpaper off again and put up something new. That was wasteful, in my opinion. That's all. I'm surprised no one had the idea before."

The business of the summons was much more complicated, he said.

He was sitting in the streetcar on his way home. Two young men boarded, wearing the Stars and Stripes and US army insignia on the sleeves of their jackets. They made a racket and cracked dirty jokes so that everybody could hear. An old Comrade with Party insignia the size of a one-mark coin on his lapel, called to them to shape up. They retreated to the rear platform and whispered together but kept quiet for the time being. Then at one of the next stops they left the streetcar and started making noise again. They stood in front of the windshield. One of them spit at the window glass, grinned and spit, aiming at the face of the Comrade right behind it. The streetcar bell rang. "I grabbed at the emergency brake and was out in a flash. I no longer know how it happened. I punched the two in the face, right and left. 'Nobody gets insulted here, not when I'm around!' Then I hit them, Merker. And I'm not worried about what the laws say about protecting young people, either."

Eddy said: "Hey guy, you're really putting me on the spot!"

"Write the truth."

"That's why I'm here."

"No, no. I know you. From more than twenty years ago."

"But you were still a babe in diapers." He meant it as a joke.

"Mistake." Hille was no longer thinking about mincing words or denying who he was. "Have you ever tried to split a real log, an oak log for instance, like the one that makes up this bench? You have to look carefully to see how it has grown, and drive in the wedge along the length of the grain. It won't work if you cut across the grain, it won't work. You'll just pound your arms numb."

Eddy pricked up his ears. Once again he had the feeling that he had met this man before. But where, but when? How long ago was it, and why was his memory deserting him now?

Hille asked: "Do you know why Alfons failed back then, right after he and our brigade received a decoration?" And before Merker, the artful dodger, could reply, he added: "Because you all stole his name. The multiple shift system was his method. But then you named it after Steffens, the leader of the neighboring brigade."

"But we couldn't describe it as the Wein method. Just think about it. Wein! Everybody would have turned it into a joke. They would have said it was a method for boozing or for crying."*

"And that was enough of a reason for you to sideline him for good?"

Eddy could not think of a reply. He put down his spoon. The photographer took a snapshot of him looking perplexed.

"But you're barking up the wrong tree with me. Either you write everything about me or nothing. And I insist that I want to see the article first before it's published. I want to know in advance what you are turning me into."

But there was no time left for that. If the sketch was to appear in the holiday issue as planned, it had to be typeset by the day after tomorrow at the latest. Regaining the power of speech, Eddy tried to explain that to Hille. He kept fighting for his assignment and tried to save it, but without success. Hartholz, almost a head taller than he, bent down to him, clapped him amiably on the shoulder and said goodbye. His two sons were just leaving the imprint of their shoes in the asphalt, and he had to give them his attention.

Only when he was out on the street, and already in the car on his way back to work, did Eddy Merker realize what had happened to him. Something is different, he thought. Something has changed since that time long ago . . . An uncomfortable feeling came over him, the feeling that he had been standing still and had failed to move on.

Translated by Jan van Heurck

---

*This is a pun on the name "Wein," which as a noun means "wine" and in the verb *weinen* means "to cry." The name "Hartholz" means "hardwood" (which cannot be split against the grain). "Merker" is ironic because the German noun *Merker* means someone who notices and remembers things: the opposite of Eddy Merker.

Werner Bräunig

On the Way

We are moving, at any rate. Here are our transport papers, here is
the thermos bottle, this is the autobahn. It is ten o'clock, you listen
to the weather report. Poetry and Truth and all the rest.

To be specific, it's raining. It has been raining since Zwickau, it
let up a little outside Leipzig, got heavier by the Schkeuditz inter-
change, and now it is pattering its way across the Elbe. The sopo-
rific sound of the windshield wiper. The monotony of the road.
Karl was just thinking it would be nice to have another driver with
him. His colleagues are expensive, too expensive. And then he saw
someone standing by the highway next to a little suitcase, wearing
a scarf and a little coat against the rain that whistled over the stone
pines, in the middle of the Fläming hills. Surrounded by nothing
but woods and moorland. Nothing but stone pines and rain and
sand and wind. Karl already had his foot on the clutch. He had
never seen a hitchhiker in this area before.

She shoved up the little case and climbed in. Karl said: "First
off, you'd better wring yourself out." He let his rig taxi along,
pushed by the trailer. This stretch of road sloped a bit downward.

Now she was sitting there in one of those pullovers, combing
her hair. Hmm. How does a person end up in this area? You bail
out, or somebody throws you out. Sure enough you have your
reasons. The Fläming is a low-curving part of the Southern land
bridge, formed in the Ice Age, relatively sparsely settled, a region
of pine forest. That's what he can still remember. You store up all
sorts of things in your memory. And she is bound to talk about
herself. Seeing this weather, how would she feel about a cup of

coffee? She unscrewed the cup from the thermos, drank in little gulps and said: "Not bad." That was all she said, for the time being. Now and then she cast a sidelong glance his way. And so it went until they got near Niemegk. Then Karl asked: "Where do you actually want to go?"

Keep going north. That was one answer, of course. To Rostock or Helsinki, who knows. Something seemed to be troubling her. Or maybe she was annoyed, how should he know? He would cheer her up a little if he knew how. He could sing for instance, if he had the knack. Strange ideas she was giving him.

Or try this story. Once there was a guy, his family sent him to college, and during the summer holidays he went to work for three weeks so his family could have a summer vacation, too. But this work was a hauling job, and it happened that on his first trip, the guy was supposed to deliver two transformers from Zwickau to Magdeburg, with no return freight but double-quick. So he sets out, and in Magdeburg he learns—ain't we got fun?—that the folks there need only one of his transformers. So he phones up Zwickau, finds there's a little misunderstanding. The second transformer has to go to Rostock. So the guy heads for the coast. When he gets there, it's almost night and nobody in the firm knows anything about his delivery, but after three hours they do find him a free bed. Next day it turns out that they really are desperate for a transformer, but a different kind. So once again, Philipp Reis's invention, the telephone, comes in handy. For a long time nobody can figure out what to do, they talk about having him come back to Zwickau and then they change their minds, because it seems that Eisenhüttenstadt is waiting for a transformer, and it would not be so far out of his way. The rest is unbelievable, although there is solid evidence that it is true. In Eisenhüttenstadt they did indeed need this transformer, the only thing is, they already received it three weeks ago. We'll pass over the scene the guy made at his office the following day. We'll just say that from then on, he had the nickname Odysseus: Odysseus Meyer. Although his name was really Karl. Now wasn't that a nice story?

She smiled, at any rate. And said that even if the story wasn't true, at least it was a good one. She wanted to know what Odysseus had been studying at college. As for herself, she said, she was studying architecture.

Rain, acid rain smearing the roadway. No, she did not ask about Penelope. His trailer looks funny in the rearview mirror. A Wartburg passes him and some lookout sends him signals that no doubt are intended to be perfectly intelligible. He pulls over to the edge of the woods, jumps out into the rain. Now we really are in for it.

She looked out from the front seat and asked if she could help. "Not that I know of," said Karl. He put up the warning sign and fetched the tools. She got out anyway. She had put on her scarf again, and donned Karl's old denim jacket, rolling up the sleeves: she looked amazing. And while Karl got out the spare tire, she was already setting up the jack, and in the right place. Karl loosened the nuts and she screwed them down. She mentioned in passing that her name was Sabine. It's true what they say, that work brings people closer. And now she had the inevitable spot of oil on her face and was helping to take off the old tire and put on the new one. She did it all rapidly. Of course Karl asked if she had done this before, maybe on a regular car. She smiled and said: "Not that I know of."

That was near Beelitz, and they were both soaked to the skin. Somewhere along the way they fixed themselves up a bit, and warmed themselves a bit, too. Then they passed Potsdam on their right, went by Nauen, ate their midday meal in Oranienburg—even though Sabine said that this area made her uncomfortable. "I know it's nonsense. But whenever I see people over forty, in Weimar for instance, I wonder. They had a concentration camp right in front of their noses and they can't say they didn't know anything. What was going on inside them, and what's going on inside them now?"

On the other hand, there are things a person knows and yet does not understand—perhaps does not want to understand. There are things that you can see and check out and still not grasp. There is this girl Sabine, and thereby hangs the following tale:

I was little and used to play by the water. The water belonged to me and was called the Rhine.

That was her childhood. Then they moved to another city where everything was strange—to another country, it turned out later, another world. When she was ten, Sabine learned the meaning of the word "camp." When she was thirteen, she visited Buchenwald with her school class. And now she knew what had happened to her father three months before she was born, in March of 1945.

Later came a time when she felt ashamed—she who had done nothing and prevented nothing, she was not even born yet—ashamed that it was her father's death to which she owed the privileges that were accorded her in this country. From then on, her life seemed to take a different course. She became more serious, more strict, sometimes even unjust, as she recognizes now. When her civics teacher talked about the "new, peaceful Germany," she embarrassed him by remarking that peace is more than just an end to the shooting. She admired Fidel Castro and Ernesto Che Guevara. She attacked the lukewarm, and this gained her friends. But she attacked the prudent even more harshly, and this isolated her from most people. A few weeks before she took her high-school graduation exam, she circulated at her school leaflets that she had made herself, expressing what later were called "sectarian and revisionist demands." In the investigation that followed, she accused several teachers: "They keep talking about struggle, so as to better conceal that they are doing nothing." She had applied to study architecture, because her father had been an architect. Although she passed her examinations with a mark of "Very good," she was notified that her application had been "deferred because of overenrollment." She grew suspicious and bitter.

Then she met a man who had known her father in the camp. For a long time she had been trying to find people who could give her information and complete her picture of her father, because she wanted to be like him: "Someone who won't knuckle under. Someone with whom you can go into the trenches, without having to be afraid that he'll run away or desert or shoot you in the back of the head." This was precisely the image that Ernst Runge painted of her father, and yet it was different from how she had pictured him in the past: less reckless, less heroic, greater. "He was a helpful and deeply cheerful person right up to the end," Runge said. That coloring that did not seem to fit in her image of antifascist struggle. Commenting on what he called her guerrilla action at her school, Runge said: "Hey kid, this isn't the Wild West." That reawakened her suspicion. All the same, she took his advice and went to work for a year in the chemical combine where Runge was foreman in electrolysis. She was close-mouthed and dismissive to begin with. But after a few months, she began to understand that there was a world here to which she had had no real access before. She suddenly realized what it means for someone to do his job his whole life long, often in a profession that does not fulfill him. She found entrance to a world where chlorine, carbide or some type of aluminum was produced every day, frequently by hard labor, and where many people did more than just what was required, and worried about production figures, political work, union problems, qualifications, even culture—for fifty years and more. They got up early in the morning and came home at night to family, children, obligations, had three weeks of vacation a year plus the weekends: that's the salt of the earth, what gives us life. She talked about it with Runge. For the first time, she had the feeling that she really belonged somewhere and was useful. But soon she found contradictions here, too. The driver at her plant, a man who could work hard and was always a leader in competition along with his squad, told her flat out that in this place they had "taught many a hotheaded revolutionary the error of his ways." "What counts with me is work, nothing else: all the rest is nonsense," he said. They often had disagreements. When he was asked to evaluate her progress in the work brigade, he described her as quarrelsome and arrogant. Sabine had almost expected that; but she did not understand why no one in her brigade spoke up and said the evaluation was wrong. She fell into a paralyzing indifference. She did not even reapply for college. When he found out, the ever-prudent Ernst Runge got angry: "Who taught you to give up so easily? Besides, the man has five children and a sick wife, and you're judging him as superficially as he does you. And the reason that the brigade didn't speak up for you is that they know what a tough time he's having and how carelessly you brushed that aside." All Sabine could say was, "I didn't know." "Exactly," said Runge. And he showed her the written evaluation, in which all that remained of the phrase "quarrelsome and arrogant" was, "She sometimes passes hasty judgments." Runge also went with her to her college entrance exam. That was how she began her studies . . .

"Yes," said Karl, "I understand."

"Odysseus," she said, "I don't know. I no longer completely understand it myself."

Then back to the road, the transit road from north to south; back to the rain. Who taught you to be so modest? Oh yes, Karl understood a lot of what she had said. When he went to work in the factory after his first year of university, his pals wanted to know what his grades had been like. Three A's, two B's, one C, that's good enough for me. "So," said Merten, who had initiated him into the mysteries of the auto mechanic's trade, "so a C is good enough for you. Who the devil taught you to be so modest?" Yes, there really were lots of parallels between his story and hers, even if they had taken completely different roads. Life is like that.

Anyway: architecture. And it almost seemed logical that at this college, she had met someone who finally seemed all of one piece. He stuck by what he said. He kept his promises. He admitted the things he did not know—even though he was head assistant. He did not stammer over tough issues. He did what had to be done. He had the right people behind him—many right people—and the right people who were against him were few.

His name was David Kroll, and what he wanted to achieve he achieved. And love, people say, has no end. David Kroll and Sabine Bach did not announce their engagement, engagements are petty bourgeois; they just said, Hey everybody, this is how things stand with us. The autumn was the best ever, the winter was terrific, and only the spring was a little less great than before. Because now he was wrapping her in velvet and silk—and there was nothing you could say against that. I love you. I need you. There was only one thing that regrettably he never asked, namely what she needed, what she expected from life, where she wanted to go in the world. Imperceptibly but relentlessly, she saw that he did not challenge her but took her over. He arranged her life, he protected her, left her standing there with her arms dangling. He thought that nothing was too good for her, and his steep, straight path began to look different to her when she observed that his father, a national laureate and builder of cities, had inexhaustible funds at his disposal. The summer was cool. He heaped her with attentions and marks of tenderness, he wanted her all to himself, and he lost her.

For months they had planned to use the summer vacation to explore the coast, and to personally investigate the North German, brick Gothic architecture which last winter's books had proclaimed it was essential to see. They were already sitting in his Wartburg, already on the highway. "Hey girl, this may turn out badly, it simply isn't the right weather. Probably it will be hard to get rooms anywhere." (Didn't they have a tent in the trunk?) And look, in his pocket he had the key to the amazing summer house of his father, the national laureate—we would really have time at last for ourselves, we would finally be alone, we would have peace and everything we need. She asked him to stop the car. She got out. He stood for a long time in the rain, reasoned with her, did not understand but did not get angry—not even that—and finally drove away. What else could he do? What else could anyone do?

And now they are at Neubrandenburg, where the roads go in different directions. The Stargarder Tor and other gates. The old city wall. Lots of new things, too, lots of things to see, for a woman who was coming especially to get acquainted with this area and its buildings, and who knows what else.

"Well," she said. "Here we are."

"Yes," he said.

"So take care of yourself." She hesitated. "And thanks a lot for letting me ride with you."

"Na," he said. "More the other way around."

He saw her standing in her little coat, just a girl along the road, waved again and stepped on the gas. This is Highway F-96, it's three P.M. and we're on our way. A point on the road edge, receding in his rearview mirror. Sabine Bach, Weimar, university, he thought. Will that be enough of an address?

Translated by Jan van Heurck

Fritz Rudolf Fries

Description of My Friends

My friends live in the city. There are three of them. Richard is the eldest, around thirty. Regine is five years younger. The youngest is Sabine, their daughter. She is still so small that everyone goes down on their knees when they want to talk with her. Only Richard stays on his feet and bends down to her. His left leg is in a brace, which a mechanical device nevertheless makes so mobile that he is able to sit down. His leg shifts into place with a clicking sound, and he seats himself at a right angle. Richard refuses to use a cane in the apartment, but he uses stable nearby objects—chairs, tables, the edge of a chest of drawers—to move around. His hands are strong and large. His upper body has too broad and too heavy a torso for his overloaded legs. His eyes are very clear and light like Sabine's. The father and daughter communicate in glances. Regine's eyes, on the other hand, are quite dark, almost black. If Richard looks at her too severely, Sabine has only to look at Regine to be comforted. Sabine needs less comforting now that she has met large numbers of other children. She also knows many more songs than before. "Before" was a time when she was very small and people could still tell untrue stories about her. "Before" was when Richard and Regine were still studying. They studied medicine at Karl Marx University and helped each other through the exams. The story goes that Regine often had an easier time of it, because of her eyes.

I have been known to stay a couple of days at their place. A year ago, they got an apartment in a suburb which a few speculators filled with rows of houses for lots of people with rather little money, back in 1911. So the apartments turned out small; dark in front because the view is blocked in every direction, dark at the rear because of the inner courtyards which rise up like mineshafts. From the kitchen on the fifth floor, you look down on carpet rails and rubbish bins. The yards are paved with brownish brick on which mopeds and motorbikes have traced long dirty marks.

I sent a postcard to let them know I am coming. I ring the bell and mechanically read Richard's surname and *M.D.* title on the brass nameplate. The dark gleam of wax, brighter here than down on the first floor, shimmers up from the ground. No one is home. In cases like this, we have agreed that the key to the apartment will be left under the doormat. I bend down and grope for the key. After all, I am an old friend of this house, I enjoy the trust of its three inhabitants. So I open the door for myself, and hang my coat on the hook in the closet. The hall smells like the apartments of our childhood, of floor polish and artificial honey. I go into the kitchen, where Regine has put the furniture her parents left her. The smell of artificial honey is especially strong here, but it is a ghostly scent of memories from the forties, when Regine and I, the same age as Sabine is now or maybe a little older, sat in these kitchen chairs and, in between two air-raid reports, tasted the world to see if it was sweet. Artificial honey. But a jar of bees' honey is standing on the kitchen table, along with a couple of unwashed teacups. I look in the fridge to forget childhood, and take a bottle of Adlershof vodka from the shelf. There are glasses in the living room. I know my way around here. As always, I pause in the hall in front of a Van Gogh reproduced by the VEB Seemann Publishing House. To enter the living room at last, I push aside a teddy bear which is blocking the entrance. Then I think it over, pick up the bear, and set it on the sofa holding a bar of chocolate that I take from my jacket pocket. The Adlershof is cold enough to taste like the Soviet vodka I have brought as a present, or almost as good. Now I feel at home, I smoke, turn on the radio, look for a record in the cabinet. They have bought a confusion of everything, Bartók and Ray Charles and *The Flying Dutchman*. Doctors conscientiously pursue education, I think, and decide on Ray Charles. The apartment is arranged so that the tenants can make the best use of it. The only thing it does not have is a bath, and the toilet is on the stairs halfway to the next floor. Nineteen-eleven was an uptight year.

I look out the window. It's raining. November weather. The front of the house opposite mimics the symmetry of the Medial Section, with its window facades framed by stucco ornaments. A coffin store on the corner. I had not expected that; the last time I was here, a green tree was standing in front of it. Richard's desk looks like the desk of a man who only uses it to pay bills for new purchases, and to write the occasional letter (but not to me); who will sign his name to report cards that his daughter brings home in a couple of years, while her glance looks to meet Regine's eyes, depending on the results of the report card. I am forgetting the prescriptions he writes out here for his friends—vitamin pills, headache tablets.

Holding my second glass of Adlershof, I have to laugh to myself about the oil painting on the wall. I laugh because the picture is of me, although I really don't know what there is to laugh about. So I drink a third glass and catch the sound of a key in the door. Richard has arrived, and I can hear him leaning his cane against the mirrored wall of the closet. He comes in, his blue coat is sparkling with rain, he shakes hands with me with his rain-damp hand, and I can see his eyes even in the shadowed room. He turns on the light and looks at the bottle. I offer him a swallow, and the ice is broken. I felt almost like an intruder when he looked at me. But this look belongs to Richard's profession, and for that very reason I find it unpleasant. After all, I'm healthy, I tell myself, smoke another cigarette and look at the oil painting of me, which now is brightly lit. Now it doesn't look so good any more.

Richard is staying a long time in the kitchen, or in the bedroom to put away his tie and put on a cardigan. Or maybe only to give me time to get used to his presence. He is a master psychologist. It has always amazed me that he wants to go on busying himself with his patients' hearts and kidneys.

He has not come back yet, when suddenly a child's voice brings all the objects in the room into sharp presence. (Or is it only that I am called back to reality from my Adlershof wanderings?) Anyway, Sabine comes through the living room door, because she has recognized my coat. Timid at first, we haven't seen each other for a long time, maybe by now I am no longer the person she thinks I am: let's just check out what sort of face this guy is putting on today.

With a sidelong glance she sees that the bear is holding chocolate. I make a very friendly face, and she withdraws, reassured, to the corridor, where Regine is waiting to help her out of her shoes and coat. Regine's voice is as dark and soft as her eyes. The only thing that gives away her presence is the fact that Sabine is there, and is talking to someone out loud. I allow them time. I have pushed my way in here. Admittedly I warned them I was coming, but this evening ceremony of seeing each other again, of rediscovering each other after each has spent the day in a different place and in different occupations, is something that must not be disrupted.

"Aha," says Regine as we shake hands across the doorway. "Aha" means: So you're already here, it's nice that you're here, you're already here of course, you have already been drinking, do you like it here with us?, wait your turn, you can see we are a family. Aha: You don't have our troubles; by the way, what is troubling you?

We have understood each other quite well without words, ever since we ate artificial honey in her mother's kitchen, before or after an air-raid warning.

Sabine looks through the door at me once more, and then goes to tell Richard that I am here.

Regine comes into the living room, looks at the record jacket as if she is seeing it for the first time, and feels tired. Richard comes and sits down at the table, and we all wait for the clicking sound from his orthopedic brace, but it doesn't come; he lifts his powerless limb with his hands and places it on a chair. The three of us sit under the way-too-bright lamp, while Sabine unwraps her chocolate. I sip my Adlershof, Richard pours himself a full glass, Regine declines. Slowly the room accepts them as something that belongs. They sit in their armchairs as they have done on many previous evenings; once again they recognize me as their guest; at least for this evening they do not need to concern themselves about my health. And for today they have done what they had to do, plus a little bit more, at their different stations in different hospitals in the city. Tomorrow they will find out if the medications they prescribed confirm their diagnosis or not. During the night, while they sleep in their marriage beds, Sabine in her crib under the Ten Little Indians, I on the couch where I am sitting now beside Sabine and smoking, the drugs will be working in their patients' bloodstreams; will fail or succeed. Invisible combats will take place, which must be planned anew the next day; new orders of battle will have to be drawn up. I look at them, their attentive weariness. Regine is assistant physician at a tuberculosis sanitarium at the other end of the city. She knows the circumstances there, she herself lay in one of the institution's beds for a year. Every doctor should have had their patient's illness. Richard had polio when he was twelve.

I am more rested than they are, so I tell them whatever there is to be told. After all, everybody has their little troubles with reality, including me. I have done a portrait of Sabine from memory. I meant it to be more than a copy of this face with its almost imperceptible nose, its bright eyes and hair—more: a child kept by universal care, the care of her parents, her kindergarten teacher, her future teachers, and by people who plan houses with other things in mind than those that were built in 1911. The picture has been accepted. It is being hung together with other pictures in a big hall.

"We are going to move some time," Regine said, "but after all, we like it here too, and the people in the building know whose door they can ring at night if they get stomach pains."

Richard goes to the cabinet, keeping his hand on the chair back, and shows me their newly acquired records: Bartók, *The Flying Dutchman*. Ray Charles is on the turntable.

"Everything a guest could want," says Regine, and goes into the kitchen. Richard lets Ray Charles do his thing, Sabine follows Regine to wash her hands. She will be first to bed, and gets her supper in the kitchen. In bed she sings her new song, loudly so that we can hear it in the living room. Richard looks at the clock and goes in to her to warn her, after the final stanza, to go to sleep. I go along and get a goodnight kiss. In the hall we pause in front of the Van Gogh, and I tell about a colleague who saw the original in the museum in Amsterdam. Regine utters her "Aha" from the kitchen while she turns the omelette in the pan over onto its back. We are handed plates and silverware, and carry them to the dining table. The silverware is a new acquisition, I am asked to appraise its colored pattern and style.

We sit and eat. November rain falls invisibly behind the window panes. We drink tea, and I praise the seal on the Soviet vodka, which can be opened so easily that a child can do it. Now Regine is absolutely determined to hear the Bartók, and I wonder when and if and how she is a happy woman. I believe she is so, at this hour of the evening, when the day lies in clear view. (Whereas Richard looks as if he is still reflecting on a syndrome that new symptoms have rendered unclear.) If I were sick, which I by no means am, I would rather be treated by Richard than by Regine, whom I have known so much longer. Everyone says that Richard is a doctor by passion, and predictably will have a great career. Regine, on the other hand, sitting in the park at her tuberculosis sanitarium, has too much time on her hands, I think. Her patients' life histories concern her as much and more than their diseases. The dying ones, she says, have an optimism about life that cancels all the house rules. When she has night duty, she gathers all the sleepless ones around her, drinks tea with them and has them recite the intricate twists and turns of their lives; interposing little soft-spoken questions now and then. It would indeed be mistaken to believe that only tubercular patients have remarkable fates. But the mere fact that they have to lie for so long in a horizontal position, makes them think that the life they lived when vertical is stranger than the lives of others. To Regine it is a marvel to walk on two legs and to live, to work and to ride in streetcars through a changing city, to stand in stores and pick things out, to have children and a household and a record cabinet and vodka in the fridge for evening visitors. Here under the lamp in the evening, she believes that she has a uniquely beautiful and happy life. But next day reveals all that is necessary to maintain this life; and I believe that it is partly for the sake of this evening feeling, for her own happiness, that she distributes medicines during the day, gives injections, does all that she can, and telephones Richard in the intervals to hear his voice from the other end of the city, and to ask him to pick up Sabine from kindergarten, and not to forget the milk and the white bread at the co-op, because she is coming home later than they had thought.

We go to bed at ten. Fresh sheets are put on the sofa. Richard turns out the big light and opens the window. A streetlamp floats dimly down below. Regine carries the heaped ashtray to the kitchen.

We wish each other good night.

The alarm rings at six. I hear it through the door. Motorcycles are traveling on the street. Soon after, Richard's shaver drones from the kitchen. Sabine is crying because she has to get up. Regine turns on the gas stove. She collects onto a tray what is needed for breakfast and brings it into the living room. I can continue to lie there, the couch is placed so that if I rise halfway, I can serve myself from the table. In any case, I don't like getting up at six. Regine turns on the big light and I look at her from eyes that are creased shut. Her eyes are large, dark, unchanged. She is fully dressed, her hands emanate a scent of soap and cold water as they distribute the cups and plates.

"The gentleman's tea, if you please," she says, and puts it down near me.

We agree on what I should buy and where I will find the proper store. The Adlershof is still struggling with the Soviet vodka inside my head.

Richard, too, comes into the room fully dressed in a white shirt and tie, one hand on his sleeve buttons, and I feel as if we are going to celebrate a party where, for some incomprehensible reason, I have turned up unshaven and wearing pyjamas. Sabine is amused to find me in bed. She gives me her bear because he is still tired. I lay him on the pillow and tell him what I will give him for lunch. "Milk," decides Sabine.

Richard butters bread for Sabine and Regine. Sabine drinks milk with honey to ward off colds.

"So, how did you sleep?" asks Richard

"I'm not sure."

"You should get married," says Regine, "then you'd have a better idea." I nod and look at her. The tea is separating the spirits that are fighting in my head.

They leave the house at seven, Sabine in little boots and a coat with a hood, Regine in a pale trench coat, Richard in his blue overcoat. Propping myself up, I shake hands with them. The apartment door locks behind them.

Richard takes Sabine to kindergarten. His journey to the clinic is shorter than Regine's, she has to travel through the city for an hour on several lines of streetcars to reach her stop under the bare trees of the park. At this hour the streetcars are full of rain-soaked people who live up to their idea of life by doing their jobs today, plus a little bit more. I can no longer see Sabine's face among the faces of other children emerging from the husk of their hooded coats. I no longer see Regine's face distorted by X rays, no longer see Richard's face but only his eyes, receiving the first patient at his office. At ten o'clock I telephone Regine. She is just ordering the release papers for a patient. "Tuberculosis," she says, "is a disease that can be conquered." Her voice on the telephone sounds as if she has won a battle.

Translated by Jan van Heurck

Jurij Brězan

The Christmas Story

The Editors of the Culture page were in trouble. Not that they were caught unprepared by some campaign, such as SAVE ON POSTERS, PRINT BOOKS! or AIRMEN, QUIET DOWN OUR SKIES!; nor by an imminent anniversary, nor even just a special "day"—Railroad Workers' Day, or Streetcar Workers' Day, or Highway Workers' Day. The newspaper would have known how to handle anything of that sort. They had enough poems which were appropriate for any number of campaigns, anniversaries and special days, if one simply assembled the page properly. And ever since trained scholars of German literature can be found on the editorial boards of mediocre daily newspapers (however extraordinary the circumstances that may have led them to this pass), our nation's cultural heritage has been called on to fill the breach—or get hacked to pieces, if you prefer—with ever greater frequency and daring. But literature has its uses, the successes prove it.

So, the reason for the trouble was none of the above: the trouble was Christmas. Christmas is a laborious holiday which ought to be eliminated, as a poet demanded twenty years ago. I can write my fingers sore composing songs about peace and people will go on singing "peace on earth to men of good will," but economists have their own song to sing about the problems that Christmas brings, and even doctors issue public warnings about the hazards of the Yule season.

Maybe all that is tolerable. You can survive it if you are well organized—organization is something we have a lot of in our country—and tradition is helpful, too.

But things are different for the culture editors of a newspaper. On the one hand, at Christmas time certain concessions must be made to the petty-bourgeois genotype which has amassed over centuries (although we cannot be held responsible for it), and they cannot be made grudgingly. On the other hand, concessions are concessions and ought not to take over the whole show: that is my first point. The second point is, concessions ought to run out eventually: maybe not right away but gradually, over many years. But they should come to an end.

"So," said our editor-in-chief of the Culture page, "we have two pages. I think we should make one entertaining, in the higher sense of the word of course, and the other page instructive. A big crossword puzzle. One column each for Practical Hints on What to Do if Your Living Room Catches Fire, and for Legal and Moral Aspects of Exchanging Christmas Presents."

"And problems of digestion," said the editorial staff secretary, who had held the job for twenty-one years and knew all its ins and outs. She weighed one hundred and two pounds and came from Old-Ugelow; but that was a long time ago.

For the second page, they had on hand a poem by a shipbuilder. It could just as easily have been written by a free-lance poet, except that everyone could understand it. After the poem was read aloud and approved unanimously, a silence ensued. But thank God, a trained scholar of German literature was on the scene. Admittedly she was a minister's daughter and had written her degree thesis on E. T. A. Hoffmann, but despite this she was, generally speaking, a reliable person, and capable of further development. "*Augusta, the Christmas Goose,*" she suggested.

"I think we already had that once," said the editor-in-chief. But he could not exactly remember either the goose herself, or when they had had her.

"Nineteen years ago, twelve years ago, and most recently, five years ago," specified the staff secretary.

"So, still too young for our pot," someone said and laughed, but it was no laughing matter. Around midnight the chief said that they had to cut the Gordian Knot or grab the bull by the horns. And he thought he had: "We must find a writer who does not yet own a little place by the seaside and ask him to write a story for us, in exchange for our booking him a holiday on the Baltic."

They found a writer and wrote him a letter describing the precarious situation of their fine arts section as it faced the threatening advance of Christmas. To begin with, they did not let him glimpse the glow of a holiday place by the sea: for you ought not to fire all your powder in the first shot.

They received no reply. The scholar of German literature repeated her suggestion about Augusta the Goose, and mentioned E. T. A. Hoffmann, who had been able to invent imaginative stories. And then the mail brought a letter with a twenty-penny stamp on it, for which they had to pay the remaining postage. After all, it weighed too much to be a mere letter of refusal.

They read the story: "The Holiday of Love."

Christmas and spring differ in a number of respects. At Christmas we have pepper cake, in spring we have Easter eggs. At Christmas we are apt to get colds, in spring we may suffer from spring fever. In spring, poets send heaps of poems to editors, and at Christmas, editors send heaps of letters to writers, asking for Christmas stories.

This contradiction between the spring supply and the Christmas demand, is one of the few genuine conflicts in our ordered society which only a conference of literary scholars could resolve.

In any case, it is no solution to expect a Christmas story simply because I do not write any poems in the spring. That is an example of linear thinking: it runs like a streetcar.

So, you want a Christmas story.

No stories occur to me. I sit here doodling little Christmas trees on my pad, some covered with candles and some with snow. Three pages full of little trees, and not one tinsel strand's worth of a story. I throw the barren little trees in the wastebasket.

I draw a new tree on a fresh sheet of paper. It's a pretty little tree, its needles look quite natural. A little tree all alone. I doodle a stick figure next to it. That could be me. Another stick figure, with a sumptuous beard under his chin. At first I am thinking of the fur-clad legendary Knecht Ruprecht who brought gifts and warnings to children at Christmas time. But then a line goes wrong and Ruprecht acquires a shotgun. Now maybe he is a forest ranger. I cross-hatch a bit of fury into his face, and draw two laugh-lines in the face of the other stick figure, who is me. The conflict is there. Now all we need is the story to go with it.

A third stick figure. This one gets a skirt, a bulky pullover, and hair to which I give a sort of Beatle haircut by mistake. But that doesn't matter. I half close my eyes, and the stick-figure with a skirt becomes a girl with black hair, maybe a bit skinny, but well-rounded in all the places where it is necessary and pleasant. A sweet face. But it only looks sweet. The shaggy black mop has been combed onto her forehead especially to hide the look of blatant stubbornness. At least that's what her father says, the stick-man who is the Chief Ranger. Also I did not get her mouth quite right. Looking at her, you could think: "That mug is made for sarcasm, or for kissing." I think it's both.

In fact I know it is. I know quite a lot about her, probably more than her papa with his shotgun. He notices only one thing about me: I will never make a forest ranger, but at most a poacher. Anyway, that's what he called me once when he caught the two of us in the meadow, when Anne and I thought he was three miles away at the Black Pond, on the lookout for wild pigs.

Since that day—actually it was night, but that isn't important in this case—he always leaves his pigdog Wotan at home when he goes into the preserve. Wotan the pigdog follows hard on Anne's heels, and instead of wild boar, he has specialized in tracking me. Anne and I were already starving to death until— and now the stick-figure Christmas tree gets into the action.

It was the custom in my family, more as a sport than for reasons of economic need, not to buy our Christmas tree from the ranger's tree lot, but to take it from his woods, with a hand-saw we had hidden under our jackets.

Anne and I wanted to see each other at Christmas at least, and I wanted to put onto her finger personally the cheap little silver ring set with a coral. We also wanted to share a Christmas kiss—a kiss at the very least.

At that time I was a casual laborer, not by choice but under duress from a higher power, so to speak. In any case I had a lot of time before Christmas. I used to stroll continually around the chief ranger's house, in a highly conspicuous way. I would greet the ranger ten times a day, irritate the pigdog, who could not do a thing to me, and wave and gesture at the house, regardless of whether Anne had appeared at the window or not.

The pigdog gave up getting cross and grew used to me. One day he even barked at me in greeting, and wagged his tail in a friendly manner.

The ranger, firmer of character than his dog, was forced to take sedatives in order to put up with the sight of me.

Shortly before the holiday, I made a bet publicly in the inn with my friend Paul. I bet that I could take a Christmas tree from the ranger's woods right under his nose. Naturally, the ranger was told about the bet and decided to put a stop to my seeing Anne once and for all, by getting me into court.

My friend Paul and I, when we put on our identical jackets, stuffed our trousers into our short boots, and shoved our identical hats down low over our faces, looked so alike that not even our mothers could have told us apart, from one hundred yards away.

On the misty afternoon of Christmas Eve—there was no snow but it looked very much like snowing, as if the Christmassy stuff would start to drizzle down at any moment—Paul positioned himself behind the corner of the barn, at the ranger's place.

I went into the yard. A dozen little trees still stood there. "I'd like a beautiful Christmas tree," I said to the chief ranger. Wordlessly he showed me his collection. I criticized and found fault with every one. "In my family, we would not put such stunted trees into our living room," I said. "Simple folk though we are, at Christmas we treat ourselves to a tree that is beautiful and symmetrical, like those you deliver to the church."

But in the midst of my criticisms, the handsaw fell out from under my jacket. "I plan to take it to be sharpened," I told the ranger, trying to stammer a little. Then I petted the pigdog, wished the ranger a merry Christmas, and made a beeline out of the yard. Behind the corner of the barn I changed places with Paul, and Paul marched off rapidly in the direction of the pine wood, looking around in a cautious way now and then. Three minutes later, the ranger set out in pursuit, with his gun on his back and his dog at his side. I watched the bold hunter from the rear as he stomped toward his revenge: an eye for an eye, a tooth for a tooth. And his hand was already on the bolt, so to speak, to bar Anne from me, or me from Anne, whichever you prefer.

Paul has half a bottle of rye schnaps in his pocket, the handsaw in his jacket, and solid boots. No doubt he will look at lots of little trees while holding the handsaw, but none will suit him. The ranger and his dog have a long hunt ahead of them. In the end, Paul will cross over a forest lane, cut down a dwarf fir that belongs to Farmer Wukasch (for which Wukasch has already been paid), and then—We don't know, but Anne and I hope that the ranger will not have a stroke when he recognizes Paul.

Anne thinks the ring is beautiful, I think her mouth is more beautiful. Her shaggy black mop of hair is very soft, and the hay in the ranger's barn is very soft, too. Anne is in a very Christmassy mood, Joy to the World, God Rest Ye Merry, and it's the hay that is singing or maybe it's something else, and then the dog barks, Anne leaps out of the barn toward the yard, I jump out through the dormer window, stroll into the yard, and tell the ranger in a perfectly friendly way that I would like one of his leftover stunted trees after all. The ranger yanks the gun from his shoulder, drills me with a look of fury, croaks to Anne, kicks the dog, and bangs the door of the house behind him.

Anne gives me a kiss, and as a bonus, the least deformed of the little trees, and then it starts to snow, and it's Christmas.

A disconcerted silence followed the reading.

Then the secretary said: "Things happened like that in Old-Ugelow, too."

"In *Old*-Ugelow," said the editor-in-chief.

"But you *did* all laugh," she stated. When someone has been in a job for twenty-one years, she is apt to turn stubborn.

"I have rarely laughed so much beneath my level," remarked the scholar of German literature: a comment which later was recorded as a plus-mark in her personnel file.

"Write to the author," said the chief editor. "Do it cautiously, just feel him out."

The scholar of German literature wrote cautiously, just feeling him out:

Dear Author,

We thank you for your Christmas story. However, this version does not seem to us entirely suitable yet, so we would like to suggest a few minor changes.

First, we would recommend that Anne be given blond hair, blue eyes and a fuller figure, so that people along the coast may find their own reflection in art. We consider this essential to establish the typology, because you have written the story for residents of the northern regions, of course, and one does not as a rule picture them as thin with shaggy black hair.

Second, we have reservations about the use of the word "pig-dog," which normally occurs only in the vernacular. We suggest that you replace it with "boarhound."

Very truly yours,
The Culture Editors

The special-delivery reply came only three days later:

Dear Friends!

Many thanks for your helpful hints! Attributing black hair to Anne can only have stemmed from an error of memory. Of course, she is blond. And your own city in particular is famed for its striking blondes . . . I agree to the use of "boarhound."

Cordially . . .

"He shows insight," said the chief editor. "We can work with him." And he dictated his own special-delivery letter in reply: "Most Esteemed Colleague, Mr. A. N. Witsend . . ." The author's name, in fact and in law, was Anton Norbert Witsend, but the chief editor of the Culture page thought that the name was a good joke if not a bad omen, coming at this time. He also thought of an appropriate Latin proverb, but unfortunately he had only a hazy idea of how it went, so he just said that a name is mere sound and fury, signifying nothing, and continued to dictate:

Despite the proposed changes, your story unfortunately cannot be published in its present form. After lengthy consultation in our collective, we have concluded that your introduction, although very nicely done, is not functionally linked enough with the actual story and thus would only confuse our readers. We would agree to have it cut. Further, we have a question: Is the ranger meant to be a typical figure? Would it not have been possible to supply more of a motive for his resistance? Also: surely your young hero is not meant to be a "love-'em-and-leave-'em" type?

"I wouldn't say that if I were you," the secretary commented. "It's old-fashioned."

"No skin off my nose," the editor-in-chief grumbled. "So write:

. . . hero is not meant to be an irresponsible and promiscuous lover? I hope he will marry his blond Anne at Easter? If not, then we regret that as an author, your tendencies seem indistinguishable from the dubious Western sex craze. If the two do plan to marry, then it would be appropriate to at least hint at how the conflict will be overcome. For example, the ranger could build a room onto his house for the future couple. (This suggestion is in no way obligatory.)

Requesting a quick reply,

Cordially,
The Editors of the Culture page

P.S. And couldn't we make the pigdog (preferably boarhound) a poodle instead? This is a Christmas story, after all! Besides, this would be a creative way to build on the classical tradition!

The author sent this telegram by return mail:

Esteemed Colleagues, If absolutely necessary, cut introduction. Will use it in one of my next novels. Marriage unfortunately not possible, as young people not yet eighteen. Their age also motive for ranger's wrath. See no way out at this moment. Am in creative crisis.

Witsend

After a stormy all-night session in which fundamental questions were not evaded, the scholar of German literature—who was the youngest and who had to pass the post office anyhow—mailed this telegram in reply:

Dear Colleague Witsend,

Have just realized you dismissed chance to ground characters in concrete historical base—STOP—We do not wish to worsen our relations with literary critics as a result of this story—STOP—Are disturbed by metaphysical touches ("higher power," etc.)—STOP—Clear-cut social context also missing—STOP—In any case had been thinking more of a Christmas story set in the here and now—STOP—We take liberty of proposing following summary as guide to writing of contemporary Christmas story—STOP—Boy loves blond ranger's daughter Anne. Ardent kisses make her forget homework. Father gets angry. Sets poodle to watch her. Goes to work. Boy lures poodle with sugar. Misses more and more workshifts. Anne gets bad grades. Father arranges meeting with young man and his Free German Youth Group, and with Anne's schoolmates as well as her teachers and instructors. They all recognize that the young couple have a genuine affection for each other. They go hiking together through the winter woods. Anne and the boy see that they are understood, and promise to study hard and to do well in their technical training exams and college entrance exams. Snow. Christmas.

The reply which the editorial staff received took the form of a box with a puppy in it. They could not determine clearly if it was a poodle or a boarhound. Thereupon, the chief editor moved Augusta the Goose into the vacant spot, having already set her in type as a precaution. No one complained. After all, no other animal symbolizes a German Christmas the way a goose does.

Translated by Jan van Heurck

Helga Königsdorf

Property Damage

At 9:20 P.M. of a November evening, a middle-aged woman climbed out of the bus and walked toward home along a street in a newly-built district. An alert observer would have noticed that her left leg was dragging a little.

The shrubs in the gardens were already bare. Only the thorny mahonias always stayed green. The woman felt glad that everything looked so tidy. Their last gardening assignment had been to prepare the beds for the winter.

She had been living here for more than ten years now. Before this, she had lived with a man in a spacious apartment in an old building. Back then she did not have a limp yet. The limp began with the birth of her son: a forceps delivery. The baby died when he was a few days old. The doctor said that it was better this way. And anatomically (he claimed) she was not built for bearing children; and the problem with her hip would go away eventually. Later, the man had a child by another woman, and she was left alone.

That was when she switched apartments with a young couple. They paid her moving costs, even though the old building was much less comfortable and there was no central heating.

The woman liked it here. The sky spread wide outside the window of her one-room apartment. She could see all the way into the center of town. At first she often used to feed the seagulls. They would pick up pieces of bread from her without breaking their flight. She even gave names to especially skilled divers, although she was never quite certain that they were the same birds.

Then the people renting the lower floors complained about the mess, and a decree from the co-op board forbade the feeding of birds.

Most people in the building were friendly. In the first few years, the woman had helped out as a babysitter now and then. Some families gave her money in return, others gave her chocolates. Now she wondered whether the children she had cared for were already old enough that she ought to address them more formally. Her services were no longer required. But the people still remembered. They greeted her affectionately and would ask how she was, as they passed by.

Ten years ago, no-parking signs still lined the streets. Now cars stood along both sides of the road like beads on a necklace and even blocked the driveways, although this had led to repeated arguments. The woman did not ever expect to own a car. But she felt proud that everyone was so well off, as if she belonged to a large family.

There were hardly any children playing in the sandboxes any more, on this side of the street. On warm summer evenings, the boys and girls stood around together in groups, and the woman felt a little bit fearful when she had to pass them. Admittedly she had never had cause for complaint, but one heard stories, at the hairdresser's and from the neighbors.

This November evening was gloomy and chilly. The street was empty of people. Only a married couple got out of the bus with the woman, and walked along past the houses on the opposite side of the street.

Suddenly the woman saw a ghostly-looking moped appear between the new apartment towers about one hundred yards away. It flew through the air with a peculiar rolling motion, its wheels lifting off the ground briefly, and then skidded across the road on its side, as driver and vehicle melted into a strange uniform gray. She had already begun running before she heard the muffled crash. She felt slightly relieved when she saw the driver get up, and then stagger as he struggled to push his vehicle off the road. Only now she noticed that the couple across the street were running to the scene, too.

"Stop, stay where you are!" the man cried in a vigorous and commanding voice.

The moped driver stood bent over the handlebars, and it was hard to decide if he was supporting the vehicle or it was supporting him.

"You stay here!" the husband ordered, somewhat out of breath. And he emphasized his order by pointing his right index finger at the sidewalk, several times over.

His wife moved her face close to the boy's head, sniffed and said: "I thought so, he's dead drunk."

The husband returned to the other side of the street, to appraise the damage to the Lada, which was parked right by the intersection.

The woman with the limp took a little longer to reach the scene of the accident. "Why, he's still a child," she thought in shock when she saw the boy, who stared at her, eyes wide with fear. She put her arms around his shoulders and felt his whole body trembling.

"Do you feel sick?" she asked.

"He's drunk as a skunk," the other woman said in a cross voice.

The woman took her handkerchief out of her bag and wiped the blood from the boy's nose and the corners of his mouth. As she did so, she saw by the light of the streetlamp that the area around his nose was turning black-and-blue.

"Do you live far from here?"

The boy did not answer, but it seemed to the woman that he was shaking his head no.

"I'll take you home," she said. "Your father can pick up your motor scooter." But it was not clear whether the boy understood her.

"Approximately eighty marks' damage," the husband announced, returning from the Lada, and this assessment appeared to satisfy him somehow. "Go and telephone," he said to his wife. "I'll stay here and see that he doesn't cut and run."

The woman with the limp had finally managed to prop the heavy moped against the pole of the streetlamp.

"I'm so cold," the boy stammered.

The woman stroked his arm soothingly and said: "Give me your I.D. So we'll know your address."

When the boy did not respond, she searched the breast pocket of his jacket, found his I.D. and flipped through it. All with one hand, because she was still propping him up. She read his name and address aloud, and suggested that they fasten a note with his address under the windshield wipers of the Lada.

"I'll take the boy home," she repeated

"Absolutely not!" protested a man in uniform who was approaching rapidly. "Drunk driving is bad enough, without fleeing the scene of an accident, too. He stays here until the police come!"

"We saw exactly what happened," a woman said.

Lights were on now in the entryway of the house across the street. Gradually a crowd collected. The woman with the limp felt shocked. She realized that she had been about to aid and abet a breach of the law. She continued to hold the boy, who was shaken by a shivering fit.

"May he sit down over there on the stairs in the entryway?" she asked the man in uniform.

The man looked startled, then nodded with a slightly puzzled expression and asked: "Is he your son?"

"It all comes from people spoiling their kids. You really have to put your foot down," someone said.

"No," the woman with the limp answered hastily. "I don't know the boy." And she let go of him.

The man in uniform helped him to cross the street.

"Boozing it up and then passing out," commented the man who had been the first to arrive at the scene of the accident.

"And putting other people in danger, too!" said a younger, trim-looking woman.

A man in a track suit had been examining the damage to the Lada. "My car has been standing outside the repair shop for three weeks already," he said grimly.

The woman with the limp took off her shoes outside the door of her apartment and put on her slippers. As always, she switched on the radio and set the table for supper. But she had no appetite. She sat at the table and thought about nothing in particular. Anyhow, later she could not remember any specific thought, just that she suddenly felt very anxious and excited. With trembling hands, she put on her shoes and coat again. Hobbling more than before, she hurried back to the place of the accident.

Nothing remained there to recall what had happened, except perhaps the dent on the rear fender of the Lada. But you had to get close to see it.

Translated by Jan van Heurck

Helga Schütz

The Earthquake at Sangerhausen

During the journey they get to know each other better,
   Michèle Charrel says she has been in Rostock before for Baltic
Sea Week, and now she is here in the Mansfeld area and wants to
see it.
   "And you, where are you from?"
   "We're from Berlin."
   "And what will you do?"
   "Probably make a film."
   "What's the film called?"
   "Either—but don't misunderstand, these are only working ti-
tles—either 'False Pretenses' or 'Bailing out the Boat while the Rain
Pours in.'"
   "And you Michèle, what do you want to see?"
   She says that first she wants to see what it is that she wants to
see. She doesn't know yet. For now she is just happy to be here.
L'Humanité publishes far too little news from the GDR. And it
publishes even fewer interesting articles, and people know next to
nothing about GDR literature. Especially they know nothing about
younger people.
   Michèle Charrel tried to explain more but failed. Her thinking
was blocked by a wall of language; the subject grew so complicated
that she could no longer find the words. "You have a very avant-
garde operation," she managed to say.
   But Josephine made her thumbs-down signal, gesturing at the
driver up front, and also gave explanatory glances to indicate that

nothing must be said to let the man know exactly who we were. Michèle Charrel guessed what was meant and kept silent.

But Karl Schüler said, "Go ahead and let her talk. Let him hear." And then loudly: "This cinder-block paving is dangerous to drive on. It's slick. We're skidding, Herr Rennebart, it's a dangerous surface."

"I'm already adjusting to that," says Herr Rennebart, "but I don't like driving here. It's a nasty stretch of road."

And Josephine says: "By the way—Rennebart? That's an unusual name."

"There aren't many," he says, "but in Norway there are lots of Rennebarts. When we were there, in Tyssedal, there were Rennebarts on every corner. Also a big hotel, the Grand Hotel Rennebart. I was supposed to go there, I had time off especially to go, but I didn't dare. Maybe it was a mistake but I didn't dare, because we Germans weren't well-liked there, we were hated there." (Herr Rennebart can't help being surprised even today; he still regards this hatred as a national peculiarity of the Norwegians.) "The Norwegians just hated us." Once, he says, he took the subway to Holmenkollen, and he explains what it was like when the subway train suddenly popped up from under the ground and how the mountains reared up ahead; they were gigantic. A sun of a kind you don't see here; but the Norwegians hadn't wanted to sit next to him, one after another they stood up, he had had four seats to himself in the packed train.

"I didn't feel comfortable," says Herr Rennebart. Karl says, "The Norwegians probably had a reason," but Rennebart is barely listening, he has to concentrate now. A policeman is standing on the center line of the road with a walkie-talkie and a stop sign. He raises the red signalling disk.

"What's up?" says Rennebart.

"Bear right," the man with the red signalling disk says through the lowered window, and he indicates the same to the vehicles following, using a whistle and hand signals. Everybody stop. Bear right. But why? May we know?

On the field to the left, a large contingent of civilians is busy putting up barriers. Posts are being driven into the ground, cords stretched, little red flags hung up, night reflectors installed. People are taking photos and measurements.

What is happening here?

The earth's crust has blinked an eyelid. The earth has batted its eyelash. Briefly and gently. But distinctly. What was it?

A geological event. The most recent of its kind. And not in Chile but here at this spot, here outside Sangerhausen, some two hundred yards from the road. It will still be detectible millions of years from now. The people in the area won't forget it for days. One particular family won't be able to get it out of their heads for years, they'll calculate and argue about it all their lives. How did it happen? Who is to blame, who is responsible? No one except the Almighty, who is questioned harshly and often: How could you? And if you had to, why was it us, why was it our son my husband our father? In the first few days there are even more people asking questions, work colleagues, for example—asking: Why our Horst, why on our land, and if it had to be, why under these circumstances? And in our time, when we have already gone to the moon and so on, why, almighty God, why? Not only the Almighty but others too are asked for information. The long-distance trucker has to give details. "I saw the tractor in the field—a potato field, wasn't it?— I know there was no trailer, no equipment attached, that is there was only the tractor, yes that's right, it was around noon, close to twelve-thirty, yes, almost exactly twelve thirty, I know I drove off from the Red Horse at twelve, that's where I had my noon break, I drive approximately forty miles an hour when I have a load."

"If he was driving without a cultivator, then he was already on his way home," says the weeping widow.

So, another custom-tailored job by malicious nature and her hasty pimp, time. Not amid chaos but on the margins; but a thorough job all the same. Let those understand it who can. It dawns on us: In all that has happened to us in our lives, we have each time escaped this final minute, who knows how. We are the survivors. Horst Hofrat has met fate. It caught him on his way home.

"I always say we stand every day with one leg in the grave," says Laubisch the tractor driver, the one who loaded ammonium nitrate on the same tractor yesterday by the edge of the field not far from here.

"Her husband's lifeline had a worn spot in it," says the head agronomist. "There's just no other explanation." The pastor of three parishes plans to argue along similar lines. He is basing his Sunday sermon on Jeremiah. "When he uttereth his voice, there is a multitude of waters in the heavens, and he causeth the vapours to ascend from the ends of the earth; he maketh lightnings with rain, and bringeth forth the wind out of his treasures. Every man is brutish in his knowledge: every founder is confounded by the graven image: for his molten image is falsehood, and there is no breath in them." Building on this text, Pastor König continues with themes of his own: the tractor driver Horst Hofrat of Fraunau parish, for example. Where is he? Has he gone to hell?

"The first thing I thought," says the long-distance trucker, "was, that guy is going at quite a clip, he must be trying to break his neck, that boy must be tired of living. That's how it looked from a distance; it all happened in fractions of a second. When I got a bit closer I could still see, for heaven's sake, am I drunk or something, the guy is slipping along with the field. When I picture that now, then that's how it looks, as if I could see from the outside how the earth is turning. Then a cloud of dust rose up, although there was no wind. At the same moment I stepped on the gas and got every ounce of speed I could out of the old crate. I heard noises behind me, I couldn't imagine what they were. At most I thought, did you maybe overlook a detour sign, maybe they're using a new method of blasting; because that wasn't the usual dynamite explosion. I could tell that because I worked on the blasting squad once myself, in Halle. So at most I thought, they're doing something there—honestly, it didn't even occur to me that something must have started moving there on its own."

"And you saw the tractor clearly?" the wife asked again.

"Clearly. I had a clear view to the electricity plant. It was one of those little old pioneer tractors, if I'm not mistaken. But I could be wrong."

"And what direction was it heading?"

"In the opposite direction to me, as I said before, parallel to the road, about two hundred yards away. But as I said, I was going fast, and he was going pretty fast too, and I didn't think any more about it, and when he was past me, the cloud of dust came up. At least I didn't see anything more behind me, in the rearview mirror. All I saw was gray."

"He was already on his way home," the wife says, and cries or screams or laughs sounds of some sort that perhaps are meant to be words and to have a meaning.

"Everything was gray," the long-distance trucker says, speaking past the wife to the others, and to the wife he says softly: "But it may have been someone else."

"Who!" shrieks the wife, and then she begins to explain loudly and precisely: "This morning before he left, he said, 'If I really push I can get the field by the bridge done by noon.' And I said, 'Then come home and eat.' If I hadn't said that—if!—he would have headed toward Arnstadt, to the office, and would have gotten a new assignment from his work-brigade chief, and then he would have gone to eat in the kitchen. If he had finished five minutes earlier he would have reached the road. If. If this morning he had not had to come back for the vehicle papers. If Laubisch had taken the tractor as planned. If? If *he* had driven the early potatoes to the train station instead. He would still be driving. And tomorrow he would drive again."

Long speeches. Many an If is retracted. One IF remains, is repeated: If I hadn't said he should come home. The wife sees the dawn of a false knowledge. I switched the points. I am the determiner of fate, the setter of courses.

"If," screams his wife.

His father is silent. And his two little girls open their eyes wide and know nothing and for the time being they are told nothing. His mother goes to Frau Kalkuhl's house because Frau Kalkuhl has the magical mandrake root in her home, inherited from her mother. She'll know, she'll be able to tell her. Who else?

The long-distance trucker says: "After I had been driving at top speed for about six miles, my head slowly cleared. I thought, maybe something has happened to the tractor, maybe there's been an accident, you have to go back. I thought, who knows what's going on there?"

The first person who tried to pass by Mile Number Forty before the Autobahn approach ramp—that mile which has now become infamous—was a passenger-car driver, a woman doctor from the district hospital riding in a blue-gray Wartburg.

She says that she didn't notice anything at first.

Well yes, she did wonder a bit about the dirt on the road, but she thought that maybe a poorly-loaded soil-transport vehicle had lost part of its cargo en route. That could be. But then she couldn't figure out what had become of the Brückensee, the little lake that had always lain like an eye in the landscape, that she had always found so beautifully unused, untouched. But then she thought up an explanation right away: they had filled in the beautiful lake to raise the ground-water level, and immediately she felt annoyed at this procedure. And because, as she believed, the work had been undertaken in the middle of the growing season, she thought that once again the beautiful fields, all the beautiful work had been for nothing—couldn't they have waited until autumn, until the harvest had been been brought in? But then she had to stop because a big rock had blocked the road, it had rolled down the sloping fruit orchard from the right, you could see the path clearly. Uprooted apple trees had fallen across the road ditch. The ditch itself had been partly covered with folded turf. A truck had stopped opposite her, the truck of the long-distance trucker who had returned along the same route. The man had gotten out, come over to her very confused and had reported his observations rapidly and with horror. The landscape had changed completely in a short period of time, he said; green hilly farmland had suddenly turned into a flat desert strewn with rocks and boulders. The man was trembling all over, she said, and was pale as if he were suffering from a neurocirculatory dystonia. She had calmed him down and given him some sedative tablets—barbiturates—and then she had turned her car around and gone to the nearest town to call in a report to the district police.

The long-distance truck driver meanwhile had not moved from the spot.

The police and fire department were there one hour later. Two hours later, geologists arrived with instruments for measuring and testing. Three hours later the region was black with human beings. The police had set up makeshift cordons.

And Frau Hofrat and the other Hofrat kin want to hear from experts that it was impossible for a tractor to be swallowed up here along with the tractor driver, that such a thing is unheard-of, that the earth alone could not manage to do it. But the geologists eagerly snap up the data from witnesses and instruments and from their own calculations, and base their findings on it. They say that if the truck driver's testimony is correct—that is if it is true—then one has to accept it, especially as no other trace has been found so far. Or could Horst, her husband, possibly have left the field and driven somewhere else? the wife asks. The wife herself is in the best position to know that—she or her husband's work-brigade chief, is the reply. The brigade chief shakes his head, at a loss; he knows nothing, he says; all the same, one can still hope until evening. Even the geologists allow for accidents. They utter a sentence which Jean Paul advises writers not to repeat: There are more things in heaven and earth than are dreamt of in your philosophy.

The experts agree among themselves: The earth has swallowed up and devoured the tractor driver Horst Hofrat along with his tractor, with its iron and chain track. The earth has blinked an eyelid. This was a collapsing earthquake, a small, localized quake triggered by none other than gravity. Natural cavities have filled themselves, and now measurements and tests are made to determine the size of the field and whether further collapses can be predicted. The experts are now able to state that they can forecast, with a degree of probability bordering on certainty, that no more such collapses will occur.

So the roadblock here should be viewed as a preventive device or a safety measure. Multi-lane motor vehicles may pass the danger point only in single file. The police officer waits for the signal from the man at the other end. A green signal. The road is clear. Go ahead. Please drive slowly, keep to thirty miles per hour, and put on a proper outside mirror when you get the chance.

"I'll do that," says Rennebart.

The highway has been cleared. The boulder is lying tidily at the edge of the road. The road service workers are fortifying the road bank. The locals are sawing apart the uprooted apple trees. Children and grandfathers are loading the wood into handcarts. Michèle takes notes. *L'homme perdu. Le tremblement de terre de Sangerhausen.*

Translated by Jan van Heurck

Reiner Kunze

My Friend, a Poet of Love

He is one of the boldest between the March and the Moldau, a taboo breaker, a dogma-subverting ironist. In his writing he had helped to bring about the Prague Spring of '68.

"Around three A.M., a woman stood outside the door calling my name. And it happened to be the very night when Alena was with me," he said. He is married to Alena. They did not live in Prague, he was only working here and had a room here. "You know how jealous Alena is," he said. "Fortunately she sleeps as deeply as a child. The woman outside waited and I thought about who it could be: Jana? Evička? . . . Daša? I had only met Daša a couple of days before. She's a terrific girl, too! But when you have slept with a woman once, you don't recognize her voice right away. She called again, knocked. Then Alena stirred. I put my hand on her mouth and said she was not to move, that probably it was someone who had been closed out of the bar and who wanted to go on drinking. Then I heard the woman outside going away. At six-thirty, a knock came on the door again. The same voice.

"'I'll go and open the door,' Alena said.

"'You can't,' I said and tried to deflect her.

"'But I'm curious,' she said, and put on her dressing gown.

"When I saw that there was no way to avert the disaster, I withdrew into the bathroom. Alena came back looking pale. 'Prague is under military occupation,' she said. 'Soviet tanks have moved into Wenzel Square.' Man, if you only knew what I was feeling. I was so glad that it was only the tanks!"

Translated by Jan van Heurck

Günter de Bruyn

Forget-Me-Not

Business was just getting properly under way when the young woman who had annoyed him so much before came back. Seiffert saw her coming along the main road, more slowly than good breeding prescribes, pale, dressed in black, carrying the borrowed basket on her arm, and he felt surprised that she had finished so quickly planting the flowers on the fresh grave.

It was ten A.M., and the crowd which was usual on the first sunny Sundays of the year had begun to arrive. People thronged to the entrance—mostly women, only rarely accompanied by a husband or child, and never men on their own; forced themselves to adopt the slow cemetery stride once they had cleared the shadow of the wall; looked to the left at the pots and boxes arranged in square and rectangular fields; paused, reflected, walked on, came closer, examined the wares, compared the prices; and every minute or so, one of them joined the line of customers where Seiffert hurried back and forth, helped them to make their selection, packed it up and took the money. It was rare that one of them knew what she wanted right away. Usually they first asked what something was, how and when did it bloom, what did it cost, does it live through the winter, do you have to water it often, give me ten of those, no, only five plus five of those, do the two of them look all right together, why don't you sell cut flowers, what do you mean not yet, why are there greenhouses; and then what they paid was not worth the cost, and the waiting customers grumbled although when their turn came they behaved no differently, and old Seiffert grew silent with fury at these bereaved people who could not get up an hour earlier for their dead in order to arrive before the rush hour.

The young woman had been there earlier. She had had plenty of time to spend on her dead husband but little money. Having studied Seiffert's meager wares for a long time, she silently made her calculations until he broke in to dissuade her from taking the pansies— only sixteen pennies the pot and in great demand—and instead recommended the plentiful forget-me-nots, fourteen pennies each, or a median-priced alternative; because roses appeared to be out of the question. At first she had wanted common heather at sixty-one pennies, but she did not have enough money. Then he had to explain to her in detail why there were no primroses. Next she decided on the pansies, but while he hobbled off grunting to the shed to fetch the last ones, they started to seem to her too colorful for her serious spouse. So it would be forget-me-nots after all! And how many? Forty? She had looked shocked, as if he had tried to palm off more on her than she needed.

And now she was already coming back again. She tried to bypass the queue of waiting women, but someone said something to her, and she turned around and silently took her place at the end, even though the only thing she had to do was return the basket. Seiffert wanted to order her to come to the head of the line, but refrained because he felt that so much shyness deserved to be punished. He planned to take the basket from her wordlessly when her turn came, toss it behind the field of rose-pots, and ask the next woman in line how he could serve her. But when her turn came at last, he could not avoid her helpless look, and could not immediately understand her soft-spoken words.

"Please take back the flowers!" she said. He already had taken the basket in his hand and noticed its weight, but only now he saw that it was still full, that the forget-me-nots were still lined up as he had arranged them. He had had to press the root-balls together to get them all inside, and had placed the last three plants on top.

"Flowers can't be exchanged," he said and gave her back the basket. "Next, please!"

She had already robbed him of plenty of time earlier, in exchange for two marks. Now the fuss and bother with her would start up again, and the line would get longer and longer.

"I don't want to exchange them, I want to give them back!"

"Even better!" he said and stuck a bouquet of roses under the nose of his next customer, who examined it from all sides as if she knew something about roses. "All sales are final! And in case you went to the wrong cemetery, you're allowed to plant forget-me-nots in the cemetery next to it, too. Those are a superior variety of roses, dear Madam. You won't get them anywhere else for that price!"

"I didn't go to the wrong cemetery," the young woman said softly. "The grave already has flowers planted on it."

"None of my business!" he said.

He had bought too many forget-me-nots, he would not get rid of them on a Sunday. They were not blooming yet, and people who did not visit their graves often wanted them to be beautiful right away, not later on when they could no longer see them. The still budding forget-me-nots were for the weekdays, for elderly women whom he knew by name because they came almost daily, women for whom the cemetery also served as an entertainment park and an allotment garden.

"But what shall I do?"

"Plant them in the garden."

"I don't have a garden."

"On the balcony."

"I don't have a balcony either."

"Then get back your money from whoever played this trick on you."

"I don't know who it could be."

"Maybe your mother-in-law."

"We don't have any relatives here."

"Maybe someone from his work place."

"Impossible."

"Then rip the stuff out and plant your own."

"I couldn't. It's much more beautiful the way it is. Blooming heather, the good-quality kind!"

She looked around searchingly to show him the flowers, but found none of that kind. He had not had the good-quality heather at all so far this year, for some reason the co-op had not delivered them. The young woman's eyes filled with tears. Seiffert could not stand to look at her again. He went on selling, and while he was counting and selecting and wrapping things up, he heard her sobs and felt irritated by the obstinacy with which she stood there bawling at the customers, just because of a couple of marks. And then it suddenly occurred to him that he had spoken as if only another woman could have planted the flowers on the husband's grave. His assumption had been unintentional, and he had made it without thinking, simply because men rarely came to his shop; because women for the most part are tougher and are the survivors; because bereaved men never remain alone, and forget faster; because they lack a good relationship with the dead and with flowers; and because they usually earn more money, and thus are more likely to contract with a gardener to care for a grave than to plant and hoe and water it themselves.

And as he packed up the roses he said: "Good-quality heather, you say? Planted over the whole grave? In the past few days I've only made one sale of that kind, to a man, he said it was for an old friend."

The woman grew still, wiped her nose, waited until Seiffert had taken the money for the roses, and asked: "A tall man?"

"Yes, he was tall."

"Dark?"

"Yes, tall and dark."

"Did he have a trace of a Saxon accent?"

"Yes, a trace."

The young woman smiled and set the basket down on the ground. "Alfred, of course it was Alfred," she said, and then she left. Old Seiffert went on serving his customers, saw the woman vanish out the door, and said to the next customer, who did not look as if she were in the market for roses: "Forget-me-nots, forty plants already packed up, only four marks, without the basket of course."

Translated by Jan van Heurck

Wolfgang Hilbig

Solid Ground

For U.K.
"Sickness in Peace"

Wordlessly and without my asking, the waiter set down a large glass of beer in front of me as he hurried past. I found this strangely touching, as I had not yet been sitting at the table for long; but I was almost too exhausted to spend a thought on it. Still echoing in my ears was the heavy crashing blow that had come out of the deep blue sky, after which the air seemed to fall on me like a rain of glass splinters, driving me unnerved into the restaurant on the west side. Now in front of me stood one of those tall-edged, damp and smooth pint glasses with a narrow, tapering base that is roughly just half the diameter of the upper rim. I reached for it with all the requisite caution, but the tips of my fingers had barely touched the cool glass when I overturned it.

Not that I had been especially nervous that day. I intended to go to Berlin to pay one of the agreed monthly visits to my child, but for unfathomable reasons I had missed the last of the frequent midday trains. Now they were waiting for me in vain. I had brought ruin to a score of pleasurable plans. In less than three hours, the resentment of my unfaithfulness would erupt again. In the evening, arriving far too late, I would hardly be able to counter the resultant reproaches with explanations about unreliable street-cars and buses, and part of my brief visit would be spoiled. Besides that, I would be reckoned as the spoiler: a father who destroyed the already meager joys of his little daughter.

It was one of the hottest days of this summer so far. Almost fainting with the hectic chase from one form of jammed traffic vehicle to another, I had seen the train pull away without me, and with guilt feelings that were still muted, I searched the schedule for the time of the next train. Then, recognizing at last with resignation that I now had more than three hours to wait, I sat down in the big railroad station restaurant.

It was a trivial thing no doubt, hardly worth mentioning. When so many trivial things keep going wrong, you cannot attach any special importance to one more. And so, too, there was no need for me to exaggerate my former wife's predictable bad humor at my lateness. The cooking fumes in the restaurant, which seemed to put a strange wobble into the noise made by the voices of several hundred people, and the pounding of my pulse, which drew all my attention and and kept me in suspense with fits of sweating that broke out at intervals, may not have interfered with me more than anyone else in this crowd. Perhaps the temperatures, the smells, the overall twilight of stagnation in the giant waiting room were impoverishing the emotions of every person present. But when my beer tipped over and flooded the table, I began to suspect for the first time that this Friday was marked out to be something special for me.

In the chair to my right sat a little girl dressed in blossom pink who looked to me only a little older than my own daughter, and who was spooning up mouthfuls of multicolored sorbet. My wave of beer rolled toward the child, broke foaming at the foot of her ice-cream cup, surged with perfidious energy above its plastic oval and spilled over its contents, sending spray in a wide band across the girl's dress as she stiffened with shock; and enough was left over to reach her mother, who waved a purse at me in horror and settled at once into a cold, speechless rage. I had turned pale and was drenched in sweat. Murmuring an apology—although I did not know if it could be heard—I fumbled for my wallet, determined to pay for all the damage, then winced with embarrassment as I realized that I would fail in this, too, because a short time ago I had spent most of my money for my ticket. But the mother, punishing me with her deepest contempt, took the girl's hand and pulled her away.

When the waiter removed the tablecloth with a disgusted look, I had the impression that everyone in the room had started to watch me.

A little later, the waiter appeared again with a full tray, bent halfway down to me, and used his free hand to pick up one of the glasses of beer, meaning to exchange it for the empty glass that stood on the slick surface of the table in front of me. To help him, I reached for the empty glass. It fell over. Propelled by its bulging curves and gaining momentum as it went along, it bounced diagonally across the slippery table, getting higher with each bounce. I lunged after it, and by a chance that was almost more incredible than the whole perverse incident, I caught it after its last noisy landing, before it dropped off the edge. As I set down the apparently unbreakable vessel, I saw the waiter struggle for words. Bellowing so that everyone could hear, he asked me if I was "dead drunk," and just as rudely, he announced that he would no longer serve me. I paid him for the beer with my eyes shut and left the table.

Keeping my eyes on the ground, and feeling as if I were in an odd waking dream, I went to look for a seat up in the restaurant gallery, which you reach by climbing a staircase at the back of the room. From there you can look out over the crowd in the lower part of the room—the atmosphere is usually a bit quieter—as if you are looking down from the bridge of a ship. Climbing the stairs, I felt unsteady on my feet, if such a word as unsteady still conveys any meaning after the situation I have described. I could not rid myself of the notion that the boards underneath me, after several seconds of peculiar swaying, had tipped to the left, making me afraid that I would lose my footing and slip sideways. But before I was really overcome by terror, I reached the top of the stairs and saved myself by sitting down—thereby earning the mute censure of an elderly gentleman from whom I had stolen the last free chair with my lunge.

The man turned to go back down the steps; I turned my head away, incontrovertibly certain that I would see him fall down the steep staircase at any moment. Then came the clattering crash I expected, I saw the eyes of all those sitting around me fly in his direction, I saw the old gentleman sway as he bent toward a monstrous black umbrella that he had dropped.—The waitress arrived with a pinched smile to take my order; I ordered coffee and a cognac.

"Probably the gentleman plans to go to a funeral." The sentence was spoken by one of the three ladies at whose table I had captured a seat. All three of them looked to me to be over sixty. They were dressed flimsily and I assume expensively, and they were drinking wine. "You can tell when someone is going to a funeral, there's no mistake about it," the lady continued, and the other two nodded in agreement. "Isn't it much too hot for coffee? Coffee wouldn't agree with me in this heat . . ." This time she undoubtedly was addressing me. "And don't you at least want cream? Tell the waitress, surely she'll bring you cream. No, not that one . . . ," she said as I reached for the little porcelain jug on the table. My hand flew back as if it had been bitten by a snake. "Not that one, there's a fly in it, a fly drowned in it." She covered the opening of the jug with her fingers.

"Were you referring to me?" I asked. "I mean, did you want to know if I'm going to a funeral? No, I'm not going to a funeral."

"We meant the friendly old gentleman who wanted to sit down at our table. It occurred to me back in Nuremberg, when he got on the train this morning. Dressed that way, I thought, he must be going to the same funeral as we are. It seemed to me that I knew him."

The other ladies kept nodding incessantly, and drank from their wineglasses with cautiously pursed-up mouths.

"You must know," the lady went on, "we're taking advantage of this opportunity, we're only sitting here because we enjoy it. I was a waitress here twenty years ago, and my two friends wanted to see where I worked."

"Here, in the main railroad station?" I asked.

"Nothing here has changed," she said, "only . . . I suppose it's gotten worse, much worse." Her two friends showed startled expressions. "There are no longer any of my old acquaintances here. No doubt the staff back then all disappeared in good time. Or have you a different opinion? We would be interested to hear what you think."

"We don't notice it," I said. "Or only sometimes, maybe today. Some time or other we reach the point of noticing that railroad stations are a disaster."

Perhaps they felt that my answer was exaggerated. They had turned away from me, and what they were saying no longer was pitched loud enough to reach me. Probably the woman had hoped that I would contradict her, I thought: hoped for an explanation from me which would prove that the restaurant of the main railroad station, where she used to work, was in great shape despite all appearances to the contrary. But I had not given her this satisfaction. On top of that, I could not really substantiate what I had said. And I myself, my own appearance, clearly was not recognized as proof of the disaster I alleged. Not only that: in this whole railroad station there was not actually the slightest proof of the existence of a disaster. If the train I had missed had left behind schedule, then I could at least have pointed to it as a disagreeable circumstance, but . . .

Besides, it seemed I was feeling okay, anyway I had already ordered my third coffee, along with my third cognac. Or it was already the fourth of these set menus?

The disaster thus would not come until it was time to pay; but by then the ladies might already have gone.

Something, some centrifugal force or an anomalous form of it, had thrown me backward against the back of the chair. I was lying in the upholstered chair more than I was sitting in it; and something inside me was lying in wait, wholly intent on registering the physical changes that were coursing over me. The shivering that stemmed from the inevitably recurring thoughts of my inadequacy in so many situations; the boiling emotions that poured over my skin so that it hardly dried before it was immediately covered with moisture again, probably with a red moisture.

My inadequacy in situations, in every situation was—so I believed I had realized long ago, and if I did not know it now, it was merely a recurrence of an old inadequacy—one instance of what possibly was a very widespread inferiority of the human being relative to his insanely well-functioning world, the world which this being, the sorceror's apprentice, had created himself. The inadequacy was innate in this being, and he could cope with it only by designating it a disease. The problem was, the diagnosis brought no prospect of cure. And moreover, this inadequacy vis-à-vis the self-created world was revisable, it seemed, only if a disaster would befall it. As long as the disaster failed to happen, the inadequacy persisted.

If, for example, I could not pay my bill in this bar, as I already predictably could not, it would logically extend my decline, which had started on this Friday just as on most days it started at one time or another . . . and almost always at a moment when I lacked the strength to give it the boot. While the world calmly continued to function, my stagger down this steep path had already begun. It only needed the slightest impetus . . . railroad stations are the outstanding examples of such an impetus . . . to land in the depths of the city, behind the railroad station, the place where one escape may easily bring on the next. I was quite familiar with these derelicts who turned up in the restaurants each night as if the shadow world had spit them out, once the transport police had finished their last round; who shared one cup of coffee among two or three; who, tattered and bleary-eyed from lack of sleep, put their heads down on their earth-gray forearms and tried to steal an hour's sleep while under the table their feet, retaining water because of their nonstop wakeful striding, popped thickly swollen out of their split-open shoes. Until they were hounded out again, sweat-soaked and surrounded by swarms of flies; and it was a mercy if no more happened to them than being chased. They were all waiting—ever since the first day when they harmlessly evaded paying a bill—for a disaster to befall the world at last instead of them.

"You look pale, young man," said the talkative lady, who to my surprise was still sitting at the table with her friends. The waitress had just come and brought me another coffee and another cognac, again with a suspicious, pinched smile. "Are you feeling unwell? . . . Maybe you should go out and get a little air, we'll tell the waitress . . ."

"I'll go and sell my ticket," I said. "If you want to go to Berlin, I would let you have the ticket at half price."

"Oh no," she answered in a tone of amusement, "Whatever do you mean? We're feeling very comfortable here, aren't we?" The other two, who had looked at me with great uneasiness, hastened to nod agreement. "No doubt it was more pleasant here in the past, but we should not take too black a view of it, I believe. At first I thought, he's just in a doomsday mood because he's not feeling well. I know how that is, I used to see it in customers in the past. You could tell right away when something was wrong. Especially at night, a lot of them popped up, who knows where from. That's no longer our problem."

Perhaps the lady was right and this doomsday mood, as she called it, would disappear if I could identify the cause. In my slanting position, it cost me unusual effort to turn and look at the standard clock that hung over the exit at the other end of the hall. Admittedly I managed to read the time, but it suddenly seemed to me impossible to relate it to the departure time of the train I had planned to take. No, there was no point, I had to stay here, and here await the doom on which I could not clearly put my finger . . . Moreover, this doom alone would make it unnecessary to pay my bill. The pleasure of all great dooms was that bills became irrelevant. Looking at things that way, the most asocial could calculate like an emperor, once he saw the doom was coming.

Yes, it had already begun when I was still sitting a floor lower down, in the seething hell of the the lower deck, knocking over my glasses like a madman and listening to the cracking sound which presumably came from fighter planes breaking the sound barrier high above this monstrous edifice, in the pale atmosphere of the summer sky, causing the vibrations to pass on into the fibers of my body, while outside the giant windows where I gazed, a snow-white glistening wall of fog seemed to drift slowly past, without being noticed by anyone.

Maybe it was just that somone had opened one of the windows, letting even more boiling heat flow in and make the dirty discolored banners of the curtains billow inward at a slant—but for a moment I had the illusion that the whole giant ship of the railroad station had tipped over onto its side.

Was it really on a Friday? . . . I had no idea if I was saying these words aloud. In any case, I did not receive any answer. Was it a Friday? It simply must have been a Friday like today. No matter if it was Friday or Tuesday, they quietly went on celebrating in the still well-heated halls, their human dignity had suddenly been restored. No one any longer had to wait for a bill, nothing more would need to be paid, unless it was with one's life. They all knew it, since that strange cracking sound had come from above or from below, from somewhere outside.

"Oh, don't worry about us," the lady interjected. "You're probably cross now because we're in such good spirits. Perhaps you don't believe that we plan to go to a funeral. But if we're going to a funeral over on the other side, we thought . . ."

You can't talk about a funeral in this case. Do you know our position? Forty-one degrees forty-six minutes north, fifty degrees fourteen minutes west, if I am measuring the angle correctly. Do you know where that is? There is no earth under it. Only water, water and sometimes ice, real proper squadrons of icebergs. Pretty inhospitable, nothing can survive there. Nothing stays on top, it goes down, down to the fishes. Just keep on celebrating, we are sinking. But please hold on tight to your glasses so they don't fall into my lap when the list increases. The water probably will come in below, through the entrance, not through the windows there. No doubt water is already standing down on the stairs—just listen to the shouting down below there. The half-strangled voices of the supervisors, who want to keep order. Now people have built this monstrosity, safe, weatherproof, fireproof, bombproof, a model for all Europe, but there is no hook in the sky to hang it on. Will we touch down gently, when we get to the bottom? Nearer, My God, to Thee. Are You down there, below this compass point at which this marvelous structure is drinking its fill? Do you know the name that this giant coffin will have later: *Titanic*. Rightly understood, that's where we're sitting now: the *Westside Titanic,* already listing considerably. Yet it is immaterial which side went down first and most likely it will not be reported.

"Will you be able to manage that?" the lady asked with concern when the waitress, already shaking her head, brought me another coffee and cognac. "Are you trying to get drunk by main force?"

"That is no longer important," I replied. "Not in this position."

At least let us go down without discord . . . and especially without becoming unjust. Think of your fellow-waiter down below there, he accused me of being drunk. Ridiculous, my beer tipped over, after all. And I was so dumb I paid for it anyway. Tell me, don't you want to buy a ticket to Berlin? You still have the chance. Women and children first, they always say. And it may still be so, even here, on this solid ground where a person forgets where he wanted to go.

Translated by Jan van Heurck

Günter Kunert

Love Story—Made in the GDR

Just a casual thing, you can't say that such an affair is anything else. It's better to leave out the word *love:* that is much too big for the mediocre feelings whose sporadic appearance reminds you of a recurrent infection. It is more honest just to lie side by side in bed, isn't it, Kläre? (her name isn't really Kläre), without solemn oaths and protestations, even if you had nothing of that sort in mind a couple of hours earlier. Don't you think so?!

Asked a question like that, you first have to light a cigarette to gain time—reflective, but unconcerned that sparks might leave a permanent tattoo on the brashly flowered quilt, or on the breast bared at the side as you reach for the pack. After the first puffs, Kläre voices the same opinion, and emphasizes besides that the fact that people today get together without inhibitions, represents progress over earlier times. Only when it comes to intimacies that "extend the employer–employee relationship into the private sphere," that can get her vicious, that sort of thing is too "cheap"!

He had directed his question at the ceiling to start with, but her answer now compels him to steal a sidelong glance at her. Did she mean that ironically? But in all good conscience, he cannot believe that he has abused his position as her employer:

"But surely you don't think you have to tell me that, Kläre? On the contrary: I am against sexual relationships inside the same department, regardless of whether I am the head of the department or not." But what he can no longer clearly call to mind, is how this thing that he bluntly and strictly opposed nevertheless came to pass. Two weeks ago, Kläre was "assigned" to him as secretary:

a minor miracle, because the profession was dying out. In the system of organized scarcity, secretaries were even rarer than telling the public the truth; and all those he had encountered so far were sullen and dismissive, or possessive and clucking. Not one had been ironic, until that day two weeks ago. Perhaps that was what had attracted him: her matter-of-factness plus wit. Also, they had eaten together right away in the canteen: fish fillet with vegetables, an unusual introduction to a romance without romanticism. It looked like a real stroke of luck that she had been sent to him in the supplies division. Other department heads envied him, because often they had to type their own letters using the hunt-and-peck system. He really was a lucky dog. Without her seeing, he stretched out his right hand to the edge of the bed and noiselessly tapped the wood with the knuckle of his ring finger: knock on wood! Yes, secretaries had become as scarce as storks in the countryside. This simile had no sooner occurred to him, than he realized why he had been thinking of storks. For some time now—ever since they completed that act whose principle had proved so successful that it now threatened to wipe out mankind—he had been wondering what she did to prevent this principle from taking effect in her own case. He had not thought about it before then, of course, because it would have seemed to him too clear-headed and businesslike, at the moment when "his passion surged," as it was described in boring books which he had given up reading—to ask her coolly whether she was taking the Pill, or had inside her one of those plastic spiral devices that people referred to as a "death coil." That would not have been an appropriate time for such a question, at least not as he perceived it. He was not familiar enough with Kläre; and everybody knew that women were especially sensitive the first time, psychologically speaking, so that you could not treat the act as one of assigning materials. At the same time, he feared that such a question—even if he succeeded in phrasing it to indicate concern about her and not about himself—would hardly express the gratitude which he genuinely felt.

As she lay beside him on her back—half covered, physically close, so that feeling its oddness he noted her skin like the cooled soft shell of some object manufactured for the seaside, like a rubber animal—tobacco smoke rose at irregular intervals out of her insinuatingly opened mouth: Like Indian smoke signals whose meaning he did not understand.

"Of course I take the pill, you silly little boy!" and with this apparently teasing diminutive she interrupted his hypothetical reflections about undesired offspring, and at the same time established once and for all her superiority, whose source he thought he knew: her self-confidence, which enabled her to get out of bed unabashedly, unembarrassed by her nakedness, after stubbing out the remains of her cigarette in the ashtray beside her with the gesture of having solved a problem. Like him she was no longer as young as she used to be, as you saw in the moment before she swung her legs out over the edge of the bed, while she sat with her breasts supported by her belly, a solidly built woman, by no means deliberately immodest; and also her rear end, which was turned toward him and which he followed with his gaze as it trailed its owner out through the bedroom door, seemed only to announce: nothing human is alien to me!

Meanwhile, he self-consciously pushed his pale thighs forward under the covers, keeping his back to the door, grabbed his underpants from the floor mat and, even though he was unobserved, put them on as he got up, lifting his rear hastily, not without feelings of embarrassment at finding himself naked in strange surroundings, and doubly ashamed because he was not able to free himself from these feelings. No sense of authority, dear boy! He was already beginning to get annoyed, which speeded up his dressing. He could hear outside in the bathroom how someone was singing cheerfully and splashing water, someone about whom the details were already beginning to slip from his mind. What color were her eyes? What shape were her hands? Who was she, anyway? A woman over forty, who wrote his letters and unobtrusively (he noticed) corrected his mistakes in grammar. It's true, with a better education he would not be stuck in the no-hope department of supplies. He was nevertheless grateful for her discretion. And when he accepted her invitation to supper—yes, that's how it happened, that was clear to him now—he not only counted on an opulent meal but also on what then in fact occurred: his hopes were fulfilled without further delay. So he had been right. Maybe he was not especially good in German, but he was not bad in psychology. That was useful in the supplies section, too: you knew exactly how to deal with reluctant suppliers and when you had to give them inducements. But before he *left* her—what an ill-omened word that was for his departure—he felt afraid that she might demand verbal testimonies of his affection (if such there was), or even ask if he intended to marry her, a question which admittedly always sounded natural in movies or on TV but which, outside fiction, never lacked an inquisitorial undertone, and at the moment of its pronouncement converted every reality to something unreal, to a badly done amateur play.

But Kläre—whose name was not Kläre, who some time in the now clear-cut eternity of the past two weeks had told him her real name, Erika or Annemarie, some remnant of her parents' conformity with whatever name was considered the going thing at the time—amiably accepted his reserved goodbye. He did not even dare to kiss her, because of his concern that she might mistakenly interpret it as an invitation to try to ferret out his feelings for her after all.

So, see you tomorrow, see you tomorrow morning at the office! See you tomorrow evening at my place—You'll see that bachelors can cook too! I'm famous for my goulash, an original Hungarian recipe, I brought it back from my vacation at Lake Balaton. Nothing but meaningless ribbons of words that he wraps around her, tying her up with them so that she cannot move, so as to ward off the danger that he does not even know exists. She smiles at everything, but with unmistakably dilated pupils that consequently are darker in the twilight of the corridor, and stand in contrast to the calm expression on her face.

This contrast still continued to preoccupy him out on the street, on his way home, and even after he stepped inside his own four walls, and all the while became more mysterious. His memory, persistently reproducing her strange expression against his will, condemned him to speculations which, if they had any probability of being true, should actually have made him feel proud. Any attempt to interpret her expression ended in the conclusion (because a person's eyes do not lie, as our parents teach us: "Look at me, Heinz, and don't blink!") that her gaze was saying what her mouth carefully did not say—perhaps merely out of consideration for him and with the intention of saying it later, because it was not expressible in banal everyday life. The department head fell asleep uneasily, still poring over this undismissable conclusion.

Before washing, shaving, brushing his teeth he determines, as he does virtually every morning, that he really does not look like someone who has slept through the night but rather as if he has been run through a mill without knowing it: so creased does he appear in the mirror, and at the same time so bloated. Sleep is supposed to improve your appearance, but there doesn't seem much hope of it working with me! He says it without resignation, matter-of-factly, he is old enough for that. But as he shaves, his customary appearance is restored, along with a sense of self-satisfaction which is also customary but today is enhanced. Why shouldn't a woman find his unremarkable but solid proportions attractive? A face that inspired trust, denoting reliability and seriousness. His sparse hair tended rather to intensify this impression, which he assumes is what moved Kläre to everything that happened between them yesterday evening. After all, she might have made her feelings clear to him. She had been very reserved when they said good-bye, he would have liked a "tender word"—as he now called it, in contrast to his self of yesterday. Anyway, even without any show of tenderness on her part, his self-confidence had expanded uncommonly in the past twelve hours.

And even after he had climbed into his minicar with its cardboard bodywork, and his protruding belly, thickened by suit and coat, would hardly fit between the seat back and the steering wheel, he did not notice that his person, which at favorable moments he regarded as something impressive, seemed gauged only for the reception of praise and blame, without his being aware of it; and when he received neither one nor the other, the result was that he felt insecure. His efforts to understand things merely led his memory to secretly falsify events that had just occurred, so that he could fit them into his own alternative scheme, so that he could grasp and file them away. Obviously, she liked me and purely out of shyness, she refrained from saying anything about it. She is a shy person. But on the other hand, what contradicted this laboriously devised explanation was the fact that she got undressed pretty fast for a shy person, and had not been at all timid, had she? Who can understand women? That had been his father's view, and the father had imprinted the saying on his son, as a way for him to escape having to think about it.

In the office, no time was left for problems of this sort because the paper ration was being cut once again (by twenty percent—madness!), which threatened to turn their production plan into total chaos and make it impossible to fill the export orders. In some way, the available paper had to be "juggled" so that there was enough for the assigned purposes. This "fact of life"—as people referred to unavoidable disaster—reduced Kläre to her professional function, so that between the many urgent letters that had to be written there was no time for anything but to say briefly: "So see you at my place this evening!"

At the noon break he arrived late and found a place only after some searching, then noticed Kläre on the opposite side of the hall near the door, talking almost boisterously with a co-worker to whom indistinct rumors ascribed shady activities that were never exactly spelled out. Hearsay like that could of course be based on an error. That sort of mistake happened, and the person involved could never get free of the taint, of which he himself was often not even aware. More than once Heinz had wondered if these whispered rumors were not spread deliberately, partly to create the impression that there were more disguised conspirators around than there really were, and partly to create a distrust of certain individuals, so that others would avoid contact with them. He imagined that he himself was the victim of a widespread false allegation, and the notion made him feel anxious. Every denial was tantamount to an added confession that you were guilty of exactly the thing that you were trying to ward off. A vacuum came to surround you, so that you could no longer get any air. Unbearable isolation could result from the lack of any tie to this side or that side of a boundary line which was invisible. Thus it made sense that if you wanted to recruit someone, you could first use rumors to drive the potential co-conspirator into such isolation that presumably he would be happy to belong to a group again.

But what Kläre was casually discussing with the aforesaid co-worker in the canteen, was most likely something completely trivial, about food brands or vacation vouchers. All the same, when she was sitting in front of his desk again later with pad and pencil, he felt sure that he could not ask her about it. After all, she was a new employee, and he would have had to explain to her who the person was with whom she had been talking, or rather who people said he was. That went against his grain, because in case the person was really innocent, it would be as if he had condemned him. It was impossible simply to comment: "Be careful what you say to him, it may be passed on!"

Shortly before finishing work, he crossed the corridor again to fetch the last typed letter from Kläre's room, not wishing her to come to him but rather to keep working until the closing bell so that she could complete the final pages. He found her office empty. In the middle of the desk lay the only sign that anyone inhabited the sparse and purposeful interior: her handbag, with the clasp open like a waiting frog's mouth with no frog behind it—or like someone's gaping, silent amputated jaw. It seemed to be waiting for someone to reach inside. He stood there, sensing that this might be the moment, perhaps the first and only moment, to make sure about things, but sure about what? After all, he had no reason to be suspicious of her. Or rather he had, without being aware of it. He admitted that for some time he had been suppressing a secret amazement that he, of all people, should have been given a secretary all of a sudden, and on top of that, someone to share his empty evenings or nights; and the admission sent an unpleasant hot flush over his whole body. He left hurriedly to avoid being caught, went along the corridor, and only when he pressed down his own door handle, he became aware that he was still clutching his handkerchief, which he had used to mop his brow. Once he was crouched behind his desk again, he felt ridiculous. What an over-the-top reaction to the handbag, which had been left invitingly wide open and so testified to the harmlessness of its owner. Unless this had been a particularly clever ploy to lull him into a false sense of security. This was absurd, he must pull himself out of it at once. Who could possibly be interested in him? You aren't harboring any secrets, you keep account of supplies, which you carefully classify and distribute. Don't start seeing pink elephants! Your conscience, or whatever people call this black box, is pure, chemically pure however much you rummage around in it. And it is unthinkable that this can have anything to do with that letter from Cologne. Cologne, you remember, from a relative so distant that you had forgotten his existence and for that reason had not listed him in any questionnaire. You had met him once some time after the war, and now this man, who was a high-ranking civil servant or whatever damned thing he called himself, felt his heart beating for German unification and wrote him some brotherly lines. He had thrown the rubbishy thing away right after he received it, and now it seemed to him that this was a mistake. As if he wanted to cover up something wrong by getting rid of the evidence. Or was there something else that someone could accuse him of? And how could anyone know about the letter?

A question as easily answered as who had built seven-gated Thebes. An involuntary shrug of the shoulders, a lifting of the hands, a raising of the eyebrows—those are the gestures that directors ask actors to perform to show helpless resignation, while inaudibly and scornfully they repeat the question: "How could they know?" And in fact that is just what people do in real life.

Five o'clock, time to stop brooding. You're not getting paid for it now, and you can't afford to idle your time away.

Instead of the hot meal he had promised, he served sandwiches, saying that he got home late and no longer had the time to cook.

"If all women would behave that way . . ." Kläre commented on the frugal supper, but did not explain what the results of this unhousewifely behavior would be. Possibly all the husbands would starve, or get divorces, which they did anyway; and wise aphorisms of this kind do not lift one's spirits. They needed the help of a bottle of Riesling, and it took disproportionately long for them to get back something of the harmony they had felt before. He obeyed her invitation to join him on the couch. During the foregoing conversation, she had already let him know that she had put on a new brassiere especially for him. A Triumph Bra: you know, "It crowns the figure"! Imported! Very expensive! And so he made an effort to appreciate the honor shown him, and also was required to feel the object, to evaluate its design and material, and to hear that people in this country could not achieve the same thing in a hundred years. That did not sound like a very optimistic view of the future, but could the manufacture of brassieres be considered the criterion of a social order? Did she think that he thought as she did? Was she looking beyond pleasure, for common views? Could they get closer that way than they already were?

"Did anybody ever ask you what you want, Heinz, what you need in order to live . . . to really live?" She is making a probe of his conscience, accompanied by a veiled look with which he is now familiar and which seems to intensify the inquiry. But when the object of the probe thinks it over, he detects no stirrings of conscience. What inside him was supposed to rebel because it has been suppressed and tied down for so long? No, it is only a reflex, it has been worn away ever since he was young, so that in its place you can hardly even see where it used to be.

He turned his attention to tangible matters to evade the question, and the other questions which might follow. His diversion succeeded, and while his fingers mechanically carried out unsupervised movements along her smooth curves, he stared with inappropriate attention at the tufts of hair, not unlike the straw used to stuff armchairs, which were pressed to the side of her left temple, above a flattened ear which he had never noticed with such exaggerated clarity before, and which he felt strangely moved to see, as if he were looking at something made of wax that he had observed once in the hygiene museum, where a great deal more involving man and woman was also displayed for general viewing.

At the same time he felt her hand at work on him, but as if not he but someone else were the object of this increasingly impatient manipulation. He had been removed, replaced with a counterfeit version of himself that wanted to act in accordance with expectations; but naturally this did not work because it did not act like the original. On the other hand, the real Heinz was afraid that Kläre might notice the substitution and figure out what it meant. Even as he struggled to get rid of his suspicions, which were bound to give rise to countersuspicions if they became known, he supported the false Heinz in his intention to behave uninhibitedly. The result was an untalented simulation of physical arousal which was contradicted by his body itself. He found it impossible to free himself from the image that he was being asked to copulate with the gaping handbag, between its brass clasps, which although it had no teeth had the look of a trap.

I want to be an animal! Where there's a will, there's a way! But such sentiments are rarely voiced by life's practitioners. Instead they come from people in study rooms who never put themselves in hopeless situations. Should he confess what his body had already admitted? His only hope was that this wordless confession would be misinterpreted, as were most of the coded messages that came from the kingdom of hormones. To the mute sharer in his failure, he offered reasons that she might find credible: overwork, troubles resulting from the new supply cut, a headache. Anything but she herself had caused his inhibition—as yesterday evening proved. But as his explanations became more detailed, he saw that the woman beside him, without stirring from the spot, was moving farther and farther away from him. He felt that she would never lie beside him in this way again. His chattering just prolonged the minutes before she would get up, get dressed and leave. Already he had made up his mind that as soon as the apartment door closed, he would go and take out of the freezer the bottle of vodka that he had started, to escape his brooding, which was as futile as it was exhausting. Admittedly, next morning at the office he would be a bit tired and dry in the mouth, but the canteen sold Bitter Lemon for just such occasions. His secretary no doubt would be glad to fetch him a couple of bottles before she began to type his letters and correct their mistakes. No more talk of lost possibilities. In the future everything would go as it ought to, and probably soon he would no longer understand why the sight of her handbag had bothered him, once upon a time.

Translated by Jan van Heurck

WOMEN IN THE GDR

Friedrich Wolf

Anna and the Men's Strike

Anna Berger, the twenty-five-year-old mayor of L., was so tired that she could hardly see straight. The autumn seed had to be sowed; there were the lists of delivery quotas to deal with, the trees to be felled in the forest, the highway to be graveled, the new schoolhouse that had to be built. Anna was on her feet from morning till night. She wore a leather jacket that had once been elegant but was now completely discolored from wind and weather, over her two-piece suit, which she still had from her time as bookkeeper in the office on a Berlin construction site. In the past, Anna had always been dressed to the nines, but now her whole life was consumed by work for her home village. Nowadays, "luxury" for her meant climbing into a big tub of hot water each evening to scrub and wash herself, after which she would tumble into bed, often too tired to eat.

Anna was not a prima donna, and this was not the first time that she had had to tackle hard work. But these days, work had a whole new meaning.

Then one noon came a phone call from the main town in the district, from Herbert Schwenk, a returning soldier. He said that he wanted to talk to the mayor. Anna held her breath for a moment. "Hello, this is the mayor speaking."

"What do you mean? That's a woman's voice."

"Yes, well. This is the mayor's office, the secretary speaking."

He asked her to inform his brother that he was arriving tomorrow.

So he was coming home. How much had happened in the interval, in the past six years since Herbert had been sent to the front with his tank corps! Her life in Berlin, where she had worked her way up from stenotypist to bookkeeper, then the bombing of her office, the evacuation into the countryside—which was not hard for her, because she came from a farm family and she had even retrained as a bricklayer, so she had both feet on the ground. Then came Germany's collapse. She struggled her way back to her home village, where she worked for the old mayor, keeping his books, lists and charts. She made a success of any job she tackled. Admittedly, the old mayor thought that he knew better than she how to do everything. So they had lots of disagreements, until one day Anna said that she preferred to farm her fields and would work as a bricklayer on the side. But the townspeople, seventy percent of whom were women, would not have it, so the youthful Anna was elected mayor. She still faced many challenges, but she was able to handle them.

Only this noon, when Herbert telephoned, she had done something that was not right. Why had she not told Herbert, who was her childhood friend, that she was the mayor? He would find out tomorrow anyway. Their friendship had persisted even during the war. She had sent him little packages and letters, and when he visited her in Berlin during his last leave, they had spent marvelous days together. That seemed an eternity ago. Why had she lied to her friend today?

Well, the matter wasn't so tragic after all. Herbert, who had gotten rather skinny but was still the high-spirited daredevil he had been before, simply laughed at the "Miss Mayor." And when she asked him to come next day to the town hall to register his details, Herbert clicked his heels in military fashion and said: "Yes sir, my Lady Mayor! At your command, sergeant sir!"

Herbert was happy to be home, and people gladly allowed him to get some rest. He had so much to tell about his experiences in the past six years. In the evenings, young people would gather at his brother's house to listen to his stories. Only Anna, the "Miss Mayor," had little time to come, and that irked him, so late at night he would go to visit her. She listened to him for a while and then said: "Oh, Herbert, forget about the war! Think about our work here. It's a constant battle, too, but for something worthwhile."

"At your command, sergeant, sir!" Herbert whipped out. He grabbed her wrists to show her that he was still the man here, and pulled her to him, trying to kiss her. But Anna held him at arm's length. He could not get the better of this powerful girl.

"Aha, so lady mayors are no longer allowed to kiss!" Herbert said mockingly.

"All in good time!" said Anna. "And when I want to."

He left, slamming the door behind him.

The building of the new schoolhouse had to be speeded up to get it all under cover before winter. Herbert was among those assigned to the building work, but he did not come. When he was summoned to the town hall and the mayor asked him why he was staying away, he replied that, first, he still had his farm work to do, and second, he did not give a damn about the school, particularly seeing that he would have no children himself and that he was neither a day laborer nor a bricklayer. He preferred to go to the city in his free time and buy a couple of bottles of red wine. He needed that, he said, to get his strength back after six years of war and captivity, and that was all there was to say about it!

The mayor, of course, could have imposed a penalty on him. But she merely said: "Whatever you think." Then she went on writing her accounts as if he did not exist, as if he were not there.

Herbert was furious. He went around to his war buddies and stirred them up to refuse to take any more orders from a "skirt"! By the fifth day, none of the men turned up any more at the building site.

A woman who was Anna's neighbor advised her to call a meeting of the town council, where the women held the majority, and there to pass a resolution to turn over the matter to the district magistrate. But Anna opposed the idea. The men had declared war on them, she said, and the women ought to use their own power to fight back. Did the thirty women who were working on the building think that they could do the job if they worked overtime, and gave crash training to the young girls to be their assistants? Women had done harder jobs than that before, she said. She spoke with such fire and conviction that they all felt enthusiastic.

Next day, more than fifty women and girls appeared at the building site, and slaved away like mad. The mayor herself, who was a trained bricklayer, instructed the young girls how to prepare the mortar and pass the bricks along a "chain." She supervised the work and pitched in herself everywhere on the site. The men walked past and cracked jokes. Admittedly, they were taken aback when the women did not come home at midday, and also did not prepare their meals. Instead, the women had set up an old cooking stove on the site, and they cooked together for themselves and the children in a big kettle. Now the women as they feasted could grin at their men, who had to fix dinner for themselves. A few domestic tyrants turned up and tried to fetch their womenfolk home. But the fifty women workers stood ready with their trowels, and the men had no desire to be smeared with damp mortar and exposed to ridicule.

This trench warfare went on for a week, then two weeks.

The walls of the new school were rising. What luck that the frame was already standing! Anna thought about whether she had not acted somewhat rashly after all. Who was going to frame and cover the roof later on? Suppose the carpenters and roofers stuck by the men? Her head ached with thinking. All day long, she spent every free minute she had at the building site. From her heated office in the town hall she would race outdoors dressed just as she was, exposed to wind and weather, and hurry to the site. Then she would have to stay up late at night to finish the paperwork for her job as mayor.

It was too much, even for her robust body.

One morning she had a trembling fit. Nonsense! She went to the building site anyway. Then she really started shaking, and suddenly she felt dizzy. She had to sit down, her teeth were chattering with a chill. She was taken to bed. The doctor found that she had a temperature of over 104 degrees and double pneumonia. She was critically ill. She kept raving about the new school: "The school is as important as the fields . . . the children must have the very best!" The women took care of Anna like their sister. They took turns watching over her day and night. Once, two bottles of red wine were left at the front door. No note was attached and no one knew who had put them there.

Anna was getting well. She was only too eager to go to the building site, but they held her back. The women followed the doctor's orders strictly. Week after week went by.

Finally one sunny winter day, she was taken out to the site. Anna stared at the building transfixed, then looked up: the roof timbers had been framed above the upper storey, and from a pole on the gable hung the garland of pine branches with bright-colored streamers that crowned the rafters at the topping-out ceremony. And on the roof ridge, among the carpenters, sat Herbert. Down below stood the other men of the village, and beamed at their mayor.

In the evening Anna said to Herbert: "Do you know what helped me a lot while I was sick?"

"What?"

"The red wine."

Herbert looked at her with a smile.

Translated by Jan van Heurck

Irmtraud Morgner

White Easter

My labor pains were coming every twenty minutes by the time I reached the station to change trains. The crowd pushed their way out the train doors and toward the exits. I set down my suitcase by my right calf and waited at the end of the platform, which was mounted on a bridge. The bridge shook as the train pulled out, leaving an unobstructed view of the two platform roofs which intersected the bridge at right angles. The roofs were ringed by a lighted well that lifted them out of the darkness. Between the platforms lay two pairs of tracks, with several other pairs to the right and left, and the wind swept snow off the blooming forsythia bushes which grew along the railroad embankment. When the crowd had drained away in the exit tunnels, I warily picked up my suitcase again and went down the steps slowly to the island platform on the right. A labor pain caught me by surprise. I headed for the nearest bench but could not make it and sat down on my suitcase. A man and three women occupied the bench. Remembering the advice from my childbirth class, I remained seated on my suitcase and memorized psychological techniques of pain prevention. Although the instructions were to get to the clinic without delay if your water broke prematurely, the train was late anyhow. Then it dawdled on the way. The taxi driver drove at thirty miles an hour at most, and I also had to wait outside the door of the maternity ward, ringing the bell several times before a nurse opened up. I handed her a card which certified that I had completed the course in reduced-pain childbirth, and told her why I had come. The nurse stuffed the card into her apron pocket, took my suitcase and carried it along a hot, conspicuously polished corridor that smelled of Wofasept disinfectant, echoed and was too brightly lit. The white walls were blinding. So were the nurse's stiff apron and pleated cap. She looked starched and antiseptic, as if she had just come out of the wash. In the admitting room, she made herself coffee while I undressed. I shut my clothes into a locker, hoping that soon they would no longer fit me. Trained as I was and up on all the literature, I did not feel surprised to be granted a nightgown without bathing first. Presumably it covered the thighs. Then I waddled over to a platform. All very pregnant women waddle, with legs spread wide and belly thrust forward. My belly had already shrunk, and I climbed onto the platform with the help of a footstool. The nurse cleared away the coffee things, handed me a thermometer, took my pulse, pressed a cold metal stethoscope against my hot abdomen, and sat down satisfied behind the desk. There she recorded my personal details, and asked me about childhood illnesses and others, operations, previous childbirths, miscarriages, abortions, the history of my pregnancy, the term date, when the pains began, how long they lasted, how far apart they were. I guessed I had dilated to the size of a one-mark coin. The nurse slipped a rubber glove onto her right hand and soon reported: "The size of a hazelnut." She was laughing out of both sides of her mouth, but I did not let myself show any disappointment, because the literature says that disappointment lowers the pain threshold. The nurse wrote my name in chalk on a blue blackboard. The blackboard was as wide as the wall and about six feet high. Information about all the day's admissions was written on it in chalk. The number 21 stood in front of my name. The nurse wished me luck in the remarkable event that lay before me, and escorted me into the delivery room. On our way there via the highly polished, echoing corridor, I wondered where I had seen those people before. The man had been nodding forward in the corner of the bench, the three women were talking together, the breath coming from their mouths was turning to vapor. When the suburban train to Mahlsdorf pulled in, the women rose and signalled to the man to wake up if he wanted to travel with them. Then the eldest of the women thumped his stomach, arm and back, and finally seized his shoulder and shook him so that his head banged against the white-enameled sign above the back of the double bench, where the name EASTERN CROSS was written in large black letters. The door labeled DELIVERY ROOM stood open, a male nurse wheeled a stretcher into the corridor, on the stretcher lay a woman with matted hair. The male nurse told the female nurse that the head physician was stuck in the snow in his Mercedes. "The Director's patient," she said, and I was led into the small delivery room. A room with light-blue tiled walls, two empty beds with night tables at the head, and little tables at the foot end with chromium-plated instrument cases on them. Next to the cases were lidded basins hanging on racks; a screen between the beds, a water boiler and washtub opposite the frosted windows, and a clock on the front wall. The clock showed seven minutes past midnight when I climbed into bed. In less than a minute, a woman wearing a neck brooch entered, came to my bed and greeted me with a handshake. I took her for a midwife, but actually she was the director of midwives. She shaved me immediately, gave me an enema, and grumbled about the unseasonable weather. Then she handed me a thermometer, took my pulse, pressed a cold stethoscope against my hot abdomen, and sat down satisfied behind the desk. (Because there was a desk in the little delivery room, too.) Then she recorded my personal details, and asked me about childhood illnesses and others, operations, childbirths, miscarriages, abortions, the history of my pregnancy, the term date, when the pains began, how far apart they were, how severe they were. "Tolerable," I said. The size of a hazelnut: many men like modest women. The chief midwife slipped a glove onto her right hand and soon reported: "The size of florist's wire." She described my labor pains as not serious, advised me to sleep to conserve energy and wished me good night. Then she turned out the light and left, leaving the door open. The door led to the large delivery room *cum* nursery. I rolled over onto the side where I felt no movement, in a relaxation posture—once you're trained you're trained, and a maternity bed is hard—and squeezed my eyes shut to conserve energy. The head physician apparently had turned up. I heard female voices call out his title repeatedly, and a male voice said "Beautiful Sunday." Moans, cries, commands, babies howling, I felt annoyed that I was still searching my memory for the data bank which the man and the three women refused to vacate. The man had a round skull where thin pale hair and a fringe beard were growing. His eyes, eyeglasses, skin and suit seemed of the same pallor and sparseness as his hair; at least all that struck you in the light was his red, abundant growth of beard. Its brass-colored sickle divided the man's shape. Someone was saying he had a hammer, the women called for a doctor. Approximately once an hour, a doctor with a rubber glove came to my bed, every half hour a nurse came with a metal stethoscope and a timer, at least once every fifteen minutes I heard a baby give its first cry. The only report on my baby was that it was okay, the head in the right position. It kicked my diaphragm. All the doctors who raised my blanket that night, said that they would start charting my pains and give me a penicillin injection. They expected that grand rounds would be at eight A.M. At five, the cleaning woman came and pooh-poohed the notion that all your trouble is forgotten once the baby comes. You don't forget drudgery like that, she said: she had gone through labor six times, and you couldn't put anything over on her. "Had you taken a course in low-pain delivery?" I asked.

"Heaven forbid," she said. "Eleven boys tonight, the box of boys is open today—if you hurry, you can get another one. My husband was furious when the first kid was a girl. This is your first, isn't it?"

"Yes," I said.

"Uh-huh," she replied. "Lots of husbands haven't come to visit their wives when they had girls. That's why the nurses aren't allowed to tell the fathers the baby's sex over the telephone. It's orders from the Director. I have four sons and two daughters. What do you want?"

"A person," I said.

"And your husband?"

"I want a healthy person of moderate intelligence," I said.

"Some days, more single women give birth than married ones," she answered. "I married at eighteen and had the kids one after another. My mother had eight. When they were grown and my father was dead, she made a nice life for herself."

We wished each other good luck and went to work. She wiped and polished, I breathed per instruction. At seven they smoothed out my blanket. At a quarter past eight, the Director appeared with the head physician, a female head physician and the chief midwife. The assistant doctors had to stay outside. The Director said, "Pain chart, penicillin," and asked me if I had seen the painting exhibition. We exchanged views about Paula Modersohn-Becker. After the consultation the chief midwife brought me three pills, a glass of water, a hypo of penicillin, a second handbell, and said: "The things that happen! A girl came here in the evening not long ago, you could already see the baby's head. The girl arrived with her mother and mother-in-law and her husband, a married girl, maybe seventeen. Her husband was not much older and couldn't speak from excitement. I said to him, 'Didn't your wife complain about the pains?'—dilation pains really hurt, most women feel their dilation pains worse than the final-stage pains that make you bear down to push the baby out—'Your mother-in-law must have noticed that it was time, why did it take you so long to get here?' But he couldn't say a thing. We hardly got her clothes down before the baby came. The things that happen!" In one of the books I had read, it said that we have to raise a generation to whom the idea of "childbirth pains" does not even occur, and to achieve this, the phrase must be neither spoken nor written but must be replaced by "childbirth contractions." Naturally, a painless or brief delivery would not interest the gossipy type of women who prefer to talk about abnormal and complicated births. But an expectant mother ought not even to listen to such descriptions in the first place, because (the book said) they strengthen the conditioned reflex to experience pain, and the station master called out that the medical orderly had been notified, and all the people who had sat on the rear side of the double bench, rose abruptly and grabbed their bags. A whirlpool formed in the river of humanity that streamed down from the platform one floor up. Those caught in its undertow were drawn into a circular crowd whose center was the man. I know him, but where from? His head was bent over so far that his brass-red beard lay on his shirtfront like a bib. Three pills once an hour, slowly they were beginning to work, the female head physician said: "Let's just see if you can manage it on your own."

"And if I don't manage on my own?" I asked.

"Then we'll have to take it out," she replied. A mentally-retarded man used to help out in the fruit-and-veg store: a forceps delivery. In the past, Anne says, the prospects were not good when your amniotic membrane broke prematurely: as a rule they would have dismembered the child to save the mother. I felt freezing. I remembered that my friend Anne had recommended woolen socks for the delivery room. My friend Anne is a nurse. "People who shout don't work," she said. I decided to work. That was in my period of unemployment, medically designated as the first stage of labor. The machine is working, powered by pills and injections, it is working hard. Five weeks too early. The concept "childbirth pains" did not enter my mind, I was thinking ahead: Sunday, the first Sunday after the first full moon in spring. Never again, I thought.

"We'll get the job done in two hours," the chief midwife said. I won't stay on the job another two hours, I thought. Out with it, alive or dead. The three women had laid the man on the bench, probably using up too much of their strength, his limbs were dangling, and when the bearing-down pains began, the professor appeared with the female head physician, the anesthesiologist and the chief midwife. The chief midwife was in command. When the pains came, she raised my head until my chin hit my breastbone, and ordered me to breathe in and to push, three times at each go. "Breathe when you push," she scolded me, all I heard were orders and scolding, and I clasped my knees as tightly as I could. Sometimes my sweaty hands slipped off and I was scolded for that, too. The pains came one right after another now, the contraction hardly relaxed any more, in the short pause I trembled as if I had the ague. "Keep going," the midwife said. "God is a man, a woman would have figured out a better way to do it, keep going, keep going." Injustices must be met with rage, keep going, keep going, keep going, you can already see a bit of the head, now you can see it clearly, now you can really see it, a head with black hair, I was supposed to grit my teeth and shit on the creation. Fine. Before the ether mask knocked out the pain-giant, I had him down for the count: one, two, three, four, five, six, seven, eight, nine. When I woke up, I was lying stretched out in bed, my feet crossed, a warm, unwrinkled blanket on top of me. The professor said: "All through."

"And the afterbirth?"

"It's all over. Congratulations on your son. Hey, show her the little guy." The anesthesiologist and the female head physician congratulated me. The chief midwife said: "I'm hungry." When my son was brought I felt frightened, but I merely expressed surprise that such big bellies produced such small people. "Six pounds thirteen ounces isn't small," the professor said. I saw the head and genitals, both disproportionately large being most important. Next, rather red, powdered skin, a flattened ear, eyebrows, big eyelids squeezed shut, lashes, a tin ID tag engraved No. 21, teaspoon-sized hands, fingernails, cuticles. "Is everything there?" I asked. Because professional experts were observing me, I decided to touch one leg with the tip of my right index finger. The leg was wrinkled at the thigh. The skin on the upper arm threw wrinkles, too, and elsewhere it mostly hung loose, as in animal cubs. I stayed in the delivery room for two more hours, listening to the babies crying. My son growled. He lay in an incubator in the nursery. I lay alone in the little maternity ward and waited for food. I had not eaten for twenty-one hours. The midwives were busy, so I had to wait a long time. I heard their orders, moans, cries, yowls, growls. Two, three hours went by on this day when I did not regret being a woman. It occurred to me that the man lived adjacent to my aunt's garden. In the summer he used to live in an arbor with his mother, his mother's sister and a woman named Maria. Maria had arranged his legs, which were clad in black corduroy, on the bench so that his knees and ankles touched. The mother's sister crossed his hands in the hollow under the thorax. The mother exhorted his yellowish glowing head. The eyes of the carpenter stared fixedly at the planks of the cross which roofed the train station. I struggled to understand that I had a son.

Translated by Jan van Heurck

Maxie Wander

The Fear of Love

I was terrifically dependent. It wasn't until the seventh or eighth grade that it began to dawn on me. Man, I thought, you're not that dumb, do your own thing. It just came, no one ever asked it of me. I've always had too few demands made on me. I used to hide in my room when we had visitors, because I had no idea what to say. I was so scared of people that I couldn't hold my fork when I had to eat out. Why, I don't know. My sister Susanne is younger than I am but she has more nerve. Sweet, pretty Susanne, naturally people are attracted to someone like her. An old bachelor guy thought I was sensational, when I was in the ninth grade. He said to Mama, "I'd marry Petra in a flash." And Mama laughed and said, "But you can't have her." After that, I didn't think I was so terrifically ugly any more. All of a sudden I was relaxed, I simply didn't put on my made-for-visitors face when someone came. "Hey, Petra sweetie, fetch the sugar, fetch the coffee." It was just too much. Then we moved. Suddenly I began to go dancing a lot and even found some people who thought I was cute. I made the most of it. When Charley came along, he was putty in my hands. He cut work for me, and told lies. It felt fabulous to have so much power over other people all of a sudden. With my new teachers, I thought: They'll think I'm a wallflower, I'll put on a real act for them straight off, and make them believe what I want them to believe about me. There I was with my own boyfriend, and the gang that thought I was cool—I was somebody now! And dumbbell that I was—because I wasn't so sharp, after all—I let a little of that show through. From then on I was sunk with the teachers, I was marked for good as calculating, insincere, stuck-up. All I did in school was argue, I was downright rude, not a trace of submissiveness left. In the eighth grade I didn't have the nerve yet to raise my hand when I knew an answer, I always just whispered it to myself. And all of a sudden this fantastic self-confidence. That wasn't entirely healthy, either.

The time with my gang was really fabulous. There were seven boys and me, the only girl. We went dancing in the villages. One guy had a car, a Trabi, with all of us crammed into it. Sometimes we cruised on our bikes, weather permitting. For Mardi Gras they hung balloons and paper streamers all over me. I never had money, I knew they would take care of everything. When I broke up with Charley, I had to leave the gang, and he looked for another girl. Now she's having his baby. Sure, that hurts me a bit. Then I went on the prowl with Susanne, just the two of us. But a gang is different, there you know you can do anything you like, with seven guys protecting you. Today that group wouldn't do anything for me any more. There's such a funny attitude in the group. Inside, no one takes the others quite seriously, practically anything goes, even if it's stupid. But everybody is all the more demanding toward outsiders. Outside the group, everybody's a nerd; inside, they're all great.

School was a breeze for me when I started to go my own way. Of course I played truant a lot, and I don't know how many times I was summoned before the collective, wow! Then I played sick every time, until my teacher started yelling, "These disgusting excuses of yours, I can't listen to them any more, get out!" Then I was out again. I didn't understand it myself. Teachers make a mistake by taking us too seriously, on the one hand. They weigh every detail and keep harping on the same old subject when we've already moved on to something else. On the other hand, they don't take us seriously enough, they only see what they want to see. In tenth grade I took a rest, until it was almost too late. I can't really complain about difficulties, I believe that a smooth path from high school exams to university, a degree, a profession, and someday a Ph.D. is not the way for me. But then we always try to justify our situation. I was simply rotten lazy. And now I realize that I don't know how to do anything. In the Expanded High School they made a big thing of me, we felt we were an elite. If I had started my university studies right away, I'd be with people my own age now and I'd have an easier time.

Now I'm doing a bit of data processing. There's a machine with numbers in it, and I transcribe the numbers onto punch cards, using the keyboard. That's pretty dumb work, and then on top of that there's a bonus that depends on how many you do. I said right off that I don't intend to ruin my nerves just for an extra fifty marks a month; my nerves are already ruined. Now I have a first-class hole puncher. It's too slow for the other women, you don't get an achievement bonus using it, but it does a better job. I see people only during breaks. So I talk to the machine. Today I was sitting there and it honked all of a sudden. "Shut up," I said. "Don't bleat now, I haven't done this bit yet." But no, it short-circuits on me! It was insulted because I didn't listen to it. Working with the machine irritates me precisely because I'm not like a machine, I'm a bit slapdash. But what I'd like more than anything is to get a job that's terrifically absorbing. I don't have any exact idea. A husband isn't so important, there's time to get one later. Besides, I have this habit. Whenever I see a film or read a book, I think: the woman comes off badly compared to the man. I always see everything stacked against the woman. I think, if I get to know a guy really well, I have to marry him right away. I look on marriage as an insurance company, a boardinghouse or a cemetery, depending. I'm happier if I know that I'm alone and have to be strong. The moment I have a husband, I'll get comfortable. Then I'll get in the same grind as all the others, then I'll be done for. I can see it in my older sister. I don't understand Claudia since she got married. She calls for her husband the minute she has the slightest little problem. I said to her once, "Come on, let's take off, let's put the kids to bed and go swimming or dancing or something." And she enjoyed it so much! Until her husband said to me, "You're ruining my wife." Isn't that something? Claudia already has a complex that nobody wants to dance with her—and she had so many admirers, she's the best-looking of us sisters. She's going to end up like all the others, when they get old they wail "Oh, if only I'd done this, and why didn't I do that?" After all, I could have stayed with my first guy, too, I cared a lot for him. But the moment it was settled, I thought, Hey, now I have to do something for him in return. That's how guys could get me into bed so quick. I just wasn't good at saying no. But you mustn't put up with surrenders, not on either side. Many boys even accepted my faults, then it was too much for me. Another weird thing about me is that if I need a guy a lot, the way I needed Bert back then, then I need to show him that I don't need him. Then I go dancing with other guys, and no one understands that. I don't either. Maybe I want to prove to myself that I don't want to live like other people. One time I hurt a guy so much doing that, that he got drunk and said to his pals: "She's dead as far as I'm concerned, I won't put up with it." Maybe he just didn't want to knuckle under.

I always wanted to be a boy. They can do what they want and nobody interferes. If a girl changes partners pretty often, right away she gets a bad reputation, especially with the girls. They have no opinions of their own, they're so terribly adaptable, they always rank themselves lower. At home I could never go into a bar alone. Susanne got away with it, but with her looks you can get away with anything. People simply don't believe that all a girl wants is to sit down and drink her beer. "Oh, did you get stood up?" That's how they read it. Actually I have no desire to go to a bar alone, my only concern is that I should be able to if I want to. These freedoms that one has or doesn't have as a matter of principle, are very important to me. If I hadn't joined that clique, no doubt I wouldn't have learned so much from watching the boys. They all believe that girls aren't to be taken seriously, they're only there to sleep with, and for fun. And I saw how well they get along on that basis. I wanted to be that way, too. Although there also are some guys who love a woman they sleep with. Only that involves obligations, and that scares me. I must say that sometimes I simply need to go to bed with someone. Susanne wouldn't understand that, or Claudia either. And yet it's quite natural. Why shouldn't women have that right? I have simply taken it.

Maybe you're right. Sometimes one needs a man friend one can talk to. But basically I don't sleep with men friends I can talk to, no matter how much they want it. If you can talk to somebody and sleep with him, that's already love, and I'm afraid of it. I smoke like a chimney. I do everything like a man—drink, smoke, change partners, be lazy. At the same time I know it's not good for me. I don't know how I changed from a shy girl into the person I am now!

The first time I kissed, a soldier brought me home, you always get those types. I was fifteen and started to bawl. I thought I was in trouble, although I knew the ropes. Then I met a guy by the Baltic Sea, he got terribly drunk, and meanwhile I lay down in his tent and said to myself, well I'll just wait, I'd like to know what happens. Naked. I didn't think anything was wrong with it. Suddenly he came in, looked at me, naturally he thought this girl wants something from me. And then I got so scared I shouted at him as if he were trying to kill me, and I took off. So, once again nothing happened. Then I met Charley. He hadn't ever slept with a girl, what could he teach me? But he had a friend who was experienced, you can tell about that sort of thing. Then I thought: You don't need to be afraid with him, and one night I stayed with him. Man, people always think it's something out of this world, but I was just mad. "Get lost," I said, and after that we didn't even say hello to each other. I didn't draw any conclusions right off, I thought maybe it was the boy's fault that I didn't like it, and then I tried it with Charley. Yes, I admit I did find one guy it was great with, but with him it was clear from the start that we only wanted to sleep together. I'd have liked to hold onto him. But a boy can practically sleep with every girl, why should he want to hold onto one?

Everywhere I see that we women come off badly. Our mama fired off a few rounds a while back. Somebody who didn't know her would think, What a liberated woman! But she only talks that way, she scolds and makes a fuss, and then she goes back to doing what Papa wants. Papa actually isn't the domineering type, he only wishes he were. Besides, he's so funny. But Mama herself is to blame, too. She could have made more out of her life. Papa didn't oppress her all that much. He adapted, too, and that turned into a vicious circle. Mama has this obsession, Hey, now we have a woman in the family who's qualified for university! She does so many things that she isn't keen on. She's obsessed with being liberated. She has felt oppressed for a long time, with lots of kids and the housework and never enough money. Now she'd like to get one up on Papa by doing everything that other women do: go to work, have a lover, join the Party. I'm a person who never beats around the bush, but Mama's view is: "Do everything that's asked of you and keep your mouths shut, kiddies, otherwise you'll never get ahead in the world." She's incredibly naive and anybody can influence her. Even as children we knew that if we said one thing, such-and-such would happen, and if we said something else, we could get something else to happen. That always annoyed us. If I wanted to pursue certain things, the best course was not to say anything at all and simply do them. I didn't really have a proper upbringing, in that sense. Of course there is the risk that you will spoil everything for yourself if you have so much freedom. We didn't get a lot of guidance. Books, yes. The books came with Papa, he read a lot himself. Susanne and I used to recommend books to each other. I expect now she'll read *The Sign of the Stones** and she'll be enthusiastic about it, too. It's about a young woman who comes to work in the synthetic rubber plant or some sort of men's factory like that. She meets a man there, he's married and a Party secretary. Later they go on and report that they have a relationship. Then he is expelled from the Party, even though he was so open with them. Also there's Balla, who wasn't for an East German state at all, to begin with. And in his work brigade they're all devil-may-care types, they do a great job in their work but otherwise they have no interest in anything. Balla falls out with the Party secretary, and it takes incredibly long before they get on the same wave length. Then Balla turns into a completely different person, he says he has read the "sign of the stones" from their beginnings. That was the first time I had an interest in a man who's not as young as me. To be honest, I have to admit I've fallen for a guy like that who works in our firm. He's almost forty, he's married too. Really masculine, sometimes gay and sometimes serious, with this fantastic vitality like somebody in the thick of life who can cope with anything. And then again, he's so concerned and paternal and takes responsibility for everything. After all, who worried about me at work? I came there, they gave me some brief instructions, and then I was left to myself. The women are much older than I am and only talk about their children or what they are cooking on Sunday. Only this man bothered about me. Unless he behaves like a creep to his family, he must see that it won't work with me, even if I do make eyes at him. Besides, he's not handsome, he has wrinkles already and he's too short for me. I believe he thinks he's a father to me. But I'm not a child any more, I have quite different feelings. Or don't you agree?

Translated by Jan van Heurck

---

*Popular 1964 novel by Erik Neutsch, later made into a film.

Sarah Kirsch

A Remarkable Example of
Determination in Woman

Frau Schmalfuss was twenty-eight and did not have any children yet. The reasons were as follows:

It is a commonly held view that every woman has six small beauties. This assertion apparently is borne out by statistics, but like all statistical claims, it does not apply to each individual case. Frau Schmalfuss had four beauties: (1) slanting eyes whose corners reached right to the hair line, (2) hands which deserved to be painted, (3) a rear end with a tidy and well-balanced curve, (4) her legs. Unfortunately, her legs ended perpendicularly in long, broad, low but not flat feet. Although these four beauties, taken each on its own, were such that many another woman might envy them, and now and then did so, their arrangement relative to each other was so unfavorable, and the distance separating one beauty from the next was so extensive, that the disturbing elements in between overshadowed them and drove away the glances which would have realized their beauty if they had lingered longer. For this reason, Frau Schmalfuss had been unable to form an intimate association with any man.

A person's good points do not have to be exclusively physical. Her colleagues and co-workers regularly showed marks of respect to Frau Schmalfuss for her work performance and her comradely behavior. In the canteen they would comment, "You have to admire the effort she makes!" or "She could have used a bit more luck!" In unsupervised moments, on summer evenings as she made her way home, or under the shower, she would sometimes confess to herself that she would have preferred less respect. Once when she was walking through the allotment gardens, an old man, apparently drunk, was swearing at his wife behind a hedge of lilac. She felt that she would have liked to change places with this woman for the fraction of a second. But she had herself firmly under control, and she looked for happiness in work. In her hallway hung documents certifying her as a winner of competitions, an activist, and a graduate of a number of training courses. Because she had no husband and children as yet, her colleagues, without having given it much thought, considered her especially suited to represent them at official and honorary functions. Her name was heard at every social occasion, she was called on for information, and at office Christmas parties she had for years played the role of Knecht Ruprecht, Santa's assistant, handing out presents to the children of employees in the various departments.

She fulfilled all the tasks imposed on her conscientiously and without deriving any personal advantage.

In March of last year, she put on her baggy camel-hair coat, which she wore when she visited new mothers on behalf of the women's committee, and took a Number 17 bus into the suburbs. When she had dropped off the little package, adding some tiny mittens which she had knitted herself, and stood once again on the narrow concrete path that wound between the houses and gardens, she felt strangely stirred. The snowdrops were swaying, the iris were pushing up the soil, water was running along the trunks of the bare trees, wind-driven black clouds raced at the antennas, and in the middle of this churned-up, joyous landscape she would have liked to see a little white baby carriage and feel that she was the one pushing it: her knees still weak after her recent delivery, and her back aching pleasantly from nursing the baby or from washing diapers every day.

From then on, images like this presented themselves to her more often. She would look into every baby carriage, and on the one hand she felt satisfied if she could just glimpse the hint of something small down under the covers, protected in its hollow, while on the other hand it annoyed her that the object of her affection hid from her in this manner. When she realized the state she was in, which of course was merely psychological and not physical, she decided to do something about it.

She proposed a theory that obligated her personally to be even more useful to society than she had been before. I earn good money, she reckoned. I have a modern, well-furnished two-room apartment. I have undertaken a number of major trips, once into a neighboring socialist country. It would be irresponsible to continue living such a selfish life. Yes, she wanted to have a child.

Frau Schmalfuss was not thinking about marriage. If she had been unable to move anyone to such a step in the past, how could she succeed now, when her early youth lay behind her, when she had become an independent person, and when, as a result of living alone for a long time, she had acquired idiosyncrasies which she could no longer get rid of, and which would no doubt prove detrimental to a marriage? But what she did do was to mentally review a large number of men, letting them file one by one past her beautiful slanting eyes: all the men she knew who were of an age to beget children, and whom she respected deeply for their industriousness and honest conduct. Friedrich Vogel, the manager of the foundry division, carried off the victory palm. He was unmarried and had a very attractive physique. Thus she would not need to engage in adultery, even though her purpose of serving society would in her opinion have entitled her to do so; and she could rest assured that she had done all she could, in good conscience, to select a father with above average qualities of character and body, for her future child. For she believed in heredity, as well as in the influence of a socialist environment on the child whom she was designing, so to speak, on the drawing board.

A not insignificant element in her choice was the fact that Friedrich Vogel had a wooden leg. He had mastered his situation so well that he ran around like any other man of his age, even when the weather shifted and caused him pain, and even when the streets were covered with ice. His prosthesis was not a flaw in her eyes, on the contrary; and she believed that it would make it easier for her to carry out her plan.

She decided not to make any claims, either financial or nonmaterial, on the father of her child. She would be the one to raise her son or daughter, and she considered telling the child a credible story to explain the absence of its progenitor. Perhaps he had been killed in an auto accident? Or had he been a soldier on border patrol, slain by an enemy bullet? But of course there were many families which consisted only of a mother and child. And why shouldn't Friedrich Vogel appear on the scene one day—the social-ist coming-of-age ceremony for young people was the traditional occasion—and give the child a valuable wristwatch?

Yes, that was the solution. Because Frau Schmalfuss's heart pounded with alarm when she thought of pushing the child's father under a car—even if she only did it with words—-or exposing him to enemy attack. She had spent so much time thinking about Friedrich Vogel that she felt warm and tender feelings for him whenever he came to mind. And although she had not yet acted on any of her plans, a time began for her when her eyes filled with joy during the day and she had strange dreams at night. She who, once all her work and social responsibilities were over, used to fall quickly into dreamless sleep and then got up again, now dreamed of bizarre landscapes and rooms with staircases in them. In the morning she would try to remember, to hold on to the pleasurable state of her dream—but what had it actually been about? A giant avenue of poplars, huge pedestals—but she lacked all the prerequi-sites for interpreting such dreams, and actually had no idea what to make of them. So she felt amazed and forgot what she had seen.

Now she had to move on to action. Frau Schmalfuss bought a collection of bright colored scarves, every day she tied a different one around her head and appeared in the foundry. The crane driv-ers whistled, she climbed through haze and heat carrying all sorts of paperwork, and cornered Friedrich Vogel in the coremaking section. They would sit down in front of the molding sand and talk about union business. Frau Schmalfuss hinted that she would like to talk with Vogel about another matter of pressing import to society, but not here where there was so much noise.

"Where?" Friedrich Vogel asked. "Maybe at my place? We won't be disturbed and we can drink a sloe vodka." He had intended this as a joke. Her head scarf bulged in such a quixotic way over her slanting eyes, twists of it flowed down her neck, and the black lozenges had a gay look. But then "OK!" said Frau Schmalfuss, "I wouldn't mind not seeing the plant for a while," and she moved her beautiful hands into full view.

They agreed to meet in the evening, which could help to further her plan. But how should she proceed? What words should she use to make her request? Ought she simply to trust in the sloe vodka which Vogel meant to serve? That would be inconsiderate to a colleague. There was no way around it, she would have to give him an explanation.

In the days before their appointment, Frau Schmalfuss attended anxiously to her work, made a thorough inspection of her wardrobe, took in a skirt to the express drycleaners, bought a red pullover. And each evening before going to sleep, she would compose the words to address to Friedrich Vogel, only to discard them again the next day.

She did not want to leave the creation of her child to chance. On the other hand, she did not feel glib-tongued enough to convince Friedrich Vogel on a single evening. And what if he wanted to visit her again? She forbade herself to think about that, her apartment was too small for three people. But she would see him every day at work. "Oh nonsense," she said, and she told herself that all that was necessary was to present everything the right way, that would eliminate any embarrassment.

The evening arrived, it happened to be a Wednesday. But she did not put on the skirt and the new pullover as she had planned, but rather a lightweight, feminine woolen dress. She draped her coat and pocketbook over her arm and walked to Vogel's apartment.

There was a small hallway with the kitchen on the right, then straight ahead stood the door into the main room. The furniture was a standard model, the armchair where Vogel led her was upholstered in black and yellow. Friedrich had gone into the kitchen. She looked along the walls: a quantity of books, Amundsen, a volume on the polar ice caps, von Humboldt's account of his travels—probably the child would turn out to be a boy—and in between, pictures pasted together from straw, showing ships and palm trees against a black background. Her host returned with a tray and steaming glasses of tea. Yes, he said, he had made the pictures himself. You soaked straw, split and pressed it, and glued it into the pattern you wanted. He went to a cabinet with many drawers, opened the top one, took out a picture and handed it to Frau Schmalfuss. This time, very pale straw piled up behind the glass to form massive glaciers by a frozen sea, and a background of ice was riddled with black fissures. An icebreaker, a heavy vessel made of dark straw, seemed to roll forward laboriously, and a red-ink sun was glued above the glaciers.

"Here, I treated plastic drinking straws the same way as the straw," Friedrich Vogel explained. "You have to be very careful when you're ironing them." He gave her the picture of the icebreaker as a present, and she took it as a good omen. Later, she would tell her son: "Your father is doing difficult, responsible work on a vessel of this kind at the North Pole, surrounded by polar bears." But right now, the father was not yet the father.

Frau Schmalfuss yanked herself out of her dreams and asked for a sloe vodka, because she needed a bit of support to put her proposition to the man. This time, Friedrich Vogel opened the lowest drawer and took out a bottle which he placed on the table. Both had partaken only moderately of the tea, Frau Schmalfuss because she was afraid of getting herself too keyed up, Friedrich Vogel because he had only served the tea thinking it was appropriate to a visit from a woman.

"She's really a lovely person," he thought, and looked her up and down. "So, what's the problem?" he asked, and she looked down at her feet and felt the blood rise from the center of her body up into her face. She sighed and started to talk—rapidly, so as to get to the end before he could say anything.

"Oh, Friedrich, we've known each other a long time. We both began to work at the plant on a small scale, before it started into the export business. Now the pumps we make go all the way to Guinea. But that's not what I wanted to say. I was just thinking that I've run around the world a bit too, almost as if I were on a big ship like your icebreaker. Well, I went to Murmansk once, and I earn good money . . ." She talked and talked, and tugged herself slowly through her trips, her prosperity, her apartment, her social responsibility, until she reached the point: ". . . so I really must have a child, and I thought you would see the sense in it and and produce the child, completely without obligations, I'll let you have that in writing!"

Friedrich Vogel felt rather as if he had been struck by lightning. Although he did not cease to respect Frau Schmalfuss after this proposal, on the contrary found it quite moral, and was even flattered by her reasons for choosing him, all the same he could not hide from himself the fact that he felt she was asking a bit too much of him. The case was too exceptional, he knew of no precedents from which he could draw support. He simply lacked the tradition. He drank no more vodka that evening, turned on the television shortly after, and watched a film about penguins with Frau Schmalfuss. "You know," he said to his colleague as he escorted her out of the apartment, "I have to think all this over thoroughly. Perhaps we can do as you say, perhaps not. Give me a week to consider it. I'll tell you next Wednesday."

Days went by. Frau Schmalfuss read pocket books about reduced-pain childbirth, and looked forward with suspense to Wednesday. Vogel's friendly, understanding words had made her happy and led her to think that her plan was feasible. But on Wednesday, Vogel did not appear, nor on Thursday, and on Friday she went to the foundry. She did not find Friedrich: he was in the scrapyard, he was walking across the track, he was unloading steel rods, he was in the office of the editor of their plant newspaper. She looked for him on the days that followed, called for him over the plant telephone, waited in the manager's office, scouted out various meetings. Vogel had flown the coop. It was not hard to guess why. All the same, it surprised her that he had not given her his refusal on Wednesday. In the canteen, she heard rumors that after quitting time, Friedrich Vogel was laying wall-to-wall carpeting at Elvira's place. Elvira worked in the lathe operator's section. Yes, she was always a lot of fun. Frau Schmalfuss went home feeling perplexed, went over to the couch and looked for a long time at the picture of the icebreaker. But she could not make up her mind to throw it away, she had too rarely received a personal gift.

"Everyone wants to see an example," Frau Schmalfuss said to herself, "but no one wants to give one." Also, it was a mistake to have approached Friedrich Vogel honestly. She would have done better, she thought, to have trusted to the sloe vodka rather than to reason. She compensated for her sadness by working diligently and doing overtime, and during that quarter period, her electricity bill was so low that the cashier had her meter checked.

Then summer began. The heat attacked her ferociously in the plant, in vehicles, from buildings, and she could take several cold showers a day and yet not rid herself of the feeling that she was going around dressed in fur.

One Sunday when the windows were open and it was ninety degrees Fahrenheit, Frau Schmalfuss was lying on the couch under the picture of the icebreaker. A lawn sprinkler was turned on outside the building, in an effort to save some newly-planted shrubs from drying up. It hurled the jet of water into the air, the drops burst and spattered, the water cannon revolved, squeaked and tossed the innumerable drops up into the air once again. Half asleep, Frau Schmalfuss saw the avenue of poplars, jumped up, quickly closed the window and ran out of the house. She took the subway into the city, sat there in a cafe, heard falling water again, this time from a fountain, hurried to the zoo, listened to the peacocks screaming as if they were mad. She came very near to walking off with a baby carriage that was standing on the terrace. The baby had laughed at her, raised its little fists in her direction and showed her its toes: ten pink peas.

On Monday she telephoned work to say that she could not come in today, and she went to a doctor.

He was a gynecologist, an old professor who gave his clients a feeling of confidence and was obsessed with bringing lots of children into the world. She believed that if she underwent a thorough examination and found that everything was all right and that she was quite capable of carrying and bearing a child, her problem would soon be solved. She would then have met a good eighty-five percent of the preconditions for having a child, and this would weigh more heavily on one side of the scale than the remaining fifteen percent would weigh on the other side. It would send the fifteen percent up with a jolt—Frau Schmalfuss could actually picture the scales jumping, and the lighter one turning a somersault— so that the fifteen percent would hop out of its container and join the heavier side.

In the waiting room, she saw the pretty women in their billowing clothes. "Oh dear, I'm feeling nauseous!" said one, "I haven't got that far yet!" said another. Frau Schmalfuss went into the doctor's office barefoot, having taken off some of her underwear in the changing room as prescribed, and as she shook hands with the doctor she said: "Hello. I want a child." The old gentleman was glad, looked at her and thought about what to reply. He led her to the chair where you sit on your back, and examined her thoroughly.

"There's no reason why you shouldn't have one," he said, and noted the topography of her four beauties. So, she in fact possessed the requisite eighty-five percent, while at the same moment the other fifteen percent vanished from view. But no doubt she had been dreaming. She asked the doctor about the results of research on artificial insemination. "The experiments have proved successful. Yes indeed, it's certainly possible!" said the old doctor and nodded. "We can talk more about it, young woman," he went on, and took her hand.

When she left the changing room, she did not go back into the doctor's office but walked home under the trees. Old plane trees which had been so cropped in the winter that nothing was left of them but the trunks, were now sprouting prodigiously, somewhat later than usual but with even larger leaves. The trees had shed some of their bark, their trunks looked like maps of river estuaries.

And what about heredity? How could you know what you were getting? What about the fun, the passionate embrace? Once again, there was a lack of examples. Well, of course there was the Virgin Mary. She read Luke's gospel in her apartment, found it all very complicated, decided to rank heredity far below the influence of the environment, and made up her mind to adopt a child.

The effort involved in an adoption was considerable, too. She filed an application, had the agency view her apartment, obtained a health certificate from a female doctor, her firm wrote out testimonials, and throughout the summer she waited hopefully for a decision.

But there were many people trying to adopt children, and all of them wanted a child of the tenderest age, so that difficulties and waiting periods resulted, and Frau Schmalfuss could not yet purchase any tiny shirts, jackets and hats, because she did not yet know either the size or the sex of the baby.

Finally—just when she was on the point of taking a three-year-old child, when she was ready to give up the experience of a baby's first steps and first clumsy phrases addressed to her, to give up having it when it was still toothless and helpless—a miracle happened. In the autumn, the social worker rang her bell and told her that they had found a boy two months old, a handsome child with black hair and large nostrils. "You're an angel!" cried Frau Schmalfuss and wanted to go out and fetch the boy at once.

But a child does not come so quickly, not even when you know that it is definitely on the way. It takes nine months, or seven, or at least another three months as it did for Frau Schmalfuss. Twice a week, she attended a course for expectant mothers to learn about infant care. In order not to miss any lessons, she was forced to disappoint the chief accountant, who had expected her help in drawing up the final accounts after closing time. So she felt dejected while she was testing the water temperature and bathing the large plastic dolls, and while she learned to prepare the many small meals or how to wrap the lower legs in hot compresses. On those Saturdays when she did not have to work, she journeyed to various districts of the city to buy all the things the child would need in the first stage of his life, chief among them being an imported baby carriage, a light-blue plastic bathtub, underwear and rattles. Once a month she was allowed to visit the state orphanage to see the child who would be hers. (The final adoption would take place after a year's trial.) He was put into a carriage, and Frau Schmalfuss was able to stroll around with him in the park under the beech trees. First the leaves were green, then they turned color, and finally only a few were left and looked like leather.

These were now the hours when she felt happy. At work, things were different. Her good reputation had suffered, not because a colleague had observed her buying a baby carriage—after all, the directors knew about the intended adoption and were obliged to approve it—but because her co-workers could no longer give Frau Schmalfuss their unrestricted praise and approbation. She would go home almost on the dot, she put in less overtime when there was a deadline to meet, and her account statements were less detailed than previously. The head of her department, and the shop stewards, now refrained from asking her advice and assistance. And all this was happening before she even had the child in her home. It made her suffer, and on top of it there was the waiting period for the baby. So she became nervous and would easily fly into a rage. Occasionally she would not take time to eat breakfast, then later she would race into the canteen, buy fish rolls and gobble them up. She behaved like a pregnant woman, and gave rise to comment. "This has to stop," Frau Schmalfuss said to herself one day. She had finished her course in child care and completed all the preparations. Now it was time to rejoin the life of her colleagues, in fact to enrich it. She decided to organize an art excursion, and studied brochures and catalogues for her project.

"Well done!" said her colleagues and co-workers during the bus ride, at the highway rest stop, and while looking at the Blue Wonder and the Kronentor Gate in the gallery: "Good for her, she's back to her old self again!" As they walked through various sections of the painting collection, Frau Schmalfuss enjoyed the gigantic still-life portraits—gleaming grapes, bursting pumpkins, on the side a bird's nest with two eggs in it and a third egg outside the

nest, broken, with a bright yellow yolk. She looked at the shifting
landscapes, the never-ending succession of trees that looked sometimes grim, sometimes friendly, and the varying skies above them.
She observed everything cheerfully and without concentration, and
did not linger by any of the paintings. They were stations along
the way to her goal. She looked at what was beautiful so as to be
able to endure the very beautiful. Coming to the naked woman
kissing the swan, Frau Schmalfuss walked faster to avoid feeling
any discomfort. A new hall opened before them. She felt her heart
stir, saw the picture on the rear wall and stepped to one side, letting
her colleagues pass her by. She did not listen to the explanation
from the tour guide, and prolonged the pleasure of anticipation.
When she was alone in the room, she sought out the best vantage
point and then looked up at the woman. The cloak was an even
more beautiful blue than the reproduction in her calendar. The
second woman and the old pope were sinking away into the clouds.
The Madonna was lighter, you could see each of her toes, even
though she was carrying the weight of the child. The woman with
the child looked approachable, not especially holy, almost like one
of Frau Schmalfuss's women colleagues. Her husband was not in
the picture, he played no role. Frau Schmalfuss remembered having
read in the Bible that Joseph had required a sign from heaven
before he would accept the pregnant Mary as his wife. Today, Mary
would have stayed alone, thought Frau Schmalfuss. And then all
she could feel was her hands, as if all her blood had flowed to that
one place; she felt the child, nothing else. His skin was warm,
slightly damp after his bath, and seemed to smell of soap. The
baby had to be dressed first, on the way to the changing table. A
glance in the mirror as she went by. From the corners of her eyes.
Pressing the child against her. She saw him and herself in the mirror, and was startled by her own beauty.

The identification was so brief that it did not surprise Frau
Schmalfuss but only gave her joy. She followed her colleagues,
purchased an illustrated book about the gallery, and set out for the
Italian Village. The fountains were taking a winter break. The
street lamps switched on in a long-drawn-out movement, and the
first snow began to fall. The sky was white, the snowflakes looked
gray or black by comparison. We need a sleigh, thought Frau
Schmalfuss.

In mid–December, the first snowfall was followed by a second and a third. Owing to Christmas, a personnel shortage in the orphanage and her own persistence, Frau Schmalfuss was able to take the child home with her, even though not all the formalities were completed. In the evening she sat in the kitchen, and instead of drinking a beer as had been her habit until a few days ago, she drank two cups of milk. A whole day was spent in doing everything that the director of her child-care class deemed useful and essential for a five-month-old baby, and then some. She wondered whether people at her plant would bring her a gift as they did to other new mothers, and who would come to call on her. She had taken an unpaid leave from work and was unaware that her colleagues had agreed on the usual sum of money, and had already assembled her gifts (sleeping bag, set of child's cutlery, and soft shoes). She felt tired and happy. The flickering images from her TV hardly reached her: Every day for two years, a woman brings her child to the day nursery, every day she travels two commuter train stations to reach the place and two commuter train stations back; walks up and down four flights of stairs; four strangers, men or women, help her to carry the baby carriage. Sometimes people scramble to get the carriage, and now and then the woman has to wait. One time she thinks: "People in the culture department should introduce a new superstition: *whoever carries a baby carriage in the morning has good luck all day.*"

She was going to experience all of that.

Translated by Jan van Heurck

Irina Liebmann

Sibylle N.

A young woman with bouncy black curls opens the door, a tiny baby curled up like a caterpillar in her arms. The mother streaks energetically into the living room ahead of me wearing a snug sweater with a belt buckled tight at the waist, a full skirt. Sibylle N. is enjoying her child-care year and is always glad to receive visitors.

Immediately she tells me about all the furnishings in the apartment. The bright-colored children's furniture belongs to her, and so do the kitchen things. She is only telling me this to set things straight, she says, because when a person has been through hard times she turns cautious, and besides, "I'm only staying here."

Her own apartment is one room in the Berlin district of Pankow, but she has been living in this other apartment since 1978, when she met Bernd, an auto mechanic. This two-room place was granted to him after his divorce. Sibylle is divorced, too.

After looking at the apartment, we sit down at the table. "You can write better here," Sibylle says and asks if I know Bernau, which is her home town. She grew up in a single-family house with a garden—"No comparison to here!" she says, and rolls her eyes briefly.

In Bernau, Sibylle trained to be a nurse, got married, had a child, and got a divorce. Then she moved to Berlin, to the room in Pankow. This apartment in the rear of the building tops off the list, so small, so dreary, and only one tree.

By now they have installed a shower and hot water, the door frames are painted white, the walls hung with bright wallpaper, and the floor is lined with green felt. The door onto the balcony stands open, the sun is shining down onto the baby carriage.

Sibylle sees that I like it and is glad. But "It's not a permanent solution," she says.

She knows what would be a permanent solution: a two-room apartment in the front of a building along the tree-lined Pappel-allee, with a bathroom and storeroom: "After all, I am alone with two children."

Right now while we are talking, her boyfriend is working in the new apartment. He has already gilded the stucco, the apartment is turning into a dream of a place.

Sibylle's boyfriend wants to marry her, but she doesn't want to. The plan is for him to keep this apartment where we are sitting, even if it means that she has to work more. That is how important it is to her to have the possibility of being alone when she wants to.

"Do you think that's wicked?" she asks in a slightly coquettish way. But I think it's fine!

"He and I are not really apart," she says.

Sibylle was twenty-four when she got divorced. Hers was the first divorce in her extensive family. Her mother ends every sentence she speaks to her daughter with the phrase: "After all, you are divorced."

"I was fed up with that," Sibylle said, "and with the shift work in the hospital, too." She moved to Berlin and found other work, as the checkroom attendant in a government ministry.

In the checkroom you meet journalists, diplomats, politicians. But receptions are not held nonstop, so you have to be a cleaning woman, too.

Her work zone is described as "The banqueting-hall area."

By now Sibylle has passed a second technical exam and qualified as a window and building cleaner. After her maternity leave, she will be earning more than her boyfriend.

Her area includes some seventy rooms. Straightening the furniture, emptying the wastebaskets, vacuuming, dusting, cleaning the windows twice a year—that is her work. By now she knows all the women secretaries, and also the peculiarities of their boss. There is no shift work, but there are special bonuses. What could be nicer?

"I want to enjoy my life," Sibylle says. "I don't have any psychological problems, being a cleaning woman."

The doorbell rings. Her little daughter has come home from school. She does not have to go to the day nursery and she can eat at home, too. Sibylle has cooked meatballs, potatoes and vegetables. She sets the table for the little girl, who is wearing a red-and-white checked summer dress.

Sibylle herself will not eat until her boyfriend comes, and she goes on talking about her workplace. It's really terrific that nobody is looked down on there, she says. In fact it is just the opposite. One time she helped to lay out the food in the banqueting hall, and when the reception began, she went to take one last look at the buffet with its beautiful dishes and salads while it was still intact. Then Willi Stoph came over to her and said: "Hey little one, don't you have any champagne?" and he gave her his glass.

"Of course you don't forget that kind of thing," Sibylle says.

She does not look down on anyone either, she tells me. She likes to talk with foreigners whom she has met at work, she has listened to what they said about Vietnam, about Portugal, and she remembers especially clearly a Chilean man who said: "If only our women were as advanced as you!"

"It's true," Sibylle says. "We've changed so much in the last few years. We do what we want to!"

Her boyfriend had said the same thing not long ago: "You women are impossible. You do what you want!"

For example, her child on the balcony there, two months old, is a wanted child. Her boyfriend wanted to have another child of his own, and Sibylle thought it was a good idea, too. But she has not gotten married because of it.

"We love each other," she says, and laughs. She has calculated that she alone with the two children—that is, with the support money for two children—would have about a thousand marks a month. She could live really well on that, couldn't she?

In the small bedroom stands a wooden cradle for the new child. The older child has finished eating and is sitting next to her mother, her hands lying on the table top. One can see that they are Sibylle's hands—very narrow with tapering fingers. The daughter is tiny, she does not look like a seven-year-old schoolgirl. Sibylle does not look like a thirty-year-old cleaning manager.

They sit opposite me and giggle a lot as they talk, both with angular shoulders and smooth white faces.

The baby on the balcony is a girl, too.

Translated by Jan van Heurck

Angela Stachowa

This Winter

This winter, Teresa has brought order into her life. She intends to meet the cold, damp, snow, overcrowded streetcars and all other injustices with composure and dignity.

Regularity is the hallmark of this winter. Teresa always swims, takes walks, rides her bike to the sauna on the same day of the week, at the same time of day. Every day she sleeps for ten hours. She goes to bed with the chickens and gets up correspondingly early. She is satisfied with herself: such a healthy life, at this rate she will live to be eighty. Last winter, when her life crashed down around her ears, she thought now and then that she would live to be forty at most. Teresa hurriedly represses thoughts that sometimes occur to her, such as: If you live like a chicken, don't you turn into one eventually?

This is a restful winter. She does not tell the man she was with all summer: "Please understand, Fritz needs me so much." Nor does she let Franz accuse her of keeping Ferdinand on the back burner to move into Franz's place when she gets tired of him. And she no longer goes to bed with Filip merely because for weeks on end he has proved to her each day how he suffers when she does not go to bed with him.

This winter, like all the winters before this, her last winter's lovers introduce their new sweethearts to her saying, "This time, it's for keeps." And they demonstrate this to her in graphic terms, while Teresa meanwhile smiles her old-maidish smile: God bring you happiness, dear children. Then next day she goes swimming early, she storms across the twenty-five-meter basin at the public swimming pool as if she were trying to break a record. The other, peaceful morning swimmers move out of her way in shock, they have only seen her when she was quiet.

Teresa has shown forethought and has dealt with all the loose ends of summer in the autumn, in preparation for this winter.

On the winter weekends, she takes the Number 29 bus each afternoon out to the forestry lodge at Kaschwitz and chases through the woods for hours. That gives her time to think. The fact that her thoughts revolve exclusively around Friedrich, is something that does not please her about this winter, but it probably cannot be changed.

This winter, there are no dissolute weekends when two people spend the period of Friday to Sunday evening almost uninterruptedly together in bed. Also, there are none of the heart-rending good-byes when the weekends are over. As compensation, she gets to skip those hours on Sunday evenings when, freezing and trembling, she would run for miles to get home from the railway station. In a metropolis like this, and with snow to boot, you can no longer get a taxi at that hour, and she had to take the very last train.

This winter, she does not wait with deadly despair in her heart for the telephone to ring, she does not lift the receiver time after time to make sure that the phone is still connected. This winter, she knows who will phone her, and above all she knows that the calls will not cause her heart to pound any more than is normal.

Teresa rarely dreams this winter, and when she does, the dreams are friendly. There is nothing like the dreams of last winter, in which every night while she was wrapping packages, she would fall into the water, be caught immediately by a whirlpool and get sucked down deeper and deeper, until at last her head disappeared under the surface while she gasped for air. The awfullest part were the variations in this dream that came when he was sleeping beside her. In the morning, he would sometimes tell her that during the night she had once again called out words that he could not understand.

This is no longer a winter in which Teresa lies on the sofa, wounded, and really wants nothing except to die. Nor one in which she races back and forth in agitation, and feels so bitter that she can hardly breathe: This man knew exactly what he needed to say to her, to hurt her deep inside. (Of course she was an expert in that, too.) Two days later, their telegrams kept crisscrossing at regular intervals: "Please come, I need you."

Now there are no more of those confrontations when everything in Teresa would rebel as he said in his irritating, factual tone: "Human beings are bad, bad. If you weaken and fall down, you get devoured." And now Teresa no longer has to shout back: "No, they are good!" and pound him with her fists as a way to defend her belief in the goodness of man. (Besides, she did not want to think about the possibility that in fact it was not so simple, after all.)

This is a serious winter, stripped of any excess of emotion when it comes to dealing with fundamental issues. Once again, Teresa has only her books, where things are clear, known and unharmful.

This winter, every argument will not end with him blaming and accusing her of having grown up with a book in her hand, dreaming behind a high white wall, while meanwhile he was running his head against the wall on the other side, or no, worse yet, while others grabbed his head and rammed it against the wall.

This winter, Teresa is not continually forced to call herself and everything else into question. (But she is shocked to notice that this has turned into a habit.)

Teresa is very hardworking this winter. She finishes every task with care and precision, with the correctness and the accuracy that she loves. She has the infallible sense that every project she tackles succeeds. Teresa is up to date on the secondary literature and things of that kind. So there is no possibility, this winter, that the same thing will happen that happened so often last winter—that with a snap of his fingers he managed to keep her busy from dawn to dusk so that she had to face twenty students unprepared, and during the hour's lecture, which she delivered with an air of confidence, her only fear was that someone might stand up and ask her a question, and then everything would fall apart. But oddly enough, this winter she does not get any more done than last winter, when everything seemed merely a slide from one disaster to the next.

Now, Teresa attends opera performances and concerts every week, and tries to get used to the public, who are so preoccupied with themselves. Last winter, the two of them went to the movies one time at most; usually they were too tired. Once she even fell asleep in the train with her mouth wide open. Friedrich thought that was just darling.

This winter she spends a long time, morning and night, doggedly doing calisthenics in front of the open window. She makes sure that she eats moderately, mostly apples, bananas and corn flakes. Before, she had no time even to think about stuff like that.

Teresa does not forget the birthdays of any of her relatives, replies almost immediately to all letters, and actually sends Christmas cards to all her friends.

Much more often than in all past winters, Teresa is seized by the compulsion to go shopping. Then she cannot help running from one store to the next, she climbs up to every floor of the downtown department store, rides the escalator from the ground up to the sixth floor at The Consumer, and rummages and burrows and buys. A day later, she does not want to ever look again at the stuff that she finally took home.

Teresa bothers to take care of her place again. Once again, she has the apartment all to herself. And she no longer gets slightly irritated the way she did when he was present in it for more than a week at a time. During those spells he would plaster the walls with posters and dubious slogans. Teresa no longer has to pick up objects that he has scattered around the room, or fastidiously gather overflowing ashtrays and hurl them into the bin. Also, she no longer scrubs thick layers of dust off the cabinets, groaning. This winter, she goes over objects with the dustcloth every day.

Sometimes Teresa feels she has been released on parole to go home to her pale yellow, imitation flat-varnished furniture. This winter—she is bored.

Translated by Jan van Heurck

Christine Wolter

I Have Married Again

I have gotten married again. This news has surprised my friends, the ones who know me well. To be exact, no real marriage ceremony has taken place, the circumstances do not allow that. But our life together corresponds to all the principles of a modern marriage, which is supposed to be based on mutual affection and respect and to assist in rearing children to be harmonious human beings.

The children are what concerned us both. My concern was for Martin, four years old, very intelligent and very attached to me—too attached, because in the long run it was impossible for me to work with Martin sitting in my lap for hours, believing that whenever I went to my desk, the whole purpose of it was to hold him. Also, Martin was a bit neglected; I keep forgetting to cut his hair, so that strangers take him for a girl. Rosa brought Ines, two years older than Martin, a sweet, solicitous girl, an ideal playmate for Martin. Ines needed a family. Rosa was so gentle that she sometimes had put up with too much from Ines, but that will not do in my house.

I met Rosa by chance; she came from other circles than mine. If I had not met Rosa, my life would never have gotten back to normal. Things are a bit wild in my circles, I don't know why that is. Perhaps we all try to meet the extraordinary demands of our work with an extraordinary private life—so extraordinary that it corresponds to everyone else's. Actually, one cannot call them circles, that sounds closed, solid. It's more a matter of fields, which—

to stick with the technical jargon—continually shift. I had assured these fields that I would never remarry, and they had all accepted it.

My life with T. was a model. People used to envy us. No one guessed what gradually sprouted in the cultivated atmosphere of our apartment, among the antique furniture and the few good pictures. From the seeds of dissatisfaction grew—if I may keep to the metaphor—an impenetrable hedge. A sort of aversion developed, to use the jargon. Was it because we both were at the height of our powers, because we had to continually advance in our professions, had to be creative? I can only speak for myself here, because in general I prefer to stick to definite facts, to clearly distinguish hypotheses from what is proven: that is part of my nature and of my profession. Experiments indicate that aversion leads on to explosive separation. Possibly the problem was that our energies were directed along the same lines. We matched each other in experience, education, talent. T. wanted and was capable of the same things I was. Suddenly, T. began to do nothing but lie in front of the television, without doing a lick of work in the apartment. I could not accept this in the long term. T. refused to do the laundry, even though we had a beautiful washing machine—(I still have it, Rosa was thrilled when she saw it)—and claimed that a certain degree of creative leisure was essential, whereas uncreative leisure was unacceptable during this segment of life, which was so important for professional creativity. T. explained all this to me while smoking and lying on the couch, and grew calmer and calmer while I raced back and forth in the apartment, bumping into furniture that had never stood in my way before.

I became increasingly irritable. Actually, no loud words were heard between us, we were both too matter-of-fact and too objective for that. The explosion did not take an acoustic form, but it happened. I knew that T. was working under pressure. But was it really T.'s right just to watch television in the evening, or produce little oil paintings with bits of toys mounted on them, leftovers from Martin's toy chest? The laundry, the tidying up and cleaning that we had shared in the past, was left to me. It was not a lot, but I got sick of it because I had to do it while T. had managed to slip out of the trap of household chores. I consider it very desirable to work out physically, but I would have preferred to go back to the tennis club or go bowling.

T. took charge of other things. For example, T. decided who could use the car. Imperceptibly, I was excluded from joint owner- ship and made incapable of driving. T. would make ironic remarks. Every time I drove the car, I was supposed to wash it. T. had lots of ideas to keep me on the run. T. decided which social invitations we would accept, which parties we would attend at work and when I would stay home. To take care of Martin, T. said. I always had to go along to the boring evenings with T.'s work team, but when it came to people I liked, it turned out that I had to stay at home.

Suddenly T. disappeared. A love affair, people said, very passion- ate. They felt sorry for me.

I knew better. I walked with relief through the half-empty apart- ment, I aired it for days to let out the last traces of the smell of T.'s disgusting cigarettes. I don't know if it was good for T. that we separated.

Admittedly, there were a couple of unpleasant results for me, too. First with Martin. Naturally Martin needed T., too. And in our field of acquaintances, T. had pushed me to the margin, turned me into a companion figure. Everyone thought of us in combina- tion, I counted only if accompanied by T., as I noticed with an- noyance and dejection. It took a while before I rediscovered my old form.

I returned completely to my old self through Rosa, and I found Rosa by accident. I had taken a holiday place in the mountains for Martin and me. It snowed for two days, then the sun shone and I romped around with Martin outdoors all day. A little girl was standing shyly at the edge of our wild games. Step by step she came closer, rolled down the mountain with us as if by chance, hit me in the neck with a snowball as if it were unintentional, and let us both give her a good lather. She howled, ran away, came back. It was Ines, pampered and cowardly, but a good kid all the same. Ines lived with her mother in the same vacation lodge as we did. The two of them ate in a different dining hall, and I was glad of that because I do not like holiday friendships. I needed nothing but air and the wild battles and chases in the snow. I could not comfort a lonely woman. Rosa would sometimes walk by on the upper meadow path to the mountain where Martin, Ines and I were tram- pling down the snow. Our sled stood forgotten on the rim, we did not need it. Rosa and I would never have met, if one sunny after- noon when Martin and I had eaten a mountain of cake at the lodge and were starting outdoors again at once—if we had not found Ines outside the lodge with her mother and a heavy suitcase. Ines was crying, her mother was at a loss what to do. Their taxi had not come, and their train was due to leave the main town in half an hour. I fetched the car keys, we hurtled at fifty miles an hour along the icy curves where gravel had been strewn only at some spots. I was driving confidently again. Martin kept quiet, with an air of expertise. Between sobs, Ines asked all sorts of silly questions, talked about baby deer and hares, pinched Martin and asked every five minutes whether we could catch the train if I drove so slowly. We found the train standing in the station. I pushed Ines, the suitcase and the mother inside. As the train started up, the mother with her penetrating, gentle eyes asked for my address, and I murmured the street and the house number.

As we were returning to the lodge, I thought over what I had liked about the mother and what I had found so comforting in our race to the station. Rosa had not asked questions, not sighed, not looked at her watch. She looked attentively straight ahead as if she wanted to help me to drive fast and safely. She was too soft with Ines, I saw that, too. The girl needed a strong word now and then. But the beneficent stillness that emanated from Rosa stayed in my memory.

You will have noticed that I have not mentioned Rosa's outward appearance. It's true, back then I did not see her. I remember only Rosa's quietness, like a soft musical triad, like the distant pealing of bells that reached us in the snowy mountains on Sundays and made us stop our wild snow play for a moment. What was that? we wondered, because we could not hear it any more. When Rosa visited me later, I again had this elusive sensation.

Ines and Martin became friends. That is the best thing one can do for two only children.

The harmony at home is indescribable. I am completely back to my old self again. Rosa's nature radiates peace. She relieves me of many burdens, that's true, but she does it gladly, voluntarily. In return, I give her the security of a family, and my experience. I feel how serene I am, how the rows of formulas flow from my pencil. I am no longer smoking, I play tennis again, I no longer snap at Martin.

Each evening when I come home, I feel the change that Rosa has brought us. The children are playing in the living room. Rosa is puttering in the kitchen, there is a wonderful aroma of roast onion. I put my case away, set the table along with the children, and while Rosa is still tasting things to see if they need more seasoning, I almost enjoy tackling the children's torn trousers in the mending basket. By the time we eat, I manage to sew on at least two knee patches using a rapid cross-stitch.

Rosa knows me. She comes into the room and knows immediately what kind of day I had and whether my computations were successful. In the beginning I told her that I am a difficult person. She looked at me with her large eyes, smiling softly and nodded. Where does she get this talent? Her job as a head of retail sales is definitely not easy, but she behaves as if the daily throng of people in the store brought her ever-increasing peace and contentment.

We had some difficulties to start with, when Rosa and Ines moved in with us. They brought an incredible amount of junk, dust-covered bunches of chocolates, a ship in a bottle, two Dutch kitchen clocks, a collection of bright-colored rummer glasses, a guinea pig, a whole nation of dolls with beds and a cooking stove. It was all an alien presence in my cool, symmetrical apartment. But after a few weeks, this caravansary had already become part of our lives. I took down the abstract painting *Bird Cries* from the wall in the hall because it had grown foreign to me, and in its place I hung the ship in the bottle.

As I already told you, our relationship has not been legalized. And why should it? Our communion is so natural and good that it does not need the slightest compulsion.

Really, it's amazing that you have not yet met me and Rosa. Since we have been together we go out often. The children get along magnificently without us.

We get a kick out of seeing how people stare at us when we enter an apartment. A couple of guests are already there, they have set up a bar, someone puts on a record and goes still. Rosa has a remarkable charm, I am only now beginning to notice it. She is shorter than I am, buxom, with strong hips. She loves rare, rich colors, violet, turquoise, orange. I am somewhat taller, and in the evenings, after running around all day in jeans and a white smock, I like to wear long dresses which emphasize my slender waist and well-developed chest.

So we walk in, and the air crackles for a second. We stand there, two women whom you could not help but call blooming. But that's not all, we don't just glow with the sap of our youth (we are still young), we glow because we are intelligent, self-confident, and solidly anchored in our jobs, and we serve society as we are able.

T. used not to like it when I went to parties in my inconspicuously daring dresses and then stood there that way—that pleasurable moment when your tongue has the foretaste of the evening ahead. He used to claim that I was putting myself on display, posing on stage, which was unworthy of a woman and harked back to the social games of the late bourgeoisie. T. would add that the men were undressing me with their eyes. That was nonsense: that was never necessary, with the clothes I wore.

So Rosa and I stand side by side at this moment, we test the wind to see what the mood is. We look around to see where the people we like are sitting. We enjoy going to Bert's place, he is a brilliant, witty conversationalist. All my colleagues were there when Bert announced at the lab: "You can all come to my place tomorrow evening." At Bert's people discuss things, dance and drink a lot. Rosa and I are not worried by the shady light we stand in. It comes from the eyes of a few squinting and short-sighted people. My school friend Roswitha, the director of the Berta von Suttner High School, says: "You always were a little crazy," and she smiles a tolerant smile.

I confess that I am beginning to see Rosa's outward attractions as well, which I did not notice when I met her. I look at Rosa now with different eyes. Could this be a temptation? I don't believe so. Rosa is as intelligent as I am, or I am as intelligent as Rosa. Our family life is happy. Sometimes I say to her, or she says to me: "Hey, I've got it bad." That can mean various things. But it would never change the harmony of our common life. There would never be distrust or confessions or hints about morality, about being discreet and what people think.

Bert's party is getting jolly. The crackling we noticed when we arrived still clings to our clothing like an electric charge. Many people are receptive to it. We each go our own way, but we remain allies. What a difference from before, from my evenings with T.! He is here today, too, alone, and we nod at each other.

Later, when I am sitting in the small circle that has formed around Bert, and people are dancing behind us, Rosa whisks past.

"Hey," she says.

"Yes?"

"Do you mind if I stay out till morning?"

"You'd have to pick up the children in the afternoon. I have a meeting with the research association. Which one is it, anyway?"

Rosa shrugs her shoulders in the direction of the hall, where a tall man is throwing a trenchcoat over his shoulders. I recognize T.

Rosa's eyes are big and sweet. "Do you mind?"

I can't help laughing.

"It's a beautiful evening, Rosa," I say.

Translated by Jan van Heurck

COMING TO TERMS WITH THE NAZI PAST

Franz Fühmann

The Jew Car

How deep down does memory go? A warm green, I think that is the earliest image in my memory: the green of a tiled stove whose upper rim supposedly was ringed by the relief design of a gypsy camp. But I only know that because my mother told me. However I rack my brain, it will not bring this picture back to me. But I kept the green, a warm winebottle green with a dull shine. Whenever I recall this green, I feel myself floating lightly in the air above the floorboards. Mother told me that I could only see the gypsies if Father lifted me up, as a pint-sized two-year-old.

The next thing in my memory is something soft and white on which I had to sit still for an endless time, while meanwhile I could not help staring into something black that was bending up and down. And then comes a cave of elderbush, with a bench and a man on it who smelled of adventures and who let me ride on his knee and pushed into my mouth a piece of wonderfully sweet sausage which I chewed greedily. And this memory is linked to a scream and a storm which suddenly tore the man and the leafy bower away from me, to whirl them headlong into nothingness. Of course it was no storm gust, it was my mother's arm that tore me out of the green cave, and the scream was her scream of horror, because the man who was rocking me on his knee was a figure of mockery in our village, a large-scale farmer who had fallen on hard times and who, swaying along on legs bent like sabers, used to go through the villages begging for bread and schnaps; and the smell of wild adventures was his breath with brandy on it, and the sausage was scraps from the horse abattoir. In any case, it must have been splendid to ride on his knees. This is the first image that I can still see quite clearly before me. At that time I was three years old.

The images grow denser and denser, from then on: the mountains, the forest, the well, the house, the stream and the meadow; the stone quarry in whose grottoes lived the spirits I invented; toad, hornet, the owl's call, the avenue of mountain ash outside the gray factory, the annual fair with its aroma of Turkish honey and the hurdy-gurdy cry of the hawkers at the stalls; and finally, the school with its whitewashed corridor, which was always dim in spite of its tall windows and through which human fear crept out from all the classrooms like a swathe of fog. I have forgotten the faces of the teachers, all I can still see are two grim gray eyes above a long, razor-sharp nose, and a bamboo cane notched with rings. And the faces of my schoolmates have become pale and indefinite, too, except for one brown-eyed girl's face with a thin, barely curving mouth and short light hair above a high forehead: the face before whose eyes I cast down my own eyes, confused for the first time by a mysterious power. I do not forget it, even if bitter events came after.

One morning in the summer of 1931—I was nine years old at the time—our class gossip, black-braided Gudrun K., who always arrived a few minutes before the bell rang, chattering like a frog pond, once again stormed into class crying, "Hey you guys, hey you guys, have you already heard the news?" She panted as she spoke, and waved her arms about wildly. Though she was running out of breath, she still cried, "You guys, you guys!" and as she cried out, she gasped for air. As always, the girls rushed over and surrounded her abruptly the way a swarm of bees throngs around its queen. But we boys paid little attention to the fuss she made. Too often in the past, gossipy Gudrun had proclaimed as sensational something that turned out to be unimportant, so we did not let her disrupt our activities. We were just discussing the most recent adventures of our idol Tom Shark, and Karli, our leader, was showing us how to do away with the most dangerous wolfhound in a flash, Tom-Shark-style: You get a firm grip on the jaws at the point where the fangs are the sharpest, then holding onto the upper jaw you pry down the lower jaw, twist the skull around and give the animal a kick in the larynx. Then we heard a shrill scream from the swarm of girls.

"Yeek, how horrid!" one of the girls had shrieked, a sharp, squeaking yeek of panic shock. We whipped around and saw the girl standing there with her hand in front of her wide-open mouth, naked dread in her eyes, and the group of girls stood bent over with horror.

"And then they mix the blood with crummy flour and bake bread out of it!" we heard Gudrun report hurriedly, and we saw how the girls were trembling.

"What kind of junk are you telling them?" Karli cried in a loud voice. The girls did not hear him. We went over to them hesitantly.

"And then they eat that?" one girl asked in a hoarse voice.

"They eat it on their holiday, they all get together at midnight and light candles, and then they say a magic formula, and then they eat it!" Gudrun confirmed with gasping zeal. "What kind of magic formula?" asked Karli and laughed, but his laugh did not sound genuine. Suddenly I felt a strange fear.

"So tell us!" I yelled at Gudrun, and the other boys yelled, too, and we crowded around the girls who were crowding around Gudrun, and Gudrun repeated her report in hurried, almost shrieking sentences. A Jew car, she spluttered, had turned up in the mountains, and at night it drove around roads that were not much traveled, to catch little girls and kill them and bake a magic bread from their blood. It was a yellow car, completely yellow, she said, and her mouth and eyes were twisted with horror: A yellow, completely yellow car with four Jews in it, four black murdering Jews with long knives, and all the knives had been bloody, and blood was dripping from the running board, too, people had seen it clearly, and so far they had butchered four little girls, two from Witkowitz and two from Böhmisch-Krumma. They had hung them up by their feet and cut off their heads and let the blood run down into pans. And we crowded on top of each other, a clot of horror that croaked and quivered, and Gudrun drowned out our dread with her shrill owl's voice and avidly assured us, although no one disputed her tale, that it was all really true. When she went to Böhmisch-

Krumma yesterday to deliver some homemade articles, she said, she had seen the Jew car with her own eyes: yellow, completely yellow, with blood dripping from the running board, and I stared into Gudrun's face, which was red, and thought with admiration that she had been fantastically lucky not to be slaughtered; because I did not doubt for one moment that the Jew car was driving through the fields catching little girls.

Admittedly I had never seen a Jew, but I had already learned a lot about them from the conversations of adults. All Jews had hooked noses and black hair, and were to blame for everything bad in the world. They used low-down tricks to get the money out of honest folks' pockets, and had caused the depression that was threatening to strangle my father's drugstore. They had the livestock and grain taken away from the farmers and bought up cereal grains from all over, poured denatured alcohol over it and then poured it into the sea so that the Germans would starve to death, because they hated us Germans beyond measure and wanted to destroy us all. So why shouldn't they lie in wait in a yellow car along the country roads to capture little German girls and butcher them? No, I did not doubt for a moment that the Jew car existed, and when our teacher came into the classroom and dismissed as improbable the report of the Jew car that was shouted to him from every mouth, his words changed nothing. I believed in the Jew car. I could see it, yellow, completely yellow, driving between two grain fields, inside it the four black Jews with long sharp knives. And suddenly I saw the car stop, and two of the Jews jumped out and headed for the grain field, at the edge of which sat a brown-eyed girl plaiting a wreath of blue corn cockles, and the Jews, with their knives between their teeth, grabbed the little girl and dragged her to the car, and the girl screamed, and I heard her scream, and I was in bliss because it was my name that she screamed. Loud and desperately she screamed my name. I hunted for my Colt but I could not find it, and so, armed with only my bare hands, I jumped out from my secret passage and sprang at the Jews. I smashed the first one to the ground with a blow against the chin, and struck the second in the back of the neck with the edge of my hand after he had already lifted the girl off the ground to roll her into the car; and he collapsed, too. The Jew at the wheel stepped on the gas, and the car shot toward me. But of course I was prepared for that and jumped aside. The car shot past, I leaped onto its tailgate and with a blow of my fist I smashed in the car roof, twisted the knife out of the hand of the Jew next to the driver as he thrust it at me, threw him out of the car, overcame the Jew at the wheel, put on the brakes, jumped off, and saw the girl lying in a faint in the grass beside the grain field. And I saw her face, which lay motionless in the grass in front of me, and suddenly I saw nothing but her face: brown eyes, a thin, barely curving mouth and short light hair above the high forehead. I saw cheeks and eyes and lips and brow and hair, and I felt as if this face had always been hidden and I were seeing it naked for the first time. I was seized with shyness. I wanted to look away but I could not, and I leaned over the girl who lay motionless in the grass and touched her cheek, lightly as a breath, with my hand, and I got hot as fire, and suddenly my hand burned. I felt a sharp pain. My name roared into my ear. I gave a start, and the teacher struck the ruler over the back of my hand for a second time. "Stay two hours after school," he snorted. "I'll teach you to fall asleep in class!" The class laughed. The teacher struck me a third time. My hand was swelling up, but I gritted my teeth. Two benches ahead of me sat the girl whose face I had seen in the grass, and I thought that now she would be the only one not to laugh at me. "Sleeping in class! Does this fellow think the schoolbench is a bed?" The teacher had said this as a joke, and the class roared with laughter. I knew that she would never laugh at me. "Quiet!" the teacher cried. The laughter died away. The welts on my hands were turning blue.

When I finished staying after school, I did not dare to head home. As I slowly walked up the village street, I pondered, trying to think of a credible excuse for being late, and finally I hit on the notion of telling them at home that I had gone in search of the Jew car. Then I turned off the road so that I would arrive home not from the main street but from the fields, and walked up a country road toward the mountains, with grain fields to my right and meadows to my left; and grain and grass waved above my head. I was no longer thinking about staying after school, nor about the Jew car. I saw the girl's face in the waves of grass, and in the grain I saw her light hair. The meadows had a fragrance that bewildered the senses, the plump flesh of the Canterbury bells swayed blue at the height of my chest. The thyme sent out wild surges of intoxicating scent, swarms of wasps buzzed angrily, and next to the blue corn cockles glowed the poppy, a scorching narcotic in the hottest of reds. The wasps whizzed fiercely around my face, the sun was steaming; the crickets chirped a mad message to me, big birds shot up abruptly from the corn. The poppy glowed threateningly beside the corn cockles, and I felt confused. Up to now I had stood innocent in nature as one of her creatures, a dragonfly or a drifting straw, but now I felt as if she were pushing me away and a fissure were opening between me and the world around me. I was no longer earth and no longer grass and tree and animal. The crickets chirped, and I could not help thinking that the chirping came from wings being rubbed together, and suddenly that struck me as shameless, and suddenly everything was changed and as if I were seeing it for the first time. The ears of grain rattled in the wind, the grass blades rubbed up against each other softly. The poppy glowed, a mouth, a thousand mouths were in the earth, the thyme seethed with a bitter vapor, and I felt my body as something alien, as something that was not I. I trembled and ran my fingernails over the skin of my chest and ripped at it. I wanted to shout and could only groan. I no longer knew what was happening to me. And then a brown car came driving slowly down the country road, pushing the grain and the grass aside.

When I saw it, I jumped as if I had been caught committing a crime. I snatched my hands away from my chest, and the blood suddenly rushed to my head. I collected my thoughts with difficulty. A car? How did a car get here? I thought with a stammer. Then all at once I understood: the Jew car! A shudder ran over me. I stood there paralyzed. In the first moment, I had imagined that the car was brown. Now, horrified and impelled by a gruesome curiosity, I saw that it was more yellow than brown, actually it was yellow, completely yellow, a lurid yellow. At first I had seen only three people in it, but surely I was mistaken; or perhaps one of them had ducked down, definitely one of them had ducked down, there were four in the car, and one had ducked down in order to jump at me. And then I felt a deathly fear. It was a deathly fear; my heart was no longer beating. I had never felt it beat, but now when it beat no longer, I felt it: a dead pain in my flesh, an empty place which, as it convulsed, was sucking out my life. I stood paralyzed, staring at the car, and the car came slowly down the country road, a yellow car, completely yellow, and it came toward me. And then as if someone had switched on a machine, my heart suddenly started beating again, and now it beat at breakneck speed, and my thoughts somersaulted at breakneck speed: scream, run away, hide in the corn, jump into the grass—but at the last second it occurred to me that I dared not awaken any suspicion. I must not give any sign that I knew this was the Jew car. And so, shaken with dread, I walked at a moderate pace down the country road, at a moderate pace in front of the car, which followed dead slow, and sweat dripped off my forehead while at the same time I was freezing; and so I walked for almost an hour, even though it was only a few steps to the village. My knees were shaking, I was just thinking that I was going to keel over, when I heard a voice from the car like the crack of a whip: someone calling to me, perhaps a cry or a command, and then everything turned black before my eyes. The only thing I could still feel was my legs running and taking me with them. I saw and heard nothing more, and I ran and shouted, and not until I was standing in the center of the village street among houses and people did I dare to look around me, gasping, and then I saw that the Jew car had vanished without a trace.

Naturally, in class next morning I told everyone that the Jew car had chased me for hours and almost caught me, and that I had escaped only by doubling back on my tracks in the most marvelous way. And I described the Jew car: yellow, completely yellow, with four Jews in it who were brandishing bloody knives. And I was not lying, I had personally experienced it all. The class listened breathlessly. They crowded around me and looked at me with admiration and with envy, too. I was a hero and could now have taken Karli's place as leader, but I did not want to. I only wanted one person's look, and did not dare to seek it. Then the teacher arrived. We screamed the monstrous news at him. Feverishly I described my experiences, and the teacher asked me the place and the time and the circumstances, and I was able to supply them with the greatest exactness, without trickery and contradictions, with nothing but irrefutable facts: the yellow, completely yellow car, the four black passengers, the knives, the blood on the running board, the country road, the order to capture me, the escape, the pursuit; and the class listened breathlessly.

Then the girl with the short light hair looked up, and I dared to look her in the face, and she turned around halfway on her bench and looked at me and smiled, and my heart dissolved. This was bliss. I heard the crickets call and saw the poppy glow and smelled the fragrance of thyme, but now all this no longer confused me. The world was whole again, and I was a hero, escaped from the Jew car. And the girl looked at me and smiled, and said in her quiet, almost reflective voice that yesterday her uncle had come with two friends to visit them. They had come in a car, she said slowly, and the word "car" shot into my brain like an arrow. They had come in a brown car, she said. And in reply to the teacher's hasty question, she said that they had driven down the same country road at the same time when I claimed to have seen the Jew car, and her uncle had asked directions of a boy standing by the edge of the meadow, and the boy had run away screaming. And she passed her tongue over her thin lips and said very slowly that the boy by the road had been wearing exactly the same sort of green lederhosen I did. And she looked at me, smiling in a friendly way, and I felt them all look at me, and I felt their glances whiz angrily as wasps, swarms of wasps above thyme bushes, and the girl smiled with that quiet cruelty of which only children are capable.

Then a voice came roaring out of me, "The silly goose is nuts, it was the Jew car—yellow, completely yellow, and four black Jews in it with bloody knives!"—and through my roaring I heard, as if from another world, her quiet voice saying that she herself had seen me running me away from the car. She said it very quietly, and I heard my roar break off abruptly. I closed my eyes, it was deathly still, then suddenly I heard laughter, a sharp, giggling girl's laugh, shrill as the chirping of crickets, and then a roaring wave raged through the class and washed me away. I raced out of the class and ran to the toilet and locked the door behind me. Tears poured from my eyes, I stood numb for a while in the caustic odor of chlorine, and had no thoughts and stared at the black-tarred, stinking wall, and suddenly I knew: They were to blame! They were to blame, they, only they. They had made everything bad in the world, they had ruined my father's business, they had caused the depression and poured the grain into the sea. They used their low-down tricks to take the money out of honest folks' pockets, and they had played one of their low-down dirty tricks on me, too, in order to disgrace me in front of my class. They were to blame for everything, they and no one else! I gnashed my teeth. It was their fault! Bawling, I said their name: "Jews!" I screamed, and again: "Jews!" How it resounded—"Jews, Jews!" And I stood bawling in the toilet cubicle, and screamed, and then I threw up. Jews. They were to blame. Jews. I retched and clenched my fists. Jews. Jews Jews Jews. They were to blame for it. I hated them.

Translated by Jan van Heurck

Johannes Bobrowski

Mouse Party

Moise Trumpeter is sitting on the little stool in the corner of the shop. The shop is small, and it is empty. Probably because the sun keeps coming in and it needs space; and so does the moon. The moon keeps coming inside, too, whenever it passes. So there's the moon, too. The moon has come in through the door. The shop bell tinkled only once and very softly, maybe not because the moon came in but because of how the mice are running around and dancing on the thin floorboards. So the moon has arrived and Moise has said, "Good evening, Moon!" and now they both are watching the mice.

The mice are different every day. Sometimes they dance one way and sometimes another, and all of it with four legs, a pointy head and a narrow little tail.

"But dear Moon," says Moise, "that's by no means all. They also have a little body and everything inside it! But maybe you can't understand that. And besides, it isn't different every day. It's always exactly the same, and I think that's just what's so strange about it. More likely it's you who are different each day, even though you always enter through the same door and it's always dark before you sit down here. But now keep quiet and pay close attention."

You see, it's always the same.

Moise has dropped a crust of bread at his feet. The mice flit closer, one little stretch at a time; some even rear up and sniff the air. See, that's how it is. Always the same.

The two old fellows sit there and enjoy it and at first they don't hear the shop door open. Only the mice hear it straight off and vanish, vanish completely and so fast that you can't tell where they ran to.

A soldier is standing in the door, a German one. Moise has good eyes, he sees it's a young person, no more than a schoolboy who really does not know what he wants here now, standing in the doorway. Let's just see how the Jew folk live: no doubt something like that is what he thought, when he was outside. But now the old Jew is sitting there on his little stool and the shop is bright with moonlight. "Won't you come in, Mr. Lieutenant sir?" says Moise.

The boy shuts the door. He feels no surprise that the Jew can speak German, he just stands there, and when Moise gets up and says, "Come sit down here, it's the only chair I have," he says, "Thank you, I can stand up." But he takes a couple of steps into the middle of the shop, and then three steps more to the chair. And since Moise once again asks him to sit down, he sits.

"Now be perfectly still," says Moise and leans against the wall.

The crust of bread is still lying there, and look, the mice are coming back. Just like before, not a whit slower, exactly like before—a little stretch, another little stretch, and rearing up and sniffing the air and giving a tiny little snort that only Moise hears, and maybe the moon, too. Exactly like before.

And now they have found the crust again. It's a mouse party—small-scale of course, nothing special, but not quite commonplace either.

They sit and watch. The war is already a few days old. The country's name is Poland. It is quite flat and sandy. The roads are bad, and there are lots of children here. What more is there to say? The Germans have come, too many to count, and one of them, a very young one, a babe in the woods, is sitting here in the Jewish shop. He has a mother in Germany, and a father, also in Germany, and two little sisters. So now we are doing a bit of traveling, no doubt that's what he is thinking. Now we are in Poland, and later maybe we'll go to England, and how very Polish this Poland is.

The old Jew leans against the wall. The mice are still gathered around their crust. When it has gotten even smaller, an old mother mouse will take it home with her and the other mousies will run along behind her.

"You know," the moon says to Moise, "I have to move on a bit."

And Moise knows that it makes the moon uncomfortable to have this German sitting here. But what does it expect? So Moise just says: "Aw, stick around a while."

But then the soldier gets up instead. The mice run away, you can't even tell where they all could have vanished to, as quick as that. The soldier thinks about whether he should say goodbye, so he goes on standing in the shop a moment longer, and then he simply goes out.

Moise says nothing, he waits for the moon to start the conversation. The mice are gone, vanished. Mice can do that.

"That was a German," the moon says. "You know what those Germans are up to." And because Moise goes on leaning against the wall just as before and says nothing, the moon continues more insistently: "You don't want to run away, you don't want to hide, oh Moise. That was a German, you saw that. Don't try to tell me the boy isn't a German, or at least not a bad one. That doesn't make any difference any more. Now they have descended on Poland, what will happen to your people?"

"I have heard," says Moise.

It's all white now, inside the shop. The light fills the space up to the door in the back wall, where Moise is leaning, all white, so that you could think he is becoming more and more one with the wall, with every word he says.

"I know," Moise says. "You're quite right about that. I'll get into trouble with my God."

Translated by Jan van Heurck

Anna Seghers

The Reed

A small farm on a lake near Berlin had belonged to the Emrich family for a long time before the war.

Vegetables were their main crop. Their well-kept one-story house was separated from the shore by a narrow lawn, the only strip of uncultivated land. The bank was shallow, sloping down very gradually to the thick reeds that ringed almost the whole of the lake. A gravel path led from the boat dock to the glassed-in porch that had been built on to the house in a time of prosperity. Usually, people used the path that led from the highway through the truck garden to get to the house. From the small forecourt you could step into the parlor or into the kitchen, and from the kitchen, a trapdoor let you down into the cellar. The outside cellar door, which faced the lake, was no longer used. It was blocked by all sorts of equipment, and the cellar window, too, was so obstructed that it admitted hardly any light.

Formerly, the Emrich family had also owned a tavern in the next village, and the smithy opposite, where horses were shod and plows and farm equipment were repaired.

Shortly before the war, father Emrich died after being kicked by a horse. People say that misfortunes rarely come singly. Perhaps he was a shade less careful than usual because he was troubled by the death of his wife, which had caught him by surprise not long before.

His two sons were called up for military service. The war extended their service indefinitely. One took part in the march into Poland, the other in the landing at Narvik.

Meanwhile, distant relatives had bought the tavern and smithy. The only daughter, Marta Emrich, looked after the farm. Her ambition was to do everything by herself, as far as possible. Only occasionally she would hire a day laborer, for example to paint the house so that it would look well-kept when one of her brothers came home on leave. She not only did most of the work in the truck garden, but also papered the walls, and tarred the boat, which for the most part lay unused at the dock. Viewed from the lake, the white house with its dog roses looked pleasant and inviting.

Marta worked hard from the first ray of dawn until it got dark— not only to save money and avoid debt because the family already had lost the income from the tavern and the smithy, and not only because she told herself that work was her purpose in life, but also to forget her loneliness.

Her distant cousin, a farmer's son from the next town who was considered her fiancé, was one of the few Germans killed on the Maginot Line. Had the two married, the tavern and smithy might have been reunited with the Emrich property. Admittedly they had not yet made a public announcement of their engagement, but when the news came: KILLED IN ACTION, Marta felt abandoned and almost hopeless. She had always been a person of few words, now she turned completely silent.

She was in good health and used to managing alone in all circumstances. In the third year of the war she was twenty-six years old, coarse-boned with a broad, flat face. Her brothers' letters from the front, and various meetings in the village kept her in touch with the outside world. She raised the flag for each victory like her neighbors.

Her younger brother was killed on the Eastern Front. Although he had been her favorite, more good-natured than the older one, she did not feel his death as keenly as her fiancé's. It felt to her more as if his leave had been canceled indefinitely.

On a rainy, hazy evening in the late summer of 1943, she was sorting out potatoes and root vegetables in the cellar to prepare food for tomorrow.

Suddenly she heard a soft, unfamiliar noise in the reeds, and then in the hedge. She had the sensation that a shadow had flitted past. It flashed through her mind that someone could think the house was empty because there was no light except the dim lamp in the cellar. She called out: "Who's there?"

There was no reply, so she climbed up through the trapdoor into the kitchen and walked through the little parlor into the glassed-in porch, and from there outside.

On the narrow strip of land between the lake and the house stood a strange young man. He was quite neatly dressed, as far as she could see. She could not make out his features in the twilight. He asked hurriedly: "Does a Mrs. Schneider live here?"

"No one of that name here," Marta replied, and added: "Or in the village either." She scrutinized the unknown man, then asked, "How did you get here?"

"By boat," he answered.

"How?" queried Marta, for looking through the dusk she could see no second boat at the dock.

"Oh, I got out a long way back. I hoped that Mrs. Schneider lived only two villages away, and then I asked directions."

They heard the noise of a motorcycle on the highway. He took Marta's hand and said softly but firmly: "Don't give me away, if anyone asks."

Marta pulled back her hand and said angrily: "Oh, so you've been up to mischief."

The motorcycle did not stop but went on far into the distance. The stranger took her hand again, and said rapidly in a low, fierce, penetrating voice: "I haven't done anything bad. Just the opposite."

Now they heard the noise of an engine on the lake. "Do I look like a bad person?" he went on.

She tried again to distinguish his face, as if a face could ever guarantee the man who wears it. Living alone so long, and having to deal with all sorts of people, had taught her as much. But she believed she had never encountered a face like this.

The motorboat had receded into the distance. "Why are they after you? If you haven't done anything?"

He continued to speak without hesitation, very rapidly and always in the same fervent tone: "Someone distributed material against the war, at my workplace. And today they hit on the notion that it was me."

"Listen, if there's something to it, then you really ought to be locked up," Marta replied.

No matter what she said, the stranger went on in the same unfaltering, ardent voice. Its tone pleaded and threatened at the same time. Had she not lost anyone in the war, he asked—never waited for someone until the news came: KILLED IN ACTION?

He deserved to be locked up for saying such a thing, yes locked up, if not in prison then in a madhouse, Marta answered, and the two of them pressed against the wall side by side.

"Should we wait until all the men are killed?" he asked. He had not waited, not he, he said; and now those people were after him. "Haven't you a heart in your body? Listen, let me take a breather here in the hedgerow, you don't need to know a thing about it."

She hesitated for a moment. "Go into the house, go on!" he said. "You haven't seen a trace of me, you don't know anything about me. Go on."

Then Marta turned and went back into the house as if they had not spoken, and set about the work which his coming had interrupted.

That's how it began. All she did was to get up earlier than usual next day, to check whether he was still in the hedgerow. She half hoped that he would have gone by now. That first morning, she could perhaps have imagined that no one had ever been there. But she found him squatting in the same spot as before. Wordlessly she went into the house, then came back with some hot food. She watched how greedily he swallowed, choked, and bit his hand to stop any sound when he was shaken by a coughing fit. Then he looked at her. It was light enough now to see his face. He said nothing, just moved his lips a little and watched her with his unswerving gaze. She did not speak, went back into the house as if no one was sitting in the hedgerow, and did her work the same as always.

That summer, a boy was working for her as a day laborer. He came from the village, limping as he had done ever since a bout of infantile paralysis. He told Marta that the police were hunting for a pickpocket, and had issued warnings in every village around the lake. That afternoon, in an early mist, Marta motioned the stranger to follow her through the door into the cellar. She had already laid in stores of wood and coal for the winter. Now she cleared a tiny hideaway, saying nothing, as if her actions would become real only if she talked about them.

The hired boy was disappointed when August ended and Marta did not book him for September. But no one was surprised, they had known for a long time that Marta Emrich could manage any work alone, and that in fact she was eager to do it.

The fugitive's name was Kurt Steiner. He did any noiseless and painstaking work there was to do, peeling, cutting up, and sometimes repairs, in his hiding place between the woodpiles. Sometimes Marta left the cellar trapdoor open and switched on her radio so he could hear. Gradually she got up courage to go down and listen to his comments. He thought of many examples from world events and from his own life, to help her understand the things they heard. It all sounded like fairy tales and legends to Marta, who knew nothing but her own existence. At first she was confused by his urgent voice, then she started to pay attention to the meaning of his words, too; she contradicted and asked questions and thought things over.

One night when everything around them was stiff in winter sleep and ice and snow, she brought him up into the house. For a few moments he glimpsed the parlor which was her pride, in the glow of the flashlight. And her bed was fresh and pleasant.

Trembling, and nestled against him, she watched at night, through the cracks in the shutters, an aerial bombing attack on Berlin.

Little by little, Marta Emrich became familiar with the thoughts of her companion Kurt Steiner. She was convinced that she had done the right thing. Given the choice, she would do it again.

She felt guilty only because she was rather relieved to hear news that her older brother Karl had been imprisoned on the Eastern Front: she did not know how she could have hidden Kurt Steiner if her brother had come home on leave. Karl was rough and harsh, even malicious. He was the kind who would enjoy grabbing somebody by the scruff of the neck, even a fugitive.

Spring brought a new and terrible danger. Over the fence, a farmer's wife told Marta that the villages around the lake were being scoured for deserting soldiers. Half anxiously, half spitefully, the neighbor woman said that not one cellar, one garden, one shrub was omitted from the search.

Kurt Steiner went pale when Marta told him. "Now it was all for nothing, now it's all over," he gasped. He pondered, then said with desolate eyes, "I have to go, otherwise they'll catch you, too."

Suddenly Marta remembered a story that her younger brother, her favorite, had read once in a color pamphlet and told to his brother and sister. She no longer remembered where the story took place, but somewhere in it, someone had saved himself—from whom or why, she no longer knew—by diving under the water and breathing through a hollow reed until his pursuers stopped searching. Kurt Steiner said that that was fiction, it was not possible in reality. "No, it may be possible, try it!" Marta replied.

"I can't," he answered. "No, it won't work."

"You must, you must!" And Marta urged him to try it at once, before the men came. He had no other choice, she said, and therefore it had to be possible. And she made him wade into the water, and she cut a suitable reed. It was not yet afternoon when their experiments turned serious. The neighboring house had been surrounded and searched without result. Now they came to the Emrich house, and climbed into the cellar, too, through the trapdoor in the kitchen. Marta was frightened when they found the empty space between the woodpiles: perhaps they could trace a clue, a hair, even a shadow. But they only rummaged around in a furious, grim way.

"Who are you looking for?" asked Marta, retaining a grain of mockery for all her dread. "My younger brother died in action, my older brother is a prisoner."

"Keep your trap shut," said the rural police. "A woman can have more than brothers." Marta felt a deadly foreboding. Can he hold out, is he getting air? she thought.

After searching in vain outside the house as well as inside, they moved off cursing toward the next home. At last Kurt Steiner crept back into his cellar hole, which seemed to him almost cosy. But they had to be permanently ready for another raid. He was near despair, he said that he would prefer death to the unbearable suspense, and that he could not endure another raid, breathing only through the reed.

Marta spoke to him urgently, saying that the war was very close to an end now, and that the very reason he had placed himself in such danger was to see the end of the war.

Soon after, the pair learned that the villages were being searched again and that the search had begun at night.

Marta begged Kurt Steiner to risk using the reed again. Just think of all the risks he had taken to bring peace at last! And did he want to perish miserably three minutes before it would all be over? At her insistence he accepted the gamble once more, and once more he succeeded in breathing through the reed while the men came and searched.

Berlin was captured a few weeks later. The war was over. In the Emrich house, the man and the woman cried and laughed, they ate a meal together to celebrate, and drank wine, and lay down in the cool white bed like an ordinary married couple. The noise of engines no longer frightened them.

The whole area was flooded with refugees. The houses were so crowded with them that no one was surprised to see Kurt Steiner, one of many strangers who turned up. Now that her heart was calm and all the danger was past, Marta rigorously guarded her vegetable beds from the footsteps of soldiers and from refugee children.

Kurt Steiner watched smiling as she struggled again to keep her world in order amid the hopeless confusion. Now he saw her as she looked in everyday life, coarse-boned with a broad flat face.

A week later he said that he had to go into the city now, to see his friends again.

She focused doggedly on her work. That made it easier to wait, when he stayed away far too long. Then at last she heard his voice. Unexpectedly he arrived in a Russian military vehicle, bringing with him several friends whom he had found again. Two officers came with them, one of whom spoke very good German and asked Marta lots of questions. Evidently Kurt Steiner had told them a great deal about his flight and his hiding place. The officer inquired repeatedly whether everything had been exactly as described, to which Marta replied briefly: "Certainly. That's how it was." The officers looked at her in amazement; their eyes were warm. Then Kurt Steiner showed his friends the hiding place in the cellar, and also the place on the lakeshore where he held out during the search by breathing through the reed. He told everyone what a debt he owed to Marta, who not only had saved his life, he said, but had continually given him encouragement.

Marta listened mutely to it all. It did not sound to her like his voice. When she started to fix them something to eat from the various bits of food she had hoarded, Kurt Steiner said: "What are you thinking of? On the contrary, we've brought you a food package. We're all going back again right away."

"You, too?" asked Marta.

"Definitely, I have to," said Kurt Steiner. "I have a good job in Berlin now, in the new administration." He stroked her hair as one does to a child. As he was leaving he called out again: "You'll hear from me soon!" Marta listened to the car drive away. Formerly, her heart had grown lighter when the noise of an engine receded, now it grew heavier.

She had kept her thoughts to herself since she was a child, and had no ability to express herself. The people she had to deal with in order to tend the truck garden and the house, were used to her monosyllables. No one noticed that now she spoke even less than before.

One day Kurt Steiner turned up to ask how she was, and offered her any help she needed. Marta answered as she answered everyone: "I can manage alone." And when he passionately assured her of his gratitude again, she said, "That's enough, Kurt." She made her body stiff when he tried to give her a good-bye kiss.

Her brother Karl came home from his imprisonment, rougher and gruffer than ever. He did not have one kind word for his sister, and was angered by every change she had made in the truck garden. Admittedly he found the house in good condition, but he offered no praise. And yet it seemed to him a suitable place to bring a wife from a respectable family, a farmer's daughter who had lived in the next village. Marta had to give up her room for a narrow garret. The young couple exploited her. Her brother was determined to alter fundamentally everything that she had managed in his absence. He also wanted to change things because he was furious about the new "production quota" and wanted to prove that it was impossible to achieve the projected surplus.

Sometimes Marta quietly recalled the things that Kurt Steiner had explained to her, although he had not showed up for a long time. "That kind always wants more land, he wants other people's land, too. He needs war," he had said.

One Sunday she was sitting still and alone on the little bench which her brother had installed by the lakeside for his wife—the couple had gone to visit the wife's parents—when a motorboat drove up to the dock. Kurt Steiner jumped out, then helped out a young woman. Marta understood instantly that the woman was more or less the type that Kurt would want for a wife. He greeted Marta cheerfully, and said he had wanted to retrace the whole of his escape route, and explain it to his girlfriend. "And here is

Marta, too, right on the minute," he concluded. This time he allowed Marta to make coffee: he had brought her real coffee beans. They sat together for an hour. "What you and I experienced is something a person can never forget in his whole life," he said, taking her hand.

"Certainly not," answered Marta.

"If you need something, come to us," Kurt said, and he jotted down for her the address where they lived in Berlin.

When Marta's brother and his wife came home, they were indignant because Marta had entertained guests while they were away. They sniffed out the aroma of coffee. Her sister-in-law scolded Marta for using the crockery that belonged to her dowry. Then the couple grew curious, and were determined to find out what kind of people could have visited Marta. "People I met back during the war," Marta replied.

Meanwhile, something called the Farmers Mutual Aid Society had been founded in the villages. Marta's brother swore at it. "For all I care, they can——. A man like me doesn't join that kind of thing."

"A man like you, no," Marta said. In the evenings she used to cycle into the village, where sometimes a meeting was held at the tavern that belonged to her relatives. She would listen, and occasionally she would shake her head when something went against her grain.

"If you prowl around there, you can just go and live someplace else," her brother said.

"You can't throw me out," Marta replied. "Father left this place to us children. But you can buy out my share if you want to."

Karl had no such desire. He was annoyed and amazed. What a tone of voice Marta had acquired!

From then on, Marta was treated sometimes with amiable malice, sometimes as a household drudge. She felt relieved whenever she could cycle off to her farmers' meeting, even though she was afraid each time she came home again. But the meetings did not nourish her heart. Her life was bitter.

She longed to see Kurt Steiner again, and could not wait for him to come of his own accord. She longed to see his face again at once, with his mop of light brown hair and his steady gaze, this face which seemed to her different from all the other faces she knew. And she longed to hear his voice. She had many things to ask him. It seemed to her that he could explain everything on earth. He was married and very likely he already had a child, and might be annoyed if she turned up suddenly. On the other hand, he had visited her, even bringing his fiancée, and had given her their address in Berlin.

Her brother was extremely unreliable in office and written work, whereas Marta had been used to doing everything alone for years; and this gave her an opportunity. She offered to visit the Farmers Bank in Berlin, without letting her brother see how important the visit was to her. He had no objection.

She knew exactly how to get there and arrived punctually. From the bank she went to Weissensee, to the house where Kurt Steiner lived. As she climbed the stairs she thought: Should I? Shouldn't I?

But a strange name was on the door of the third-floor apartment. She searched the other doors without result. Finally she asked a woman just returning from the market where Kurt Steiner lived. "He's long gone," the woman said.

"But where to?"

The strange woman shrugged. As Marta's anxious eyes persisted in the question, the woman mockingly traced a wide arc with her hand.

Marta walked to the bus stop. She was tired, and felt bleak. He could have written me, she thought. Her shoulders sagged as if she were weighed down by disappointment, and the corners of her mouth drooped. The nearer the bus came to her village, the more faces she recognized. She pulled herself together because she felt that people were staring at her. She heard one tell another: "She was also in that tavern all alone." You all would have played a fine trick on Kurt Steiner, you would have dragged him to the Gestapo, she thought. Then full of pain she thought: Now he's gone for ever.

She walked from the last bus stop to the house. If she did not keep biting down hard, she would be flooded with misery again instantly. She showed her brother the bank papers, and since he understood nothing about them, he could not think of anything to criticize, either, except: "Why did you take so long?"

Suddenly she felt that inside, she had her compensation. She had something of her own, and she would not give up any of it. It belonged to her and to her alone; and it was not an object but an experience. She was absolutely justified in being proud of it. She straightened up.

A piece of untended land adjoined the truck garden. Its former owners either had not returned from the war or had fled in fear. The local council turned over this plot for resettlement to a man named Klein. Eberhard Klein had lost his wife when they were refugees, and looked after his only son himself. He was melancholy and quite at a loss. To be sure, he had been a gardener, but he had always worked with good soil. He could not make friends with the meager soil by the lake, nor with the temper of the people, which was as stingy as their land.

Emrich had been keen to acquire the land which Eberhard Klein was now working. So he gave Klein the cold shoulder, and if Klein asked him a question, the information he gave was sparse or even false. At first Klein believed that Marta was the same type. Many people had told him that she was rough and surly. But one day on her own initiative, she kindly gave him some over-the-fence advice about tomato pruning. At the farmers' meeting she expressed sensible views, although shyly. Eberhard Klein listened in surprise. Those are my ideas exactly, he thought. Also, he began to realize how kind and calm her eyes were.

Soon she became his wife and a good mother to his child. They lived peaceably, of one mind in their opinion of the outside world, of their own work, and of their little family.

Once, Marta received a card from Kurt Steiner, sent from Düsseldorf. He wrote that he would never forget her. Eberhard Klein asked who the man on the card was. "Occasionally we helped each other in the hard times, during the war," Marta replied, then added: "One time he got me real coffee." Klein asked nothing more and she said no more about it.

On the rare occasions when someone asked about Marta, the answer was: "She's Emrich's sister. Now she's married to Eberhard Klein." People with the same ideas as the Kleins might add, "She's a decent woman."

What else could they have said, since that was all they knew?

Translated by Jan van Heurck

Stephan Hermlin

My Peace

In spring 1948, I spent about four weeks in Moscow. On the afternoon of May 1, after the big May Day demonstration, I was invited to the home of some people I did not know, had to respond to toasts by drinking more than was good for me, and went to my hotel in the evening. Seeing the lively activity of evening and nighttime that normally concludes the holiday, I was determined to join in. I had barely returned to my hotel when my mood changed: I could no longer feel anything but a boundless exhaustion. I did not look even once more out of the window of my room, which was on the top floor just at the corner where Gorki Street meets Manege Square. I collapsed onto my bed and must have fallen asleep immediately.

A far-away sound penetrated my sleep, slowly and steadily turning up the volume. The hail of drums, the austerity of the flutes, were preceded by a singing that was sensed rather than heard, that was distant and then came nearer, and whose wild staccato finally burst upon me with a bang:

> It cannot scare a sailor,
> Never fear, never fear, Rosemarie.

At that moment I was in a deep forest in the département of Haute-Vienne about twenty-five miles south of Limoges, if I remember correctly. Three words were forming in my mind, turning into one word that repeated itself incessantly, a set phrase of the times: "Theyarehere, theyarehere, theyarehere . . . ," while at the same instant my hand groped for a nonexistent pistol, and simultaneously I was brushed by irritation, by an idiot amazement that I could have let myself be caught by surprise despite all my intentions and precautions; and the singing grew louder and louder while I knew I was already lost. Something kept choking me, it was the will to wake up, it was my overpowering sleep that was choking me; but I escaped from my sleep and its nightmare, I was in my hotel room, midnight was long past, I staggered out onto the balcony, the bellowing choir coming from a loudspeaker on the roof of the hotel above my head continued to assure us that nothing could scare a sailor, and similar messages warbled across the wide square to the walls of the Kremlin, among them this phonograph record, some bit of war booty which by chance ended up in tonight's program, not really noticed by the celebrants; and through a veil I saw far below me the spinning and whirling of the crowd, and the war had been over for three years already.

Dreams of this kind became rarer and lost their power of devastating threat. The older the peace, the more I settled into it, the more a single unending dream made its home in the varied zones of me, replacing the dreams of the past. It contained idyllic, bucolic episodes, but its terrors grew steadier, deeper, I got used to them. I had spent the last months of the war in Switzerland. Now already it was becoming a memory how, shortly after the ceasefire, a jeep from a French regiment waited for me in a wood near Singen and took me into Germany. I saw the Hohentwiel mountain; we drove alongside a railroad embankment where a burned-out German train lay and on the high-wheeled locomotive I read: "Wheels must turn for victory." In Germany I wandered around, sometimes on foot, sometimes in vehicles. I talked with countless people who happened to cross my path, with shopkeepers, returning soldiers, clergymen, workers, wives of SS officers who were hiding out, members of the resistance. For a while I still found it difficult to speak my mother tongue openly, without switching to the artificial French accent I had used with fellow Germans whenever I glimpsed a gray-green uniform. But the conversations turned more and more into monologues. The people I talked with must have gotten the impression that I agreed with them unconditionally, because of the way I sank into silence and was able to free myself from it less and less often. Every day I mutely absorbed opinions and confidences: the war wasn't over yet by a long shot, many of the Allies would soon regret having fought against Germany; there was a plan to sterilize all German men so that Germans would die out; all the institutions of higher learning in Germany were going to be closed; they had known nothing about the concentration camps; they had always been "against" them but had not been able to do anything because they would surely have been sent to a concentration camp; the gassing of the Jews of course had been an exaggeratedly harsh measure, they should simply have been deported; on the other hand, they hadn't really been gassed, it was sheer propaganda, the so-called gas chambers had been built after the Allied victory.

Once I lived for a week in a house in Munich whose owner, a middle-ranking Nazi party official, had fled at the approach of the Americans. I leafed through the volumes of his little library, there were forty or fifty of them—of course Alfred Rosenberg's *Myth of the Twentieth Century* was there and *Mein Kampf,* of course one found Löns, Hans Grimm and a widely circulated Scandinavian novel entitled *And the Forests Sing Forever;* but I also found a few German classical writers, a volume of Goethe, a volume of Lessing, even one of Heine, in the reliable common editions of the Bibliographical Institute. But each of these volumes had on the title page the stamp of the public library of a small town in Poland. I understood the route by which German culture had reached this representative of the master race.

At night I used to read the diary he had kept for twenty years, which lay in his desk: his annoyance about his superiors at the office, weddings and birthday parties, the description of outings to Upper Bavaria, the retelling of films that had impressed him. He had joined the Nazi Party in the twenties. Later he had carried on a correspondence with Rudolf Hess in the vain hope of earning the Blood Order. Next to the diary I found a photo album with the usual overlit or underlit amateur photos, which accompanied the birthday celebrations described in the diary. Beside the photos were commentaries neatly written in white ink. "Today our darling was eight years old." Time flew. A picture showed an empty country road, white as in summertime, at the edge of which lay something dark. Before I could recognize this unrecognizable thing, I read the inscription: "Jews shot during our advance on Kielce, September 1939." You could look across the desk from the lamp to the edge of the forest under the moon.

In the market square of a small town I saw forced laborers gather around trucks that were going to take them back to their countries. A group of Frenchmen were waving tricolor flags; they were singing the Marseillaise very loudly, enthusiastically and incorrectly, they were laughing and all talking at the same time, they called out to the girls, who blushed. My gay, cheeky, skeptical, brave French . . . Already I no longer dared to speak to them. For them I had already become a German among Germans. Fifty yards farther on were the Russians and Ukrainians. There were many more of them. They did not sing and talk. They stood mutely under red flags. They had suffered and fought without hesitation, without mercy, without complaint, even when no one came to their aid, when everyone had given them up for lost. Their people had won. Now they climbed into their trucks without a sound. I looked after them as they drove away eastward and they and their flags disappeared from view at a curve in the road.

A couple of months later I was in Nuremberg as the reporter on a newspaper. Every day I sat in the little press box a few yards away from Goering, Hess, Rosenberg and the others at the Nuremberg Tribunal. I took my meals with the soldiers in an American army barracks. In the evening, I shared a room in a miserable half-destroyed hotel with a former Wehrmacht lieutenant to whom I gave some of my cigarettes and who told me his experiences at Lake Ilmen and Monte Cassino. He was almost the only person I talked to. Then in the morning I would pass through military police checkpoints at the Palace of Justice and sit in my customary seat. Apart from the accused, I was one of the very few Germans in the hall. Goering, who sat closest to me among the accused, sometimes used to look at me; we got used to each other. I listened as Streicher, chewing like an old man, protested against the statement of a prosecutor: He had never been an anti-Semite, Streicher said. I saw Field Marshal Keitel, dressed in his uniform with the rank insignia removed, object to the British prosecutor's claim that Keitel had ordered Allied airmen to be shot: "I assure you by my honor as a soldier that this is untrue." And I witnessed how the Englishman listened to him quietly and then showed him the written order which Keitel believed had been destroyed: "Is this your signature, Herr Keitel?" And Keitel, white as chalk, sank down in his seat without a word. Not long after, I was waiting for my streetcar at the main guard station in Frankfurt when I noticed an elderly woman with a friendly rosy face who kept wiping away her tears. I asked her what was wrong. She stared at me: "Haven't you heard that they have sentenced our Reich Marshal Hermann Goering to death too?" Many of the fifty million victims of this war earned no tears because those who would have wept for them were themselves among the dead, but there were some whose lives were saved only so that they could mourn the guilty.

I recall how several years after the war, I tried to explain to some French friends what set me apart from them so profoundly. I said something to this effect, that the difference was that they had always felt secure in their country, in their sense of belonging to it. Of course, I said, this did not mean that their country was a peaceful refuge, everyone knew that it had been subject to the most dreadful upheavals and changes in every period of its history; but no Frenchman had ever doubted France as the center of his existence. And so too, every Briton, every Russian, every Spaniard took their nationality for granted in the little universe of Britain, Russia, Spain; and of course their sense of nationality had nothing to do with where they might be living at any one time. It was different for Germans, at least for Germans who thought about their country and their relationship to it. There has always been something indeterminate, problematic about it, I said—by which I did not mean the national borders, which reactionary forces had continually challenged, but I meant the fact that every serious German had seen his country in the terrible conflict between political reality and what was morally and intellectually possible or desirable. The fact that patriotism here had always produced inward or outward exile was a clear proof of it. You should just read our writers, I said: not just those from the Thirty Years' War, not just Seume or Schubart or Platen or Büchner, but look too at the bitter, ever-deepening isolation of Goethe and the cries and laments of Kleist, Hölderlin, and Heine. The homeland of them all, and of thousands of others who were not poets—the homeland of them all was not really Germany but the German question. My French friends smiled indulgently, but I knew that what I had said made them weary and impatient. The world had already dwelt long and often upon us Germans, and this time it had almost been destroyed by us.

Over the years I found new friends and acquaintances, mostly younger. In the past, the people with whom I was intimate had generally been older than I. In fact I had been among the youngest, or simply the youngest. Privately I had called these people my people, my real family. By now they had been lying in their graves for a long time already, in a field near Berlin where those executed in Plötzensee Prison had been hastily buried; they lay by the Jarama and the Ebro, they lay near Sainte-Croix-Vallée-Française. Many had no grave. I walked over their ashes, with which the roads in Auschwitz were strewn. I had been in the war in Oradour shortly before it was destroyed; now I went to Dachau, to Lidice, to the Slovenian mountains, to Buchenwald, to the Warsaw Ghetto. I stood on the field of the five hundred thousand at Leningrad, I climbed into the Ardeatnic caves.

My new friends were taking part in experiments to build a new society; I tried to be useful to them in this task. Many of them had been on the opposing side in the years before and during the war; some had been young Nazis. Among the latter group especially, I found several to whom I am particularly close. One of them, a writer, wrote a story about the time when he was a child and heard that Jews were driving through the villages and fields in a yellow car, abducting and murdering Christian children. His story does not describe him refusing to believe the rumor or actually helping the vilified Jews, but rather shows how he believes what he is told—in fact he sees the car himself.

In the years of peace I thought, sometimes with shame, about the demanding and self-righteous way I had often treated fellow Germans shortly after the war. Yet I had been right to demand that they recognize a truth that left them almost nothing of what had been dear to them. Only a few were capable of carrying this burden. Most took refuge in extenuation, in silence, in a regret that involved no obligations. Only gradually I understood that it is beyond the strength of most people to change, to become different people. I felt sorry for this majority. Often I thought about the words of the young Karl Marx, who said something like this: "A people who are really capable of being ashamed are like a lion that prepares his jump by going inward." At the same time I understood that my new, younger friends, by the way they lived, imposed on me the obligation to fulfill the same demands I made on them. I had to recognize truths and act accordingly.

I am glad about my new friends, glad that they exist and that they are my friends. All the same, a painful line divides us that is almost indetectible. In a conversation of whatever kind, someone may use the phrase "before the war" or "after the war," and at once I feel an irresistible force pushing us apart, because they evidently regard this time "before the war" as a better, more peaceful, almost a normal time; it's still the summer of 1939. And yet I know, at every moment of my waking and dreaming, that for me the war began on January 30, 1933, that is on a date that means nothing to them, or whose significance they have not yet begun to think about. At the same moment I know that for some unfathomable reason I enjoy an advantage, because I survived; and they, the better people, my dead friends, have been gone so long already, they are moving on farther and farther into endlessness, and I am here and have younger people around me, and I feel their nearness and for a moment, the long familiar, almost indetectible pain.

Translated by Jan van Heurck

Heinz Knobloch

Change at City Center

If you travel the Berlin subway in the direction of Thälmannplatz, get out at City Center station, walk farther in the same direction, and leave the platform just after passing the standard clock—you will notice nothing out of the ordinary.

A wide exit. Machines that cancel used tickets. Behind them, a staircase leading upward. A great many people climb it every day.

But if, as you leave the platform, you keep your eyes down, you will see a discolored area in the floor, a square shape which is roughly the size of a living room and which contrasts with the rest of the subway. It has been unable to conform to its surroundings, in all these years. That is no cause for alarm. The floor is solid, we are standing on firm ground, and the concrete is probably sound. The color difference is the only thing that will startle you. Does no one hesitate by this patch on the ground, which looks damp, as if it had not yet dried completely?

But why hesitate? This is not the floor in the Edgar Allan Poe tale where an old man's corpse lies hidden under the boards. The Tell-Tale Heart is not beating here, or if it is, then it is our own, not someone else's. Neither are we in Poe's cellar: by no means could a corpse be hidden behind the walls and every memory be neatly walled up with it, except for the Black Cat who still lives and howls behind the Tell-Tale Wall. The skeleton in the living-room closet. Are our sympathies with the person who discovers the skeleton, or with the person who mistakenly believes that he could hide it for all time?

The square patch in the floor of City Center subway station stands out distinctly from its surroundings, once we have been made aware of it. It becomes visible. Who is uneasy when he sees it? Who can make any sense of it?

It is like the Valley of the Kings.

Howard Carter is consulted. He comes at just the right moment. He sees a place which stands out, which is conspicuous, oddly enough, because of the regularity of its shape. They hack away the stones, they dig, they clear the rubble and they discover stairs. Rough stairs which lead downward until, after more digging, they find the start of an underground passage. Naturally, the museum sign—EATING AND TAKING PHOTOGRAPHS IN THE TOMB OF TUTAN-KHAMEN IS STRICTLY PROHIBITED—is not there yet, but one day it will be.

If we put ourselves in the role of Howard Carter the archaeologist, if we make his persistence our own, if we pause curiously at the west exit from City Center and look hard at the ground, if we look right through it . . . .

We can do this without a sound. We need no pneumatic drill, no pickax, no digging crew. We do not even need to ask permission. The concrete ceiling dissolves and disperses like smoke—not in a flash but gradually, as we reflect. Now the steel beams below the concrete are yielding to memory, and move aside. We can see stairs. A staircase.

". . . and it was with ill-suppressed excitement that I watched the descending steps of the staircase, as one by one they came to light." (Howard Carter)*

A broad staircase. And down below where the stairs end, a passage begins. It extends farther than the eye can reach. But now the eye does reach farther, it gazes deep into the underground passage.

"Good grief, is there really something like that under the smooth floor at the exit from City Center?" people are saying.

Every passage lures us with its ending. Especially when no end seems to be in sight.

At the end of this very long passage comes another staircase.

Are there still movie posters hanging along the way?

---

*English quoted from ch. 5, p. 32, of Carter, *The Tomb of Tutankhamen*, New York, E. P. Dutton, 1972.

Finally you come to a few more stairs. And if you go down them—it is so long ago that I can no longer remember how many there are—you find yourself standing in a subway station which is called City Center, just like the other one.

It may happen that a train is pulling in or out, or just traveling slowly through. And what if someone asks me for information: "Should I change at City Center?"

Yes, that was long ago. Once upon a time there were two transportation companies operating in this city at the same time. One routed its subway line from west to east and back, and the other from north to south and back. Somewhere, the two lines had to intersect. The place where they met was here, in the center of the city. Back then, this train station was called *Friedrichstadt*. Easy to confuse with the station called *Friedrichstrasse*. But please do not confuse them, because we will need to talk about Friedrichstrasse station later on.

The two transportation companies ran their lines alongside and one above the other, in the 1920s. The result was the construction of this long—this unnecessarily long—connecting tunnel, which would have been built quite differently, and might even have been equipped with escalators, if the interests of the passengers had been the first concern. Those were the good old days, when things were more complicated, and simpler. Each company built for itself alone. One day, the fall in dividends required a merger.

Let's take a good look at this underground crossroads. If you want to change trains, you must not go up to the earth's surface. You should simply walk through the long tunnel to the other train line. From City Center to City Center.

I ought not to put that in the present tense.

Because not everyone knows his way around. The upper train line, which is where we got out, continues on to Thälmannplatz. The other, the lower track, carries trains of the north-south-west line, and does not stop in the east. How to explain this?

Here in the two City Center subway stations under the soil of Berlin, is an international border, the other equator. As a child I planned one day to walk to the ends of the earth. And why not?

Now this dream has come to pass of its own accord. The ends of the earth lie at our front door. Enjoy it if you can.

The West Berlin subway line travels without stopping through those of its stations which lie in GDR territory.

Once more, from the beginning. You take the train that goes to Thälmannplatz, get out at City Center, but do not leave the platform.

And now it is slowly getting dark. The date is May 1, 1945. Like a movie theater, when slowly the lights go out so that you can see a different image.

Many people are sitting on the platform and the rails, people who had to flee or whose homes were bombed, war casualties of all kinds. They are not waiting for the next train but for the end of the war. The war could have been over a long time ago if the supreme commander, a few hundred yards away, had not refused to see its inevitable end. Admittedly, he created this end to the war with his first order on September 1, 1939, but he did not want to acknowledge it. This refusal, even now, is still costing many people their lives.

People are lugging suitcases and blankets into the subway, bits of household equipment, their whole kit and kaboodle, and are sitting down wherever there is still room. Even between the tracks. Why be afraid of the electrified rails, when there is no more electricity?

The next station to the west is not called Thälmannplatz, not yet. At this time it is still known as Kaiserhof.

When Ernst Thälmann rode on the subway (and he did ride on the subway), he did not dream that the signs saying "Kaiserhof" would one day be replaced by signs that say "Thälmannplatz." Thälmann certainly had his dreams, and who knows the extent of them? But it is improbable that he ever pictured this station with his name on it. Thälmann was someone it was safe to name a train station after.*

Hitler, too, when he was crouching in the underground bunker beneath his Reich Chancellery, could not have imagined the new name that Kaiserhof subway station would very soon acquire. If he had thought about it, he could have foreseen that his Adolf

---

*Ernst Thälmann, 1886–1944, German communist leader who died in Nazi captivity.

Hitler Square would be rechristened. But he would have needed outspoken, invulnerable, unimpeachably honest advisers to make him think about it, and what dictator tolerates advisers like that? And even with such advisers, he could never have guessed that a subway station would be named after Ernst Thälmann. Too bad that he never found out that the walls of Thälmannplatz station were lined with the beautiful marble from the ruins of his Reich Chancellery.

There are no hidden, walled-up staircases in that station. It was and is only a simple station like most others, one in a series. Nobody guessed that one day it would have to be the end of the line. The place where you cannot go on. "Thälmannplatz—The train stops here."

It attracts attention if you stand around in City Center station, or sit on a bench there for a long time.

Someone comes and asks you to show your I.D. You have to produce a ticket. You are asked why you don't just travel on, or leave?

"What are you waiting for?" the Someone asks.

"I'm waiting for SS Brigade Leader Mohnke."

"Who is this colleague of mine? From which work brigade? Where is it working?" asks Someone.

"You're getting things mixed up," I say. "Not work brigade chief, brigade leader."

"We don't use that term," says Someone. "We say brigade chief, or head of a work crew. So, where is this Mohnke Brigade supposed to be operating?"

"Fortunately, it doesn't exist," I reply. "I expect that you and I would agree that that is fortunate. *Brigade Leader*—you understand?" The man is young. How could he know the facts? "Mohnke is a Brigade Leader," I say. "And that is a rank equivalent to a major-general. Mohnke is a Major-General of the Waffen-SS."

"You're waiting for him? Here?"

Yes, we'll let him appear and watch what he does.

"And who told you to meet a war criminal here?"

He does not think me capable of deciding to do it on my own. "No one," I say. "I read about him and I am interested in an incident, a particular detail. I would like to show it to people."

That sounds as incredible as most writers' projects. Writers can compose something, they can invent and show things through imagery, but most lack the talent to present an outline. They cannot give an exposé because they never know ahead of time exactly what they will write. They cannot draw up the conceptual framework, the plot skeleton, the guiding theme, not even for their own use. They simply write. That's how it is, usually. And afterward, they are not able to explain what they have written, either.

The station clock shows two minutes to midnight. That is all the prehistory we have time for. When the witching hour begins, we will be ready for anything.

The reader, meanwhile, needs no magic but can picture what is happening even in broad daylight, with the help of the stopped station clock. We invite this reader to go to Thälmann Square. That is, you are not absolutely required to travel on the subway but could take a bus, or walk there from Leipzigerstrasse, from Glinkastrasse or from Mauerstrasse—yes, from Mauerstrasse is the best. But if you do decide to travel by subway after all, because it is easier to make connections, then remember, when you get out at Thälmann Square, to walk opposite to your direction of travel. You should be facing Mohrenstrasse aboveground, and Kronenstrasse will be the nearest cross-street on your right.

Between these two streets, like an island sunk in the roadway, once stood the Holy Trinity Church. In appearance it was similar to the Church of Our Lady in Dresden, and was visibly larger than the Bohemian Church on Mauerstrasse.

The German theologian Schleiermacher preached in Holy Trinity Church, and on April 1, 1831, he confirmed here a young man named Otto von Bismarck. (Every society keeps note of its important dates.)

This church, which stands out in the cityscape "by its nobility and the tasteful simplicity of its forms," is the church where von Hindenburg, the likewise simple Field Marshal and President of the Reich, used to shuffle to worship, only a few steps from his seat of office. Unfortunately he experienced no inspiration there, but appointed and empowered Hitler to become Chancellor of the Reich. Hitler at that time lived right next door, in the Kaiserhof Hotel.

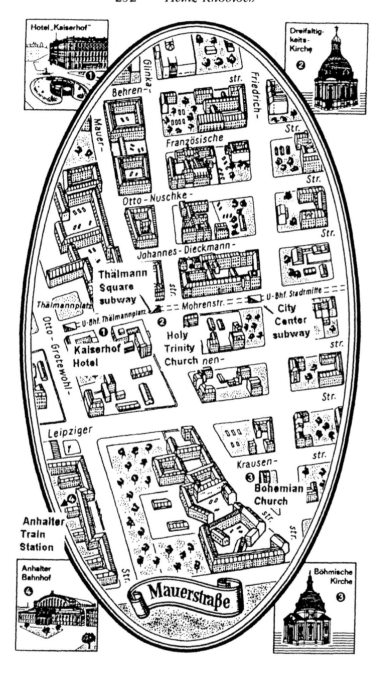

Hotel „Kaiserhof" ❶

Dreifaltig-keits-Kirche ❷

Glinka-str.

Behren-

Friedrich-

Französische

Str.

Str.

Otto-Nuschke-

Str.

Johannes-Dieckmann-

Mauer-

Thälmann Square subway

Thälmannplatz

U-Bhf. Thälmannplatz

Mohrenstr.

U-Bhf. Stadtmitte

City Center subway

❷ Holy Trinity Church

Kaiserhof Hotel ❶

Otto-Grotewohl-

nen-

Str.

Str.

Leipziger

Krausen-

str.

❸ Bohemian Church

Anhalter Train Station

❹

Str.

Str.

Mauerstraße

Anhalter Bahnhof ❹

Böhmische Kirche ❸

People are bound to ask what became of the Holy Trinity Church. So before we go on, I will tell you that this rotunda built in 1739 was destroyed in an aerial bombing raid in November 1943.

Afterward, the district leaders of the Nazi Party in Berlin had a bunker built in the crypt of the ruined church. The bunker was bombproof, it withstood attack and was taken over by the Gestapo. We read with horror that on the very day of the surrender, a remarkable number of German soldiers were found hanged in this area, executed because they had said that the war was over, and we may safely attribute their deaths to the existence of this especially secure bunker, and to the people who lived in it.

Today, this space is occupied by modern monumental buildings, embassy buildings. Leaving the subway and walking toward Thälmann Square, we come to Mauerstrasse, where the first house on the right bears a plaque saying that Heinrich von Kleist lived here— well, not in this house but in this location—and one day he left here for an excursion to the Wannsee and did not return.

On the left, where the Korean embassy stands now, was the Kaiserhof Hotel, at Number 1–5 Mohrenstrasse. When the Kaiserhof, or "Imperial Court," was opened in 1875, the Emperor was present, as the name implies. When the subway line reached this area, the station was not named Wilhelmplatz after the Emperor, nor Wilhelmstrasse to represent German foreign politics. It was named after the hotel, one of the largest and oldest in Berlin.

In travel brochures, the Kaiserhof was mentioned as one of the five best hotels, as the top of the line. From early 1931 on, the Kaiserhof was Hitler's headquarters in Berlin. The man who posed as a working-class leader lived in a luxury hotel. Other people paid the bill.

When Hitler looked out the window of his rooms on the second floor of the Kaiserhof, the target of his gaze was the Reich Chancellery building. Goebbels, the Nazi Party district leader in Berlin and later Hitler's minister of propaganda, published a book in 1934 entitled *From the Kaiserhof to the Reich Chancellery*. The title has an ambiguous ring. The Germans got rid of their emperor in 1918 at the end of World War I, but now that their Republic and its democratic institutions were being eliminated, mentally to begin with, important words like Kaiserhof and Reich Chancellery signaled something more than the names of buildings.

Hitler, once he had managed to be made chancellor, did not walk the few steps from the Kaiserhof Hotel to the Reich Chancellery. He had himself driven there: a distance of two hundred yards.

The Reich Chancellery stood on the Wilhelmstrasse in Wilhelmplatz. On a present-day map of the city, you will find this location listed as Otto-Grotewohl-Strasse in Thälmann Square. On the corner where Voszstrasse begins, Hitler built the New Reich Chancellery. Today everything has been razed to the ground, there is not even a park there.

But to understand the situation better, we need to go back to where it started.

So, in the darkness we stroll across the silent Thälmann Square, picturing it as Wilhelmplatz, jam-packed with cheering people who are calling out in chorus: "We want to see our Führer!" It sounds incredible but it is true. Even if I had not heard it myself, seen it in films—it is true. They shouted for him. Sometimes he showed himself. And when he did not appear, then everyone knew that at that moment he was working for Germany. Roaring crowds, homage, and lines of poetry which described how somewhere in the night, a little lamp still glowed in a certain room. The room was not on the street side of the hotel, of course, because powerful people like him are always scared shitless of the common man.

In the darkness we gaze at this patch of sand and imagine that it is the first of May.

The first of May is a beautiful day, as a rule. It does not rain, and the sun warms the newborn life. In the last century, great tact was shown by making this day a holiday to celebrate the working man. On May 1, 1933, it snowed, because the Nazis had debased the holiday for their own ends. Some people took this for an omen.

We, in Thälmann Square, imagine May 1, 1945, as it was when this place was called Wilhelm Square. It is evening, and probably so quiet that the birds are chirping. Hitler and his bride have changed into smoke and evaporated.

In the cellar of the Reich Chancellery, post commander Mohnke has given orders to his people. They discuss and prepare the escape of those who are still alive. They plan to divide into groups, which at intervals of twenty to thirty minutes will try one by one to get through the subway tunnel to Stettin train station.

Brigade Leader Wilhelm Mohnke, Major-General of the Waffen-SS, military commander of the government district known as the

Citadel, post commander of the Reich Chancellery—no doubt that's enough offices and titles—gives the command to escape. The survivors—all those who do not wish to follow the leaders of the dying Reich into the Beyond immediately, but want at least to risk the path to life: in other words, most of them—have formed up in the cellar.

Mohnke divides them into ten groups. The first group consists of twenty men and four women, and he leads it personally. The women are secretaries, and Hitler's Viennese dietician-cook. (Yes, Brecht, he had at least one dietician-cook.)

At around eleven P.M., they climb very quietly and cautiously out the cellar window below the balcony where the Führer, when he was alive, used to stir the crowd to cheers. No one can say whether sharpshooters of the Soviet Eighth Army are not already in position at the other end of the square.

While we, in Thälmann Square, picture how Mohnke's group is trying to reach the subway tunnel, a streetcorner tipster by the name of Rosi Nante gives us the lowdown on Brigade Leader Mohnke: stuff that presumably not even he is thinking about at this moment.

Mohnke, the last watch commander of the Reich Chancellery, was also its first. On May 8, 1933—two days before the Burning of the Books—SS Staff Sergeant Mohnke came on duty as watch commander. Wilhelm Mohnke from Lübeck, twenty-two years old with thirty-two teeth and no spectacles, and over five feet eleven inches tall, recently assigned to SS Special Command Berlin and now a member of Adolf Hitler's SS elite bodyguard.

He was headed for the top. He fought in several theaters of war, received several serious wounds, and finally, ten days before it was all over—on April 20, 1945, Hitler's last birthday—Mohnke arrived with eight hundred of the Hitler bodyguard and became post commander of the Reich Chancellery.

Now he wants to get out of here. About two hundred yards separate the Reich Chancellery from the Kaiserhof Hotel.

Mohnke's group reaches the entrance into the subway without meeting any opposition. The stairs have been shot to bits. The group slides, falls, gets a fright. It's black as pitch. Down below, you can hear people breathing.

But they are not the enemy, as the group had feared. They are fellow Germans. Berlin residents, local people, known until now as "our compatriots." Wounded soldiers, and ordinary folk: the folk for whom the plan was to use them up to the last drop.

Unimaginable that a train could travel through here. Mohnke's group sets out on foot through the subway tunnel headed toward City Center.

Let's wait for them there.

Nothing extraordinary happens. They stumble over thresholds and train tracks, and walk on the gravel in the railroad beds as insecurely as we all do, if we step on railroad tracks. But the journey takes longer than they had calculated. It is around midnight before they reach City Center station. The station is crammed with people. Doctors who have taken shelter here, are performing operations as best they can in a railroad car.

The roof is not weathertight, but who is worrying about that now? A few days ago, artillery shells came bursting through. People are afraid and are seeking shelter wherever they can find it. And now, combat-ready soldiers are back on the scene. Isn't this war over yet?

Mohnke has a doctor with him, too, Dr. Schenck. Not to mention his SS Chief of Staff, Klingemeier, and Hitler's aide, SS Major Otto Günsche.

When they reach the station, they turn the corner without hesitation and proceed to the stairs and the passage that leads to the lower platform.

All change at City Center.

More people are camped down in the lower station, waiting for the end and probably more afraid of other Germans than of foreign enemies. Mohnke's group jumps down from the platform into the rail bed without a pause, and continues north. They want to get to Stettin subway station in the north of the city.

Today, a person on foot, if he wished to avoid meeting obstacles, could follow this planned route only by staying up on the earth's surface. You would have to cross Invalidenstrasse from the corner of Chausseestrasse—which would allow you to do some shopping along the way, an advantage not to be sneezed at.

Having crossed Invalidenstrasse, you would see at the northern end of the intersection a pedestrian island with a peculiar grate, a structure which looks purposeless here in the middle of the roadway. This is the subway entrance to what in 1945 was Stettin station.

If you look more closely, you will see a staircase that is no longer open for your use. If you could go down the stairs, you would find yourself in an old-fashioned tiled train station that ekes out a dark and grubby existence under the name *North Station*. Up here aboveground where we are standing, is the exact spot where Mohnke's group hoped that they could surface, having slipped under the Soviet cordon, and break through farther on—you've got to read this twice—toward Schwerin.

But right now, they are still in between two other stations, City Center and Französische Strasse.

Meanwhile, the second group has set out, and has changed at City Center. Their leader is the commander of the Reich Security Service, Rattenhuber, or "Rat Raiser." (My God, what names!)

The third group is approaching, too. Highest in rank in this group is Martin Bormann, Hitler's chief of Nazi Party administration and domestic policy leader. Now he has no more Reich left in which to make policy. Baur, Hitler's chief pilot, has taken over the job of leading the group along their nocturnal path. He is carrying a valuable painting on his back: Anton Graff's oil portrait of King Frederick the Second, which used to hang in Hitler's office. Hitler looked at the picture over and over, but it did nothing for him. At the end of his performance, he gave it to his chief pilot. The pilot is standing with his relic of culture like a man who has bought a poster and would like to get it home without creasing it. He loosens the frame, rolls up the canvas: an impractical gift, if you have to travel by foot.

Baur knew his way around better in the air. A few days ago he had a Junkers-390 at his disposal, in which you could fly nonstop across the Pole as far as Japan. They had tested it to find out.

Baur was equipped to fly his employer out of the fray. Preferably to Manchukuo, but Greenland, Madagascar and Jerusalem were on the list, too. Hitler in Jerusalem? Anything is possible. At least Eichmann ended up there.

Who will hold it against the airline pilot that he does not know his way around the Berlin subway? The two others in his group who might conceivably know the way are Reichsleiter Bormann and Reich Youth Leader Axmann. When was the last time that Axmann used public transportation? As for Bormann, it cannot even be imagined.

Bormann, Axmann and Baur do not know that one can change at City Center. And that in their case, they definitely should. They have let other people drive them too often. They have forgotten how to walk. Admittedly, they are learning to walk tonight, but they lack the basic information that the little people know. How can they know what it is like when there is no train?

World history does offer consolation to suffering people, if they survive long enough to observe such moments of retribution. Or if we do not think that we will survive, we may read, while we still have time, about what happened in the past, and take our consolation beforehand. There is always some Friedrich or Ludwig or what's-his-name, who has bequeathed us his story. We only have to know how to interpret it.

Instead of taking the tunnel passage at City Center, Baur's group continues to walk straight ahead, in the direction of Pankow.

These people who belong to Hitler's immediate entourage, only know about one City Center station.

Even Hitler very likely would have missed the right path. And if he had popped up suddenly among the dead-tired, resigned and despairing people on the platform, would anyone have called out: "Führer, command us, we will follow you"?

Like all the women here who have not been to a hairdresser for a long time, our streetcorner tipster, Rosi Nante, ties her head scarf back on, and recites:

> The innkeeper's wife, she had a dream
> You won't believe: it was a scream.
> She heard them sing a Te Deum,
> And saw Hitler dead and stuffed
> Inside the British Museum.

The Superman of the Germans had not been seen in public for years. Not only did he not wish to be seen—as we said, that type gets scared of the little guy eventually—but he did not wish to see anything. When he spoke to the public, it was through a radio microphone. When he traveled—and that was only the short stretch from the Reich Chancellery to Anhalter Railroad Station or to Tempelhof Airport—the curtains of his big car stayed drawn. So he never saw a bombed house, never saw a bread line outside the food store, never saw prisoners in striped coats clearing away the debris.

Meanwhile, Bormann, Baur, and Axmann and their group have arrived at Hausvogteiplatz station. Here they realize that they have taken the wrong route. They do not continue forward, nor do they go back, probably because they do not know exactly how to get from City Center to City Center. They climb up to the surface, and complete the rest of their planned journey toward Friedrichstrasse station using the route they are accustomed to take in their cars.

We will not stay with them. Baur survives, gravely wounded. Axmann gets away, too. But Bormann and an SS doctor feel cornered hours later at Lehrter station and bite through their poison capsules. Whatever happened to the portrait of Frederick the Great?

Meanwhile, Mohnke's group now has fewer people. They could not manage to stay together in the darkness. The remaining members have passed Französische Strasse station, crossed underneath the linden trees, reached Friedrichstrasse station.

So far so good.

They head north. They need to pass two more subway stations under the Spree river. But one hundred yards beyond Friedrichstrasse station, Mohnke's group is halted for the first time.

At this point, let us remember once again who Mohnke is. A combat veteran SS general. A member of Hitler's bodyguard since 1933. He is wearing a steel helmet and a camouflage suit, and carries a pistol and a submachine gun, and the ammunition to go with them. His men are as badly armed as he. (Mohnke is also carrying a little bag of cut diamonds which were stored in the Reich Chancellery and were meant to be handed out as a bonus with the highest military decorations. But there is no more opportunity to confer them. The value of the "Knight's Cross of the Iron Cross" would be vastly increased if awarded "With Swords and

Diamonds." What rewards would the German leadership have had to devise, for those who already had reached the jewel-studded pinnacle of achievement? "The Iron Cross, with Bratwurst and a Sauerkraut Cluster." There was many a Berliner in the subway tunnel that night, who would gladly have given a decoration in exchange for a hot meal.)

As we said, Mohnke and his men—and the four women—have been forced to a halt under the earth, approximately at the spot where the Weidendamm Bridge begins. (Today we cross that bridge heedlessly, suspecting nothing.)

Down below in the tunnel, there was a bulkhead that may be there still. By a bulkhead I mean a large iron gate which is water-tight and maybe hermetically sealed to keep out the river Spree, should it decide to seek a new riverbed here.

At this hour—it is after one A.M. on May 2, 1945—a number of residents of Berlin are standing in front of this bulkhead and arguing with the guards, because they would like to flee northward. But that just is not allowed. Two uniformed men are on watch duty and will let no one through. They have their orders. The gate to the north remains closed unless a train is going through. And no trains are traveling on a night like this, when the Russians may already have occupied the stations at the end of the line.

We who were not there, who are the offspring and the delayed aftermath of these events, must now try with all the imagination in us, to picture what is happening.

In the glow, in the meager imperfect gleam of a few flashlights, two men bar the path of SS General Mohnke.

They are not soldiers but employees of the Berlin Transportation Company. That makes their position weak and strong at the same time. As nonsoldiers, they are not under military command. At least not under normal conditions.

The subway company would hardly have assigned unreliable men to guard the bulkhead at such an hour. These two subway employees recognize clearly that not just anyone but an SS general is standing before them. If his camouflage jacket did not tell them, then his voice would. It is the voice of a man who is used to being in command. This voice has given orders in several theaters of war. And if the rank of major general is not enough to force them to yield, to obey, then the SS double-lightning insignia no doubt will.

Experience tells us what will happen next: These two government employees will give way to force. As good Germans from the
time of the Weimar Republic, they know what is expected when
an army officer tells a government representative what to do. A
lieutenant with ten men can control a government. So they open
their iron curtain with a groan. They ask only to have the order in
writing first, if possible, so that they can account to their superiors.

Or no, the two guards remain undecided. Neither ranks higher
than the other. They do not open the bulkhead, because they have
no orders to open it.

No doubt the strange general in the SS camouflage jacket will
now call them dirty shits, and tell them to get out while the getting's good, and go punch tickets somewhere. Do two dumb-ass
train conductors and streetcar lackeys like you dare to oppose a
man like me, who only yesterday spoke with the Führer?

Will that work any more?

The two men from the Berlin Transportation Company do
not open the bulkhead. They do not give way. They go on standing where they are. The unknown major general cannot give
them orders.

Why?

Because they do not work for him!

It is particularly difficult for a German to know exactly who can
order him to do what, and when. And who cannot. And who
should be shot afterward because he followed an order, or because
he did not follow it. There are so many guidelines, instructions and
laws, and possible ways to interpret them, that no one knows exactly, at the moment when knowing is critical. No one knows or
can know.

What happens now?

The two doorkeepers refuse the order. At this point, we would
expect Mohnke to use his machine gun to instruct them as to who
wears the helmet tonight, the last night of the Berlin Reich. Two
more dead men no longer matter. The date is May 2, 1945. Two
young soldiers are dangling from the arch of the rail bridge over-
head, hanged because they resisted the orders of the SS. (You who
are reading these lines ought also to read the memorial plaque
on the bridge, although it is less conspicuously placed than an
advertising billboard.)

Meanwhile, what about the two railroad employees? Are they lying there, shot dead? No, they are still standing and refusing to open the bulkhead.

But now surely they will be "bumped off," as the German language creatively puts it. Later they, too, will be honored in some wreath-laying ceremony, for doing their duty to the last.

No, they are simply refusing to let anyone force them to open the bulkhead.

But at least someone could scare them off, drive them away, and open the gate himself.

But Mohnke does not open the bulkhead. The incredible happens. He goes away. He withdraws to Friedrichstrasse Station. Then his group climbs up to the surface. They choose the surface rail line as their escape route. They find a sidebridge by which they can cross the river. They move through cellars and courtyards, ruined buildings and passages, and get quite a long way. They escape capture until the following day, when they are all taken prisoner in a brewery in the northern part of Berlin. But that is no longer important to us.

The only important thing is this incident by the underground bulkhead. At the last moment, the cave of the dead monster gives birth to resolute people who in turn are stopped by two subway workers and forced to turn around. Forced by men who would not even be able to control all the people who try to travel without a ticket.

Two uniformed, self-important men at a lost post. Or is that not an accurate description? Hitlers come and go, but the subway trains have to keep running.

Years later, when Mohnke's imprisonment ended, he was asked what had stopped him from forcing his way through the bulkhead. He replied in these words: "As soldiers, we were accustomed to think in terms of orders and obedience. In this case, the order was that the bulkhead had to stay closed at night—even if it only came from the Berlin Transportation Company. And we obeyed." Mohnke also praised the sense of duty shown by the two subway employees. "No doubt it was our respect for their sense of duty that made us decide to turn back."

Did he see himself and them as equals?

There was this victory in the final hour. A small incident which reveals so much, partly because it is bloodless and without violence.

Two men at their workplace. Approached by armed power from a regime which still represents almost the ultimate in state violence. This power had diamonds to offer, or could produce close to fifty heavily armed men in the next half hour. And this power, accustomed to obedience, gives way to instructions from a civilian company?

Was the German secret weapon used at the end after all, the weapon that says: FORCE WANTS TO BE COMMANDED and ORDERS ARE ORDERS?

Or did the all-powerful SS reach the limit of their power to give orders, at the bulkhead under the river Spree? Were the SS taught obedience not only by the allied armies but by two Berlin subway employees? Is this the place where democracy begins again, a democracy in which there are limits to what military men can do? Or is it the same old song: one uniform won't tear the button off another?

Uncertainty. The two subway employees say, without saying it out loud, that the SS can look for ratholes to hide in wherever they like, only not here, not any more.

Or are they just showing the blackshirts the Man in Black, the bogeyman who may already be in the subway tunnel, at the Oranienburg Gate . . . ?

Are they afraid that the SS troop will blow up the tunnel in order to flood it, to block with water an enemy who has not been blocked by anything else? Are the two concerned about what will happen in the next few hours? Do they feel they must protect the precious train line from the panic of the mob who have not yet shown the white flag? Or are the iron doorkeepers in fact motivated by the sense of duty, that feeling that *To be German means to do a thing for its own sake?*

I am not at all sure. I don't know the answer.

This episode can easily be overlooked among the documentary films about the unconditional surrender, and the memoirs of fighting men. Flashlight batteries do not last long, especially when they are wartime goods.

Translated by Jan van Heurck

Heiner Müller

The Father

A dead father would have been perhaps
a better father. The best
father is stillborn.
Grass grows over the border ever anew.
Again and again the grass that grows over the border
must be torn out.

1

My father, an official in Germany's Social Democratic party, was arrested from bed at four am on January 31, 1933. I woke up, the sky black outside my window, to the noise of voices and footsteps. Books were being thrown on the floor in the next room. I heard my father's voice more clearly than the strangers' voices. I got out of bed and went to the door. Through the crack I saw a man punch my father in the face. Shivering, with the blanket pulled up to my chin, I lay in bed as the door to my room opened. My father stood in the doorway, behind him the strange men, tall, in brown uniforms. There were three of them. One held the door open with his hand. My father stood with his back to the light, I could not see his face. I heard him call my name softly. I did not answer and lay very still. "He's sleeping," my father said then. The door was shut. I heard them take him away, then the short stride of my mother coming back alone.

2

After my father's arrest, my friends, the sons of a minor official, told me that they were no longer allowed to play with me. It happened one morning when snow lay in the ditches. There was a cold wind. I found my friends in the yard, inside the toolshed, sitting on logs and playing with tin soldiers. I heard them imitating the thunder of cannon while I was outside the door. When I came in, they fell silent and looked at each other. Then they went on playing. They drew up their tin soldiers in battle lines facing each other, and took turns rolling marbles into the enemy ranks. Each time, they imitated the roar of cannon. They addressed each other as General, and after every shot they triumphantly called out the casualty figures. The soldiers were dying like flies. At stake was a pudding. Finally one general had no more soldiers left, his army lay dead on the ground to the last man. That's how they knew who had won. Then the fallen soldiers, friend and foe jumbled together, were tossed into the cardboard box along with the one survivor. The generals stood up. The victor announced that they were going to have breakfast now, and as he passed me, he said that I could not come along and that they were no longer allowed to play with me, because my father was a criminal. My mother had told me who the criminals were, but also that it was not good to say it. So I did not tell my friends. They found out twelve years later, when great generals sent them into the fire and the roar of countless real cannons, to kill and die in the last terrible battles of World War II.

3

A year after my father's arrest, my mother was granted permission to visit him in the camp. We took the local train to the end of the line. The road ran uphill in curves past a sawmill that smelled of freshly cut wood. The way to the camp led off from the flat cone of the mountain. The fields by the wayside lay fallow. Then we stood outside the wide wire gate until they brought my father. I watched through the wire mesh as he approached along the gravel street inside the camp. The closer he came, the more slowly he walked. His prisoner's clothing was too big for him, so that he looked very small. The gate did not open. He could not put his hand through the small mesh. I had to come very close to the gate to see the whole of his thin face. He was very pale. I can't remember what we talked about. Behind my father stood the armed guard, with a round rosy face.

I wish my father had been a shark
who ripped up forty whalers

and I had learned how to swim, in their blood
My mother a blue whale, my name Lautréamont
Died unknown in Paris, 1871.

4

My mother could not get work, because she was his wife. So she accepted the offer of a factory owner who had been a member of the Social Democratic party until 1932, to let me eat my midday meal at his table. Every day at noon I leaned against the iron gate outside my benefactor's house, climbed the broad stone stairs up to the second floor, hesitantly rang the white doorbell, was escorted into the dining room by a white-aproned maid, and was seated at the big table by the factory owner's wife, beneath a picture of a collapsing stag attacked by hounds. Ringed by the voluminous shapes of my hosts, I ate without looking up. They treated me cordially, asked about my father, gave me sweets, and let me pet their dog, who was fat and stinking. I had to eat in the kitchen only once, when they had guests who objected to my presence. It was raining, the last time I leaned on the iron gate until its hinges creaked and yielded. I heard the rain falling as I climbed the stone steps. The husband did not sit with us at the table. He had gone hunting. We had potato dumplings with beef and horseradish. While I ate I listened to the rain. My last bit of potato dumpling split on my fork and dropped onto the carpet. The wife noticed it and looked at me. That same moment, I heard the noise of a vehicle on the road outside the house, then brakes and a scream. I saw the wife go to the window, then rush out of the room. I ran to the window. The factory owner was standing next to his car, in front of the woman he had run over. I went into the hall just as two workmen carried the woman inside and laid her on the floor. I could see her face, her twisted mouth with blood running out. Then another workman came in with the quarry, hares and partridges, which he set down on the floor at some distance from the bleeding woman. I could feel the horseradish coming back up my throat. There was blood on the stone steps. I did not make it to the iron gate before I threw up.

5

My father was released on condition that he kept away from his former district. That was the winter of 1934. We waited for him on a snowbound country road two hours from the village. My mother carried a bundle under her arm, it was his coat. He arrived, kissed me and my mother, put on the coat and walked back through the snow, bent over as if the coat weighed him down. We stood on the road looking after him. You could see a long distance in the cold air. I was five-years old.

6

Because my father was unemployed, my mother resumed her work as a seamstress. The factory was two hours from the village, where we had a room and an attic. The house belonged to my father's parents. Once my mother took me with her to the bank in town. She paid in three marks at a window. The man at the window smiled down at me and told me that now I was a rich man. As we were leaving, I saw a man next to me stuff a thick wad of paper money into his coat pocket. My grandmother was standing by the stove in the kitchen when I showed her the savings book. She read the figure and laughed. "Three marks," she said, and threw a big chunk of butter into the frying pan, then put it on the stove. "Yes," I said, and watched the butter melt away. She cut a second, smaller chunk and put it in, too. Because my father was against Hitler, I had to eat margarine, she said. Taking potatoes from a pot, she sliced them up and dropped them into the seething fat. Grease spattered onto the passbook I was holding. She would not eat margarine, she said, and: "Hitler gives us butter." She had five sons. The three youngest died on the Volga, in Hitler's war for oil and grain. I was there when she got the first telegram. I heard her scream.

7

When Hitler started building the Autobahn, German school-children had to write essays about the project. Prizes were offered for the best ones. I told my father about it as I was coming out of school. "You don't have to get a prize," he said. But two hours later he added, "You have to try." He stood at the stove and broke an egg into the pan, then, after hesitating, a second one and finally, after looking at it and holding it in his hand for a long time, a third. "That makes a good meal," he said. We ate and my father said: "You must write that you're glad that Hitler is building the Autobahn. 'Then my father is bound to get work again, he has

been out of work a long time.' That's what you must write." After
the meal he helped me write the essay. Then I went out to play.

8

Thirteen years later, we were living in one of the main towns in
Mecklenburg. Sitting at our table was a baroness, the widow of a
general who was executed after the failed attempt to assassinate
Adolf Hitler on July 20, 1944. She asked my father, an official of
the recently founded Social Democratic Party, for help in opposing
land reform. He promised to help her.

9

In 1951, my father traveled via Potsdam Square into the American
sector of Berlin, in order to stay out of the class war. My mother
accompanied him as far as Berlin, leaving me alone in our apartment. I sat by the bookcase, reading poetry. It was raining outside,
I heard the rain while I was reading. Putting away the volume of
poems and donning my jacket and coat, I locked the apartment
and walked through the rain to the other end of town. I found an
inn with a dancehall. The noise was audible from far away. As I
stood in the doorway of the dancehall they announced a pause, so
I went into the lounge. A woman sat alone drinking beer at one of
the smaller tables. I sat down beside her and ordered brandy. We
drank. After the fourth brandy I touched her breast and said she
had beautiful hair. She smiled obligingly, so I ordered more brandy.
Next door in the dancehall the music had started up again, the
percussion boomed, the saxophones whined, the strings cried. I
pressed my teeth and lips onto the woman's mouth. Then I paid.
When we stepped into the street, the rain had stopped. The moon
hung white in the sky, spreading a cold light. We walked in silence.
The woman's face wore a stiff smile as she undressed without
ceremony next to the double bed in my parents' bedroom. After
the sex I gave her cigarettes, or chocolate. "When will we see each
other again?" I asked to be polite. "Whenever you want," she
answered, and almost bowed to me—or maybe to the position she
thought my father still occupied. He found the peace he sought
years later in a small town in Baden, paying out pensions to men
who had murdered workers, and to the widows of men who had
murdered workers.

10

I last saw him in the isolation ward of a hospital in Charlottenburg. I took the metropolitan train to Charlottenburg, walked down a broad street past ruined buildings and tree stumps, and was led through a long, bright hospital corridor to the glass door of the isolation ward. They rang the bell. A nurse appeared behind the glass, nodded mutely when I asked for my father, walked up the long corridor and vanished into one of the end rooms. Then my father came. He looked small in the striped pajamas, which were too big for him. His slippers flapped on the stone tiles. We stood looking at each other with the glass between us. His lean face was pale. We had to speak in loud voices. He pulled at the locked door and called the nurse. She came, shook her head, and left again. He dropped his arms, looked at me through the glass, and did not speak. I heard a child crying in one of the rooms. As I left I saw him standing behind the glass door, waving. He looked old in the light that came through the big window at the end of the passage. The train ran fast past the debris and building sites. Outside was the iron-gray light of an October day.

Translated by Jan van Heurck

Hermann Kant

For the Files

I've had it easy. That's not meant as a reproach to anyone, not even myself, it's just a fact.

When I came home, I registered with the police, and the employment office, and for ration cards, and with the Party.

There was no ceremony about it, neither in the offices I went to, nor in me. When a man has been away for four years, he has to report his return, and if he has been where I was, he should report to the Party, that's what I thought.

I just had it easier than most people. I mean that exactly how it sounds.

"Poor folk," a phrase from a fairy tale. We were poor folk. We lived in a summerhouse, and six of us slept in the bedroom, my father and mother and four children. The toilet was out in the yard; a bucket stood in the bedroom.

We ate margarine on our bread, not for reasons of health, and had liverwurst on Fridays. We kept rabbits and a goat, and once we had a sheep. We did not starve, but one morning when I found fifty pennies, my mother wept with relief.

Sometimes we had to borrow money, five or ten marks, and then we were in debt.

I have often told stories about my father, but I'm afraid they were mostly a bit too jokey. In 1933 he was hounded out of his job and became a garbage collector, and later a streetcleaner. He would come home dyed up to his ears and eyebrows with rust-yellow ash. We had a handpump in the entryway.

I doubt that my father was in a joking mood at the garbage dump, or in the gutter with his broom. He only joked around with us. That's why I made the mistake of telling funny stories about him later on.

There's another way I had it easy: nobody in my family could stand the Nazis. My father had no bias against any party, but that did not stop other parties from having a bias against him. A permanent theme of all family gatherings was: should Paul join something or not? My father had been given the word that he could be a gardener again if he would show that his ideas were a bit more in tune with the times. So, should Paul join something?

He didn't. He didn't even stay in the volunteer firemen. The Nazi theory for putting out fires did not suit him.

I had it easy. I grew up among bricklayers, stokers, gardeners and stevedores, and with women who worked at Essig-Kühne and the Reemtsma factory. We also had a civil servant in the family, a forcibly retired policeman, Uncle Ludy, who was the second-loudest Social Democrat I've ever met. The loudest was Grandpa Schmidt, who had raised my mother. He was considered wealthy because he used to drink four bottles of beer on Sunday.

None of them were quiet-voiced people, and no one had trouble hearing what they thought of the Nazis. I heard it, too.

I knew what a concentration camp was, and who had burned Willi Hagen to ashes in Fühlsbüttel, and who had chopped off Hermann Fischer's head.

That made a lot of things easy for me. The names of the dead didn't come out of books, they were the names of neighbors and relatives. My family never disagreed about Hitler. But we did about Ebert and Thälmann,* and sometimes it got so bad that no one gave Hitler another thought. I had it easy when I came home, because I no longer had to choose between my grandfather's party and my uncle's. The thought that I could also choose between my party and no party, never occurred to me. That was decided long before.

My grandfather, uncle and father differed on many points but agreed about me: He is going to go to war! My uncle was alone in his view: he is not going to beat Moscow!

---

*The debate is between Social Democrat and Communist policies (Friedrich Ebert, 1871–1925 was a Social Democrat and first president of the Weimar Republic; Ernst Thälmann, 1886–1944 was a German Communist leader).

He did go to war, and he did not beat Moscow. It came to pass as it had been told to me. I did not have to rely on faith.

I didn't know much. I only knew a handful of stars out of a whole skyful. That was enough to point me in the right direction but not to guide my path.

But it helped that my father was already dying from the war when I had to go in. I was a soldier for four weeks, and a prisoner for four years. I was extremely lucky once again, with my imprisonment, because I went to a place where the war had been extreme. My camp was in what once had been the Jewish ghetto, in the city that once had been Warsaw.

If you're not a clod incapable of feeling, you will either die of dread in a place like that, or you'll begin to think. Begin at last, or begin again.

I was twenty. I was old enough to know a thing or two and young enough to start over.

I am proud that the first political article that was nailed to a board in our labor camp in the former ghetto of burned-out Warsaw, was written by me.

And I had to defend what I wrote. And I wrote more articles. And found allies. And lost friends. And when there were six of us in a camp of two thousand, we formed an organization, the Antifascist Committee of Warsaw Labor Camp. Today, people sometimes ask me if a person can be both a writer and a political official. Well, that's how it was for me.

And the question: Should he join something? did not arise when I came home. All I had to do was check in. I had been involved for a long time.

My checking in was not a ceremonious affair. The results were typical: they immediately sent me to school. That's how it was for me in Poland, too. The first three Party members I met in my self-appointed roles of writer and functionary, were three incredible teachers. One was Karl Wloch, who had been a prisoner in Esterwegen and had survived what his friend Ossietzksy could not.* The other two were women, a Latvian and a Pole. Edda Tennen-

---

*Carl von Ossietzky, 1889–1938, German writer and pacifist, won the Nobel Peace Prize in 1936 and died in a Nazi concentration camp.

baum, who had been Clara Zetkin's political co-worker, and Justyna Sierp, known as Elsa in the French Resistance.

The women were both Jews. The ghetto whose cinders lay under our school, had been home to many people with the same names. I could not possibly have wanted to join any party but theirs.

I had it easy.

Translated by Jan van Heurck

THE END OF THE GDR

Christoph Hein

I Saw Stalin Once When I Was a Child

Various methods exist to learn the condition of a society. In German lands, it has always been instructive to scan the writings of the native historians. Another method that is not without merit, is to look at the games people play.

One game involves asking people the question: "What would you take with you if you were going alone to a desert island?"

I do not like games and questions of this kind. Hypothetical cases distress me, and the dreadful limitation distresses me even more. I do not intend to live on an island, still less to live there alone, and I have no urge even to imagine it. (Before long, I am afraid that my dentist may ask me: Which teeth do you want pulled and which do you want to keep?)

I do not wish to give up any of my pictures, books, and books of pictures. One gives me one thing, another something else, and only all of them together give me what I really need.

The dilemma of being unable to choose just one picture, because this excludes so many that I would not wish to forfeit, is relieved when I think that the "ZEIT 100–Picture Museum" is also intended to be a time-museum in pictures. And so, I choose the picture *I Saw Stalin Once When I Was a Child,* by Komar and Melamid.

I can say little about the painting and nothing about the painters. It surprises and confuses me that two artists are listed as its creators, because it is hard for me to imagine how two people could have collaborated on this canvas. Neither can I comment on the official artistic stature of the painting. I do not know how it is ranked by art historians and gallery owners, whether it is considered first-rate or is one of those works which already change owners for five or six million dollars at auction.

I have chosen this picture for the gallery of the ZEIT Museum for a reason that is naive, almost illiterate: its subject. This picture, a portrait of Stalin, is for me an image of my time, of my century.

The painting is in warm colors, almost a genre scene. It has the look of a pleasant childhood memory, of something you glimpse as you walk or drive past: an unforgettable and seemingly indelible experience whose significance is apparent from the start, however drastically its meaning may change later on. The picture looks to me like the memory of a wintry late afternoon in Moscow. Left-over daylight, or a streetlamp, is making the colors glow, and allows you to recognize the man in the car—a car which looks old-fashioned today. An affable older man is giving the child a look of encouragement which radiates not just kindness but an indulgent understanding of the importance which their meeting holds for the youngster. A statesman, a father of his country, a benevolent papa smiles at the child—and at the viewers of the picture. The car, for us an antique, emphasizes the cosiness, the grandfatherly goodness, the apple-pie security.

This is the portrait of a man who shaped the hopes and the crimes of our century, its seemingly limitless dawn, its homicidal end, and a desperate awakening. A man who probably has a better title than any to stand for our times.

The workmanship certainly is not significant. As a painting, this work is hardly original. Instead it is traditional and conforms to the canon. Considering when it was painted—1981–82—you could even call it an academic painting, or worse yet, hackneyed. And yet there is something provocative in the treatment, there is a troubling, perhaps even an exasperating point of view. This looks like a remote, isolated glimpse of Stalin, a glimpse that knows nothing, that is confined to the child's vantage point and has learned nothing more since the days of childhood.

Seeing its astonishing ignorance, we might shake our heads and pass the picture by. But something compels us to turn our heads again, to walk back and linger. This picture confuses us in some way: its deliberate littleness, the tiny scale of the excerpt, the small car window emphasized by the broad canvas frame, a format which contradicts the real format and seduces the viewer into thinking that it is a miniature. The insignificance of the event, its look of an amusing and nostalgic anecdote which is no different from any other, and which has the endearing charm of lace doilies on bric-a-brac shelves in our grandparents' day. The pleasantness of the picture clashes with the horror we have stored up inside us. Our very different heads hold very different images of Stalin. No doubt they all are painted in the color of blood.

What would a picture of Stalin have to look like, for us to accept it? We know that a grand painting of warriors' butchery is incapable of capturing the horror on canvas. The technique which Goya used to depict war is inadequate to describe all-encompassing, everyday terror, a terror which destroys the psyche before the body and which forces the victim to pass sentence on himself. Perhaps one artist comes to mind who could portray the commonplaceness, the banality of the machinery of murder: Franz Kafka. But if we think about it, we soon realize that this depiction would omit an important element, without which the scene would be incomplete and thus uncomprehended: hope. Hope boundless and then disappointed. Our hope or the hope of others. (And the lesson which our century is still laboring to teach us, is that the blood and the hope of other people are ridiculous and worthless.)

And slowly we realize that all of us once looked at Stalin in the way that Komar and Melamid have recorded. Independently of everything we knew and thought, independently of our attitudes, our faith, our ideology—we saw him like that child, like the painting's unseen author. Whether it was hope we felt or loathing, admiration or despair, hatred or reverence, or mere lack of interest—all of us once saw no more than this friendly face. And what looks like the portrait's limitation to the surface, and the resultant clash between the portrait and our knowledge of history, makes us interact with it in a way that brings us insight. The painters compel us to do follow-up work on their painting, on the image of Stalin; on the image of a head of state smiling amiably at us from an imposing state coach; on the portrait of our century. And finally we glimpse the hidden fate of that child who, the evening after the meeting, may have wondered with pride, and later perhaps with a squeezing dread—whether He also remembered the child. Whether He, too, did not forget, but remembered: I Saw a Child Once When I Was Stalin.

Translated by Jan van Heurck

Erich Loest

I Have Never Drunk Champagne

I have never drunk champagne, until now. My successor gave me the bottle. More precisely, she presented it to me in the name of the school faculty. I worked in the school system for forty-four years. First as a novice teacher, then came my first- and second-level teacher examinations, then I was deputy principal, then principal for more than twenty years, finally demoted because my son ran away to the West. I was a Party member, of course. Then came the unification. They talked about giving me early retirement but they did not let me go, because there was no other music teacher anywhere around. Now the school year is over. Four weeks ago, I turned sixty-five. Not sent packing but bidden a ceremonious farewell.

So, now I will drink champagne. The cork comes out easily. I'll watch out not to spatter a drop. Of course I am familiar with Crimean champagne; the Rotkäppchen brand was not bad at all. Henkell-Dry came along with the West German currency, and now there is champagne. It does smell good. And it is bubbly. And it tastes good, too.

What do *we* know about wine? We had Balkanfeuer, Hemus and Natalie, and at best, Meissner Domkeller. But Laurent-Perrier—now that has an impressive ring to it. We were a country of beer and did not even know how bad our beer was. In the north, people drank schnaps, too. Hanne used to love cold wine punch. I believe that she would be as bewildered by champagne as I am. Since she died, no one here has made cold punch. Here's to you, Hanne!

Now I am thinking about It again. When I stood by her coffin, I thought: Now I'm the only one who knows about that damned business. I told her about it, I had to lean on someone. My parents knew, of course. And Bremer, too. I had to share my burden with Hanne. I did not want to lie to Hanne. Young love and marriage at twenty-two. Head over heels, like a lot of people right after the war. We were determined that there should be nothing but trust between us.

And Bremer. I did not recognize him after thirty years, but he recognized me. I felt that he had grown shorter, he had a fat belly and awful teeth. I was sitting with a couple of colleagues by the Kriebstein Dam. It was a day of radiant sunshine, we were thinking that maybe we would take a motorboat ride, too—when he walked over to our table and said: "Excuse me, are you Steinbruck? Gernot Steinbruck?"

"Yes," I said and waited for him to go on. He pulled a face. It did not look like a smile. For a long time I have pondered what to call it. Sorrow was mixed in it, and maybe contempt. But it was not a sneer either. Then he said: "Hirschbaude." We looked at each other and did not say another word. I knew what Hirschbaude was, on the north slope of the Eulengebirge in Silesia, where the Hitler Youth were given a training course in shooting in the spring of 1943. We were working to earn our sharpshooters' badge and receive some sort of certification that we were qualified to administer examinations. That's where it all began. And that man had been there. Three days later I remembered his name: Bremer. Heinz Bremer, I think, but I could be wrong. Maybe it was Hans.

He raised his eyebrows for a moment, then he walked away, in and out among the tables. One of my teaching colleagues may have asked who he was and what Hirschbaude meant, and maybe I said that I didn't know. We did go for a motorboat ride. No one noticed how the incident had sent a shock deep into my bones. So, someone was still alive who had been there and remembered, who had survived as I did. And most or maybe all of the people at the table with me were Party members, including Kessler, whom we later threw out of the Socialist Unity Party for giving false information on a form.

I had hoped that everybody who knew me from that time was living in West Germany. It was simplest for me that way. But now one of those people, Bremer, was in the German Democratic Republic. After popping up on that summer day, he disappeared again. He would not talk. But the fright lasted for a year. I do not know if I told Hanne about that meeting, probably not.

It's right for me to be drinking the champagne out of a long-stemmed glass and not from a bowl. The carbonization holds up better this way. A trail of bubbles is still rising. I hold my nose right over the spot.

I liked the farewell address they gave me earlier. It's not easy these days to make speeches. The old movable stage sets are no good now: Our Socialist Homeland, Loyalty to Our German Democratic Republic, Our Staunch Alliance with the Mighty Soviet Union. Once long ago, Stalin still figured in our speeches, and then Comrade Walter Ulbricht, all served up with a poem by Weinert or Becher. Now Sarah Kirsch* is a good choice for a poem. In today's speech they said that, undeterred by many changes of fortune, I had devoted forty-four years to the education of our youth. And no one admitted that the whole thing was a flop, that we did not get rid of Margot Honecker, and that we teachers have been a cowardly bunch of conformists, including me. Including me. No one quoted my title: "Meritorious Teacher of the People." Gernot Steinbruck, still on the job a year and a half after the unification, and now retired with a good thousand marks a month. Here's to you, Gernot. It all could have turned out badly at the end.

Sometimes I think that if things had "followed their lawful course," as the phrase went—if socialism had triumphed and capitalism had rotted away, and if we had turned out to be history's victors, as we always called ourselves, and had marched into a bankrupt West Germany—would we have failed to put people there into internment camps? After all, we Marxist-Leninist revolutionaries knew that we had to smash the old bourgeois state machinery. We would have stuck West German party leaders, generals, millionaires and captains of industry behind barbed wire, and emigrés from East Germany, too—no doubt including Sarah Kirsch, the traitor; and Edzard Reuter of Daimler and Hahn of Volkswagen, and Blüm and Weizsäcker and Lafontaine and Grass and my son Hartmut. And then, with our people, we would have built everything the socialist way. Hardly anybody realizes it, here or

*Sarah Kirsch, contemporary woman author (born 1935), first lived in East Berlin but then left the GDR to write in West Berlin.

over in the West. No, I really won't drink to that. It would be irrational to complain that the West Germans are giving us a hard time.

Yes, we expelled Kessler from the Party. After that he was not allowed to be a teacher any more either. He worked in the building trade, then took off for Berlin where no one knew him. His wife did not want to go with him. It could be that their marriage broke down, I don't remember exactly. The affair was crystal clear: Kessler joined the Nazi Party when he was eighteen. He told us everything, perfectly calmly. After all, he knew how the hearing would end. Then we debated, and I said that no one among us would reproach him for his Nazi Party membership and that in fact, I myself had been a Hitler Youth leader; but he had *lied to the Party*. Everyone said: You lied to the Party, you gave false information in the questionnaire. "I simply wanted to be a teacher," Kessler added. "And would I have been allowed to be one, in 1946?"

"No, you wouldn't," others objected, "but two years later, maybe you would. Couldn't you wait?" Brownshirt affiliation was not so serious any more, but he had *lied to the Party*. How we all used to say that phrase: *the Party*. There was a sanctity about it, as if Bebel and Liebknecht were looking down upon us from the clouds above.* We voted unanimously to expel Kessler. During the proceedings, I took neither an especially prominent nor an especially retiring role. I contributed to the debate, factually and dependably. And I didn't kick either, when I was dismissed from my job as school principal in 1980. Our son Hartmut had taken off for the West via Yugoslavia, and I was unable to prove that I had known nothing about his plans. For a while it even looked as if I had helped him. They could have put me in prison for that.

The military training camp at Hirschbaude is where the thing began, and today it is finally over. They can no longer throw me out of the Socialist Unity Party because the party no longer exists, and I am not a member of the PDS.† They cannot kick me out of the school because I am retired. And the school is completely

---

*August Bebel, 1840–1913, German labor politician, and Karl Liebknecht, 1871–1919, German socialist politician.

†PDS, the Party of Democratic Socialism, formed in 1989 after the collapse of the ruling Socialist Unity Party, included what was left of the former communist government, especially those who had shown independence of the old regime.

changed now. Now the question they ask is whether you helped the Stasi, that's the acid test. We belong to the Federal Republic of Germany; there are different standards now. But for more than forty years while this was the German Democratic Republic, I had this knife at my throat. Today I drink to it. Today I could stand in the public square and shout: "I was in the Waffen-SS!" But I will take care not to do that.

The scar under my arm has turned pale. In Westerwald, a doctor surgically removed my blood-group number. He gave me six other small wounds, and a sizable one down on my hip. He was cutting it all away, I was under a bit of local anesthesia, and he kept joking that it would be even more convincing if he amputated my finger— and which one did I think it ought to be? I changed clothes in a warehouse. The Waffen-SS man turned into a navy infantryman. I tore holes in my shirt and jacket, I ripped the bandage from one of my smaller wounds to get a little blood. Everything looked really authentic. The Americans had pushed past us into central Germany, they simply did not want to climb up to the village and take us prisoner. Then I got scared that a Werewolf troop or even Waffen-SS might chase us back into combat again. I walked down to the road. American tanks were driving by, and the men looking out of the hatches showed me where to go. A guard standing at the crossroads sent me into a field where infantrymen crouched on their backpacks. They asked me where I had come from, and I said that I was a sailor from the *Bismarck,* which had not sunk but at this moment was sailing up the Rhine to change the course of the war; and I had been caught because I came on land to try to get hold of some fresh vegetables.

It all began at Hirschbaude. The Waffen-SS officers were recruiting for their squad, using both soft and hard sell. The Waffen-SS was the best military unit in the world, they said: equipped with the newest weapons, superbly trained, elite. They were not chary of derogatory comments about all the other branches of the service. If the SS would finally get its own fighter planes, they would clear the sky of Allied bombers (they claimed)—and wasn't it the SS who had halted the Russians again and again? Now a new division of Waffen-SS was being created, with a name to live up to: the "Hitler Youth." It would be equipped with Panther and Tiger tanks, and sharpshooters would of course be needed for the mechanized infantry regiments. The division (they said) was being groomed for deployment in the West: after all, some time or other the Yanks and the Tommies and the Canadians would try to crack the Atlantic Wall. The Hitler Youth Division would lead the counterattack and kick those guys into the sea. So, who wanted to be there when it happened?

I am almost certain that Bremer was the first of us to volunteer. One boy insisted he must ask his father, a general of artillery. They had a family tradition going back to the time of Frederick the Great, he said, and he wanted to be in the artillery, too. Naturally the Waffen-SS has artillery, was the rejoinder. Then two more boys signed up. They were given time off immediately, and were allowed second helpings in the canteen. This really meant something to us, because we were always hungry. I didn't care much where I ended up. Basic training would be tougher in the Waffen-SS, everybody said, but I was attracted to the idea of getting better training. And I refused to be shipped off to a desolate troop somewhere on the Eastern Front to be slaughtered after four weeks' training as an infantryman, as had happened to several boys in the class above me. I signed up without a qualm. It's crazy how a signature you write at seventeen can oppress you your whole life long. Today all that is over. Anyhow I'll pour myself another, and drink to that. It really is strange, I had to reach sixty-five to drink champagne for the first time.

If I try, I can hear again the songs we used to sing back then. Some ten years ago, I came across them in the course of my music teaching. How was that again? Probably some film showed the German army singing while they marched: "The rotting bones are trembling." Idiocy, of course. I tried to make that clear to the students. The German army, and the Waffen-SS, too, loved sentimental sob songs. "For home sweet home I'm pining." Probably I could still sing all the verses of that straight through. Or "Lonely sinks the sun 'neath heaven's tent; a blackbird . . ." Was that "lonely" or "slowly"? I sang songs of that sort to the students, accompanying myself on the piano. They listened with disbelief and also reluctance. They did not want to know the Nazi time in *that* form. The version they knew was: a fascist war for plunder, and the Soviet Union liberated us. Their parents may perhaps have told them that the Americans were the first to march into our city, but they did not hear it in school. I played and sang to them: "One day I'll come back to my homeland again, at early morn as the sun is rising." I pictured myself marching around the square in this barracks in Franconia while our drill instructors yelled: "Louder!" I had not fought in the International Brigade in Spain, in fact I was too young, so I had not sung: "Spain's skies spread out their stars above our trenches." That song goes on about our faraway homeland. I think there may be some girls in it, too. And now these GDR children heard me sing it, their Comrade Principal who still used to give a few music lessons so as not to get out of practice. Wearing my Party badge on my lapel as I always did, for forty years. Of course I did not reel off my entire repertoire. When I stopped, a girl said meditatively: "All that doesn't sound so bad." And another girl giggled.

Not that everyone signed up for the Waffen-SS during our sharpshooter training. Quite a few got harangued about how they did not love Germany and its Leader as they ought to. One boy sat bent forward and shook his head, saying "No, no." The two Waffen-SS officers asked him why he did not volunteer: what concerns or questions did he have? But he went on shaking his head and insisting: "No, no." He was short and physically frail. At that time, the Waffen-SS no longer required recruits to be at least five feet seven inches tall. Nowadays you have to explain to the students that back then, five feet seven inches was equivalent to five feet eleven today. I was a little over five feet five.

Suddenly the recruiters ended their campaign. Ten young men had signed up, and maybe that was their norm per recruiting day. In the evening, many of us took part in a heated debate, and defended our decision to volunteer. I remember that I felt numb.

The label on my champagne bottle says: "Laurent-Perrier. Domaine de Tours-sur-Marne. Brut L.P." "Brut" means "dry," I know that much at least. "L.P.": I've no idea what that is. Twelve percent alcohol, a three-quarter-liter bottle. So not too much for one elderly gentleman. Here's to you, Mr. Steinbruck! To your good health!

When I think of the send-off I got! Several of my colleagues envied me, I'm sure. Especially the ones who have been teaching history and civics; and teachers of German, too. Many teachers of Russian are rapidly switching over to English. But people who praised Lenin in the past are badly off now. Those who said that Neutsch was a major author, and now are obliged to admire Uwe Johnson, had better guard their backs. With music one can still manage. "Heaven praises the honor of the Eternal." We used to sing that, and we will go on singing it. I have not thought about that piece for a long time; but it was stored in the back of my mind. The belt buckles of the Waffen-SS used to carry the motto: "Loyalty is our honor."

If the facts had come out during all those years when this was still the German Democratic Republic, the first thing I would have been asked is whether I had had anything to do with concentration camps, with Jews. I could have answered with a clear conscience: nothing whatever. Our Waffen-SS training continued for a pretty long time, because the armored personnel carriers which were destined for our use would not arrive—they kept telling us—until tomorrow or next week, and then the week after that. I was in combat twice, but without those vehicles. What was the model called again? I can't remember for the life of me. The "Caesar"? Or was it a woman's name? We were sent into action one night because some Americans had broken through to free prisoners. It was a confused mess. The Yanks did make it to the prison camp, but we blocked their return route. We lay in wait at a crossroads. Their first tank hit a mine that ripped off one of its tracks so that it rammed through an avenue of trees into a field, where it was shot to bits by bazookas. The second tank turned around, was hit in the rear by a bazooka, and burst into flame immediately. I don't think anyone got out. I fired my automatic rifle at the two trucks, which were now wedged in. I was scared. After all, this was my first time in combat. In the glow of the burning tanks we led the prisoners back to the camp. There were close to twenty. We counted the dead. Six. One of them may have died because of me. If I can be charged with anything, it is this man's death. But accusations of that kind were never brought: "At the front you killed Poles, French, Serbs, Russians, Americans or British, you shot them dead, you bombed them, burned them up with your flamethrower, drowned them in the sea." No doubt that was one crime too many to attribute to the beaten German soldiers and their mothers and wives.

I had my second combat experience on the hills above Remagen. The Allies had expanded their bridgehead there some time ago. Our plan was to dent it from the north. It would have been crazy to try to eliminate it altogether. But one general still had a couple of hundred men, plus mortars and cannons and three tanks. Per-

haps the Führer personally ordered our attack against the Sie-
bengebirge hills on the border of Westerwald. We attacked in the
morning fog so that the fighter-bombers could not detect us. Our
tanks halted at the edge of a wood and we were right behind them.
We were two companies of Waffen-SS, and our assault position, of
course, was at the center. "When all betray, we stay loyal." The
Waffen-SS had chosen that for their anthem. Then we had to go
out onto the field after all, where we were caught by artillery fire.
Their shells reached our lines of riflemen from the very first volley.
The Americans must have had an excellent field observer in one of
the houses on the other side of the open area. Under his direction,
their fire tracked us with diabolical precision. The grain was just
a hand's breadth high, a densely sprouting crop. One of our tanks
took a diagonal path, in a heroic attempt to protect us. An antitank
gun tore off its turret. Then at last our leaders shouted to us to
retreat. We assembled in a ravine and marched through thick
broad-leaved forest and a series of crevasses. It was a German
forest of beeches and oaks, the forest of dragons, knights and
witches. The fighter-bombers hissed above the treetops, and the
German forest rescued us from them. I was convinced that I no
longer had long to live. "We'll die together," we all said. Many no
doubt were thinking of a heroic, senseless suicide attack. Once I
cried. I was just eating out of a can of meat, and my tears fell onto
my spoon. I thought about home and about Hirschbaude. I knew
that if I had not signed up there for the Waffen-SS, I could have
let myself be taken prisoner like all the regular soldiers.

When the Berlin Wall came down, I naturally visited my son
Hartmut, who lives in Wuppertal. There, for the first time, we
were able to talk about everything that happened after he fled to
the West through Yugoslavia. I met his wife and my two grandchildren, and on the third day he drove me up to those hills above
Remagen. Of course I did not tell him in which unit I had fought
there. A little cemetery stood at the edge of the woods, enclosed
by a low wall, well-tended, with a Cross in the middle. The names
and birth dates of some eighty dead were listed, without their
ranks, so no one could tell whether SS men were buried there. That
day I realized that my life had been saved a second time. "I could
have been buried here," I said. And Hartmut asked: "Would I have
been born then? Or would I have had a different father?" No
philosopher and no clergyman can answer that question.

"Do you know that I couldn't stand living there with you people any longer?" Hartmut said that evening. "I would have died."

I had not realized that he felt so strongly. As a child he was often rebellious, stubborn and could get into a white-hot fury. I had more problems with him than Hanne did. He studied mathematics. Occasional radical cutbacks were made in his branch. Suddenly, far fewer data experts were needed than had been estimated. So he went into the production end, for which he had not been trained, and became a shift director, a buffer between the higher-ups and the workers, in a foundry that had been established in the nineteenth century. The workers worked for only six hours a day, or four, as it suited them. Anyone who had filled his quota went to take a shower. Workers who had done only eighty percent of their quota, asked Hartmut to record that they had done one hundred and ten percent. The department heads basically were indifferent. Hartmut poured out his heart to me, and I responded with nothing but worn-out adages. Once, I encouraged him to write a letter to the government minister who had jurisdiction over his firm, and to say that his father, a Party member since '47, agreed with him. This in turn led the Party to the notion that I had encouraged Hartmut to leave the country through Yugoslavia.

People who were in the Socialist Unity Party are familiar with this kind of charade. They needed to make an example of someone. In my circle, they needed a case like mine to prove to their superiors that they were on the alert for signs of disloyalty. None of the faculty members favored tough action, but instructors came and went and my colleagues thought that if they did not dismiss me from my post as principal, the district council would do it and might take a much harder line. Today, what seems to me the worst thing is that I distanced myself from Hartmut. That was the term I used: to distance myself. I did not play my trump card and tell them that the people who had put Hartmut into this damnable position should get it into their heads that he did not leave for the fun of it, but because he could no longer tolerate the slackness and fraud in his foundry. *There* was where they should make a clean breast of things; and if that happened, I would ask Hartmut to come back. But instead I said, and maybe even wrote: "I distance myself from the action of my son Hartmut in running away from our Republic." I even said: "I distance myself from my son." That was a hundred times worse than signing up for the Waffen-SS in Hirschbaude.

Our daughter Christa kept a correspondence going with Hartmut so that we would know the main facts: where he was living, how he went back to college again, how a foundation gave him a grant that allowed him to complete his studies with very good marks, and how he worked as a bartender while he was going to school. I had some concern about this job of his, but when I visited him later, I learned that he had enjoyed mixing drinks, and that once he had even won a prize for inventing an unusual cocktail. So there was nothing sleazy about it, it was a student prank. He served me his cocktail, which he called "Steep Iceberg." Champagne tastes better.

Hanne suffered more than I did at the separation from our son. Of course, photos of our grandchildren stood all over. When Hanne died, Hartmut was not allowed to come to her funeral. At that point, I considered throwing away my Party membership card. My memory of this is ambivalent, because today I wonder to what extent I was deceiving myself. That is, I did not throw the card away. Maybe I just pretended, worked myself up deliberately— artificially, that is—so as not to have to think too meanly of myself. We all like to remember our moments of defiance. Surges of emotion which lead to nothing. Then we can say: "Back then I *almost* . . . ." This ridiculous Almost is all there was.

I was dismissed from my post as principal and was censored by the Party for lack of vigilance. I accepted the punishment. That was another dirty trick that I put up with. "Comrades, I say this by way of self-criticism . . ." It's a good thing that there is no tape recording of the proceedings. Or maybe I ought to look at it the other way around: It's a damned shame that there are not tapes of *all* such proceedings. The people who took part ought to listen to the tapes today, to hear the speeches they made, the oaths of loyalty they swore, and their contempt for the class enemy. "If the West Germans, bent upon retaliation, should dare . . ." No doubt the most exciting thing would be to confront a Christian Democratic Union party official who is sitting in the united German parliament today, with what he said back when he represented the same party in Saxony or Mecklenburg.

It is clear to me what I am doing: I am pointing a finger at other people. Everyone knows other people who were even more rotten than themselves. It's a widespread game.

Many a year went by without leaving a mark. One year we got our Wartburg car; another, the prize of a trip to Kiev. For a while I was a member of an armed industrial militia which belonged to the firm next to our school; the firm acted as our school's sponsor. Each time I buckled on my waistbelt, I would think of the Waffen-SS. I could feel it coming on beforehand, and tried to push away the memory with other thoughts; but I failed. One time I was rated the best marksman in our squad of one hundred, and I was supposed to take part in a district elimination round in another town. My dreams were invaded by the popguns going off on the hills above Remagen. I was afraid that the next time I came onto the shooting range, I would scream that I could not stand to listen to the bang-bang-bang any more. I managed to avoid the conflict: my gall bladder started giving me trouble. My body is helping me, I thought; my gall bladder is smarter than my brain. For four weeks I lay in the hospital, and the complaint cleared up after I had been on a special diet for two years. I was assigned to garrison duty in the industrial militia, then I dropped out. Not much fuss was made about it. There were plenty of malingerers around who were trying to cheat their way to an industrial militiaman's pension.

In Wuppertal I finally met my daughter-in-law. She comes from Amsterdam. We visited her parents there for a couple of days. Hartmut warned me beforehand that like a lot of Dutch people, they were not very fond of Germans. He said that they had never talked about whether they had suffered under the Nazis. Maybe their attitude was based on a collective experience which made them attribute to Germans a collective guilt. We spent our time together in polite probing, and afterward we were all glad it was over. I ate white herring and wonderful cheese, and meanwhile I tried to imagine what would happen if I said, "Just to let you know, I served with the Waffen-SS." I suspect that they all would have stood up looking deathly pale, and silently left the room.

If I had not drunk too much, I would look for a bit of music. Jazz, of the kind that was played after the war. For us, jazz meant the opposite of standing at attention and shooting a gun, of hand grenades and burning tanks. Louis Armstrong and Big Ella Fitzgerald. I am afraid that if I stand up now, I'll find that the champagne has made my legs wobbly. No more than two glasses are left in the bottle. A couple more swallows and I would get even more sentimental. It was a good time, when we played music on the dancefloors in the years after the war: "I feel such a yen for the Kurfürstendamm. . . ." Bully Buhlan and Rita Paul and Paul Henkels in Leipzig—surely they healed us faster and more effectively than Marx and Papa Stalin.

For Christa's sake, too, I will not stand in the public square and shout: "I served in the Waffen-SS!" Politically, everything was clear-cut during her childhood. Father was in the Party, Mother was in the Women's League, we all were in German-Soviet Friendship, and Christa was in the Young Pioneers. She became a teacher and would have remained one, were it not that she quickly had three children and that her husband, as a physician, was financially independent of any extra income she could bring in. They lived an almost idyllic existence amid the hustle and bustle of the GDR. They traveled to the Black Sea and to Leningrad for holidays, and because Christa's husband was a top-notch doctor, he was also allowed to attend a conference in the West now and then. He almost went to Japan, but only almost. What if I told him I was in the Waffen-SS? He has to establish a practice now, he has no interest in anything but his debts. I ought to discuss it with Christa. She would understand me, no doubt. Hartmut would say: "You lied to me for forty years." It would be terrible for his wife and her family.

Is there anyone whom it would help to know?

Ilona? Man, what a really weird notion that is. Ilona my wild granddaughter, who ran away from the university in 1988 and then worked in every possible forum from the feminists to Bündnis 90,* searching for truth, banging her head against every wall, and suddenly ended up a member of the state legislature, wondering whether she ought to return to her studies or go into politics right away. I should give her the facts straight between the eyes, so she will see how tangled life's course can be, and so she will not think she has already understood everything. Always going flat out against the PDS and the old stallions of the bloc-vote parties. Should I tell Ilona?

---

*Bündnis 90, or Alliance 90, was one of many groups that put up candidates for the parliamentary elections in the GDR in March 1990. A coalition, it included New Forum and other citizens' groups that had led the November 1989 revolution, but it differed from regular parties in that its members aimed not to hold government power but to act as a pressure group. Most wanted the GDR to take a new independent line rather than immediate unification and absorption by the conservative parties of the Federal Republic of Germany.

There goes the last swallow of champagne. Will our granddaughters make a better fight of it? I must give that careful thought, but not any more today. Perhaps I simply want their absolution, perhaps I would like to lean on them the way I used to lean on Hanne? But not after a bottle of bubbly. Probably I will take my old tale with me into the grave. It won't do anyone any good any more, not even Ilona. It is my problem, not hers.

Now I truly have drunk champagne.

Translated by Jan van Heurck

F. Hendrik Melle

I.M.*

1

Before we begin, this last bit of self-indulgence: I would rather have held my tongue. I would rather have flowed down time's river as a mouthful of turbid broth and not had to chew over this story again.

Some people may call this cowardice. Why not? Everything could have turned out okay. Socialism going forward, unstoppable by ox and donkey; the Federal Republic becoming somewhat more colorful, stylish, easier to maintain over the years, a sort of plumper, more complacent Switzerland. And little me living high off the hog.

But that isn't what happened. You should never take a stand against oxen and donkeys. And now I have to, because otherwise I can't stand it. Because otherwise I can't stand myself.

I was Sebastian Edelbrink.

Is that the doorbell ringing?

It isn't the doorbell. Sebastian Edelbrink is not "Mischka," "Rose" or "Heiner." He won't make a splash in the news. He's taking a nap. He is napping in one of the myriad files of the Gauck Commission.

---

*"I.M." is "Inoffizieller Mitarbeiter" or "informal collaborator," a term referring to ordinary GDR civilians who fed information about their fellow citizens to the state security forces ("Staatssicherheit" or "Stasi"). After unification, the Gauck Commission was set up to investigate these cases.

Alas, he is being waked up!

Nothing will happen if they wake him up. No one of rank or name will lose face. No one will resign. No one will be upset. Just one more petty little accomplice in a petty gang in a petty little age.

Only me.

I'm upset.

Even now, years after his death.

I'm waking him up. Sebastian Edelbrink was one of them, an I.M., an unofficial collaborator of the Ministry of State Security.

2

I was eighteen, had school behind me and the army ahead of me. In between came a last trip to Bulgaria, a last summer.

It's the summer of the year when the mad spray-painter is skulking through Zurich, John Lennon dies of five bullets, and Dire Straits brings a few new sounds to rock.

The night before leaving on my trip—I planned to take the train to Prague and hitchhike from there—we were sitting in the attic of a friend's house drinking red wine, smoking Karo cigarettes, and the future lay before us like a racetrack.

It was a dream, in that last naive summer, to be allowed for once to look out over the edge of the pot on whose bottom we were all living, and to glimpse the shadow of an adventure. To be allowed for once to get a quick look for oneself, if you please, and see that there is no better alternative—free by Engels' definition: to make a decision based on knowing the facts.

A few hundred miles beyond Budapest there is a fork in the road. Both roads lead to Bulgaria. To the left you travel through Rumania, to the right to the border of Yugoslavia. I had a visa for Rumania. Rumania too lay at the bottom of the pot we were living in. I knew the stretch of road through Rumania by heart. Yugoslavia stuck out a bit beyond it.

There was never much said about Yugoslavia. It belonged to the same group as our country but not properly. Belonging to us so little, it was alien and mysterious enough to be something different.

I didn't think a lot that day. The sun was too hot and too bright for that. This inexplicable, absurd sun a hundred yards before the crossroads. Let's just see where the first car that stops is headed, I thought.

I dropped my backpack on the asphalt, raised my hand.

A red R4 stopped.

The oracle spoke: Take the road through Yugoslavia.

Two hours later Bernhard Helfenöter and I were sitting on the meager seat boards of a Hungarian border post a hundred yards from Yugoslavia. A guard stood outside the door. He stood there as if by chance, smoking. A Kalashnikov hung at his side. Not very dangerous. There to inspire respect.

"Don't get into any discussions," Bernhard whispered between pursed lips.

I shook my head.

"You must stay tough!"

I nodded.

Another border guard appeared and fetched me.

I was taken to a jeep. The jeep took me to a barracks. My room was a room, not a cell. Three times a day the guard changed outside the door. Four times a day you got something to eat. Countless times I asked what was going to happen to me. No one could give me an answer. No one spoke German. The sky in the window was whitish blue in the daytime, black at night. The window had no bars yet.

"Take off," a part of me said. "At least try."

"Don't be a fool," said the other half. "Don't get any deeper into this nightmare."

I hadn't a clue.

I was never a hero except in dreams—a rock star, dragon-slayer, liberator of princesses and nations. Never a man on the run. I became that later.

I got in deeper.

A bus brought me under guard to the next-biggest town. What I could see of the town was beautiful. The building they took me to was yellow. It was the prison.

After the first week I was taken before a judge. He was an old, heavy man with black hairs growing out of his nose who spoke German with a hint of a Viennese accent. He read out the investigative report: Bernhard Helfenöter had not picked me up until the crossroads. We had talked about Paris in May, Trotzky and literature. I had wanted to go to Yugoslavia, Bernhard and the investigative report knew nothing of any intention to flee the German Democratic Republic. Herr Helfenöter had left Hungary two weeks earlier.

The freedom of others makes you happy too. I wept for a friend whom I had known for two hours, wept for that one sentence of boundless intimacy: "You want to go to Yugoslavia? Let's try."

The old man shook his head. "You're still young," he said. "I'd be glad to release you. But we've already reported you to your people, haven't we? They'll come and fetch you soon. Tsst, tst, tsst."

I was taken back to my cell.

3

My journey home began at dawn. I had to clean my cell the evening before. "Yo-uu ha-ave to cle-ean like at home," the guard said, "spick and span." That night I slept badly, restlessly. I didn't have any nightmares. The whole time I was behind bars, I only had nightmares when it was light. The nights were islands of stillness.

The days were not so still: the key would crunch in the lock. An officer would bark at me to come outside. Face to the wall!

Always face to the wall.

Down we went into the cellar. Along the corridor walls to left and right were wooden lockers, rabbit cages without wire grates in the doors. I was locked inside one of them. And was no longer alone. To left and right, the cupboards were full of people experiencing the same things as I: the hubbub of voices, whispers, shouts of someone's name, cries of encouragement shouted down by orders: "Where did they catch you?"

"Shut your trap!"

Wait until you all get back home!!!

It was an Icarus Bus from Interflug. It was a bus full of captured escapees, would-be runaways, attempted refugees from our Republic.

"You weren't running away, just going to Yugoslavia. You'll have to explain that very clearly to your people," the border patrolman had said. Now I understood.

I didn't know!

I wasn't the exception, I was the rule!

And the rule provided that an IL 62 would be waiting on a remote runway at Budapest airport. And the rule provided that each prisoner should be assigned a guard. And the rule also provided that during the flight the prisoners had to wear handcuffs. And the rule provided that no one spoke during the flight. And the rule provided that the plane would fly at least twice a month during summer.

This was the first time in my life that I had flown in an airplane.

Let this damned plane crash, I prayed to the god of Marxists. Let this damned plane crash and the rescue teams find a pile of corpses imprisoned in handcuffs.

Never mind that nonsense, I prayed: Don't let anything happen. Anything is better than being dead.

When I landed in the clink in my home town thirty-six hours later, after we spent hours driving over decayed highways in small dark transport cages inside B-1000 transport vehicles, I was cooked soft like spaghetti in a factory kitchen.

My socialist fatherland had reclaimed me.

4

Number so-and-so, come out! Face the wall! Turn left! Up the stairs! Right turn! Left turn! Face the wall! Go on, wait!

In the room where I was led six weeks after being captured in Hungary, a man sat at the desk bent over a few papers. Sunlight poured through a barred window. Without looking up he greeted me with a nod. "Sit down!"

I sank into the chair, my heart was racing. On the small table under the window lay the scattered ruins of my last summer—the rucksack cut open on the side, my shirts and underpants, the books I had with me. The notebooks to which the youthful poet confided his lyrical soul: "I'd like to be a point-mass, a theorem zinging through everything. . . ."

"Sit properly, if you please!" snarled the Desk. A brief glance from his gray eyes and I knew he loathed me, even though I had not said anything yet.

A second man entered the room, inconspicuously garbed in circular-knit trousers like the first. They whispered together. Then the whispering was over. The topic was me. "Izze the one?" asked the Circleknit Trousers.

The Desk nodded: "Would you ever have thought that that guy would end up here?"

The Circleknit Trousers said nothing. They both stared at me.

I gathered all the strength at my command. Folding my arms on my chest, I stared back. "Would you mind if I . . . ," I tried to intervene in the conversation about me.

"Hands on the chair!" the Desk bellowed instantly.
I jumped, my hands darted to the wood.

5

Number so-and-so, come out, hands up! Face the wall.

Circleknit Trousers was the one who acted as host. "I had the feeling that you would get along better with me than with my colleague." Circleknit Trousers was smoking. "Tell me about it," he said.

I wanted to talk. After eight weeks in solitary there was nothing I wanted more than to talk. It wasn't easy: the crossroads beyond Budapest, the glittering sun, Engels' idea about making decisions based on knowing the facts, and this one last summer. Everything I had been given A's for writing in my essays, head glowing with inspiration; everything I had learned to believe in for eighteen years. It was anything but easy. "I wasn't trying to run away!" I said.

Circleknit Trousers nodded. "You wanted to go to Yugoslavia. What did you want there?"

"To see, to look, to be there . . . I don't know."

The Desk appeared right on cue. "I do-o-n't kno-ow," he aped me, then at once bellowed so that his carotid artery threatened to burst, "He wanted to run off, to sneak off and do a bolt, to take the easy way out! He doesn't even have the guts to just say it . . ."

Circleknit Trousers raised his hand, turned to the Desk. "Take it easy, I can manage him alone. . . ."

The Desk vanished, muttering under his breath and banging the door behind him. I started to relax. Circleknit Trousers had saved me. He was trying to understand me! It wasn't a question of having the guts to run away, it was a question of the guts to stay. Is there anyone now who believes that once upon a time, that was a question too?

"Scared?" asked Circleknit Trousers. He had ordered two coffees over the intercom. The first coffee I had had in months!

I nodded. I was scared.

"Why?" asked the Stasi.

"Because I'm here." The whole truth.

"Yes," he set down his cup. "Let's start with that. Why are you here?"

Good question. Why was I here?

I wrote out some personal notes about what I had wanted in Yugoslavia.

I wrote out some personal notes about why I had wanted to go to Yugoslavia.

I wrote out some personal notes about what I had wanted at the crossroads past Budapest.

I wrote out some personal notes about how a red R4 had pulled up.

I wrote out some personal notes about what I had talked about with Herr Helfenöter.

I wrote out some personal notes about why I had spoken to Herr Helfenöter.

Circleknit Trousers helped me do it. Sometimes when it was going well, we smoked a cigarette together. When it wasn't going so well he had to shout a bit because I was so stubborn, and for three to six days I vanished into my hole, my twenty minutes' round of daily exercise cancelled, alone with myself, my fear, my bad conscience.

That was only the beginning.

6

Youthful poems on my interrogator's desk were read aloud, not unsympathetically. A man who reads all of someone else's journals and letters can get very close to him. Especially if he does it with a professional interest: "That isn't hostile to the state. You've read quite a bit of Rilke—youthful melancholy. But it isn't hostile to the state, now is it?"

"No, that is, no, no." What was I supposed to say? That day I wasn't especially on top, even though the lightbulb shone in a friendly way and not one little cloud sailed across the ceiling of my cell.

My sentence had been pronounced.

"Less than a year," my interrogator said, "less than a year. You can do that standing on your ass. More cookies?"

He meant it seriously. I could tell that by looking at him. He had seen so many people pass through here that he had completely lost his sense of time. And there were plenty of years for the enemies of the Workers' and Peasants' State.

And I sat there in my funny outfit, stuffing myself full of cookies, and could feel the snail of time crawling over my skin, leaving its trail on me with each day that dragged on. "A year." I grabbed a lebkuchen. I always did love Christmas. "A year is five percent of my whole life so far."

"It doesn't matter," my interrogator said. "Any quantity of time is always subjective."

He was right.

No one was closer to me than my interrogator.

Not entirely by my choice, I admit. But he brought me unlimited possibilities: of being allowed to talk.

So one day we were sitting there again—I still remember it was only a few days till the Feast of Peace, the low-hanging December sun tinted the window bars gold, time slowly grew short, soon I would begin to serve my sentence and then it would be time for us to say goodbye, we who had shared all my secrets together. And so, shortly before the holiday and saying good-bye, Circleknit Trousers too wanted to make peace with me and the world. He asked how I felt about the time under his care, and warned me to be honest.

How could I have lied to the person who knew more about me than anyone else? "The food was okay," I said. That was true.

"We need good people. People who are capable of deciding for themselves what benefits this country and what harms it. No blind informers who bring us a few names. We need people who'll tell us the reasons for what goes wrong in this country. Do you know what I mean?"

I felt something contract inside me. I knew.

"We trust you," said my Stasi. "We need you!"

Now it was out. I, without a place in the world, assigned a number and a sentence, locked away behind a steel-rimmed door, led around for twenty minutes a day under a barred patch of sky, I who felt I was the most useless of things, useless to myself, useless to others—I was needed again.

I had never been able to say No when someone needed me.

For a moment I felt something like happiness.

It was no more and no less than feeling as if the gate had been pushed open again, the gate that I had banged behind me at the Yugoslav border. And for a moment I could see through the open portal to all the impeccable champions of mankind's welfare whose light blinded me.

I was not yet lost.

And as an archangel at the one gate, so another stood at this other gate. He was tall, calm, and a cheerful glow lay upon his face. "I'll be your control officer," he said, "the one to whom you tell everything and who trusts you. Nothing will separate us." He held out his fountain pen. "Sign here!"

I signed.

I was Sebastian Edelbrink.

7

A year after that summer in which I departed from the path of virtue, I reentered the realm of relative freedom with 136.80 marks in my pocket that I had earned in the laundry room of Brandenburg Prison.

The exact date of my release was not revealed to me until the last minute, for reasons of my own safety, my jailer said. This reason was as universal as a concrete slab. It could be used for anything.

No one picked me up at the train station.

I got out of the train, inhaled the sooty air. The billboard advertizing Narva oil lamps was still broken. The loudspeakers were still blaring incomprehensible phrases. I looked around, searching for my first human being. My heart stood still. Not I but Sebastian Edelbrink was being picked up. By his control officer.

He was standing next to a newspaper kiosk; two inconspicuous young men with neat short haircuts stood beside him, just hanging around, simply there. In the hall of the train station, amid the commuter traffic, my control gave me a little display of conspiratorial behavior: spoke to me as he walked past, asked the time, refused to shake hands, whispered an address, a day, a time, vanished.

I admired his disappearance in the crowd.

I was shocked.

I don't know how I had pictured it; in any case not so concrete, not as if the class war were raging in the middle of this cold, draughty train station. And how it did rage.

> Of all our comrades none was so dear
> and so good as our little trumpeter,
> a cheery
> young Red Army guy.

I wasn't coming home. I was arriving to carry out a mission.

One of the clean-jawed young men walked up to me from behind while I was still standing frozen in the crowd, holding the bag full of my earthly goods.

"Keep walking," he growled.

I obeyed.

I went to eat a grilled sausage with as much mustard as they would give me.

8

The meet took place in a newly built apartment. Some name like Müller or Schmidt was on the door.

"So here you are," said my Stasi.

"I was just in the neighborhood," I said and tried to swallow the lump in my throat.

My control led me inside. My hosts had been busy. They had laid a doily on the sofa table. A thermos flask of coffee stood waiting with a plate of cookies and a bottle of 60-proof rum. My control pulled his trousers up above the knee and made himself comfortable in an armchair. He asked me to go ahead and sit down.

How was I doing, my control wanted to know. Had I any problems?

"Not a one," I said.

"We made every effort," said my control. "But you have to want it too. There's no point if you shut yourself in. You have to go out, mix with people, otherwise you'll do yourself in."

We drank coffee, I drank rum.

My control drank a toast to me. He could not quite manage to feel content. He didn't like the look of me. "What's wrong?" he asked.

Face the wall, go out, go in! I pulled myself together. "I don't want it."

"What don't you want?"

"This thing here, these meetings."

"Your conscience is getting to you, right? You think you're betraying your people?"

I nodded.

"You're not betraying any friends. You just have to watch out not to betray yourself." He paused. "There are no resignations in our division."

I knew that tone. It was usually followed by solitary confinement. Face the wall. "What's that supposed to mean?" I asked.

"A joke," said my control.

We both laughed loudly and heartily. Shook hands at the door as we said goodbye. "Do you still write?" he asked.

I shook my head. Not a line since.

"You must start up again," said my literature-loving Stasi. "You must!"

My most loyal reader.

9

Life went on.

The meetings went on.

It was the fifth, maybe the sixth meeting. I wasn't keeping score. I forgot each meeting at once, as fast as I wished for the next so that I could talk about the fact that I was a Stasi informer. Because the only person I could talk to about it was my Stasi. Each new trust would also have meant a new dependency. No one was as close to me as my control.

"There are some people in your circle of acquaintances—who may belong to your circle, that is," my control corrected himself, "whom we are not at all clear about. We suspect that they are involved in antisocial intrigues."

"What kind of intrigues?"

"Bad business."

I listened. I had learned to listen. These were the people with whom I used to sit night after night, working on the little baroque frescoes in our Workers' Paradise: a bar that stayed open at night, a stage open to all, a few thoughts to help you endure the world— by seeing it on a more existential plane. All these post-evangelical GDR words: hope, longing. Nowhere. The laughing Man of Sorrows under the red flag, Father, Father, why hast Thou forsaken me?

"No, the name doesn't mean anything to me." I wasn't lying. I had trained myself not to react to names. It's effective. Today I still have problems remembering names. So-called delayed effects. One of these people might turn up one day.

If a name could not help but mean something to me, I would write up a sketch of the person. "Just write what you think of him," and apart from the feeling of impotence, I experienced the tiniest feeling of power.

And now we I.M.s, we "unofficial collaborators," put our hands over our hearts and are honest enough to confess—Wasn't it a great feeling: I write, therefore you are. I am important. I know that they are interested in you. I know more. I cover it up with my hand. I pull my hand away. Who is our equal, who can separate the true faith from subversive elements!

There was also the other side of the coin: How did my control know about my shifting circle of acquaintances? How did they know what, where, whose shoes I had puked on? Who had seen me going here and there, who had noted down the person I went with? Who wrote the sketches of me; who was sitting after me on Schmidt's or Schulze's sofa?

Only now do I understand the full extent of the tragedy.

Me too.

10

It was still afternoon, the city was already wrapped in night, the apartment looked like all the apartments where we had met in the past. The wall of cupboards in the "Neustrelitz" model, the furniture suite in the "Oberhof" design. The coffee in the thermos bottle was hot, my control's bosses were satisfied with me. They sent me their greetings. "A sketch you wrote put an end to a certain person's antisocial intrigues." My control reached out to shake hands. My control always attached great importance to physical contact. Trust-building measures. Perhaps he really loved me too.

"Who was it?" I asked.

"You don't have to concern yourself with that." His hand was still there.

"But I do." No hand. I wanted to know at last.

"Beate F."

"No. *No.*"

That had been my first assignment. "Go there, it's a new youth club," my control had said. "Look it over and tell me what you think of it." I went. The club was in a street in the district of old buildings behind the train station. The building was among the few that had been renovated in the past few years. The gas lamps outside had not yet been sold to Japan by Herr Schalck.* There was a doorbell. The door stood open.

The sound of running water came from behind a door. There was a clattering noise, and a young blond woman with a wide smile, a rather crooked upper incisor, a mole above the left corner of her mouth, green eyes and a skirt so short it was forbidden walked out of a black-painted door and asked if she could help me.

I shook my head. Either this was a different Free German Youth group than the ones I knew, or this was not a youth club. "I'm just looking around," I said.

She said that was okay, went back to her desk. I was extremely interested in the paintings. We exchanged our two smiles.

She was older than I. She came over to me. "Are you an artist too?"

I nodded.

"May I ask what you do?"

"Poetry, that sort of thing."

She asked my name. She knew it. "Nice that you found this place," she said. "We need people like you." Her name was Beate and she explained her philosophy, which was quite simple: to remove a few blocks from people's heads, to make a few things possible. Simple things: you like this or that music? I'll get it for you. You want to read this book? There is a way. You need a video camera for this project? I know where you can get one.

"Yes," I said, "that's it exactly! Yes, yes, yes."

I came back again. There was something about Beate and her group that I had not encountered before: relaxation. I felt the frozen corners of my mouth loosen up. I have never claimed to be especially relaxed. Here for the first time I got an impression of what a wreck I was.

"What sort of people go there?" my control asked me at the next session.

"People like me," I said.

"Write it down," he said. Paper and pencils were waiting.

I wrote it down. And I wrote that I loved Beate. That I pictured the new human being we needed for our new society as being like her.

---

*Schalck-Golodkowski ran shady international business operations for the GDR and is thought to have absconded with GDR funds at the time of unification.

Antisocialist elements, said the Stasi.

The man in front of me now, who was saying "Good work," was afraid of this new human being. He was glad to have the old human being under his control. "Good work!" He radiated pride of workmanship.

I stared at him. Whatever had I believed?

11

Dear Beate,

I am sorry. I am still sorry now, almost ten years later. I didn't want that. I believed I could be useful to you. But I wasn't as clever as I thought I was. They just used me like a divining rod in reverse—Where I got enthusiastic about something, is where they set the spade to drain away the water.

I resent that.

But also there is no excuse for letting oneself be used in that way. Maybe an attempted excuse: There was a time when I believed in good and evil.

Dear Beate, sometimes more knowledge can be packed into a single breath than one had learned in a lifetime. This letter is an attempt to describe such a moment.

Thank you for giving me the kick to get out of this circle.

P.S. Forgive me that you had to pay part of my debt. I still owe you something for that.

12

I don't trust the dispositive of my memory. Because what happened next looks too heroic. It's a bit too far off my usual form. It looks as if I grabbed the little sofa table, knocked it over, jumped up, grabbed the Stasi, who was having trouble catching up to the change in my mood, spit my NO into his face making the walls shake with it, and ran out into the winter, seething with rage and shame, failing to get myself under control, a man on the run at last.

Maybe that's how it was.

Maybe it was different. Maybe I was just so helpless I was at a loss. Certainly I was desperate. Certainly I didn't manage to get a word out. In any case I struck sparks, dyed my red flag black.

I don't want to overdramatize this, but on my way through the snow something was going through my head. My control had always jokingly told me that the resignation rate for operatives was nil, that the only way to leave was if the Ministry left you. I had heard stories about people who wanted no more contact with the Stasi, and how they had died. Whether the stories were the complete truth I did not know. That was their way out. I knew other bits from other stories. Face the wall, go out, go in.

What I'm trying to say, without beating the drum, is—my final decisive NO that day could have cost me.

13

When I arrived in West Berlin in the mid-eighties with my cardboard suitcase full of unreadable manuscripts, the Federal Information Service asked if I knew where the Soviet SS 20s were stationed. Everyone got asked that. And whether I was a member of any secret service. Everyone got asked that too.

I said no twice. I was only half lying. It seemed to me too complicated to explain the other half.

Later everyone asked me how I got across the border, how I had lived on the other side. No one asked what I had left behind.

My personal contribution to the struggle of the international proletariat sank into the sediment of memory. The struggle between systems took on a new meaning: between IBM and Apple, for example. The important thing was no longer how man can change the conditions of production. The important thing was no longer points of view. The important thing was the escape points in an open system, the important thing was initiation and a limitless gastronomic need to catch up on what had been missed.

But the thing was there the whole time, like a virus-infected file on a hard drive. And then when the Wall came down and people's hearts swelled with the last euphoric feeling of "We," I stood at the Brandenburg Gate and my feelings were very mixed. What came next didn't look good.

14

Now I am sitting here at my desk, whose position on the fringe of the city has been suddenly transformed into its center. Rents are exploding all around me and the TV tower is flashing in front of my eyes. When I think what we used to want—I'm sorry but sometimes I just can't get away from using this plural—it wasn't a lot. We wanted socialism. We wanted better music. We wanted to take this youngest of all forms of society and make it younger still. We wanted to struggle. But we wanted to struggle the same way you dance. Beautifully.

It didn't work.

Sometimes I can't help thinking about my control. I have to fiddle a long time with the dials to get a clear picture. It isn't really important what he is doing. Maybe he's working for some locks and security firm that eventually will put the doorman at the city museum out of a job. Maybe he has bought up a piece of Stasi real estate, plans to turn it into an industrial park and is driving a 500 SL.

As I said, it's not really important.

What would be important is if one of them would stand up and pound his fist on the table and say: "The GDR wasn't just the filth you're making of it. It was one of the West's dreams of salvation, and those who did not dream it will know less their whole lives long about what it is to be a human being."

But they are silent. They are letting themselves be turned into tools of fascism, without principles, without uttering any contradiction. Maybe they can't do anything different. Maybe they were what people say they are. My white shirt is stained too. It's clean, but not stainless deep into the pores.

Never mind. It's me.

Am I a perpetrator or a victim?

It doesn't matter. For a period of my life I regarded the world as changeable.

It was a good time. Honestly.

Translated by Jan van Heurck

Beate Morgenstern

The Reunion

That kind of thing can happen. You think it can't happen but it
can. It happens every day and is quite ordinary: someone disappears. Leaves the house to get cigarettes and is never seen again.
The media thrive on this phenomenon that people vanish, leave
their past lives behind them.

Not long ago I read a little poster stuck to the tiles of a suburban
train station:

*Sasha, come back. Whatever you have done can't be that bad.
We are here for you! Your Mother.*

I stood in front of the poster, could not tear myself away.

Philipp had his own room and every possible freedom. Nevertheless we understood that he wanted to lead his own life. When he
got his own apartment we thought: It's an opportunity for him to
grow up. Now he is responsible for his life, that will help him.
Philipp has never been aware of reality, he has always been a
dreamer. Perhaps he'll learn now, we thought.

I visited him every month to bring him money. I also dropped
in on him occasionally when I was in his neighborhood. He was
living with a girl. What a child! I thought the first time I saw her.
Small, thin and completely unstable, I noticed that right away. But
maybe he needed that kind of child-girl. For the first time in his
life he had someone who looked up to him. He had never had a
girl before. He had no male friends either. Not until he met these
new friends.

I assume that it was because of his new friends that he did not
want to live with us any more. He was ashamed. They were polite.

But you could tell by looking at them that they were *rightwingers,* and Philipp knew what that meant to us.

If I didn't find Philipp in his apartment, I chatted with his neighbor, an ageing actress. She looked after the two children a little . . . yes, that's what you'd have to call them. I was always kept posted.

I also looked for my son in bars that I knew he hung out in. I didn't care how people looked at me. "Hey lady, what are you after here?"—that's more or less what their glances said. But they left me in peace.

When I found Philipp in one of these bars he smiled, was glad. And I was very happy. I looked at him, this handsome shy boy, slender, two heads taller than I, a bit pimply, black-haired with big dark eyes and long eyelashes. (He got his hair and eyes from me.) For the last couple of years he has been wearing glasses. He shaves, but not regularly yet. That's my Philipp, my son, I said to myself when he smiled rather helplessly, half looking as if he were asking me to forgive him. Whatever he's doing now he can't be bad, not really bad, I thought.

Philipp took our money. But actually he didn't need it. He lived modestly. But that wasn't the only thing. Sometimes he tried to tell me about his business dealings, which had to do with his new friends. I didn't want to know. I was only afraid that he might get caught. Philipp could not have survived being in jail.

He never had money problems. Also he had manual skills. All of us set our hopes on that. Despite his miserable grades we got him into a good apprenticeship, which continued until the "turning point." (Back then of course we meant something quite different by "turning point" than it means today. But people think and believe all sorts of things in their lives.) After unification the plant didn't know whether they could take on their apprentices as skilled workers, and our son was no longer willing to go on with the training. He *chucked up* his apprenticeship as people say nowadays.

Shortly after that he was drafted. Maybe there they'll teach him that a day has a certain rhythm, that life has rules, my husband said. Philipp went to Hamburg. One evening he said good-bye to us in good spirits. But he never arrived at his unit. That was the first time the army tried to track him down. Then we had a discussion with his superior. He showed a lot of sympathy for Philipp. Somehow he seemed to like him. No doubt he deals with people like Philipp quite often. I don't know whether here in the GDR they would have treated Philipp so civilly. No, probably not. Definitely not.

They suspended the search. Philipp did his service in Berlin and came home at night.

Then when he got his pad in the Prenzlauer Berg, of course no one saw to it that he reported for duty in the morning. It was inevitable that one day he wouldn't get up. An officer called at our house. No, our son has moved out, we said. We were told to telephone if he turned up. But the officer probably didn't seriously expect us to do that. So Philipp was listed as AWOL again, and they hunted for him again.

I think they didn't take the search very seriously, they didn't watch his place day and night, otherwise they would have caught him. His neighbor told us that he and his girl friend used to climb into his apartment through an attic. They sometimes used to do that even before, if the building was locked, she said. I think the two of them crawled across the roofs out of sheer love of adventure, because he could easily have opened the door with a picklock. He's good with his hands, as I said.

Before the search for Philipp was on again, he took me once to see his new friends. I was interested. I spent the longest period of my working life with young people. I was prepared for the young men's warlike appearance. But when I heard them talk: my God, I felt sorry for the boys. They seemed so helpless, so alone. I don't know what kind of homes they came from. Of course they could have been the best homes, as you can see from our son. But they were all poor souls without hope in the future. I talked with them. "But Hitler has six million Jews and twenty million war dead to answer for," I said to them. The Führer had simply been betrayed, was their reply. And the thing about the Jews wasn't definite. And if it did happen, then it wasn't the Führer's fault. You had to see the idea, they said. Justice. A sense of community. Nowadays there wasn't anything holding people together. Everyone looked out for his own interests. Money determined everything. Strange as it seemed, I could not help agreeing with these rightwingers, these neo-Nazis. Evidently our socialist order, when it criticized the conditions that now reign all over Germany, agreed in many points with the views of the *Right*.

Are we who wanted to build socialism to blame because now youngsters are setting fire to houses, persecuting and murdering people? Are we to blame because we told the young people that ideals can be made reality? In fact we even went so far as to claim that they already were reality, even though ideals can never be realized and we didn't even come close.

A young German has to have the opportunity to learn a proper trade and support his wife and children, these children said. Foreigners should not be allowed to take away their jobs. And so on. I let them flood me with this rubbish for my son's sake. I argued against them as well as I could.

Of course Philipp had visited Buchenwald in preparation for his socialist youth coming-of-age ceremony. He had visited Sachsenhausen too, just like all young people. But if a person only believes what he wants to believe. . . . We know how that is.

I could hardly imagine that the young people who huddle together, so abandoned and forlorn, and cling to slogans and symbols, are the same ones who beat, kick and kill people. But I know one thing, Philipp will never beat up anyone. Neither out of anger nor out of fear. We never hit him. And he'll never hit anyone.

After they started searching for Philipp, I didn't find him in his apartment any more. His neighbor had moved away. I no longer knew anything about him. He phoned now and then. We didn't ask where he was, if only he was near us.

He visited us at Christmas. Our Grandma was still living with us. She was overjoyed to see the boy. Our Grandma, my husband's mother. She's going to be ninety-three, she lived through World War I, Hitler, World War II, the postwar period, socialism, and now the so-called turning point. Our Grandma, this wizened dear little woman pressed Philipp's hand. Over and over. Philipp allowed it. We gave him presents and ate with him. We didn't ask him about anything. We thought he might stay the evening, perhaps sleep overnight with us. We had already thought about what we would do if the military police came. But he left again two hours later. He gave us all a kiss and hugged our Grandma. He acted as if he would come back by the day after tomorrow at the latest.

Since then Philipp has been missing. No phone calls. I sit by the telephone. Each time it rings, I'm scared and happy at the same time. It could be Philipp! It's been nine months since we last saw and heard him. My life—what passes for my life—is much heavier, as if I had a heavy weight on my chest. My heart problems have gotten worse again. All the same I run around our area giving private lessons. At the end I worked in the Party organization, so of course opportunities are no longer open to me in this society. All the same I cannot regret the fact that in my Party post I was able to assist many young artists against narrow-minded officials, and prevented many stupidities. So I hope. But of course I was a "supporter of the system."

We have celebrated Christmas again. For our Grandma's sake we put some pine branches into vases. We didn't listen to any music, we just couldn't stand that. We ate a good meal. Also for our Grandma's sake. I thought about Philipp the whole time. Where can he be now? Perhaps in America? Or in Australia? Or in Hamburg? Or even here in Berlin, a couple of streets away? What if something has happened to him? We'll never know. I was glad when the holidays were over and I had other things to think about.

I had terrible dreams at night. But then I gathered my courage again and said: Philipp is alive.

I can't put up any posters like the desperate mother of "Sasha." The military are still looking for him. For the same reason we can't go to the police. There's nothing we can do. Nothing at all.

Philipp was a friendly, tractable child, only somewhat lacking in concentration. There were a lot of things he didn't understand. He was always on his own, sat in his room reading, making things with his hands. Airplanes, for example. I used to think about why he didn't have any friends. Probably the other schoolkids thought he was a dreamer. Children quickly eliminate anyone who is a bit different from themselves. They're no different from adults that way.

When Philipp began to go to school, I was working until late at night. After day nursery in the afternoon, he was left to himself. Many children are robust and can tolerate that. Philipp suffered, no doubt about it. I had awful pangs of guilt, in the evening or at night I would race home with only one desire, to see my son. But I didn't want to take a step down in my job. If you don't take advantage of an opportunity when it's offered, you don't get a second chance. That's what I thought. Now I smile bitterly: If I had been less committed, I would be a teacher today and wouldn't have to chase money. And I would have been a good teacher. I love my profession, I get inspirations. Neither I nor the children ever get bored. I can make children enthusiastic. I can get along with the most difficult ones—a knack for which I have to thank my former mentor. Sometimes I wanted to chuck everything when I started teaching in a school in the Prenzlauer Berg. But with my mentor's help I managed to get through it.

If only I had not been so ambitious. Maybe I could have given Philipp some support. You never know.

Our Grandma has moved out. She lived quietly in her little room, the one next to Philipp's. She kept herself busy there, I don't know with what. But old people always find something to do. Time passes much faster for them than for us. My husband—who has gone into early retirement—used to buy our groceries, looked after her when I wasn't there. She trotted out for meals, her white hair tied in a bun, always had a smile for us or a look of concern. She was like the grandmothers you imagine in fairy tales.

We miss our Grandma a lot. We were still like a family.

Her departure came quite unexpectedly. She visited one of her sons in Güstrow and just stayed there. Now she is living in an old people's home. She wants to be buried in Güstrow. Güstrow is her home town. It always was her great fear that she would have to be buried in one of the big cemeteries in Berlin. We tried to convince her that this wasn't so, but evidently her fear was greater than her trust in us. And perhaps it's quite right not to trust any more—not anything, not anyone. Today, who can give any guarantees?

We don't have our dog, a cocker spaniel, any more either. He died of old age; we don't want to get a new one.

My husband is alone all day in the big apartment. I'm out and about. I don't earn much. But for the time being it's enough to keep the apartment. We want to keep everything the same until Philipp returns.

Why doesn't Philipp phone? From New York or wherever he is. He must know that we wait for him day and night. Just one phone call so that we'll know he's alive.

Has he forgotten everything? Has he drifted into a world where there is no mother, no father, in which the past lies behind him like a country where he no longer wants to set foot? Like that country we come from, for instance, that people are now supposed to forget?

I have seen Philipp again. Even this much is not granted to some mothers. But I did not picture our reunion like *this*. Definitely not. Except in my nightmares.

I know where I can go when I want to be very close to Philipp: the cemetery in Baumschulenweg. We had him buried anonymously. They have very beautiful grounds there.

I am no longer waiting. Nevertheless I sometimes have the distinct feeling that the doorbell is ringing. Philipp is standing outside the door. I think about him even more than I used to. He is so close to me. Much closer than during the time when I was still waiting. Sometimes I think I have just been dreaming. I wake up from a long horrible nightmare. Philipp comes and says: "Mama, don't forget you're invited to my place tomorrow!"

The last time I visited him in his apartment, he cooked for me. He bought a set of expensive pots and pans just for the purpose. I thought, For heaven's sake, what is he going to do with all those pans? We had soup. The entree was spaghetti bolognese with salad, and chocolate pudding for dessert. He was so fond of chocolate pudding.

For a moment I feel reassured that I have only been dreaming. But then this nightmare comes between me and Philipp again: I am led to a sort of table with a dead person lying on it, covered with a sheet. The sheet is partly turned back. I see my son. Philipp. Deathly pale. He was always pale. Now he is deathly pale. Above his eye is a long red slash like a scar. He isn't wearing his glasses, he has closed his eyes with their beautiful long eyelashes like a girl's.

"Yes, it's he," I tell the officer. "It's he," says my husband, who is with me. But actually it isn't he. The real Philipp has gone away.

I have seen my son again. He lay there mutely, he could no longer say anything to me.

I believe he is trying to apologize to me, and that's why he is visiting me so often now.

"I wanted to phone you," he says. "All the time. How often I picked up the receiver. I would have phoned you if I had known that I wouldn't ever be able to come back to you. I would have phoned you, believe me, Mama."

"You could still be alive, Philipp. If they hadn't run away. I don't understand. She was your girl friend."

"Dead is dead," says Philipp. "It gets some people sooner, other people later. I've always had bad luck, Mama."

The conversation cannot be continued. But I am glad that he comes, that he talks to me.

Philipp has always stayed near us. His girl friend testified that he wanted to phone us but kept putting it off. Sometimes he stood in the phone booth and then went out again. Afterward he only said now and then that he really had to phone some time. Philipp and she had lived now here, now there, staying with friends. He could not go back to his own apartment. That evening at the end of April they had gone walking in Treptower Park. Philipp, the girl, and another friend. A boy around their own age came toward them. Suddenly the boy jumped at Philipp with a knife. The girl and the other friend saw Philipp lying on the ground bleeding, got scared and ran away. It did not occur to them to tell someone what had happened. They simply ran. Panic.

Philipp's murderer testified that he felt threatened when the three were coming toward him. He was only trying to defend himself. When he was asked if he felt threatened by Philipp, he said he felt less threatened by Philipp, and not at all by the girl. He felt most threatened by the other boy. And the fact that there were three of them scared him. He thought, it's them or me. He only wanted to survive. It was purely a *reflex* to take on the one of the two boys who seemed weaker to him. Nowadays you have to fight to survive, he said. That was the most important thing.

To think that a reunion with my son means a permanent good-bye! At first I believed I could never bear it. But I'm still alive. Human nature is tough. Unfortunately.

Our Grandma wasn't even able to cry, she was so shocked when we went to the old people's home in Güstrow to tell her the news. And then she went back to thinking about what had preoccupied her at the end of her time with us: "It's right that I moved to Güstrow," she said. "Philipp has to be in the big city. I'll lie here at peace in Güstrow."

People turn stubborn when they get that old.

Translated by Jan van Heurck

Stefan Heym

Property

"All that is going to change in this country," my Elisabeth says, with that gleam in her eye that I call her Intershop look, the one she always gets as soon as she enters the store and sees the selection of bright-colored products from the West that you can obtain only with hard currency. Now nobody needs the store any more, of course; now you simply go to the West, although the currency is still a problem. "Things will change a lot," she says, "especially with real estate. It's going to go sky-high."

Real estate? I'm amazed. How did she get to know that term?

"We can really be glad that we bought the house from the Local Housing Authority when nobody was thinking about doing that sort of thing yet. And for 35,000 East-marks, that's nothing! This house will be worth half a million before long, if not a whole million, and in solid German marks. Whereas our dear neighbors just went on paying their rent to the Housing Authority and so they can be thrown out any time, as soon as German unification comes with the new laws. But your property is your property, nobody can touch it, not now and not later. And who was it who drummed it into your head that you should buy, and kept pestering you until you finally got the lawyer and legalized the purchase?"

"Elisabeth," I answer. "You are the cleverest woman."

My Elisabeth loves to hear that, and the conversation very well could have continued along the same lines, all joy and harmony, if the gravel had not crunched outside the house. It is a car, apparently a pretty heavy one.

"A visitor?" I ask. "In the middle of the week?"

She goes to the window. "Oh, that's the man who . . ."

"Who?"

"Who was here before. Twice in fact."

"Why didn't you tell me before?"

"I didn't want to worry you," she says. And adds: "He parked at an angle across the street, got out, and walked around the house a few times. And several times he stopped and looked around as if he had lost something, and I wanted to go out and ask him if he was from the Stasi; but of course the Stasi has been dissolved. And before I could make up my mind, he was gone."

"You're sure it's the same man?" I answer. "Because I see two men."

She gulps. "He's multiplied."

"And which was the one you saw—the short plump one with the narrow-brimmed hat, or the skinny one who looks like a pallbearer?"

"The short one," she says.

"The short one, umm-hmm." But before I can ask why she thought that a person of his sort would have worried me, our doorbell rings

Recently we have been using a Chinese gong for a doorbell. Its deep ding-dong-dang gives us pleasure each time we hear it, only at this moment its foreign peal gets on my nerves. Elisabeth, too, stands there as if rooted to the spot, and gnaws her lower lip.

"Open the door," I say, "The gentlemen want something from us, and I for one would like to know what it is."

The two of us walk to the door hand in hand: it's better to stick together. The short man doffs his little hat and performs a sort of bow. The skinny one flashes his magnificent teeth. "Mr. and Mrs. Bodelschwingh, I presume?"

My name *is* Bodelschwingh, like the famous Pastor Bodelschwingh although my family is in no way related to him, and Elisabeth acquired the name by marriage.

"May we come in?" asks the skinny man.

Elisabeth's eyes are gleaming again, but this is a different gleam, grim and threatening: what I call her Don't Give Me Any Guff look.

The short one wipes his shoes on the doormat long and carefully: "as if he owns the place" is the thought that crosses my mind, I don't know why. And while he takes off his lightweight dust-colored little coat, he introduces himself. "My name's Prottwedel, Elmar Prottwedel, if you please."

"Pleased to meet you," I say.

"Schwiebus," says the other man, handing me his calling card. "Dr. Schwiebus, Attorney-at-Law from the firm of Schwiebus, Schwiebus and Krings, Real Estate Consultants."

"We don't need a consultation," Elisabeth replies.

Meanwhile Mr. Prottwedel goes through the open sliding door into our living room with what can only be described as a sleep-walker's steadfastness of purpose, and heads for the Biedermeier armchair which we recently restored, with great effort—just try to find a master upholsterer in this country, and an authentic fabric like this with gold stripes and little flowers on it!—then sinks with a groan onto the seat, which seems made for a rear end like his. "This was my grandpa's favorite chair," he says. "Only it was covered in green then, green with little lavender roses. My grandpa died in this chair: heart failure."

Elisabeth turns pale. Not because of the death scene, she is not so sentimental, but because of the possibility that the armchair actually might have belonged to Mr. Prottwedel's grandpa: because we did not acquire it ourselves, it came to us from our predecessor, Comrade Watzlik. When we took over the house from him, I had a right to it, as a department head, Watzlik said. "I'll leave you the armchair, Comrade Bodelschwingh, we'll get modern furniture in the capital."

"Perhaps"—Lawyer Schwiebus has a very cultivated accent, probably from the Lübeck area—"perhaps we ought to explain the purpose of our visit," he says to Mr. Prottwedel.

"High time," says my Elisabeth.

Mr. Prottwedel purses his mouth into a sort of buttonhole. "You must have noticed my previous attendance at your property, Mrs. Bodelschwingh."

"Twice," says Elisabeth, nodding. "Twice."

"I hope I did not frighten you," says Mr. Prottwedel. "I am merely concerned with memories. The happy youth I spent here with the kindest of fathers—who, please note, purchased this house together with the land it stands on."

"Thank heaven, Mr. Prottwedel lives in comfortable circum-stances," says Lawyer Schwiebus. "He is the owner of a brewery of some renown in the West where we live, and of other interests, which give him a sufficient income. So he is not in any sort of distress which might make it seem advisable for him to repossess the real estate to which actually he is entitled."

"Repossess!" The slight flush suffusing my Elisabeth's face is a warning signal that I know well. "Repossess!" she says. "What do you mean by that?"

"I am also happy to observe that you have kept the property in good condition, Mr. and Mrs. Bodelschwingh," Mr. Prottwedel says.

"And why not?" Lawyer Schwiebus agrees, nodding. "The Bodelschwinghs, who were described to us as clean, reliable people, are using the property themselves."

The pink flush in Elisabeth's face has turned to unmistakeable red. "We not only use the house," she says, "it belongs to us. Just so you know, Mr. Prottwedel, and you, too, Mr. Schwiebus: we bought and paid for it, including the chair. We have a valid sales contract, and it's all been recorded in the land register perfectly legally, you can check that for yourselves."

"Lawyer Schwiebus has already checked it in the land register," Mr. Prottwedel says. "All the same, surely we are allowed to visit the house and look around?"

"We understand your need to pursue your memories, Mr. Prottwedel," says Elisabeth, and she adds a sort of afterthought, "especially when it doesn't cost you anything anymore, not even the twenty-five marks one had to pay to cross the border until a short time ago."

"I'd really like to see the upstairs now," replies Mr. Prottwedel.

The footsteps which come now from one spot, now from another, echo in my brain. It is enough to drive a man crazy.

"Why don't I throw those guys out?" I ask.

"It isn't their house, to roam around wherever they want to," Elisabeth responds.

"They're behaving like conquerors," I say.

"And the bathroom hasn't been cleared up," my Elisabeth says. The eruption long heralded by her red cheeks, has arrived. "And to think we brought that on ourselves!" she cries.

"Take it easy," I warn. "They're not deaf."

But no one can stop her. "It's *our* house! In our house I'll shout as much as I want to!"

Then silence. Followed by the voice of Mr. Prottwedel. "Here we are again!"

"And how was your tour?" Elisabeth asks.

Mr. Prottwedel slips behind the armchair as if seeking protection from her gaze. "The layout of the rooms is just as I remember," he says.

"Memory is half of life," opines Lawyer Schwiebus.

"And the furnishings!" Mr. Prottwedel remarks. "Such good quality!"

After a pause for thought, Lawyer Schwiebus states that he just does not understand our attitude of rejection, not to say resentment. Apart from refreshing his memories, Mr. Prottwedel's only intention is to clear up with the utmost dispatch, the questions regarding the ownership of the house and lot—at this point he removes a piece of paper from behind the handkerchief in the outer breast pocket of his suit—the house and lot at 27 Marshal Koniev Street, formerly 27 Hindenburg Street.

"What is there to clear up?" My Elisabeth stamps her foot. "The house and land are our property, and property is protected by the state, always and everywhere, both East and West."

"Exactly why," returns Lawyer Schwiebus, "that's exactly why." Isn't it in our interest, too (he asks), to avoid possible conflicts that might arise once the two German states happily have reunited, with resultant effects on the laws? And from his black moroccan leather briefcase he removes a quantity of pages which he spreads out on the table in front of me. These documents, he lectures, indicate that Mr. Dietmar Prottwedel, the deceased father of his friend and client Mr. Elmar Prottwedel, legally purchased the house and land formerly at 27 Hindenburg Street, in 1936 from a Mr. Siegfried Rothmund, who soon afterward left Germany for parts unknown. The purchase price was 35,000 marks, the same sum, as fate would have it, for which we, Mr. and Mrs. Bodelschwingh, acquired it from our Local Housing Authority. And here, he concluded, was the sales contract.

"Not that it ever entered our heads to throw you out," Mr. Prottwedel assures us.

My Elisabeth's lips tremble. "Throw us out of our own house?"

"Nor to make demands of another kind on you at this time," Mr. Prottwedel smiles.

"Are we supposed to pay again for something we already paid for a long time ago?" I ask.

"By no means were we talking about money," Lawyer Schwiebus chips in. And continuing his lecture, he explains that he and Mr. Prottwedel are instead concerned about legal title, in which regard there is no doubt whatever concerning the claims which we, the Bodelschwingh Family, have upon the house and land at 27 Marshal Koniev Street, as it is now called. It is simply that Mr. Prottwedel has claims, too, and the question is, who has the older claims, and even more important in the light of the shifting legal situation, in what manner did the person or persons from whom we acquired the said property, acquire it in the first place, and was the manner of their acquisition legal and proper according to the law, which no doubt would soon apply in our part of Germany, too?

"Because the truth is, my family home was expropriated. Without compensation," Mr. Prottwedel declares, and rolls his eyes blissfully.

This damned waiting. We knew they would come back, only we did not know when. And often, when I returned home from my long-since meaningless job in my now long-since meaningless bureau, I caught myself sitting in the living room listening to every sound that came from outside. It woke me up in the middle of the night. You can tell when the person beside you is lying awake, their breaths are too short, there is a sudden movement, and you start to think. It can't be true, you think. Life just followed its course, and now suddenly what seemed permanent—well, if not permanent at least long-lasting—is falling apart. And yet the house still stood there and belonged to us. A roof was there for us to crawl under.

"No," Elisabeth says. "Things won't go the way those people think. One country or two countries, what's yours is yours. And especially for the people from the West. What would become of them if they admitted that somebody can simply walk up and say, 'That was my grandpa's favorite chair?'"

Not talking about it doesn't help. The fear has to come out, otherwise you go crazy. "But they're the victors," I say. "And we brought them into the country. We tore down the Wall with shouts of Germany, Germany! Sure, what we had before was no picnic. Year after year always being a yes-man, and always having to do what you're told, and what reward did you get for it? A privilege here and there. But at least the house they let you have was your own, and you had peace in your bed."

"You're giving up before the first shot is fired," she says. "Who is Mr. Prottwedel? A seedy little businessman, like thousands they have running around over there. But you, how many people have you been in charge of, in your department? If you had been a nobody, they would have fired you a long time ago. And do you think the people in the West, the government ministers and secretaries of state and general managers, don't need people like you who know the ropes over here, and the hookup among the different bureaus? Wait a little while, and you'll be able to show Prottwedel and Schwiebus the hole in the house for them to leave by."

That's my Elisabeth, a truly strong character and alert to every opportunity. And I realize that the rules that govern this republic are not so different from those that determine who has the whip hand over in the West. I feel really moved. "Elisabeth," I say, "you're right once again. We won't let ourselves be intimidated by people like them."

All the same, we jumped when we heard the gravel crunch again, followed shortly by the ding-dong-dang of the gong.

"It's probably the mailman," I say, thinking how ridiculous it would be if it really were the mailman. The gleam is back in my Elisabeth's eyes, and she takes my hand as she never would have done had she believed it was the mailman. And so we support each other, morally, on our way to the door.

But it is neither the mailman, nor Mr. Prottwedel, nor his friend Lawyer Schwiebus. A woman is standing at the door, dark, with remarkable features. As we step aside, surprised, she walks in and heads for the armchair with the same sleepwalker's confidence as Mr. Prottwedel showed not long ago.

"I assume that was your grandpa's favorite chair," I say.

She looks startled. "How did you know that?"

"And your name is Rothmund?"

"Eva Rothmund," she confirms. "From Tel Aviv." And she sinks into the chair, where admittedly she takes up less space than Mr. Prottwedel.

"And you, too, are here in search of your memories," I say. "Now that it doesn't cost anything any more, not even the twenty-five marks to cross the border."

"I have no memories," she replies. "Not of this house and not of Germany. Except an indirect memory of this chair. My grandfather often used to tell me about it."

"What is it that you want then?" I ask.

"I am my grandfather's heir."

"Are you?" I say. Then a wicked thought occurs to me. "Well, that puts a whole new slant on things."

"Why? What new slant?" she asks.

"You and I together, Mrs. Rothmund, are going to challenge Prottwedel and Schwiebus," I announce.

But Elisabeth seems not to think much of the idea. "But Mrs. Rothmund, didn't your grandfather sell this property to a Mr. Prottwedel?" she asks.

"Sell?" Mrs. Rothmund gets up from her grandfather's ex-favorite chair, and takes from her cheap brown leather handbag a quantity of pages which she spreads out on the table. "These documents indicate that I am the sole and lawful heir of my grandfather, Siegfried Rothmund," she says, "and that my grandfather signed over his house and land at 27 Hindenburg Street on February 23, 1936, to SS Captain Dietmar Prottwedel, after the said SS Captain Prottwedel threatened that he would be arrested and taken to a concentration camp."

"What do you mean by threatened?" Eliisabeth asks. "The determining factor in the ownership of real estate is not what was said during the negotiations but whether your grandfather did or did not receive the purchase price of 35,000 marks." And I can see what is going through her mind. The woman from Israel poses the greater danger, Elisabeth feels, assuming that she really holds the original title to our property. It would be easier to reach an agreement with Prottwedel and Schwiebus, especially now that Mrs. Rothmund has turned up. West or East, with them you were dealing with Germans.

"The determining factor, you said. The determining factor is receipt of the purchase money?" asks Mrs. Rothmund.

"We personally saw the sales contract agreed between your grandfather and Mr. Dietmar Prottwedel," Elisabeth replies.

"Here is an affidavit signed personally by my grandfather the day before his death, in the presence of a notary public," Mrs. Rothmund says, reaching for one of the papers. "It says that the sale of the house and land at 27 Hindenburg Street, along with the contract for its sale, are null and void because the buyer, SS Company Commander Dietmar Prottwedel, kept and withheld the 35,000 marks guaranteed to my grandfather by the contract, which sum in any case represented only a small part of the true value of the said real estate."

My Elisabeth gasps. "But where do *we* stand then?" she says at last, and after a long minute's pause: "Surely you must think about us, too, Mrs. Rothmund?"

I don't know whether that was exactly the right thing to say to Mrs. Rothmund, who after all had traveled all the way from Israel especially for the purpose. But what ought one to say in a situation like this, now that everything in our country is changing?

Translated by Jan van Heurck

Joachim Walther

The Raft of Utopia

The ship has sunk. Designed by waking dreamers, built as a multi-colored sailing vessel, it set sail for the goal of all desires, which had many names inside people's heads but was not marked on any map. During its centuries-long crusade, it deteriorated into a galley. Reequipped as a battleship by navigators who took over command and set its course, in the end it hardly moved anymore: a rusted chunk of iron. Petrified. Sunk at sea without a storm.

The wooden raft carries the shipwrecked sailors: perpetrators and victims together, divided between those disillusioned people who no longer believe in land, and the hopeful ones who are looking out for new isles of the blessed, and who consequently do not see the *Titanic*, which some time ago set its course straight for them in order to rescue them.

Translated by Jan van Heurck

Daniela Dahn

The Invincible Monument

HERE, BERLIN'S GOVERNING SENATE IS CLEANING UP THE HISTORY OF THE TWO GERMANIES BY CARRYING OUT A PURGE AGAINST DISSIDENTS—I read on a large placard, while the workmen from the assigned construction firm curse because their most expensive diamond drill has broken while they were cutting off Lenin's head. Sightseers troop along the builders' fence, deciphering the notes tacked to it. THE SYMBOLS OF MILITARISM ARE STILL STANDING, laments a political group from Kreuzberg. FROM THE SUBLIME TO THE RIDICULOUS IS ONLY ONE STEP, someone says, quoting Napoleon, and another has copied out Brecht's poem "The Invincible Inscription," the beautiful story of the soldier in an Italian prison who writes "Long live Lenin!" on his cell wall with a copying pencil. Despite attempts to paint it over, the inscription keeps showing through again and again, until someone takes a knife and scratches it out, thereby carving it in, and in the end, nothing can be done any more but to tear down the prison wall.

A young man who is wearing a tie and belongs to the Deutsche Volksunion, is calmly explaining to a young man wearing an earring and a Lenin cap why the statue of a man whose theories were cited by the criminal Stalin, is not allowed to stand here. The young man in the cap replies that as long as a monument makes people think, it serves a purpose. In front of a bright-colored nylon tent sit members of a vigil, radical independents, punk rockers, anarchists. They do not claim to be familiar with Lenin's work. It is enough for them that he described capitalism as withering and parasitic. "We'll stay until the last stone comes down, we owe him that much!"

With Brecht's poem ringing in my ears, the nonstop presence of a police car at my rear, and the tent before my eyes, it is suddenly clear to me what is bound to happen here:

When all the hubbub has died away, the square will be left unpleasingly bare. "Why is the square so empty?" people will ask, and they will be told, "Because of Lenin." To stop all this, soon a postmodern sculpture will be designed and erected by a famous artist, to fit the dimensions of the square. It will consist of intertwined steel tubes that jut into the sky, it will be called *Projection 13*, and it will shine beautifully and obligingly in the sunlight. For one whole week.

But on the seventh night, a radical independent will appear with a little bucket of red paint and a brush and write "Long live Lenin!" on the thick tubes at the bottom. And in the morning, on their way to work, people will pause there, annoyed or amused. A furious nearby resident will arrive with a can of solvent and wash off the paint. Only a red puddle will be left on the paving stones, and be trodden firmly into place.

Not long after, a punk rocker will sneak up at dawn and, moving along the tubes hand over hand with acrobatic skill until he gets to the top, he will pull a spray can from his pocket. Black letters saying "Long live Lenin!" will shine upon the steel, visible from a long distance. The young man with the tie will fetch a folding ladder, but it will not reach up far enough. Some days will pass before the volunteer firemen voluntarily arrive and clean the thing off amid the howling of the crowd.

But before long, there will again be an outcry at the monument. And people will ask: "What's going on there?" Someone will point at a fleeing anarchist, who this time has used acid to etch in the invincible inscription. Now, if he has not already done so, the famous artist will take precautions to stop *Projection 13* from being desecrated by the name of a shady revolutionary. He will insist that his colleague Christo wrap up the acid-etched strand of tubing, and that in the future, an armed policeman should stand by the sculpture to guard it. The city's senator for internal affairs will decline, but the famous artist will win his lawsuit, which will be followed with avid attention by the public. And from then on, the smell of paint remover, the rifle patrol, and the partial wrapping of the tubes will give the square an explosive character.

And the tourists will ask: "What's going on here?" "It's all because of Lenin," a young woman who happens to be standing there will tell them. And they will not know whom she is talking about. And she will explain, in front of the unnerved police officer, and they will ask: "Why is she smiling?"

And the city's senator for internal affairs will get fed up to the teeth with these antics and will have *Projection 13* dismantled. All that is left will be the red puddle on the paving stones, and flowers which are placed there by the punk rocker and the smiling woman. And people will not stop asking: "Who got shot to death here?"

Finally, a citizens initiative will be launched by the Deutsche Volksunion, which will save the day. A crane will be sent to recover those granite blocks concealed in a gravel pit, and hurriedly stack them up on the spot. And on that day, it will be quiet at the monument. Because it will be as ugly as it has been from time immemorial, and the people will turn away their glances and make a wide arc around the square and have nothing more to ask— exactly like the twenty-five years before. Only then will the monument be conquered.

Translated by Jan van Heurck

Joochen Laabs

Beautiful Summer

I look out the lattice windows of my old house through the shadow of the chestnut at the enclosed pasture on the other side of the road. Upholstered with bushes at intervals, it spreads out in gentle waves on all sides, flooded with light. The stinging nettles, thistles and tall grass panicles that edge the road sway almost imperceptibly. Otherwise there is no movement in the landscape, except for the cabbage butterfly which is reeling underneath the latch beam of the gate into the pasture.

Only the upper beam stretches between the posts, because the pasture is empty.

Undisturbed summer, nothing else.

It is as if it came from my imagination: that noisy chaos of downfall and upheaval which has descended everywhere and on everything, on cities, villages, on every home; that hard-to-bear mixture of defensiveness and greed, of blocked streets and blocked corridors in ex-Stasi fortresses which have been converted into employment bureaus, of falling flags and rising promises; that wild party mood and the hectic blows of the demolition machines, the unending din and nonstop funeral . . . it is as if all this were no longer true, when I turned my back on it.

The reality—a sky so full of light that it has almost lost all its blue, and below it, the expansive green waves of the meadows flowing outward. The cat is lying with sheathed claws and eyes pressed shut under the mallows, in whose wide-opened red velvet blossoms bumblebees are swarming. The land is drunk with silence, the soundless victory of nature, which, I almost think, is at bottom aware that it cannot be shaken. A white wagtail patters along the length of the enclosure rail. The question of what has happened to the cows who give the enclosure its purpose, is one that I do not allow to arise. Perhaps the cabbage butterfly is helping me in this, by multiplying into four.

Then a buzzing filters through the stillness. It intensifies into a drone that appears to break off, only to reappear the next moment, clearer and with a hardness that lacks vibration. I know this sound, and I catch myself trying not to hear it. Even now it's still going on! But it cannot be ignored, it has already formed an envelope of noise in which I am prisoner. Delicate quakes grope their way through the ground in my direction, the walls around me begin to tremble. The drone swells into a boom surmounted by a howl. The quaking turns into a stamping. The house rattles as if it wants to break free of its moorings and flee. But the first shadowed colossus is already invading my picture: a high-wheeled truck pushes in between the meadow and the chestnut, and casts darkness into my room. It appears noiseless, because the source of the din is not the truck but what follows it: clattering, rattling, rumbling, an unchained or laboriously subdued iron monster, a tank. Then a second, a third. The gun barrels, rigidly aimed straight ahead, sway up and down. The heavy, swollen iron track appears to lie still on the road. An illusion; it rises over the rear wheels, tears up the roadway, and tosses it backward in a wild veil of dust and slag. And I stand there—jumping up out of my chair is all that I am capable of doing—impotent as always.

My insignificant, harmless road is a Soviet military highway. From the repair base the vehicles transfer to their main station, and vice versa. Or so people say. The spectral procession roars past my house two or three times a month. Sometimes at noon, sometimes in the evening. At night you can see the cones of fire bursting out of the exhausts, so that I fear for my reed roof. I have lived with this, as long as I have owned the house.

The upper bodies of the soldiers stick out of the turret hatches as if they were a part of the vehicles. I do not know if they see me, these faces under the black leather caps. I see that the faces are always similar, I would prefer to say that they are the same, and I matter nothing to them. They matter to me, to the extent that they keep invading my world. In which I do not want them.

They have been there since my childhood. Back then, they brought the end of the war with them. They were part of the khaki-colored foreign tanks and trucks that stood outside our house. They fiddled with the vehicles, and built campfires next to them, then threw in potatoes and stuck chunks of meat into the fire on wooden sticks. When the potates were well roasted and charred, they would roll some of them toward us. They also invited us to climb up onto the tanks. I did not do it.

These are the leather-capped faces from that last week in June when I had to go to school running the gauntlet between rows of threateningly aimed tank-gun barrels, until the vacation set us free.

It was a long time before I got over the echo of those meetings. But now it is back again, in the form of helplessness, fear and rage. Above their grotesque presence, a soldier who no longer has a nation continues to drive the empty trappings of power.

And long after the tanks have set the pastures free again, the booming has died away into a hum, the dust has settled, and the white wagtail has resumed its seat on the rail and is wagging its tail up and down, I still cannot rid myself of a feeling of bitterness.

When I see that the cat has disappeared under the mallows, I know that there is no point in waiting for things to go back to how they were. I walk through the house into the shed and take out the bicycle to put on a new inner tube. When I am finished, I wash my hands and drink a cup of cold coffee standing up in the kitchen.

Finally I sit down at the desk again. The cat is back, too, although admittedly it has withdrawn deeper into the elder bushes, because the mallows now stand in brilliant sunlight.

This summer is something to be reckoned with. As I force myself back to the thoughts on the piece of paper in front of me, the birds have long since returned to their chirping and a rustling scurries through the foliage of the chestnut tree—and some time or other, I again hear a sound that does not belong in my surroundings.

But it is soft, almost no sound at all. And while I am still preparing for it to get louder, suddenly a car is standing in front of the pasture gate. It's a passenger car, an Audi. We have already reached the point of being able to identify the current makes of car. And it is a sandy brown, as if it knows what will blend in with the meadows, the pastures, the road.

Then the car comes to life, or rather life emerges from it. The doors spread wide, and a well-off married couple—there is no doubt that they are married—climb out of the vehicle. Straightening up seems to cost them some effort, at least the man. But then he is standing, well fed and well dressed, his beige trousers fall without wrinkles, his right arm rests casually on the open door, while at once he turns his round face, its rosy complexion hidden by a tan, toward the pastures. His gaze through dark-rimmed spectacles does not for one moment linger on my house, as if my side of the road were filled with emptiness rather than landscape. Then he removes his hand from the car door, and in two strides he skirts around the hood, which despite its quiet color is now giving off a disturbing, blinding reflection of light. He joins his wife by the pasture gate. They lean on the gate rail, first the man, then the wife, so that the long wooden beam sags.

With their backs turned to me, they look alike, although of course as man and woman they are distinct. The wife's hair has a dark tint and is animated by a permanent wave, while the man's hair is white and lies smooth. What makes them so like twins is their sturdy stature, their visible stability, the product of sixty years of solid investments. But perhaps the impression stems above all from the fact that they belong to this car, from which they emerged, and which now is waiting at their rear like a well-trained pet. It carries the number plate of a large northwest German city. So they have not come from far away. Now and then they turn their faces toward each other, then I see their lips move. The man takes his hand off the rail and makes a sweeping gesture. (Freed of part of its burden, the wooden beam immediately straightens out a bit.)

Involuntarily, I jump up from my chair again and before I am aware of it, I have crossed the room and installed myself in the open door of my house. The heat rushes toward me. I retreat half a stride. Why shouldn't I stand there? But to be honest, I am not standing there, I am building myself up, being demonstrative, making a challenge. Which admittedly escapes the notice of the couple, because their backs are turned toward me. Nevertheless I do not feel comfortable in this pose, especially because I have no right to make demands concerning the enclosed pasture.

Scraps of sound drift my way. The man raises his left arm again and points across the fields. When he pulls it back and turns to the woman, I hear the phrase: "in any case." In the wife's reply I catch the words "right away." They mention the name of our village, then that of the neighboring community. I hear "the local government," this phrase which is not yet totally familiar to us, because we used to say "town council." "What else?" I hear, and "Friday" and "welcome." Completely ordinary, innocent words. But suddenly they give off a fatal radiation, each one seems like the threat of some danger. When I hear "three hundred," all doubt is eliminated. It does not matter what three hundred are massing there across the road—three hundred home-owners in a residential community, three hundred thousand visitors to a golf course, three hundred million sales at an industrial park. . . . Once, the woman turns toward the man so far that she really must have seen me. I don't know what I expect to come of that, but whatever it is, she does not do it. No doubt it is my imagination that she is lowering her voice. The man maintains his self-confident bearing. He merely mops his forehead once or twice with a handkerchief that he is holding in his half-closed hand, invisible to me. A gray heron flies over the pasture, flapping its wings. They do not notice it, they release the enclosure rail again and turn around. Once more they ignore my house, as if it were not standing there and I were not standing in the door. And yet I could have taken the man for a perfectly amiable aging gentleman. They stow themselves away in their metal cocoon. Only when the doors close, it makes a dry, cracking sound that is out of place. The car sways onto the center of the road. When it has disappeared from my view behind the hedge, I hear a gentle buzzing which goes on only long enough to disappear.

I walk back into the shadowy interior of the house, want to sit down but continue standing. Tense, bending forward I gaze sightlessly out into the hot summer day and listen.

Could it be that I hear those tanks coming again?

Translated by Jan van Heurck

The Authors

The following notes are a brief introduction to the lives and works of the authors and do not aim to be complete.

Bobrowski, Johannes (1917–65)

Born Tilsit (East Prussia), son of a railroad employee; studied art history; in 1937 was drafted into the Nazi *Arbeitsdienst* and later into the Wehrmacht; as a professing Christian, he was in contact with the Christian resistance to the Third Reich; in 1949 he returned home from Soviet captivity and became an editor at a publishing house in East Berlin; awarded Gruppe 47 Prize (1962), Heinrich Mann Prize (1965), Charles Veillon Prize (1965), F. C. Weiskopf Prize (posthumously, 1967).

Published works: novels *Levins Mühle. 34 Sätze über meinen Großvater* (1964; Eng. *Levin's Mill*, 1970), *Litauische Claviere* (1966; Eng. *Lithuanian Pianos*, 1986); poetry *Sarmatische Zeit* (1961), *Schattenland Ströme* (1962; Eng. *Shadow Land*, 1966), short stories *Boehlendorff und Mäusefest* (1965; Eng. *I Taste Bitterness*, 1970, 1989).

Bräunig, Werner (1934–76)

Born in Chemnitz; his father was an unskilled laborer, his mother a seamstress; worked in factories; after the war charged with involvement in smuggling activities with the West and held in a youth facility; began writing in 1956; became a member of the GDR's Communist Party, the Socialist Unity Party, in 1958; studied at the Johannes R. Becher Institute for Literature in Leipzig; issued the call "Take up your pen, Comrade" leading up to the 1959 Bitterfeld Conference promoting worker–writers; criticisms from the Socialist Unity Party made him break off work on the novel *Rummelplatz*.

Published works: *Prosa schreiben* (essays, 1968), *Gewöhnliche Leute* (short stories, 1969), filmscripts, reportage.

Brězan, Jurij (1916–)
Born in Räckelwitz/Kreis Kamenz, son of a quarryman; studied economics; in 1933 became active in the Sorbian resistance movement, emigrated, returned home and was imprisoned in 1938–39; served as a soldier; joined the Socialist Unity Party in 1946; became a free-lance writer in 1949; was vice-president of the GDR Writers Union in 1969; awarded the GDR's National Prize (1951, 1964, 1976).

Published works: starting in 1951, numerous volumes of short stories and novels including the Felix Hanusch trilogy (*Der Gymnasiast*, 1958; *Semester der verlorenen Zeit*, 1960 [Eng. *The Fallow Years*, 1963], and *Mannesjahre*, 1964); *Reise nach Krakau* (1966), *Krabat oder die Verwandlung der Welt* (1976), *Krabat oder die Bewahrung der Welt* (1995), *Mein Stück Zeit* (1989); and anthologies of Sorbian literature.

de Bruyn, Günter (1926–)
Born in Berlin, the son of a store clerk; after passing the qualifying examinations for the university, he became a soldier in 1943; after the war he was a novice teacher, a librarian at public libraries in Berlin, and 1953–61 a research fellow at the Central Institute of Library Science, then became a free-lance writer; awarded Heinrich Mann Prize (1964), Lion Feuchtwanger Prize (1981), Thomas Mann Prize (1989), Heinrich Böll Prize (1990), Konrad Adenauer Prize (1996).

Published works: novels *Buridans Esel* (1968; Eng. *Buridan's Ass*, 1973), *Preisverleihung* (1972), *Neue Herrlichkeit* (1984); *Märkische Forschungen* (1978); autobiographies *Zwischenbilanz* (1992) and *Vierzig Jahre. Ein Lebensbericht* (1996); *Das erzählte Ich. Über Wahrheit und Dichtung in der Autobiographie* (1995), *Jubelschreie, Trauergesänge. Deutsche Befindlichkeiten* (1991).

Dahn, Daniela (1949–)
Born in Berlin; studied journalism; until 1981 was an editor at GDR Television; awarded Fontane Prize (1987) and Berlin Prize (1988).

Published works: prose volumes *Prenzlauer Berg-Tour* (1987), *Wir bleiben hier oder Wem gehört der Osten* (1994), *Westwärts und nicht vergessen. Vom Unbehagen in der Einheit* (1996); also radio dramas and the documentary film *Zeitschleifen—Im Dialog mit Christa Wolf* (1991).

Fries, Fritz Rudolf (1935–)
Born in Bilbao, Spain, the son of a businessman; moved to Leipzig in 1942 where he studied Romance languages and literatures; 1960–66 was research assistant at the Academy of Sciences, then a free-lance writer and

translator; after 1980 became member of the governing board of the writers' association P.E.N. and of the science academies of Munich, Darmstadt, and Berlin (until 1996); awarded Heinrich Mann Prize (1979), Marie Luise Kaschnitz Prize (1988), Bremen Prize for Literature (1991), Blind War Veterans Prize for Radio Drama (1996).

Published works: novels *Der Weg nach Oobliadooh* (FRG 1966, GDR 1989; Eng. *The Road to Oobliadooh*, 1968), *Das Luft-Schiff* (1974), *Alexanders neue Welten* (1982), *Verlegung eines mittleren Reiches* (1984), *Die Väter im Kino* (1990), *Die Nonnen von Bratislava* (1994); short stories *See-Stücke* (1973), *Der Seeweg nach Indien* (1978); *Im Jahr des Hahns. Tagebücher* (1996); children's books, radio plays, screenplays, poetry.

Fühmann, Franz (1922–84)

Born in Rokytnice/Bohemia, son of a pharmacist; became a soldier, underwent Soviet captivity and antifascist schooling until 1949, then was active in journalism and politics; 1954–63 was on governing board of the *Kulturbund* (League of Culture); became a free-lance writer in 1958; awarded Heinrich Mann Prize (1956), GDR National Prize (1957 and 1974), Johannes R. Becher Prize (1963), Lion Feuchtwanger Prize (1972), Geschwister Scholl Prize (1982).

Published works: prose volumes *Kameraden* (1955), *Kabelkran und blauer Peter* (1961), *Das Judenauto* (1962; Eng. *The Car with the Yellow Star*, 1968), *Böhmen am Meer* (1962), *König Ödipus* (1966), *22 Tage oder die Hälfte des Lebens* (1973; Eng. *Twenty-Two Days; or, Half a Lifetime*, 1980), *Saiäns Fiktschen* (1981); *Fahrt nach Stalingrad* (epic poem, 1953), *Erfahrungen und Widersprüche* (essays, 1975); poetry, drama fragments, letters.

Hein, Christoph (1944–   )

Born in Heinzendorf/Silesia; attended secondary school in West Berlin because as a minister's son he was not allowed to enroll in a high school in the GDR; lived in East Berlin from 1960 on; various occupations including film editor; 1967–71 studied philosophy; assistant director at East Berlin's Deutsches Theater and dramatic adviser at the People's Theater (Volksbühne); became free-lance writer in 1979; awarded Heinrich Mann Prize (1982), Critics' Prize of West Berlin (1983), Lessing Prize (1989), Stefan Andres Prize Grant (1989), Berlin Prize for Literature (1992), Federal Order of Merit (1994); member of the arts academies of Berlin and Darmstadt.

Published works: numerous plays, frequently with historical themes, including *Cromwell* (1978), *Die wahre Geschichte des Ah Q* (1983), *Die*

Ritter der Tafelrunde (1989), and *Randow* (1994); Hein's most successful work, the novella *Der fremde Freund* (1982, published in the former Federal Republic of Germany in 1983 under the title *Drachenblut; Eng. The Distant Lover,* [1989] was followed by the novels *Horns Ende* (1985), *Der Tangospieler* (1989; Eng. *The Tango Player,* 1992) and *Das Napoleon-Spiel* (1993); *Exekution eines Kalbes* (stories, 1994); *Die fünfte Grundrechenart. Aufsätze und Reden 1986–1989* (1990).

Hermlin, Stephan (1915–   )

Born in Chemnitz, the son of a factory owner; 1933–36 a printer in Berlin, took part in the antifascist resistance; after 1936 was in exile in Egypt, Palestine, England, Spain, and France; was interned in Switzerland, joined the "Free Germany" movement; returned home in 1945, became a radio editor in Frankfurt; in 1947 moved to the Soviet occupation zone and joined the Socialist Unity Party; since then has been a free-lance writer, adapter, and translator; has held leading posts in the German Writers Union and P.E.N.; organized peace conferences in East and West Berlin in 1981 and 1983; awarded Heinrich Heine Prize (1948, 1972), GDR National Prize (1950, 1954, 1975), F. C. Weiskopf Prize (1958), Heinrich Heine Prize (1972).

Published works: short stories and other prose works *Der Leutnant Yorck von Wartenburg* (1946), *Die Zeit der Gemeinsamkeit* (1949; Eng. *City on a Hill,* 1962), *Lektüre 1960–1971* (1973), *Abendlicht* (1979; Eng. *Evening Light,* 1983), *Arkadien* (1983), *In einer dunklen Welt* (1993); *Zweiundzwanzig Balladen* (poetry, 1947); *Mansfelder Oratorium* (1950), *Begegnungen 1954–1959* (journalist material, 1960), *Scardanelli* (radio play, 1970), *Die Argonauten* (children's book, 1974); *In den Kämpfen dieser Zeit* (1995).

Heym, Stefan (1913–   )

Born in Chemnitz under the name Helmut Flieg, father was a businessman; went into exile in Czechoslovakia in 1933 and to the United States in 1935, where he studied German literature and pursued various occupations; joined the US army in 1943; in 1952 moved from the United States to the GDR and returned his American military decorations; worked as a journalist and free-lance writer; in 1976 signed the protest letter against the expatriation of Wolf Biermann; in 1979 was expelled from the GDR Writers Union, was rehabilitated in 1989–90; became a member of parliament for the PDS (Party of Democratic Socialism) in 1994–95, then senior president of the German Bundestag; awarded Heinrich Mann Prize (1953), GDR National Prize (1959), honorary doctorates from the universities of Bern (1990) and Cambridge (1991), Jerusalem Prize (1993).

Published works: novels include *Hostages* (1942, German edition *Der Fall Glasenapp*, 1958), *The Crusaders* (1948, German edition *Kreuzfahrer von heute*, 1950), *Goldsborough* (1954; Eng. *Goldsborough, 1954), Die Papiere des Andreas Lenz* (1963; Eng. *The Lenz Papers*, 1964), *Lassalle* (1969; Eng. *Uncertain Friend*, 1969), *Der König David Bericht* (1972; Eng. *King David Report*, 1973), *5 Tage im Juni* (1974; Eng. *Five Days in June*, 1977), *Collin* (1979; Eng. *Collin*, 1980), *Ahasver* (1981; Eng. *The Wandering Jew*, 1984), *Radek* (1995); the autobiographical *Nachruf* (1988); journalistic writings *Stalin verläßt den Raum* (1990), *Einmischung* (1990), *Filz. Gedanken über das neueste Deutschland* (1992), *Der Winter unsers Mißvergnügens. Aus den Aufzeichnungen des OV Diversant* (1996); short story collections including *Auf Sand gebaut* (1990).

Hilbig, Wolfgang (1941–)

Born in Meuselwitz/Saxony, raised by his miner grandfather; military service, worked as a toolmaker, busboy, and starting in 1970, as a stoker; 1967–68 belonged to a group of worker–writers; arrested by the Stasi in 1978; a free-lance writer since 1979, moved to the former Federal Republic of Germany in 1985; awarded Brothers Grimm Prize (1983), Academy of Arts grant, Berlin (1985), Ingeborg Bachmann Prize (1989), Berlin Prize for Literature (1992), Bremen Prize for Literature (1994), Prize of the German Schiller Society (1996), Fontane Prize (1997).

Published works: short stories and novels from the GDR's anarchistic underworld including *Unterm Neomond* (1982), *Der Brief* (1985), *Eine Übertragung* (1989), *Alte Abdeckerei* (1991), *Aufbrüche* (1992), *Kunde von den Bäumen* (1994), *Die Arbeit an den Öfen* (1994); *Abriß der Kritik. Frankfurter Poetikvorlesungen* (1995); poetry in the style of Hölderlin, Rimbaud, and Baudelaire; Hilbig's most successful work so far has been the novel *Ich* (1993).

Kant, Hermann (1926–)

Born in Hamburg, father was a gardener; electrician, then soldier, a POW in Poland 1945–49, where he was active in an antifascist committee; joined the Socialist Unity Party in 1949; 1949–52 studied in the Workers and Peasants Faculty, Greifswald, then studied German literature in Berlin; worked for the student newspaper *tua res* and for *Neues Deutschland;* became a free-lance writer in 1959; from 1969 to 1978 was vice-president of the GDR Writers Union, from 1978 to 1990 was its president, also vice-president of the Academy of Arts (1969–78), member of the Central Committee of the Socialist Unity Party (1986–89) and deputy to the GDR People's Chamber, the Volkskammer (1981–90); awarded Heinrich Heine

Prize (1963), Heinrich Mann Prize (1967), GDR National Prize (1973, 1983), Goethe Prize (1987).

Published works: volumes of short stories including *Ein bißchen Südsee* (1962; Eng. *A Bit of the South Sea*, 1979), *Eine Übertretung* (1975; Eng. "Stepping Over," 1976), *Der dritte Nagel* (1981) and *Bronzezeit* (1986); best known for three novels about the GDR: *Die Aula* (1965), *Das Impressum* (1972) and *Der Aufenthalt* (1977); Kant's memoirs appeared in 1991 under the title *Abspann; Kormoran* (novel, 1994); *Escape. Ein WORD-Spiel* (1995).

Kirsch, Sarah (1935–)

Born in Limlingerode/Harz, father a telecommunications engineer; studied biology, then at the Johannes R. Becher Institute for Literature 1963–65; since has been a free-lance writer; moved to the former Federal Republic of Germany in 1977; awarded Heinrich Heine Prize (1973), Petrarch Prize (1976), Austrian State Prize for Literature (1981), Friedrich Hölderlin Prize (1984), Peter Huchel Prize (1993), Georg Büchner Prize (1996).

Published works: volumes of poetry including *Landaufenthalt* (1967), *Zaubersprüche* (1973), *Rückenwind* (1976), *Drachensteigen* (1979), *Erdreich* (1982), *Katzenleben* (1984; Eng. *Catlives*, 1991), *Schneewärme* (1989), *Erlkönigs Tochter* (1992), *Das simple Leben* (1994), *Ich Crusoe* (1995), *Bodenlos* (1996); prose *Die Pantherfrau* (1973; Eng. *The Panther Woman*, 1989), *Irrstern* (1987), *Allerlei-Rauh* (1988), *Spreu* (1991); children's books, translations.

Knobloch, Heinz (1926–)

Born in Dresden, son of a photographer; trained as bookseller, was a soldier and then a prisoner-of-war in the United States and Britain; studied journalism, became feature editor for the *Wochenpost;* member of the board of the GDR Writers Union since 1978; awarded Heinrich Heine Prize (1965), Goethe Prize of the City of Berlin (1979), Louis Fürnberg Prize (1980), Lion Feuchtwanger Prize (1986), GDR National Prize (1986), Roswitha von Gandersheim Prize (1992), Moses Mendelssohn Prize (1994), Georg Trakl Prize (1997).

Published works: numerous collections of feature articles including *Herztöne und Zimmermannssplitter* (1962), "Du liebe Zeit" (1966), and *Die schönen Umwege* (1994); short stories, biographical novels, and reportage including *Herr Moses in Berlin* (1979), *Meine liebste Mathilde* (1985), *Berliner Grabsteine* (1987), *Der arme Epstein. Wie der Tod zu Horst Wessel kam* (1993), *Eierschnecke. Dresdner Kindheit* (1995).

Königsdorf, Helga (1938–)

Born in Gera; studied physics and mathematics, was awarded a doctorate in science in 1963 and became a professor in 1974; research fellow at the GDR Academy of Sciences, then a free-lance writer; 1989–91 served on the governing board of the GDR branch of P.E.N.; awarded Heinrich Heine Prize (1985).

Published works: satirical stories based on everyday life in the GDR, including *Meine ungehörigen Träume* (1978); *Ungelegener Befund* (1990) uses the example of woman nuclear physicist Lise Meitner to examine the theme of scientific responsibility; *Im Schatten des Regenbogens* (novel, 1993); since 1989 has published numerous statements on GDR unification with the former Federal Republic of Germany, including *Aus dem Dilemma eine Chance machen* (1991), *Adieu DDR* (1991), and *Unterwegs nach Deutschland* (1995).

Kohlhaase, Wolfgang (1931–)

Born in Berlin, father a machinist; in 1947 began to work on newspapers for young people and as a dramatic adviser with DEFA, the GDR's national film company; since 1953 has worked as a free-lance writer, filmscript author, and film director; awarded two GDR National Prizes (1954, 1968), the Erich Weinert Medal, the Chicago Film Festival Prize for the best filmscript, the Lubitsch and Käutner Prizes (1990).

Published works: most important feature films are *Berlin—Ecke Schönhauser* (1957), *Ich war neunzehn* (1968), *Mama, ich lebe* (1977), *Solo Sunny* (1980), *Der Aufenthalt* (1983, based on the novel by Hermann Kant); also radio plays and *Silvester mit Balzac und andere Erzählungen* (1977).

Kunert, Günter (1929–)

Born in Berlin; the fascist racial laws barred him from pursuing his education and caused him to be declared unfit for military service; in 1946–47 studied at the College for Applied Arts, has worked as a free-lance writer since 1947; joined the Socialist Unity Party in 1949; 1972–73 was a visiting professor in Texas; in 1976 he signed the letter protesting the expatriation of Wolf Biermann, in 1977 he was expelled from the Socialist Unity Party; in 1979 he moved to the former Federal Republic of Germany; awarded the Heinrich Mann Prize (1962), Heinrich Heine Prize (1985), Friedrich Hölderlin Prize (1991).

Published works: volumes of poetry *Wegschilder und Mauerninschriften* (1950), *Tagwerke* (1961), *Notizen in Kreide* (1970), *Unruhiger Schlaf* (1979), *Abtötungsverfahren* (1980), *Stilleben* (1983), *Fremd daheim*

(1990), *Mein Golem* (1996); prose works *Tagträume* (1964), *Im Namen der Hüte* (1967), *Kramen in Fächern* (1969), *Ortsangaben* (1971), *Im toten Winkel* (1992); also *Fetzers Flucht* (a television opera, 1962), *Der andere Planet. Ansichten von Amerika* (1975), Frankfurt lecture series *Vor der Sintflut. Das Gedicht als Arche Noah* (1985), *Zeichnungen und Beispiele* (1987), *Die letzten Indianer Europas* (1991), *Der Sturz vom Sockel* (1992), *Baum, Stein, Beton. Reisen zwischen Ober- und Unterwelt* (1994); radio plays and television pieces.

Kunze, Reiner (1933–   )

Born in Oelsnitz/Erzgebirge, son of a miner; 1951–55 studied philosophy and journalism, research assistant at the university of Leipzig, then worked in various occupations; free-lance writer since 1962; expelled from the GDR Writers Union in 1976, moved to the former Federal Republic of Germany in 1977; awarded German Prize for Children's Books (1971), Georg Büchner Prize (1977); Georg Trakl Prize (1977), Geschwister Scholl Prize (1981), Federal Order of Merit (1984), Hanns Martin Schleyer Prize (1990–91).

Published works: volumes of poetry *Sensible Wege* (1969), *Zimmerlautstärke* (1972; Eng. *With the Volume Turned Down*, 1973), *eines jeden einziges leben* (1986); *Die wunderbaren Jahre* (prose, 1976; Eng. *The Wonderful Years*, 1977, 1978), *In Deutschland zuhaus. Funk- und Fernsehinterviews 1977–1983* (1984), *Das weiße Gedicht* (essay, 1989), *Deckname 'Lyrik'* (documentary report, 1990), *Begehrte, unbequeme Freiheit* (interviews, 1993), *Am Sonnenhang. Tagebuch eines Jahres* (1993).

Laabs, Joochen (1937–   )

Born in Dresden; a streetcar driver, then studied at the College of Transport and from 1962 to 1975 worked as engineer in urban transportation in Dresden; 1976–78 was editor of the magazine *Temperamente;* active in the GDR branch of P.E.N.; awarded Martin Andersen Nexö Prize (1973).

Published works: short story volumes including *Die andere Hälfte der Welt* (1974), *Jeder Mensch will König sein* (1983) and *Der letzte Stern* (1988); novels including *Das Grashaus oder Die Aufteilung von 35000 Frauen auf zwei Mann* (1971), *Der Ausbruch* (1979), and *Der Schattenfänger* (1989).

Liebmann, Irina (1943–   )

Born in Moscow; graduate sinologist; 1967–75 developing-nations editor for the foreign-affairs journal *Deutsche Außenpolitik;* free-lance writer since 1975; moved to West Berlin in 1988; awarded Aspekte Prize for Literature, Bremen Prize for Literature grant, Ernst Willner Prize (1987).

Published works: newspaper articles for the *Wochenpost* (1975–79); short story volumes *Berliner Mietshaus* (1981) and *Mitten im Krieg* (1989); *In Berlin* (novel, 1994); *Quatschfresser: Theaterstücke* (1990); *Wie Gras bis zu Tischen hoch. Ein Spaziergang im Scheunenviertel* (1995); children's books, radio plays, reportage.

Loest, Erich (1926–   )

Born Mittweide/Saxony, son of a businessman; high school, military service, after the war became an editor in Leipzig; joined the Socialist Unity Party in 1947, free-lance writer since 1950; in 1957 sentenced to seven years in prison for "forming counterrevolutionary factions"; after his release in 1964 he published crime and adventure novels under various pseudonyms; in 1981 he moved to the former Federal Republic of Germany, in 1990 returned to Leipzig; awarded Hans Fallada Prize (1981), Karl Hermann Flach Prize (1992).

Published works: the novels *Jungen, die übrig bleiben* (1950), *Schattenboxen* (1973), *Es geht seinen Gang oder Mühen in unserer Ebene* (1978), *Swallow, mein wackerer Mustang. Karl-May-Roman* (1980), *Völkerschlachtdenkmal* (1984; Eng. *The Monument, 1987), Nikolaikirche* (1994); autobiographical writings *Durch die Erde ein Riß* (1981), *Der vierte Zensor* (1984), *Der Zorn des Schafes* (essays, 1990), *Die Stasi war mein Eckermann* (1991).

Melle, F. Hendrik (1960–   )

Born 1960; studied theology; worked for underground periodicals in the GDR; moved to West Berlin in 1985.

Morgenstern, Beate (1946–   )

Born in Cuxhaven; 1964–68 studied German literature and art education, then worked as a book dealer, photo editor, and since 1978 as free-lance writer; held leading posts in the German Writers Union and the GDR branch of P.E.N.; awarded Berlin Prize (1989).

Published works: novels *Nest im Kopf* (1989), *Huckepack* (1995), *Küsse für Butzemännchen* (1995); *Jenseits der Allee* (prose, 1979), *Pellkartoffel* (radio play, 1978).

Morgner, Irmtraud (1933–90)

Born in Chemnitz, father a locomotive driver; studied German literature, 1956–58 worked as editor for the periodical *Neue Deutsche Literatur*, then became a free-lance writer; awarded Heinrich Mann Prize (1975),

GDR National Prize (1977), Roswitha von Gandersheim Prize (1985), Kassel Prize for Literature (1989).

Published works: novels *Hochzeit in Konstantinopel* (1968), *Die wundersamen Reisen Gustav des Weltfahrers* (1972), *Leben und Abenteuer der Trobadora Beatriz nach Zeugnissen ihrer Spielfrau Laura* (1974), *Amanda* (1983); short stories.

Müller, Heiner (1929–95)

Born in Eppendorf/Saxony to an office-worker father and a mother who worked in the textile industry; in 1945 served in the Nazi *Arbeitsdienst* and was briefly a prisoner of war; moved to Berlin in the late 1940s; became a literary critic, worked in the GDR Writers Union 1954–55, in 1961 was expelled from the Writers Union after the premiere of his play *Die Umsiedlerin*, began in 1959 to work as a free-lance writer and dramatic adviser for various theaters; 1990–92 was president of the GDR's Academy of Arts, in 1995 was art director at the Berliner Ensemble theater; awarded Heinrich Mann Prize (1959), Lessing Prize (1975), Georg Büchner Prize (1985), GDR National Prize (1987), Kleist Prize (1990), European Theater Prize (1991, 1994).

Published works: approximately thirty-five plays including *Der Lohndrücker* (1958), *Die Korrektur* (with Inge Müller, 1958), *Germania Tod in Berlin* (1963), *Der Bau* (1963), *Philoktet* (1966; Eng. *Philoctetes*, 1981), *Die Schlacht* (1974; Eng. *The Battle: Plays, Prose, Poems*, 1989), *Mauser* (1976; Eng. 1976), *Hamletmaschine* (1977; Eng. *Hamletmachine and Other Texts*, 1983), *Der Auftrag* (1979; Eng. *The Mission*, 1982), *Verkommenes Ufer Medeamaterial Landschaft mit Argonauten* (1982; Eng. *Despoiled Shore Medeamaterial Landscape with Argonauts*, 1984) [Eng. tr. in *Hamletmachine and Other Texts*, 1983, and *Explosion of a Memory*, 1989]; *Gesammelte Irrtümer* (conversations, 1986, 1990), *Gedichte 1949–1991* (1992), *Krieg ohne Schlacht* (autobiography, 1992).

Neutsch, Erik (1931–)

Born in Schönebeck/Elbe, father a manual worker; joined the Socialist Unity Party in 1949; studied journalism, then was culture editor of *Freiheit;* a free-lance writer since 1960; awarded GDR National Prize (1964), Heinrich Mann Prize (1971).

Published works: *Bitterfelder Geschichten* (1961), *Spur der Steine* (1964), *Auf der Suche nach Gatt* (1973), *Der Friede im Osten* (four volumes 1974–89, volume five withdrawn in 1990 before publication).

Plenzdorf, Ulrich (1934–)

Born in Berlin-Kreuzberg into a communist workers' family that was imprisoned under Hitler; after briefly studying philosophy, he became a stagehand, served in the military, and 1959–63 attended the Babelsberg Film Academy; then worked as a scenarist and dramatic adviser for the GDR's state-run film company DEFA, and as a free-lance writer; awarded Heinrich Greif Prize (1971, 1973), Heinrich Mann Prize (1973), Ingeborg Bachmann Prize (1978), Adolf Grimme Prize (1995).

Published works: filmscripts *Mir nach, Canaillen!* (1964), *Die Legende von Paul und Paula* (1972), *Karla* (1965, not distributed following the Eleventh Plenum of the Central Committee of the Socialist Unity Party, which stepped up censorship of artists); the novella *Die neuen Leiden des jungen W.* (1972; Eng. *The New Sufferings of Young W.*, 1979), completed in 1968, was adapted for the stage in 1972 with great success and made into a film in the former Federal Republic of Germany in 1976; *Legende vom Glück ohne Ende* (novel, 1979), *Ein Tag, länger als ein Leben* (play, 1986), *Freiheitsberaubung* (play, 1988), *Das andere Leben des Herrn Kreins* (documentary, 1995); short stories.

Rülicke-Weiler, Käthe (1922–92)

Born in Leipzig; business training, became a secretary; in 1950 was made director's assistant to Bertolt Brecht, 1957–64 worked as drama consultant and free-lance associate of the Berliner Ensemble theater, 1967–82 was vice-president for research of the GDR Film and Television Academy.

Published works: *Die Dramaturgie Brechts. Theater als Mittel der Veränderung* (1966); prose.

Schütz, Helga (1937–)

Born in Falkenhain/Silesia to a working-class family; trained as a gardener, then studied at the Potsdam Workers and Peasants College and the Academy of Film Arts; screenwriter for the state-run film company DEFA, and a free-lance writer since 1972; awarded Heinrich Greif Prize (1969), Heinrich Mann Prize (1973), Theodor Fontane Prize (1974), ZDF [television] Prize in Literature and resident writer of the City of Mainz (1991).

Published works: short story volumes including *Vorgeschichte oder Schöne Gegend Probstein* (1970), *Das Erdbeben bei Sangerhausen* (1972) and *Festbeleuchtung* (1973); novels *Jette in Dresden* (1977), *Julia oder Erziehung zum Chorgesang* (1980), *In Annas Namen* (1986), *Vom Glanz der Elbe* (1995); screenplays including *Lots Weib* (1965), *Die Schlüssel* (1972), *Die Leiden des jungen Werthers* (1976), *Fallada, letztes Kapitel* (1988) and *Stein* (1990); radio plays.

Seghers, Anna (1900–1983)

Born in Mainz under the name Netty Reiling, daughter of an art dealer; in 1924 earned her doctorate with a thesis on Rembrandt; joined the German Communist Party in 1928, became a member of the Proletarian–Revolutionary Writers League; 1933–41 in exile in France, a copublisher of *Neue Deutsche Blätter;* 1941–47 exile in Mexico where she wrote for *Freies Deutschland* and was chairperson of the Heinrich Heine Club; returned to the GDR in 1947, became vice-president of the League of Culture, a founding member of the German Academy of Arts, and from 1952 to 1978, chairperson of the GDR Writers Union; awarded Kleist Prize (1928), Georg Büchner Prize (1947), Stalin Peace Prize (1951), GDR National Prize (1951, 1959, 1971), honorary doctorates from the University of Jena (1959) and the University of Mainz (1977), made honorary citizen of the city of Mainz (1981).

Published works: Among her most important novels are *Der Kopflohn* (1933; Eng. *A Price on His Head,* 1960), *Die Rettung* (1937), *Das siebte Kreuz* (1942; Eng. *The Seventh Cross,* 1942), *Transit* (1948; Eng. *Transit,* 1944), *Die Toten bleiben jung* (1949; Eng. *The Dead Stay Young,* 1950), *Die Entscheidung* (1959), and *Das Vertrauen* (1968); short stories including *Die Toten auf der Insel Djal* (1924), *Aufstand der Fischer von St. Barbara* (1928; Eng. *The Revolt of the Fishermen,* 1929, 1960), *Auf dem Wege zur amerikanischen Botschaft* (1930), *Der Ausflug der toten Mädchen* (1946; Eng. "The Outing of the Dead Girls," 1967), *Der Bienenstock* (1953), *Die Kraft der Schwachen* (1965), *Das wirkliche Blau* (1967; Eng. *Benito's Blue and Nine Other Stories,* 1973), *Überfahrt* (1971), *Der gerechte Richter* (written 1957–58, published 1990); essay collection *Über Kunstwerk und Wirklichkeit* (1970–71, 1979).

Stachowa, Angela (1948–)

Born in Prague; telecommunications technician, studied at the Technical University of Dresden; free-lance writer since 1976.

Published works: short story volumes *Stunde zwischen Hund und Katz* (1976), *Geschichten für Majka* (1978), *Kleine Verführung* (1983).

Strittmatter, Erwin (1921–94)

Born in Spremberg/Niederlausitz, the son of a baker; worked at various jobs, including baker, waiter, manual laborer; self-educated; imprisoned in 1934, then became a soldier and deserted toward the end of World War II; worked as a baker after 1945, joined the Socialist Unity Party in 1947, became a public official and newspaper editor in Senftenberg; free-lance writer in 1951; in 1959 was made first secretary of the GDR Writers Union, from 1969 to 1983 was vice-president of the Writers Union;

awarded GDR National Prize (1953, 1955, 1964, 1976, 1984), Lessing Prize (1961), Fontane Prize (1966).

Published works: the novels *Ochsenkutscher* (1950), *Tinko* (1954), *Der Wundertäter* (three volumes, 1957–80), *Ole Bienkopp* (1963; Eng. *Ole Bienkopp*, 1966), *Der Laden* (three volumes, 1983–92); short story volumes *Schulzenhofer Kramkalender* (1966), *¾ hundert Kleingeschichten* (1971), *Die blaue Nachtigall oder Der Anfang von etwas* (1972); dramas *Katzgraben, Szenen aus dem Bauernleben* (1954), *Die Holländerbraut* (1961); *Vor der Verwandlung* (notebooks, 1995).

Walther, Joachim (1943–)

Born in Chemnitz, father a civil servant; completed his qualifying exam for the university, became a machinist in 1962; 1963–67 studied German literature and art history; worked as editor at Der Morgen publishing house and for the magazine *Temperamente* from 1976 until 1978; freelance writer since 1983; awarded Radio Drama Prize of the Berlin Broadcasting Studio (1991).

Published works: short story volumes *Stadtlandschaft mit Freunden* (1978), *Zwischen den Stühlen* (1987), *Verlassenes Ufer* (1994); novels *Ich bin nun mal kein Yogi* (1975), *Bewerbung bei Hofe* (1982), *Risse im Eis* (1989); radio plays *Infarkt* (1979), *Illusionsfassaden oder Welttheater ohne Notausgang* (1993); *Meinetwegen Schmetterlinge. Gespräche mit Schriftstellern* (1973), *Heldenleben* (satirical writings, 1988), *Sicherungsbereich Literatur. Schriftsteller und Staatssicherheit in der Deutschen Demokratischen Republik* (1996).

Wander, Maxie (1933–77)

Born in Vienna, father worked in a service station; left high school to work at odd jobs; moved to the GDR with her husband, the writer Fred Wander, in 1958.

Published works: *Guten Morgen, du Schöne* (1977), *Tagebücher und Briefe* (1979), *Ein Leben ist nicht genug* (1990).

Wolf, Friedrich (1888–1953)

Born in Neuwied am Rhein, father a businessman; earned his M.D. in 1913, 1913–33 worked as a ship's doctor, army doctor, and public-health-service physician; in 1918 joined the Independent German Social Democratic Party, in 1928 joined the German Communist Party and the Proletarian–Revolutionary Writers League; after 1933 went into exile, mostly in the USSR, where he worked in radio and in war propaganda, in 1943 was a cofounder of the National Committee for a Free Germany; returned to East Berlin in 1945, became a founding member of the state-run film company DEFA, of the People's Theater Association, and of the GDR branch of P.E.N.; 1949–51 he was the GDR ambassador to Poland; awarded GDR National Prize (1949, 1950).

Published works: Most important dramas include *Das bist Du* (1919), *Der arme Konrad* (1924), *Cyankali* (1929), *Die Matrosen von Cattaro* (1930; Eng. *The Sailors of Cattaro*, 1935), *Professor Mamlock* (1934; Eng. *Professor Mamlock*, 1935), *Floridsdorf* (1935; Eng. *Floridsdorf*, 1935), *Thomas Müntzer* (1953); essay "Kunst ist Waffe" (1928).

Wolter, Christine (1939–)

Born in Königsberg; 1957–61 studied Romance languages and literatures, 1962–76 worked as editor for a publishing house, then as a free-lance writer; edited anthologies of Italian poetry and novellas; moved to Milan in 1978.

Published works: prose writings *Wie ich meine Unschuld verlor* (1976), *Die Hintergrundsperson oder Versuche zu lieben* (1979), *Die Alleinseglerin* (novel, 1982), *Italien muß schön sein. Impressionen, Depressionen in Arkadien* (1993).

Translated by Jan van Heurck

Acknowledgments

Every reasonable effort has been made to locate the owners of rights to previously published works and the translations printed here. We gratefully acknowledge permission to reprint the following material:

Christoph Hein, "I Saw Stalin Once When I Was a Child"; Hermann Kant, "For the Files"; Wolfgang Kohlhasse, "Suffer the Little Children. . ."; Helga Königsdorf, "Property Damage"; Käthe Rülicke, "Hans Garbe Tells His Story"; Helga Schütz, "The Earthquake at Sangerhausen"; Anna Seghers, "The Reed"; Erwin Strittmatter, "Electric Power"; Friedrich Wolf, "Anna and the Men's Strike"; Christine Wolter, "I Have Married Again" by permission Aufbau-Verlag GmbH.

Johannes Bobrowski, "Mouse Party," by permission Verlagsgruppe Klinkhardt & Biermann.

Werner Bräunig, "On the Way," by permission Michael Bräunig.

Jurij Brĕzan, "The Christmas Story," by permission Jurij Brĕzan.

Günter de Bruyn, "Vergissmeinnicht" from *Babylon* © S. Fischer Verlag GmbH, Frankfurt am Main, 1992.

Daniela Dahn, "The Invincible Monument," by permission of Daniela Dahn.

From Fritz Rudolf Fries, *Der Seeweg nach Indien. Gesammelte Erzählungen.* © Piper GmbH & Co. KG, München 1991.

Franz Fühmann, "Das Judenauto" aus *Das Judenauto, Kabelkran. . .,* Hinstorff-Verlag Rostock 1979.

Stephan Hermlin, "Mein Friede" aus *Traum der Gemeinsamkeit—Ein Lesebuch,* Verlag Klaus Wagenbach Berlin 1985.

Copyright © 1990 Stefan Heym. From his story collection AUF SAND GEBAUT (© Bertelsmann. Germany, 1990). Reprinted with author's permission.

Wolfgang Hilbig, "Fester Grund" from *Grünes, Grünes Grab* © S. Fischer Verlag GmbH, Frankfurt am Main.

Sarah Kirsch, "Merkwürdiges Beispiel weiblicher Entschlossenheit" from Kirsch, "Die ungeheuren bergehohen Wellen auf See," © by Manesse Verlag, Zurich 1987.

Heinz Knobloch, "Stadmitte umsteigen." In: Heinz Knobloch, *Stadmitte umsteigen*. Berliner Phantasien. Buchverlag Der Morgan, Berlin 1982, 4, Auflage 1990.

Günter Kunert, "Love Story—Made in the GDR," by permission Carl Hanser Verlag GmbH & Co.

Reiner Kunze, "Mein Freund, ein Dichter der Liebe." In *Die wunderbaren Jahre*. © S. Fischer Verlag GmbH, Frankfurt am Main 1976.

Joochen Laabs, "Beautiful Summer," by permission Joochen Laabs.

Irina Liebmann, "Sibylle N.," by permission Irina Liebmann.

Erich Loest, "I Have Never Drunk Champagne," by permission Linden-Verlag.

Beate Morgenstern, "The Reunion," by permission Beate Morgenstern.

Irmtraud Morgner, "White Easter," © 1990 by Luchterhand Literaturverlag GmbH.

Heiner Müller, "The Father," from *Germania Tod in Berlin* © Rotbuch Verlag Berlin 1997.

Ulrich Plenzdorf, "The New Sufferings of Young W.," Copyright © 1979 by Frederick Ungar Publishing Co., Inc.

Angela Stachowa, "This Winter," by permission Angela Stachowa.

Joachim Walther, "The Raft of Utopia," by permission Joachim Walther.

Maxie Wander, "Angst vor der Liebe." In: Maxie Wander, *Guten Morgen du Schöne. Protokolle nach Tonband*. Berlin. Buchverlag Der Morgen 1977. Alle Rechte bei Fred Wander, Wien.